759.4
D317d

Degas

Degas and New Orleans

A French Impressionist in America

Gail Feigenbaum

Catalogue by
Jean Sutherland Boggs

Essays by

Christopher Benfey
Marilyn R. Brown
James B. Byrnes
Victoria Cooke
Christina Vella

NEW ORLEANS MUSEUM OF ART
IN CONJUNCTION WITH ORDRUPGAARD

This book is published in conjunction with *Degas and New Orleans: A French Impressionist in America,* an exhibition organized by the New Orleans Museum of Art, in conjunction with Ordrupgaard, and presented in New Orleans May 1–August 29, 1999, and in Copenhagen September 16–November 28, 1999.

Degas and New Orleans: A French Impressionist in America, under the patronage of the Ambassador of France to the United States, His Excellency François Bujon de l'Estang, is presented in New Orleans by the State of Louisiana, Department of Culture, Recreation and Tourism with individual sponsorship by Michel David-Weill, Chairman, Lazard Frères & Co., LLC. In New Orleans support for *Degas and New Orleans* is generously provided by Hibernia National Bank. Additional funding is made possible by Blumenthal Print Works. This exhibition is supported by an indemnity from the Federal Council on the Arts and the Humanities.

Library of Congress Catalog Card Number: 99-70046
ISBN 0-89494-072-4 (hardcover)
ISBN 0-89494-073-2 (softcover)

Page i: *Achille De Gas,* cat. 17
Frontispiece: *A Cotton Office in New Orleans,* detail, cat. 31
Page 2: *Children on a Doorstep (New Orleans),* detail, cat. 29
Page 22: *The Nurse (La Garde-Malade),* detail, cat. 22
Page 32: *Cotton Merchants in New Orleans,* detail, cat. 32
Page 46: *A Cotton Office in New Orleans,* detail, cat. 31
Page 66: *Woman with a Vase of Flowers,* detail, cat. 27
Page 98: *Woman Ironing,* detail, cat. 37

Edited by Wanda O'Shello
Editorial assistance by Amy Smith Bell and Elizabeth E. White
Designed by John Hubbard and Ed Marquand
Produced by Marquand Books, Inc., Seattle, in conjunction with the Publications Office of the New Orleans Museum of Art
Printed and bound by C & C Offset Co., Ltd., Hong Kong

Distributed by
Rizzoli International Publications, Inc.
300 Park Avenue South
New York, New York 10010
212-387-3400

Contents

Patrons' Preface

LOUISIANA HAS A REPUTATION for its diverse music and art and is world renowned for its unique culture and cuisine. We also have an abundance of natural beauty, unmatched entertainment, and a rich heritage. This year we are celebrating FrancoFête, commemorating three hundred years of French influence that began when explorer Pierre le Moyne d'Iberville founded the first colony in what became the Louisiana territory. We are eager to open our hospitality to you and invite you to explore as much of our state as possible.

Louisiana is fortunate to have been home to many famous personalities throughout its long and interesting history. One such notable artist, Edgar Degas, called Louisiana his home in the early 1870s. As part of our FrancoFête celebration, the Louisiana Department of Culture, Recreation and Tourism and the New Orleans Museum of Art are proud to present to you *Degas and New Orleans: A French Impressionist in America,* May 1 through August 29, 1999. Seventeen of the nearly two dozen works created by Degas during his stay in New Orleans have been justly assembled in the same city where they were completed more than 125 years ago.

We are honored to have been able to bring these paintings together from around the world for your enjoyment. Louisiana's Department of Culture, Recreation and Tourism and the New Orleans Museum of Art have gone to great lengths to provide this unprecedented exhibition. We hope you enjoy this glimpse at the very new and exotic city experienced and translated through the eyes and brush strokes of Edgar Degas, one of the most important Impressionist painters of his time.

Kathleen Babineaux Blanco
Lieutenant Governor of Louisiana

I WOULD LIKE TO EXPRESS my great delight that the exhibition *Degas and New Orleans: A French Impressionist in America* is taking place at the New Orleans Museum of Art. Given Edgar Degas's great affinity for Louisiana, the birthplace of his mother, I cannot help but believe he would have been exceedingly moved to see these carefully selected works exhibited here.

The ties that link France and Louisiana go back some three hundred years. Indeed, the exhibition, which is a part of FrancoFête, marking the three-hundredth anniversary of French influence in Louisiana, is symbolic of this historic friendship and reinforces its abiding vigor. It is fitting that the world-renowned artist Edgar Degas be associated with this particular chapter of history as he was the only one of the French Impressionists who ever traveled to the United States, much less to New Orleans, which was, at that time, one of the fifteen biggest cities in the United States and a cultural melting pot.

May I express my appreciation to Dr. Gail Feigenbaum, the exhibition's curator, for the exquisite assembling and mounting of the exhibition as well as to both Michel David-Weill, of Lazard Frères, and the State of Louisiana Department of Culture, Recreation and Tourism for having made it possible.

The viewing audience has a very special treat in store for them especially in that some of the works they will see have never been on public view, while a number of others have never before been exhibited in the United States. I warmly congratulate everyone involved for having had the vision and skills necessary to the realization of this exhibition.

François Bujon de l'Estang
Ambassador of France to the United States of America

Lenders to the Exhibition

The Art Institute of Chicago

Mrs. Amanda Belge, Augusta, Georgia

Bibliothèque Nationale de France, Paris

Fine Arts Museums of San Francisco

The Detroit Institute of Arts

Dumbarton Oaks Research Library and Collection, Washington D.C.

Earl K. Long Library, University of New Orleans

Walter Feilchenfeldt, Zürich, Switzerland

Emma Glenny, Baton Rouge

Göteborgs Konstmuseum, Sweden

Mrs. T. Ham, McLean, Virginia

Harvard University Art Museums (Fogg Art Museum), Cambridge

Historic New Orleans Collection

Howard-Tilton Memorial Library, Special Collections, Tulane University, New Orleans

John Loeb, New York

Edmund Martin, Lynchburg, Virginia

The Metropolitan Museum of Art, New York

Dora Martin Miller, Waveland, Mississippi

Hugh Miller, Chicago, Illinois

Minneapolis Institute of Art

Marie Estelle Moyer, New Orleans

Musée des Beaux-Arts, Pau

Musée du Louvre, Paris

Musée d'Orsay, Paris

Museum Boymans-van Beuningen, Rotterdam

Museum of Fine Arts, Boston

Napoleon-Museum, Arenenburg, Switzerland

National Gallery of Art, Washington, D.C.

New Orleans Museum of Art

New Orleans Notarial Archives

Ordrupgaard, Copenhagen, Denmark

Philadelphia Museum of Art

Pierpont Morgan Library, New York

Private Collection, The Bahamas

Private Collection, Bonn, Germany

Private Collection, courtesy of Portland Museum of Art, Maine

Private Collection, New York

Carol Selle, New York

Ronald Smith, New Orleans

Statens Museum for Kunst, Copenhagen, Denmark

Sterling and Francine Clark Art Institute, Williamstown, Massachusetts

Walters Art Gallery, Baltimore, Maryland

Weil Brothers, Montgomery, Alabama

Director's Foreword

New Orleans takes considerable pride in being the only city in the United States where one of the great French Impressionist painters lived and worked. Edgar Degas spent the winter of 1872–73 in New Orleans. The artist stayed in the handsome mansion rented by his maternal uncle, which still stands on Esplanade Avenue, where his brother René, who had married Estelle Musson, one of their Creole cousins, also lived in the house along with assorted cousins, nieces, nephews, and in-laws. It was a productive visit for Degas, who had as yet not achieved public success or recognition. A series of memorable, sometimes haunting portraits of the artist's New Orleans family resulted from his five-month visit, which some scholars believe marked a turning point in his life and art.

In late 1997 the New Orleans Museum of Art was invited by the State of Louisiana to organize a major exhibition of French art as the centerpiece of FrancoFête, a celebration of the three-hundredth anniversary of the French presence in Louisiana. Time was short since major international loan exhibitions usually take two to three years to organize. The subject of such an exhibition naturally suggested itself since a milestone in the history of our Museum was the purchase in 1965 of one of Edgar Degas's New Orleans paintings, the *Portrait of Mme René De Gas, née Estelle Musson,* an acquisition so wisely made by my predecessor, James B. Byrnes. Our Curator of European Painting, Gail Feigenbaum, believed that it would be possible to organize an exhibition focused on the work done by Degas in New Orleans in time for FrancoFête.

We knew that the essential loans would be difficult to secure. There are fewer than two dozen works by Degas thought to have been done in New Orleans and several of these could never be lent because of their fragility or because of the terms of their donation to public institutions. The key to our success lay in France in the city of Pau, where Degas's American masterpiece,

A Cotton Office in New Orleans, has resided in the Musée des Beaux-Arts since 1878. Dr. Feigenbaum traveled to Pau to present in person our request to the Director of the Museum, Philippe Comte, and the Mayor of the City, André Labarrère. While this great treasure rarely leaves Pau, the concept of our exhibition and the unique appropriateness of the New Orleans Museum of Art as the institution to organize it convinced Messrs. Comte and Labarrère to graciously agree to our request. Of course the exhibition would not have been possible without the generous cooperation of all of the other lenders in Europe and the United States, who are acknowledged individually elsewhere and whom I am pleased to thank collectively here.

Considering the enthusiasm with which Degas is now universally appreciated, studied, and exhibited, his New Orleans sojourn and family connections have received comparatively little attention. Perhaps this is because the New Orleans work is not typical of the Degas we have come to know so well, the painter of dancers, racehorses, and bathers. Recent books by Professor Marilyn R. Brown, of Tulane University in New Orleans, and Professor Christopher Benfey, of Amherst College, who have both contributed to this catalogue, have considerably increased our knowledge of this chapter in Degas's life. Fortunately for the success of our exhibition we were able to secure the scholarly services of the great Degas authority, Jean Sutherland Boggs, past Director of both the National Gallery of Canada and the Philadelphia Museum of Art, who immeasurably contributed to the organization of the exhibition and who wrote the perceptive catalogue entries.

After we had sent out our loan requests, we learned that we were not alone in planning an exhibition on this subject. Ordrupgaard in Copenhagen owns two of Degas's finest works from the New Orleans period and was in the early stages of a similar project. It was decided that we would make every effort to send the exhibition to the Ordrupgaard, a museum with an exquisite and highly important collection of nineteenth-century French painting. We are most grateful to Anne-Birgitte Fonsmark, Director of the Ordrupgaard, and her staff, particularly Thomas Lederballe, Curator, for working so diligently in making possible the presentation in Europe.

Needless to say the presentation of a major international exhibition could not be possible without financial support of generous patrons. *Degas and New Orleans* is presented by the State of Louisiana Department of Culture, Recreation and Tourism in celebration of FrancoFête. We are most grateful to Governor Michael J. Foster Jr., Lt. Governor Kathleen Babineaux Blanco, and the Louisiana State Legislature for providing the essential funding for the exhibition. Generous individual sponsorship was received from Michel David-Weill, Chairman of Lazard Frères & Co., LLC. In New Orleans further support was provided by Hibernia National Bank and Blumenthal Print Works. We are pleased to thank the Federal Council on the Arts and Humanities for providing full Federal Indemnification for the exhibition.

In New Orleans, history is ever present and so it is with Degas's visit. Today you may walk down Esplanade Avenue and see the fine house where Degas lived with his maternal relatives. You may follow the artist's footsteps on the way to the racecourse at the nearby fairgrounds or to his uncle Michel's cotton office on Carondelet Street. None of these places have changed much in 172 years. You might even pass one of René De Gas and Estelle Musson's descendants on your walk. It is my hope that this exhibition will bring to life a unique chapter in the three-hundred-year history of the familial and economic interconnections and the shared traditions of language and culture between France and Louisiana.

E. John Bullard
The Montine McDaniel Freeman Director
New Orleans Museum of Art

Acknowledgements

THE OPPORTUNITY TO PRESENT *Degas and New Orleans: A French Impressionist in America,* an exhibition that is so totally rooted in this unique community, would be satisfying enough. To be able to do so under the urgent deadline that we faced, however, was possible only with the grace, good humor, and hard work of a group of dedicated professionals. I have always believed that Degas attracts a particularly enlightened sort of collector and curator. This belief is now fact for me since the responses to our loan requests, both from individuals and institutions, proved to be impressively generous. We are most grateful to the many colleagues who lent their energies to help us trace lost paintings and convince reluctant lenders to change their minds.

For their support of the exhibition we are especially indebted to His Excellency François Bujon de l'Estang, Ambassador of France; Lazare Paupert, Cultural Attaché; and Pierre Buhler, Conseiller Culturel. For their good offices on our behalf we are grateful to Henri Loyrette, Director of Musée d'Orsay; Pierre Rosenberg, Director and President of the Louvre, and Arnaud d'Hauterives, Director of the Musée Marmottan. We are particularly grateful to André Labarrère, Mayor of Pau; and Philippe Comte, Director of the Musée des Beaux-Arts, Pau. Under such leadership the outlook is bright indeed for the next three hundred years of French-Louisiana relations.

To Marc Cooper, Director of the Vieux Carré Commission, I owe a particular thanks. He introduced me to the unforgettable M. and Mme Gaussens, citizens of Pau and friends of the city of New Orleans, who offered invaluable support in securing the all-important loan of *A Cotton Office in New Orleans.*

Meeting the great grandneices and nephews of Degas, descendents of René De Gas and Estelle Musson, has been one of the delights of this project. They have shared wonderful family stories and freely lent precious photographs and heirlooms to the exhibition. We are grateful to Amanda Belge, Emma Glenny, Edmund Martin, Dora Martin Miller, Hugh Miller, Marie Estelle Moyer, and Joan Prados.

Ambassador John Loeb and Walter Feilchenfeldt have been friends as well as lenders to the exhibition. Philip Conisbee, Anne-Birgitte Fonsmark, George Shackelford, Margret Stuffman, and Catherine LeGrand have been exceptionally helpful. Alison Whiting and Christie's donated their services to the exhibition. Anna Swinburne and Michel Strauss of Sotheby's responded expertly to our multiple requests for information. For their advice and help we would like to acknowledge: Peter A. Agelasto III, Joseph Baillio, Edgar Peters Bowren, Philippe Brame, Barbara Byrnes, Joan Caldwell, Richard Campbell, James Carder, Michael Conforti, Elizabeth Croog, James Cuno, Chris Deacon, Ingmari Desaix, Christopher Fischer, Sally Fontana, Bjorn Fredlund, Diana Griffin, William Griswold, Mrs. T. Ham, Ann Hoenigswold, Marianne Karabelnik, Edward L. Keenan, Thomas Lederballe, James Marrow, Hans Peter Mathis, Evan Maurer, Suzanne Folds McCullogh, Philippe de Montebello, Monique Nonne, Earl A. Powell III, Richard Rand, Sue Welsh Reed, Theodore Reff, Naomi Remes, Christopher Riopelle, Joseph Rishel, Ann Robertson, David Rockefeller, Malcolm Rogers, Harry Parker III, Maurice Parish, Berthe Saunders, James Seljic, Barbara Stern Shapiro, Alan Shestack, Marianna Shreve Simpson, Roulhac Toledano, Ken Wayne, Karen Weinberger, Robert Weil, and Gary Vikan.

The State of Louisiana's FrancoFête has given us the once-in-a-lifetime opportunity to mount this exhibition, for which we are profoundly grateful. We would like to mention the indefatigable support of the staff of the Lt. Governor Kathleen Blanco, especially Mary Perrault and Philip Jones. Support in New Orleans has been enthusiastic, extending to the accommodation of innumerable rush orders, to the sharing of unparalleled knowledge of New Orleans's history, culture, and architecture, and even to such amazing feats as Florence Jumonville's discovery of Estelle Musson's sheet music at the Earl K. Long Library, University of New Orleans. We appreciate the contributions of Thomas Bayer, Adelaide Wisdom Benjamin, Judith Bonner, Wayne Everard, Shannon Glasheen, Jenna Kuttruff, John Lawrence, Robert McCard, John McGill, Wilbur Meneray, Charles E. Noland, Jessie Poesch, Sally Reeves, Mary Strickland, Gary Van Zante, and David Villarrubia. To Mme Nicole Lenoir, Consul General of France in New Orleans, and Debbie de la Houssaye, in charge of artistic affairs, a special thanks. Patricia Chandler's help was invaluable.

As a specialist in baroque art, I am personally indebted to the more pertinent expertise of my collaborators on the catalogue. I have learned much from Christopher Benfey and Christina Vella, and I have relied on Marilyn R. Brown's help and friendship every step of the way. James B. Byrnes could not have been more informative or willing to share the fruits of his long research on the subject. He will recognize how much the present endeavor is inspired by his pioneering exhibition *Edgar Degas: His Family and Friends in New Orleans* of 1965.

From the first idea of *Degas and New Orleans* to catalogue deadline was just under a year. Though it has meant meeting impossible deadlines, endless accommodations, heroic efforts, and many, many extra hours of work, my colleagues at the New Orleans Museum of Art have been committed to the exhibition and have shouldered the burden with unfailing good cheer. Without their talent and hard work there would be no exhibition. Paul Tarver, Registrar, has worked tirelessly to safeguard the treasures in the exhibition. Wanda O'Shello edited the catalogue under intense time pressure. Judy Cooper often had to go far out of her way to take our photographs. Particular thanks are also due to William Fagaly, Assistant Director for Art; Steve Maklansky, Curator of Photographs; Pat Pecoraro, Curator of Special Exhibitions; Jackie Sullivan, Assistant Director for Administration; and Lee Morais, former Assistant Director for Education. The contributions of Joyce Armstrong, Michael Guidry, Emma Haas, Jonn Hankins, Jennifer Ickes, John Keefe, Nora Hennessy, Daniel Piersol, Carl Penny, Norbert Raacke, Ed Skoog, Annie Williams, and Alice Yelen deserve special mention. Two interns, Jill Chancey and Megan Faulk, also helped on the project.

I owe a special thanks to Sharon Litwin, Director of Development, who seized the day for *Degas and New Orleans* and made the hard work seem a pleasure. The exhibition would be a well-kept secret were it not for her expertise and the efforts of her staff. Victoria Cooke, Associate Curator for the exhibition, contributed in myriad ways to its realization. I cannot imagine how we could have finished this project without her research, commitment, and attention to detail. Most of all, I thank our director, E. John Bullard, for his untiring support and encouragement.

We are grateful to Ed Marquand of Marquand Books for turning a refractory manuscript into a book and for his patience. For being an ideal collaborator, and for conjuring the ambience of New Orleans 1872 in our galleries, thanks are owed to our designer Elroy Quenroe.

My husband, Bill, and daughter, Phoebe, provided vital moral support. My greatest debt of gratitude is to Jean Sutherland Boggs for her humanity, peerless knowledge of the field, and insight into Degas, which were truly a gift to the exhibition.

Gail Feigenbaum

Degas
and
New Orleans

GAIL FEIGENBAUM

Edgar Degas, Almost a Son of Louisiana

IN OCTOBER OF 1872 THE NOT-YET-FAMOUS ARTIST Edgar Degas left Paris for a journey to America (fig. 1). His destination was New Orleans, birthplace of his mother. There he would spend the winter with his relatives in a handsome mansion at 2306 Esplanade Avenue (fig. 2). The works he created during his visit are at the heart of this exhibition. Foremost among them is *A Cotton Office in New Orleans* (cat. 31), which has become the emblem of Degas's American adventure.

The story of Degas and New Orleans is, however, larger than this sojourn on the banks of the Mississippi. Though his stay was brief, Louisiana played a considerable and sustained role in Degas's life. The story is richly documented. It is a personal, family saga, but one that is inextricably bound up with the larger events of history—economics, war, epidemics. It is a remarkable illustration of the interconnection between French-Creole Louisiana and France.

What was the role of New Orleans in Degas's art? Was it a watershed in his career, or "a journey . . . very little else?"[1] The works gathered for this exhibition, which include not only most of those created in America but others that are closely related in date, style, or subject, encourage a new assessment of this question. Degas was anything but mechanistic in response to his world, and hence the answers are not simple or obvious. Jean Sutherland Boggs in this book offers new reflections on the meaning of New Orleans for Degas's art. Perhaps it is the very difficulty of "explaining" Degas's art, not to mention his own complicated character, that makes him unceasingly fascinating.

The story of Degas's visit to New Orleans has been told and retold. Each time it looks different according to the author's point of view, the light and shade of new evidence, and the corrections of old errors.[2] Though the famous *A Cotton Office in New Orleans,* and the sojourn that occasioned it may be mentioned in introductory art history courses, it seems an odd incident and often

FIG. 1. Portrait of Degas, copy of a lost photograph taken in 1872.

3

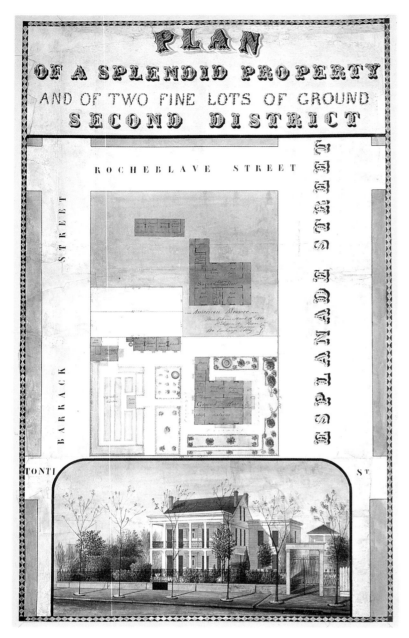

fails to survive in the memory. That Degas was the only member of the French Impressionists to have worked in North America is a fact that still takes many people by surprise.

This exhibition is not an introduction to the artist Degas, for there are several excellent publications that serve that purpose.[3] *Degas and New Orleans: A French Impressionist in America* is a "cabinet exhibition," a close exploration of a particular, and fascinating, aspect of an artist who had many facets. The concentrated topic affords the luxury of focus and reflection, of savoring of mood and nuance, of a more leisurely perusal of the works of art and their context.

FIG. 2. Adrien Persac (artist) and Eugène Surgi (civil engineer), *Plan of a Splendid Property and of Two Fine Lots of Ground/Second District* (Musson residence), 1860, watercolor, 55 × 30 in. New Orleans Notarial Archives.

FIG. 3. Theodore Lilienthal, *Private Residence, New Orleans 1867: Photographs for Emperor Napoleon III.* Napoleon-Museum Arenenberg.

The Worst of Times

As the old photographs of New Orleans and Degas's paintings attest, there was exquisite beauty to be found in the city (fig. 3). New Orleans has long been a name to conjure with, but a nostalgic, sepia-toned view of the city, a place of charm and vetiver fans, is hard to sustain in light of the miserable conditions of the postwar and Reconstruction periods. As Christina Vella's essay recounts, the city was dirty, unhealthful, and prone to epidemics that carried off at least four of Degas's Creole cousins as children and three of his nieces and nephews.

Some of the essays may at first seem surprising in their insistence on issues of race in regard to Degas and New Orleans, but in view of the history of both the family and the city, the pertinence is undeniable. Blacks were comparatively rare in Paris but constituted a large segment of the population of New Orleans. When Degas's younger brother who had moved to Louisiana wrote to his wife from Le Havre of seeing "two Negroes, the first since New Orleans," his sense of identification of black skin with the city was such that the sight made him want to take the next boat home.[4] Nineteenth-century French attitudes to race can be understood in part through accounts of travelers to America who discussed issues of race and slavery. More than one remarked on the absence in France of prejudice based on skin color.[5] Whatever the depth of truth in this assertion, it was certainly a truism applied to other European countries as well, and New Orleans's free people of color were often sent to Europe for their education. For example, René De Gas wrote that an acquaintance had sent his mulatto son for schooling near Bristol because "prejudices about color do not exist in England."[6] Edgar Degas's letters are salted with admiring descriptions of the blacks of New Orleans, yet their image is virtually absent from his Louisiana oeuvre.[7] As Christina Vella's essay underlines, French-Creole society may have been cultivated and charming, but it was profoundly racist, as was its white American counterpart in the city. Degas's relatives in New Orleans, including his brother René, were typical of their social class in this regard.[8] Those who had depended upon the plantations and the institution of slavery, including virtually everyone in the cotton business, were devastated by the outcome of the Civil War. White desperation was matched by black. After the war New Orleans's wealthy, educated, and skilled free people of color had lost much of the ground they had gained. The city was flooded with black freedmen who had little desire to work for their former owners for low wages, and who met stubborn resistance to all efforts to better their situation.[9] Other issues are raised by Christopher Benfey's discussion in this book of the celebrated inventor Norbert Rillieux, a free person of color living in exile in France, who was a first cousin of Degas's mother. Genealogical research conducted by James B. Byrnes and Victoria Cooke has uncovered further details about the Rillieux and other members of the family. This new evidence, detailed in Appendix I of this book, will doubtless be brought to bear on the ongoing discussion of how Degas's complicated attitudes to race and religion and other social issues are reflected in his art.

If the economic situation had an adverse effect on Degas's relatives, the artist himself had a more complicated response to American business, which Marilyn R. Brown explores in her essay on *A Cotton Office*. She has discovered that this painting, in a sense, portrays Degas's uncle Michel Musson going bankrupt before our very eyes. Given by the family to Tulane University, the

FIG. 4. *La Famille De Gas,* Patent of Nobility. Collection of Edmund Martin.

FIG. 5. Catherine Longchamps, *Portrait of Mme De Gas, née Musson, and her Sister, comtesse de Rochefort,* 1835, chalk and wash, 9 × 11 in. Historic New Orleans Collection.

De Gas–Musson Papers, comprised of scores of letters and documents (many of them extremely difficult to decipher), are an invaluable source for all matters concerning the two families. Brown, in her fundamental *Annotated Inventory* (1991) of this archive, has made the papers an accessible scholarly resource. In her essay for this book, Brown makes selections of these extraordinary letters easily available for the first time. Her commentary makes manifest how historical conditions affected Degas's family.

DEGAS, DE GAS, MUSSON

Edgar Degas is regarded as the archetype of the Parisian artist. His family background, however, was international.[10] Edgar's father, Auguste De Gas, was born in Naples to René-Hilaire Degas, a Frenchman living there in exile, having fled France during the Revolution, and his Italian wife, Aurora Freppa. The family owned a banking firm in Naples, and Degas's father later opened a branch in Paris.[11]

The family in Paris spelled their name De Gas, the particle indicating nobility. The De Gas patent of nobility is, in fact, a false concoction, and it has been shown that the family was descended from bakers (fig. 4).[12] Edgar changed the spelling to "Degas," eschewing the pretense to nobility.

Edgar's mother, Marie Célestine Musson, was born to a prominent French-Creole family in New Orleans. Her father, Germain Musson, had fled the uprisings in Saint Domingue and settled in New Orleans in 1809. He married advantageously into one of the oldest Creole families, the Rillieux. When his wife died at a young age in 1819 leaving five children, Germain packed them up, including the four-year-old Célestine, and moved to Paris. While providing for his children's future in Paris, Germain continued to carry on business in America, dividing his time between two continents. He was killed in 1853 when his coach overturned in Mexico, where he was attempting to make a fortune in silver mines. The Musson children were given a French upbringing and education. A portrait by Catherine Longchamps shows Célestine and her sister Anne Eugènie, later comtesse de Rochefort, in Paris (fig. 5). Célestine married Auguste De Gas in 1832. Her sister Anne and her brothers Henri and Eugène remained in Paris. Her eldest brother, Michel, studied law at the University at Göttingen, and learned the cotton business in England.[13] Michel returned to America to establish himself in New Orleans as a businessman. He had a varied career, serving as postmaster of New Orleans, and holding important positions in the insurance and cotton businesses.

Both of Degas's grandfathers had led lives of risk and adventure, fled for their lives from bloody revolutions, and made their own fortunes in their adopted cities of Naples and New Orleans. If the swashbuckling air is lacking in the lives of the next generation, an adventurous spirit as well as rich veins of rash, passionate behavior, genius, and even (in the Musson branch) madness ran through many of their children and grandchildren. No doubt these were invigorating, though at times devastating forces, in what might otherwise have been a quiet, bourgeois existence for Edgar Degas.

Edgar had two younger brothers, Achille (b. 1838) and René (b. 1845) (cats. 2, 3), for whom he had particular affection (fig. 6). Both would go to New Orleans to seek their fortunes. Edgar was likewise close to his two sisters, Thérèse (cats. 5, 6) and Marguerite (cat. 4).

In the marriage of Célestine and Auguste an intimation has been detected of strain sometimes blamed on Célestine's longing for a more active social life, although such opportunities would necessarily have been curtailed by the births of at least six children in a period of ten years.[14] It is likely that tensions were created by the exigencies of her father, Germain. An exchange of letters in the fall of 1835 between René-Hilaire Degas in Naples and his wife, Aurora, who was visiting in Paris, indicates that Germain was pressuring his new son-in-law Auguste to enter into a partnership to establish a cotton warehouse in Le Havre.[15] To start up the business, Auguste would have to secure the capital from René-Hilaire. Unwilling to commit his limited resources to only one son at the exclusion of the others, René-Hilaire offered to back the venture on the condition that Auguste take one of his brothers as a partner in the business. Auguste was not amenable to this proposal. René-Hilaire then wrote to his wife in a state of shock and dismay at the tone of a letter he had received from Germain chastising him for his selfishness. It is not difficult to imagine the stress put on Célestine by her father's failure to enlist Auguste, and the Degas family's capital, in the Musson family enterprises. Germain's intemperate reaction to the caution of Célestine's father-in-law cannot have helped matters between the young couple. A pattern of pitting one side of the family against the other was already evident while Edgar was yet in the cradle.

The links of the De Gas family with New Orleans were steadily nourished by economic ties. The children owned property in New Orleans left to them by their grandfather and mother. During the Confederacy, efforts were made to sell some of the De Gas property with the plan to invest the proceeds in Confederate bonds. Auguste planned to convert greenbacks into Confederate

FIG. 6. Edgar Degas, *Portrait of Achille in the Uniform of a Cadet*, 1859–62, oil on canvas, 25⅜ × 20½ in. Chester Dale Collection, National Gallery of Art, Washington, D.C.

bonds. Even Henri Musson urged that his brother-in-law consult him before buying Confederate bonds.

At the same time as Edgar and his brothers were growing up and being educated in Paris, reportedly tutored for some time by their uncle Henri Musson, on another continent their uncle Michel Musson was raising his own family in New Orleans. He had married Odile Longer, of the prominent Longer family (fig. 51). It was said to be "unpardonable social ignorance" not to know the married names of the eight Longer sisters, through whom the Mussons became cousins of many of the leading families, both French-Creole and American, of New Orleans.[16] This included the cousin Emma Hermann, whom Edgar's brother Achille eventually married. Michel and Odile Musson had seven children of which three daughters would survive into adulthood: Estelle, Désirée, and Mathilde. Their family would be the subject of the portraits Degas made during his visit to New Orleans.

The De Gas children's first encounter with their Louisiana cousins must have been with Désirée, when she apparently accompanied Michel Musson to Paris in 1857.[17] Edgar seems to have been in Italy and thus missed their visit. In January 1862, Estelle married Capt. Joseph Davis Balfour, nephew of Jefferson Davis, who was killed only ten months later in the battle of Corinth. Three weeks later their daughter Estelle Josephine Balfour, called Joe, was born. In June 1863, to escape the misery of New Orleans during Union occupation, Odile Longer Musson accompanied two of her daughters, Désirée and Estelle, as well as Estelle's new baby daughter on an extended visit to France.[18] It is from this three-year sojourn, much of it spent in the provincial town of Bourg-en-Bresse, where the ailing Odile's doctors recommended she convalesce, that all of the De Gas family's attachment to these women stems.

When the women first arrived in France, Edgar and René showed them the sights of Paris.[19] In Bourg-en-Bresse at least three visits by Edgar are documented: one at New Year's of 1864, another in February, and a third in January 1865. Odile and her daughters are immortalized both in Degas's portraits and in letters written by and about them. All evidence suggests that they were sweet-natured, charming, and brave in the face of the adversity that plagued them throughout their lives. The reciprocal affection between them and the children of Célestine was apparently instantaneous and genuine. Odile, as René readily owned in a letter, was a welcome surrogate mother for the children of her late sister-in-law. The adoration among the cousins was such that the eighteen-year-old René seems to have fallen in love with Estelle and within a month of the Mussons' arrival had fixed on the plan of accompanying the family back to America, ostensibly to deal with the De Gas family's property in New Orleans.[20]

Edgar was immediately at ease with his Louisiana relatives. They brought out a gentler side of his personality in contrast to the sharpness remarked on by many of his familiars. He made sketches of Estelle's baby, Joe (cat. 9). A handsome watercolor of Odile, Estelle, and Désirée is the most formal portrait from this moment (cat. 8). He is said to have been captivated by Désirée's beautiful hands, although none of the sketches he was supposed to have made of them survives. The visits of the De Gas cousins must have brought a desperately needed gaiety to a household where money to pay for living expenses and the welfare of their family in America were constant preoccupations. Estelle was at the time still in mourning for her husband. In Degas's *Estelle Musson Balfour* (cat. 10), the ache of this young widow's grief is so exposed, so unmediated by rhetorical convention, that the portrayal seems to trespass on her privacy. The artist's own phrase, "one cannot look at her without thinking that that face filled the eyes of a dying man," would be an apt colophon for the picture. Edgar manifested a particular sympathy for Estelle in his portraits. Already on this visit Estelle was having trouble with her eyes. She made a pilgrimage to Lourdes on this account, returning with a carved wooden rosary that was later given by her granddaughter to St. James Major Church in New Orleans. By 1869 she had lost all vision in her left eye. Her right eye deteriorated gradually until she became completely blind in 1876. Edgar, who also would have trouble with his eyesight,[21] was particularly attentive to her condition. His portraits of Estelle seem to acknowledge and signify her blindness. Edgar was fond of Désirée as well, and it has been conjectured that during his visit to New Orleans, she was on his mind as he toyed with the idea of marrying and having a family.

Estelle had talked about New Orleans and described it so vividly that René claimed he felt he knew it. Edgar having become an artist, and Achille's turbulent nature rendering him unsuitable, Auguste De Gas had intended René to take his own place in the family banking house. René protested that he would never make any money that way. "New Orleans is the place for young men with nerve," he proclaimed. Unfortunately for both sides of the family, René had more nerve than business acumen. Michel Musson's three sons had died in childhood, breaking their parents' hearts. Now Michel had only daughters and he was eager to have his nephew in New Orleans. The family correspondence is full of strategizing on how to convince Auguste De Gas to free his son from the obligation of entering the family business; there must not be any appearance of Michel exercising undue influence on the boy.[22] René got his way and joined the cotton factor's firm of Musson and Watt in 1865. The next year in England René made a disastrous speculation in cotton futures, losing $8,000 (worth more than ten times that sum in today's currency) of his family's and the De Gas bank's money. This debt plagued the family for years, for René was never able to pay it back. After Auguste's death in 1874, at least partly as a result of this loss and an outstanding loan to René from the De Gas bank in 1872, Edgar and his family in Paris were forced to live in conditions of utmost austerity to settle the affairs of the bank.[23]

René left for New Orleans and on June 17, 1869, he and Estelle were married.[24] At just this time, her eyes worsened and she lost the sight in one eye. They had a son Pierre in 1870, a daughter Odile in 1871. When Edgar Degas arrived the next year, he was in time to stand as godfather to the baby Jeanne who was born on December 20.[25] By 1869 Achille had joined René in New Orleans, where they lived in the mansion on Esplanade Avenue rented by Michel Musson. In 1871 Achille moved to 87 Royal Street in the French Quarter. The firm of De Gas Brothers (fig. 7) Importers and Commercial Merchants on 186 Common Street is listed in the City Directory from 1869 to 1872. In 1873 De Gas Brothers was listed as cotton buyers with an address of 3 Carondolet. De Gas Brothers was evidently doing well when Edgar came for his visit, although not well enough to build up the fortune that René had been counting on or to pay off his large debt.

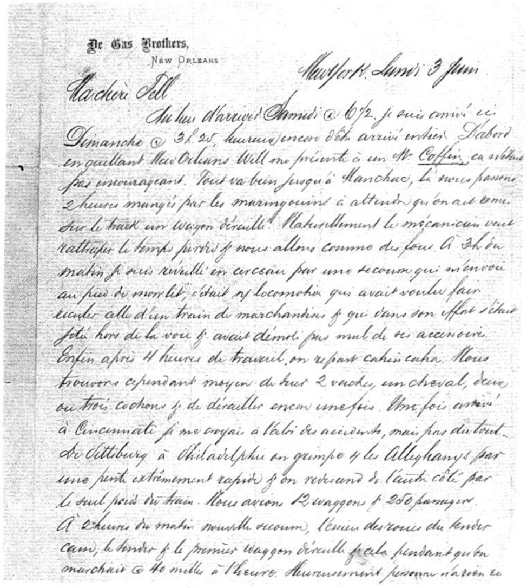
De Gas Brothers,
New Orleans

New York. Lundi 3 juin

Ma chère Tell

Au lieu d'arriver Samedi @ 6½ je suis arrivé ici Dimanche @ 3h 25, heureux encore d'être arrivé entier. D'abord en quittant New Orleans Will me présente à un Mr Coffin, ce n'était pas encourageant. Tout va bien jusqu'à Manchac, là nous passons 2 heures mangés par les maringouins à attendre qu'on ait remis sur le track un wagon déraillé. Naturellement le mécanicien veut rattraper le temps perdu & nous allons comme des fous. A 3h du matin je suis réveillé en cerceau par une secousse qui m'envoie au pied de mon lit, c'était notre locomotive qui avait voulu faire reculer celle d'un train de marchandises & qui dans son effort s'était jetée hors de la voie & avait démoli pas mal de ses accessoires. Enfin après 4 heures de travail on repart cahin caha. Nous trouvons cependant moyen de tuer 2 vaches, un cheval, deux ou trois cochons & de dérailler encore une fois. Une fois arrivé à Cincinnati je me croyais à l'abri des accidents, mais pas du tout. De Pittsburg à Philadelphie on grimpe les Alleghanys par une pente extrêmement rapide & on redescend de l'autre côté par le seul poids du train. Nous avions 12 waggons & 250 passagers. A 2 heures du matin nouvelle secousse, l'essieu des roues du tender cassé, le tender & le premier waggon déraillés & cela pendant qu'on marchait @ 40 milles à l'heure. Heureusement personne n'a rien eu

FIG. 7. Letter to Estelle Musson (on De Gas Brothers stationery) from René De Gas, Monday, June 3, 1872, De Gas–Musson Papers, ms. 226. Special Collections, Tulane University, New Orleans.

Musson's own business affairs had many ups and downs over the years. The Civil War brought significant reversals. While his wife and daughters were in France during the Civil War, their expenses were a serious worry, and Michel could not afford to get Estelle's furniture out of storage. Following the financial reversals of the Civil War, he had been forced to sell the mansion he had built on Third and Coliseum in the Garden District. He rented, for $300 a quarter, a house on Esplanade that enabled him to keep up appearances and accommodate his daughters' growing families. It was spacious and surrounded by gardens, really a suburban villa, though there were numerous other fine houses close by, and many of the best Creole families of the city lived in them (fig. 2).

In Paris meanwhile, there was the usual stream of visitors from Louisiana. French-Creoles traveled to Europe continuously. An introduction from the Mussons to the De Gas family in Paris or in Italy must have been in the possession of a quite a few visitors. In fact in 1834, shortly after the marriage of Célestine Musson and Auguste De Gas, we find the Louisiana planter Duncan Kenner in Naples borrowing horses from Henri Degas, Auguste's brother, and attending balls in his company, all of this doubtless on the strength of a Musson introduction.[26] Family friends of the Mussons from Louisiana, including the Millaudons, Ducros, and Beauregards, were visitors to the De Gas in Paris and in Naples beginning as early as the 1850s. Hardly a letter from the

De Gas family went to America without a greeting or inquiry about the Millaudons or the Ducros with whom they had become quite close. While the Creole visitors were plentiful, Edgar seems to have confined himself to making drawings and portraits of intimate friends like the Ducros and Millaudons. In 1858, during Degas's long stay in Italy, Auguste De Gas sent his congratulations on a drawing of the Beauregard twins, ten-year-olds Angèle and Gabrielle. Auguste was less impressed by the three other portraits of the twins' stepfather and mother, M. and Mme Millaudon, and that of their grandmother, Mme Ducros.[27] Edgar's father was not alone in his cool response. To eyes accustomed to the conservative portraiture tradition of Louisiana, Degas's portraits may have been viewed in certain instances with more bafflement than admiration (fig. 8).[28]

In 1867, the Paris Exposition Universelle, which we know Degas attended several times, would have offered the artist another source of information about New Orleans. There was at the exposition a New Orleans pavilion, the only one to represent a city, where large photographs of the city by Theodore Lilienthal were displayed. Their purpose was to entice foreign investment by showing the fine architecture and other sights of the city.[29] If Degas indeed looked at these photographs, and his ties to New Orleans must have made him curious, he would have seen the train depot at Lake Pontchartrain where five years later he would arrive in the city, and many of the buildings he would pass on foot or in the streetcar (fig. 9).

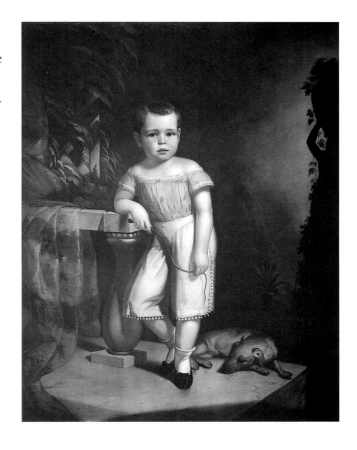

FIG. 8. Benjamin Franklin Reinhart, *Portrait of Eugène Musson*, ca. 1850, oil on canvas, 52 × 40 in. Collection of Ronald Smith, New Orleans.

ON THE EVE OF THE JOURNEY

In the summer of 1872 René was in Paris on business and spent much time with Edgar. Lively letters home are filled with news of the artist and announce his intention of coming back with him to New Orleans for a two-month visit.

In 1872, Edgar already had, as his brother put it, a few gray hairs in his beard. His career was hovering on the point of aesthetic and commercial success. He was experimenting with certain themes that would later become the focus of his art. He had arrived at the idea of the racetrack, as attested by paintings that were begun before the New Orleans trip (cats. 16, 18). Two exquisitely resolved ballet class paintings had been bought by the Paris dealer Durand-Ruel earlier that year.[30] Degas's letters to James-Jacques Tissot indicate at least a sporadic interest in strategies for placing his work with dealers and getting it sold, and making some money from his art.

Degas had not been a young prodigy, but arrived at his full powers through a long course of study and reflection, hesitation and experiment. It was not a question of technical mastery, which Degas achieved early. The problem was what kind of art to make at a moment when the French academic tradition was in crisis. His decision to become an artist had engendered a good deal of doubt in the mind of his father, who had intended his son to enter a more solid profession, urging him to law school. Edgar was determined, and continued a somewhat desultory, largely self-directed, education in art, eventually taking himself off for a long stay in Italy. It was easy for him to do, as there was family in Naples and Florence for him to stay with, and Rome was a mecca for French artists. The Italian sojourn had been an obligatory stage in a French artist's training since the seventeenth century, and its purpose was to assimilate the grand classical tradition of Italian art. Copying the antique as well as Raphael and the old masters was the standard procedure to which Degas would adhere.

Returning to Paris, Degas began to develop a repertoire of modern subjects and new ways to approach them. He met Édouard Manet and other artist friends who were also thinking along innovative lines. He had made some initial contacts with dealers who would market his work. Suddenly, in 1871, life in Paris was disrupted by the Franco-Prussian War. Degas, as did many of his friends, volunteered for the National Guard. He had hoped to be a sniper, but was dismayed to find out that his vision was too flawed. He joined an artillery company commanded by his old friend Henri Rouart. For much of the year the seige of Paris, and then the bloody and distressing confusion of the Commune, dominated the life of every Parisian. The disruption and difficulties took their toll. Something was wrong with his eyes—ophthalmia, what it was has never been entirely clear—and he was under treatment. He may have been eager for a break from life in Paris, for when his brother came to Paris the next year, Edgar determined to go back to New Orleans with him for a visit.

DEGAS IN NEW ORLEANS

"Prepare a fitting reception for le Grrrande Artiste," René wrote.[31] The epithet is the entirely affectionate mocking of a younger brother who, of all the family, may have been the only one to have recognized Edgar's genius. Shortly after announcing Edgar's plans to visit, René changed his tone and reported that Edgar's eyes were worse and he might not be in a condition to make the trip. His eyes were bothering him,

FIG. 9. Theodore Lilienthal, *Lake End Pontchartrain, New Orleans 1867: Photographs for Emperor Napoleon III*. Napoleon-Museum Arenenberg.

but it is possible, too, that the brothers were planning to surprise the family. Without a word to New Orleans both brothers boarded the *Scotia* in Liverpool on 12 October, and occupying cabin 231 set sail for New York. They docked in New York on October 23, at 6:34 A.M. (fig. 10).[32] The brothers were forced to give away the surprise of Edgar's visit when rumors of yellow fever in Louisiana prompted René to telegraph Achille to ask if there was any danger. The *Scotia* was an English ship and Edgar, speaking very little of the language, found the company on board stiff and tedious. He passed the time with his notebook making caricatures of fellow passengers and the birds flapping around them (cat. 19).

A day and a half as guest of his uncle's business associate James Watt was the sum of Degas's experience of New York. He was whisked onto the train for the four-day journey to New Orleans. Entranced by the American sleeping cars, Edgar wrote letters describing their ingenious comfort and efficiency. The train would have arrived in New Orleans at midday, in time for dinner, according to René's letter,[33] and the Mussons were assembled at the Lake Pontchartrain Depot to greet him (fig. 9).

The assembled company soon settled into the house on Esplanade and a routine described by Edgar in his letters: a morning walk to the De Gas Brothers offices to write long and eloquent letters home, and hoping for a line from his correspondents Manet, Tissot, Rouart, Frölich, and Dihau. Aside from the paintings and drawings he produced, Degas's own letters home are the chief source for our knowledge of his visit. They divulge his constant hunger for news from Paris. Degas asked that if his friend Désiré Dihau were to see his cook, Clothilde, he might ask her to write and tell him what was happening at home.[34]

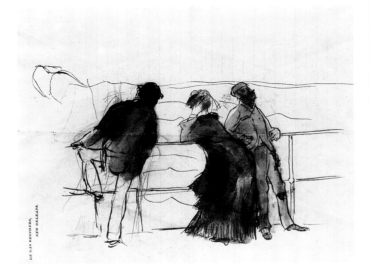

FIG. 11. Edgar Degas, *La Bastingage*, pen and wash on De Gas Brothers–New Orleans letterhead. Private collection, France.

FIG. 10. Steam Ship *Scotia* Passenger List, *New York Times*, 23 October 1872, page 8. New York Historical Society.

Passengers Arrived.

In steam-ship Scotia, from Liverpool.—Capt. J. B. Eads, Rev. J. Hughes, Mrs. E. O. Horlbeck, Mrs. J. F. Simmons, Mrs Newbrough and 2 children, A. McLeod, R. Donald, W. M. Fliess, Mr. and Mrs. C. E. Miller, Mrs. Goddard and 2 sons, Mr. and Mrs. Wistar Morris, Miss F. H. Dering, Miss E. N. Hurlbut, Mr. and Mrs. H. A. Rice, Miss N. Grant, Mr. and Mrs. A. E. Borie and servant, 2 Misses Borie, Dr. and Mrs. D. Bly, Mrs. Buckley and daughter, Mrs. H. K. Corning and daughter. Dr. and Mrs. C. Morris, Mrs. Kopper, Miss Loring, Mr. and Mrs. P. R. Pyne, M. T. Pyne, P. R. Pyne, Miss A. Pyne, Mrs. Taylor and maid, C. Connolly, A. Molloy, Miss A. Gould, Mrs. S. L. Bowman, Mr. and Mrs. S. Coleman, Mrs. Parker Jones, Mrs. Siegling, R. Siegling, S. E. Pecker, A. J. Pollard, J. H. Keene, E. W. Walgrove, Mr. and Mrs. G. C. Morris and child, 2 Misses Morris, Miss Harris, Miss Foster, Miss C. B. Smith, Mr. and Mrs. J. E. Thompson, Mr. and Mrs. Fahnestocck, 2 children and 2 servants, 2 Masters Fahnestock, Mrs. Dock, R. de Gas, E. de Gas. Mr. and Mrs. W. Sceonerzz and 2 children, Miss Schmertz, Mrs. J. Bishop and servant. Mrs. J. M. White, Master J. White, Mr. and Mrs. D. H. Wickham, J. P. Cullen, J. O'Connor, Mr. and Mrs. E. A. Livingston and servant, three Misses Livingston, two Masters Livingston, Miss A. Vad Falkenstayne, Miss G. C. Smith. Miss O'Smith and servant, Mrs. G. H. Derby, Miss Derby, Mrs. M. Pitts and servant, Mrs. M A. Brayley and two servants, 3 Misses Brayley, Miss L. Martin, 2 Misses Varicks, Miss Taylor, Miss Mohun, Countess R. de la Vaulx, Mr. and Mrs. H. Berthold, Mr. and Mrs. C. E. O'Hara and 3 children, Mrs. S. Borel and child, Mr. and Mrs. C. H. Scharfer and child, A. Wilcocks, C. H. Spang, Mrs. M. Hart, Miss Hart, R. B. Lawrence, B. Hart, D. Parish, H. A. Taylor, E. I. Sarboris, A. Sarboris, Mr. and Mrs. W. Hilton and servant, P. Ferrer, E. Harvey. Mr. and Mrs. W. P. Wright, T. I. Semmes, Mr. and Mrs. C. Pfizer and child, Mr and Mrs. J. J. Post and servant, Miss Mahoney, Mr. and Mrs. W. Barron, 3 children and 3 servants. E. Lonegan, G. H. Phelps, Miss Tobey, Miss Nash, E. J. Phelps, Mr. and Mrs. J. Kieke, 3 children and servant, Mr. and Mrs. A. G. Brown, The O'Connor Don. D. O'Connor, T. W. Strong, J. Bellows. F. Grisenheimer, M. Baird, C. O. Baird, Mrs. McDonald, Miss L. F. HcDonald, Mrs. S. Jackson and servant, Mrs. D. C. Wilson, Miss Higgins, Mr. and Mrs. R. S. Morse. Mr. and Mrs. T. Smith, B. H. Henderson, M. H. Henderson, Mr. and Mrs. F. B. Arnold, child and 2 servants, T. E. Read, Miss Read, Mrs. McCoskey, Mr. and Mrs. W. McMichael, child and servant, Miss Boyd, two Misses Massey, W. S. Massey, A. Blackburn, M. A. Frost, W. Dickson and servant, H. Brewster, Miss Brewster, Miss Britton, Mrs. Stuart, 2 children and nurse, Mr. and Mrs. D. H. Gregory, Mr. and Mrs. N. Peck, J. B. Baker, W. S. Jourdan, Mrs. J. Lamson and servant, Rev. J. Janssens, G. Lamothe, T. W. Morris, A. Leslie, J. Spence, E. Pendleton, A. Cowell, W. Tilden and servant, C. Bowles and secretary, J. T. Lewis, J. M. Keating, C. E. Schmertz, J. Stuart, F. Georg, F. Mohun, Chancellor Zabriski.

In steam-ship City of Brooklyn, from Liverpool.—Mrs. Parsons, Miss Stevens, Mrs. C. Whiteley, Mrs. Preedy, Arthur Wright, Mr. Pemberton, Wm. Rice, B. Harwood, J. T. Harwood. Mrs. Harwood and 3 children, A. Herthel, R. M. Miller, G. J. Witthians, Rev. Clarence Buel, H. C. Lockwood, Ed. Orgell T. Orgell, J. G. Baldwin, Mrs. Baldwin, Miss Baldwin, Ed. Eagan, F. McIlwain, Jos. Monte Denico, Rev. M. Murphy, T. B. Bissett, G. Appleton, B. J. Eyre, Mr. Deal, Mrs. Deal and child, J. H. Woodcock, Miss J. Caunce, Miss Nellie Herd, E. C. Palmer, Mrs. Palmer, Mrs. Mary Keye, Mrs. Jane Parry, O. W. West, Mrs. West, J. P. Beaumont, Mrs. Beaumont, Mrs. H. Milich, Mr. Enser, Mrs. Enser, Jas. Phelan, Mrs. Phelan, Mr. Phelan and five children. Wm. Hopper, Major J. R. Jennings, Mrs. Jane Pugh.

FIG. 12. *Cotton Warehouse,* 19th century, photograph. Southeastern Architectural Archives,
Tulane University, New Orleans.

Degas's moods varied. His earliest letters register his initial excitement of
the trip. He was ebullient at being reunited with his adored and adoring New
Orleans family, the abundance of new nieces and nephews, and the novelties
of the city. He described the sights, but he had to be careful out of doors as the
strong, bright light of New Orleans hurt his eyes, which had been bothering
him even before the trip. In fact the weather conditions of New Orleans proved
difficult for Degas, "climate that must be unbearable in the summer and is
somehow deadening during the other seasons." Newspapers confirm Degas's
reports of exceptionally warm winter weather, with temperatures of 24 and 26
degrees centigrade (75 and 79 degrees Fahrenheit) in December, even higher
in January. The humid heat took its toll. "One does nothing here, it lies in the
climate, nothing but cotton, one lives for and from cotton." A slight attack of
dysentery made matters worse. Degas walked, took a few excursions in and out
of town, and talked about the fascinating things he saw. Yet the exotic pan-
orama of New Orleans weighed on him. His inspiration to paint the fantastic
sights was fleeting. By turns lethargy, restlessness, and homesickness hung over
his days. His ennui seemed to accompany the realization that he was not the
artist to paint the New World. He would not paint the "Monde Illustré," referring to a periodical with prints replete with description and anecdote. He resolved to return to his own corner of Paris and paint what he knew. "One loves
and gives art only to the things to which one is accustomed."[35]

Degas's familiarity with Parisian nightlife, with the operas, cafés, and the
demimonde, is well-known. The extent to which he patronized the less varied
or sophisticated diversions of New Orleans is not known. He said little on the
subject, noting the presence of a French company with a Mlle Winke who was
a dancer; he regretted not being introduced. There was, he remarked, a company for "comedy, drama, vaudevilles, etc., where there are some quite good
people and a great deal of Montmartre talent."[36] He reported sadly that the
opera season was canceled, which was a genuine privation for himself, and

especially for the musical Estelle. He heard operatic recitals and concerts but was rather disappointed. Estelle's music enlivened the household on Esplanade Avenue. Her sheet music indicates a taste for opera and French songs (fig. 13), and it is probable that she was one of the singers in the duet portrayed in *The Song Rehearsal* (cat. 34) set in the Mussons' parlor.

The Mussons had many friends and connections in New Orleans, and even with Estelle's confinement, there were visits and dinner parties. Degas wrote to Henri Rouart that he had dined with Mr. Bujac, an associate of Rouart's in the ice-making business in New Orleans. Rouart, an engineer, had developed the machinery for manufacturing ice that was in use in the factory on Tchoupitoulas Street (see fig. 103), and Degas spoke of his intention to visit the facility.[37] Family members and friends recall stories of excursions made by Degas to the Millaudons' plantation and other homes of the Ducros and Beauregards, close friends of the Mussons and of the De Gas in Paris.

"All day long," wrote Degas, "I am among these dear folk, painting and drawing, making portraits of the family." He complained of the difficulty. The lighting was impossible and his relatives did not take him quite seriously. To get cousin Mathilde, nursing the two-month-old Willy, to sit for him was a chore (cats. 24, 25, 26). Posing little nieces and nephews on the steps was an exercise in futility (cats. 29, 30). Frustrating conditions aside, the family portraits from New Orleans form a unique group, and virtually all the works from the trip are, on some level, family portraits. Ostensibly, Degas was making the portraits to oblige the family. He says as much in his letters. Yet none seems to have been presented to the sitter. Degas either took or sent back to Paris all the New Orleans portraits. *A Cotton Office in New Orleans* excepted, he kept them in his studio, almost a substitute for the presence of the people.[38] After Mathilde's death, Michel Musson repeatedly begged for Degas's portrait of her. Putting his uncle off with promises, Degas never sent it. Late in his career, he attached strips of canvas to the top and bottom of the *Portrait of Estelle Musson*, sketching in an extended composition that he never completed.[39] Most of the New Orleans family portraits remained with him in his atelier until his death.

Degas's regard for his cousins, and his persistent portrayals of them, may have been tinged by an association of these young women with his own mother, only thirty-two years old when she died. Edgar was barely thirteen at the time of her death, his brothers even younger. It is not without significance that René promptly fell in love with his mother's niece, or that Achille eventually married a French-Creole woman. Aside from family resemblance, there was the style of

FIG. 13. *Mon âme à dieu mon coeur à toi!* Album of sheet music belonging to Estelle Musson. Earl K. Long Library, University of New Orleans.

Portrait of Estelle Musson (cat. 28), added strips of canvas, top and bottom, as it appeared in Degas's estate sale.

comportment of the French-Creole women. They were described as ineffably old-fashioned, in contrast to the modern Parisian, or even American women from elsewhere.[40] Basking amidst the domestic charms of his brother's ménage, Edgar mused, "A good family: it is a really good thing to be married, to have good children, to be free of the need of being gallant. Ye gods, it is really time one thought about it." He found the French-Creole women pretty, "and many have even amidst their charms that touch of ugliness without which, no salvation."

The notorious difficulty in identifying which cousin is portrayed in the various New Orleans pictures, even with the aid of photographs of the sitters, may point to something else. At times Degas seems to efface some of the individuality of the sitters, blurring the specific features and allowing a family resemblance to dominate. For example, in the case of the portrait in the New Orleans Museum of Art (cat. 28), had Estelle's own ex-husband not identified her as the sitter, it would have been difficult indeed to recognize her as the same woman in the portrait in the National Gallery of Art (fig. 96), or in the photographs (figs. 55, 64). In a haze of family resemblance, the individual features of the Musson cousins are indistinct. A nostalgic reception of the French-Creole women, as representatives of "a past whose perfume has barely evaporated," seems to emerge in Degas's portraits as well. Perhaps in this act of making family portraits Degas was summoning memories of his own mother. A Freudian interpretation might help to explain the sense of difficulty, failure, and wasted time that attended at least the artist's own descriptions of the process of making the portraits.

The heavy air of domestic routine and nostalgia, sometimes agreeable, other times irritating to Degas, cleared at once when he set to work on his great American project, *A Cotton Office in New Orleans*. In contrast to his frustrated accounts of the family portraits, Degas described his progress on this picture in brisk and vigorous language. He was keen to sell the work and take advantage of the international market, the milieu and source of income of the rest of his family, to make some money from his art. (The story of the picture is told by Marilyn R. Brown in this book.) With it Degas regained his energy and enthusiasm. Until this painting, artistically the trip had been "a journey I have done . . . very little else." He had not painted New Orleans. With the *Cotton Office* he had redeemed his experience: He had painted America.

"BETTER ART," FORTUNE, AND MISFORTUNE

Degas had intended to stay only two months in New Orleans. His trunks were packed to leave in early January, but he reported that he had missed his train and the ship sailed without him. Had he left on time, there might have been no *Cotton Office in New Orleans.* He was almost certainly in New Orleans for Mardi Gras on February 25. Whether his brother-in-law William Bell, who had been in Paris the previous summer, had followed René's advice to buy the costumes from the "Ballet of the Insects" for the Mistick Krewe of Comus is not known. The costumes, "all ravishing, from the ladybug to the roach," would have been perfect for the theme of "Missing Links to Darwin's Origin of the Species" which was the theme of the Mistick Krewe of Comus that year (fig. 14).[41] In any event, Degas was anxious to make the return crossing on a French ship, and probably traveling via Havana, he was back in Paris in mid-March.

It appears that Degas picked up the thread of his work again by returning to paintings, as well as subjects done before his trip. He seems to have reworked some of his earlier pictures shortly after his return. As Edmond de Goncourt put it, "after many attempts, experiments, and thrusts in every direction, he has fallen in love with modern subjects and has set his heart on laundry girls and danseuses."[42] The familiar subjects of Paris with which Degas had experimented before his trip, and had missed so much in New Orleans, were now established as themes to be studied in suites of variations. When Degas returned to Paris, he knew where he would go with his art, and there were no more false starts or hesitations. The fully realized perspectival setting with its careful plotting of figures in space, the precise delineation of forms, the fine finish of *A Cotton Office in New Orleans* represented a summa of the past. Even in New Orleans Degas had drawn a bead on the future, an affinity with the Impressionists with pictures that were more like the sketchier, second version, the *Cotton Merchants in New Orleans* (cat. 32): in his words, "less complicated and more spontaneous, better art." Collectors were buying and commissioning works.

Attendant upon the artistic gains were family misfortunes. Many, perhaps the majority of these misfortunes, were linked to New Orleans. For Degas bad luck, scandal, and tragedy, the exigencies of relatives, exerted a constant undertow from Louisiana.

Late in 1873 Auguste De Gas fell ill en route to Naples, and Edgar traveled to Turin to care for his father. Auguste died in Naples in February, his estate entangled in debt. Two years later, with the failure of the De Gas family bank, the financial situation of Edgar's entire family grew dire.[43] René's large debts to the bank now became an urgent problem, and stern efforts to force him to make good on these were unsuccessful.[44] Business in New Orleans was not thriving for either René or Michel Musson, and it appears that money to pay off the debts was simply not available. Edgar and his siblings were living on

FIG. 14. C. Briton, *Grasshopper, Procession of Comus,* Missing Links to Darwin's Origin of Species, Mardi Gras 1873, watercolor. William B. Wisdom Collection, Special Collections, Tulane University, New Orleans.

the brink of privation, giving over all their resources, selling their furniture, to honor the family's obligations.[45]

At the same time Achille De Gas became the center of scandal when he was accosted by the husband of his former mistress on the steps of the Paris Bourse and, in turn, wounded the man with a revolver. A trial, in which it was concluded that Achille had been provoked, a small fine and a month in prison were the legal consequences. Five years later in New York, Achille would marry a woman from New Orleans, Emma Hermann, a cousin of his own Creole cousins.

In 1878, the year the Musée de Pau acquired *A Cotton Office*, a far more serious family scandal erupted in New Orleans. René De Gas deserted Estelle and their five children and eloped with their married friend and neighbor, America Durrive Olivier. The white house where she lived on Tonti Street, and which still stands, can be seen at the end of the garden through the back door of the Mussons' house in *Children on a Doorstep* (cat. 29). The scandal opened a chasm between the Musson and De Gas families, and between Edgar and René.[46] René's attempts to enlist other members of the family to effect a reconciliation with Edgar were futile.[47] A rapprochement between the brothers came only after many years.

Michel Musson was nearly out of his mind with fury at René, and the estrangement of the families was perhaps inevitable. His efforts to elicit a word of support from Edgar were in vain. Edgar would not write to the Mussons, though other members of the family assured them that he had refused to see René, and that his sympathy was with Estelle and her family. Michel legally adopted René and Estelle's children, changing their names to Musson.

Meanwhile in Paris, the psychologically unstable Eugène Musson by 1876 had escalated his activities from writing long political tracts and letters to the editor, to laying seige to the wife of the minister of foreign affairs and writing obscenities. The police were involved. Edgar's friends the Camus were embroiled in Eugène's breakdown, and Edgar himself had to retrieve his deranged uncle from their house so that Henri Musson could take him to the asylum. The record is silent, but Edgar was not likely to have relished his own part of such an episode. Eugène was judged to be insane and committed to the asylum at Charenton.[48] Henri Musson in Paris took charge of his brother Eugène's welfare. When Henri died in 1883, Michel Musson's desperate pleas from New Orleans for Edgar's help in overseeing Eugène's care were ignored. Edgar refused to answer the letters (fig. 56).

In 1878, the year of René's desertion, Mathilde Musson and the six-year-old Jeanne De Gas, daughter of René and Estelle and Edgar's godchild, died of

FIG. 15. Theodore Lilienthal, *Joe Balfour*, age 18, cabinet card, albumen print. Collection of Edmund Martin.

yellow fever. In 1881 René and Estelle's son, eleven-year-old Pierre, and eighteen-year old Joe Balfour, Estelle's child from her first marriage, both died. After so much heartbreak, Michel Musson died in 1885. Désirée lived until 1902. Estelle, widowed, abandoned, blind, and grieving for four of her children, was a woman of remarkable endurance and fortitude. A house, which still stands at 1015 Esplanade, was built for her in 1881 by her cousin James Freret. She lived until 1909; her children remembering her cheerful and kind nature.

Despite the familial and financial disasters brought about by René, Edgar eventually reconciled with his brother. When the artist died in 1917, he left René half of his substantial estate. Upon René's death in 1921, the New Orleans family was heard from once more. René had been living in Paris with his second family. His children with America Durrive inherited his estate. When Gaston and Odile Musson, the two surviving children of René and Estelle, learned of their father's death, they filed a lawsuit in Paris claiming their share of the estate.[49] It came as a surprise to René's Parisian children that their father had earlier fathered a family in Louisiana. The French court eventually ruled that the estate, which was substantial, be divided amongst René's children on both sides of the ocean. In this way a share of Edgar Degas's fortune, the fruits of a successful career, returned to New Orleans after his death.

Degas's wax sculptures were cast in bronze after his death. His estate had a set of casts made outside regular commerce, marked 'HER. D,' which were expressly intended for distribution to Edgar Degas's surviving relatives. As part of the settlement of the lawsuit regarding René's inheritance, his children Odile and Gaston Musson in New Orleans received casts.[50] In the parlor of their house on Second Street, while Gaston Musson's children were growing up, were ten Degas bronzes. By this time the late artist was, of course, famous. The New Orleans family had loved Edgar, but had never treated "Le grrrande artiste" with great deference. Edgar's grandnieces and grandnephews who grew up in the house used to put plastic saddles on the bronze horses (cat. 15) and gallop them around the parlor. Their mother despaired of her husband's habit of emptying his pipe into the basin of the bronze bather, and of irksome guests who used Degas's sculpture as an ashtray.[51]

Degas's *Portrait of Mme René De Gas, née Estelle Musson* (cat. 28) is yet another New Orleans story. When the portrait appeared on the art market in 1964, James B. Byrnes, director of the New Orleans Museum of Art from 1962 to 1972 (then called the Isaac Delgado Museum of Art), led a campaign to acquire

FIG. 16. "Bringing Estelle home," 1964, photograph of fund-raiser held at the Isaac Delgado Museum of Art. New Orleans, *Times-Picayune*.

the picture by public subscription. Funds were raised, mostly modest contributions from private individuals, but on the day before the museum's option on the picture was to expire, the goal had not been met. Preparations to return the portrait were being made when an eleventh-hour donation saved the bid to "bring Estelle home"(fig. 16). In celebration of the acquisition, James B. Byrnes mounted a small exhibition, accompanied by a catalogue, *Edgar Degas: His Family and Friends in New Orleans*, to which all subsequent scholarship on the subject is much indebted. The exhibition of 1999 likewise embodies the consciousness and pride of New Orleans's unique link to an artist who described himself as "almost a son of Louisiana."

NOTES

1. See Boggs in this book. Loyrette, 1991, argued that the impact of the New Orleans sojourn on Degas's art was indetectable. The visit to New Orleans may also be considered apart from the roles played by New Orleans and the interconnections between the Louisiana and Parisian branches of the family, just as aesthetic issues may be considered separately from biographical ones.

2. See Rewald, Boggs, and Byrnes in New Orleans, 1965; Lemoisne, 1946–49; McMullen, 1984; Loyrette, 1991; Benfey, 1997, who provide accounts of the New Orleans period.

3. The literature is vast but the indispensable works are the biography by Loyrette; the *catalogue raisonné* by Lemoisne, 1946–49; the retrospective exhibition, Paris, Ottawa, New York, 1988; the portrait exhibition, Zürich, 1994–95.

4. De Gas–Musson, July 25, 1872, René to Joe Balfour, Box II, folder 46d.

5. See for example J. J. Ampère, *Promenade en Amérique,* vol. II, 1855, chap. VIII, "La Nouvelle Orleans"; D'Almbert, 1856, "Les Noirs et l'esclavage," 55–63. From d'Almbert: "nous font considérer la race noir a l'egal des autres; nous sommes fier de compter parmi nos amis des hommes de couleur, qui ont été nos compagnons d'études, nos camarades et nos émules dans les carrières sérieuses de la vie; . . . nos ne tenons aucun compte de la couleur de l'epiderme."

6. Brown, 1991, Box II, folder 47d.

7. See Benfey, 1997, and Appendix II in this book. The terms used for denoting race throughout this book are those chosen by the authors of the individual essays. An editorial decision was made not to impose either uniform or historically based usages. The Degas and Mussons generally used "Negre" in their letters which has been variously translated as "black" or "Negro."

8. The family's attitudes are expressed in their correspondence, for which see Brown in this catalogue, and Brown, 1991. Just after Degas's visit Michel Musson joined the new Unification Movement dedicated to promoting cooperation between the races. Musson's first cousin, Edmond Rillieux, a free person of color (younger brother of Norbert Rillieux) was also a signer of the Unification Manifesto. By the next year Musson, as well as his two sons-in-law, René De Gas and William Bell, were playing leading roles in the White League, a white supremacist organization. (All three men are portrayed in *A Cotton Office in New Orleans.*) See Benfey, 1997, 184–92, for fuller discussion.

9. John Blassingame, *Black New Orleans, 1860–1880* (Chicago, 1973), provides an overview of the period.

10. This brief introduction to the family is augmented in Appendix II by Byrnes and Cooke in this book, as well as Boggs's entries.

11. The story of Degas and his Italian connections is recounted in Boggs, 1963. See also the intriguing family correspondence in Raimondi, 1958, and Loyrette in Rome, 1984.

12. Sigwalt, 1988, 1188–91. It is likely the fraudulent patent of nobility in the exhibition was brought or sent to New Orleans when René was getting married here. French-Creole society put a high value on their patents of nobility and routinely brought copies with them when they moved to America.

13. "Louisiana Students in German Universities in the Nineteenth Century," *Genealogical Review* (Baton Rouge, La., June 1967). Musson's fellow student, Henry Wadsworth Longfellow, mentioned that "Musson fought a duel of 12 Gangens (rounds) with a Hildesheimer. Neither wounded."

14. McMullen, 18–21.

15. Letters in Raimondi, 12 November 1835, 24 November 1835, 9 December 1835, 104–7.

16. King, 1921, 389.

17. The trip may have been prompted by the death of the comtesse de Rochefort, Michel's sister. There is also some possibility that Mathilde had met the De Gas family either in Naples or Paris. It was usual for young French-Creoles to make a trip to Europe, and passenger lists from ships at the port of New Orleans attest to the frequency of such voyages. A young woman might travel to Europe chaperoned by family friends or cousins, and the Musson family was well-supplied with these.

18. Mathilde, the third daughter, who had recently married William Bell, remained at home this time. A nurse was also part of the Musson entourage, as the family correspondence attests.

19. Brown, 1991, Box I, folder 34d, letter from Désirée to Michel Musson, 24 June 1863.

20. Ibid., Box I, folder 34f, letter from René De Gas to Michel Musson, 22 July 1863.

21. See Richard Kendall, "Degas and the Contingency of Vision," *Burlington Magazine* (March 1988), 180–97, and more recently Philippe Lanthony, "Degas," *Pathographies,* no. 110 (1990), 2382–01, whose conclusions are summarized as follows by Loyrette, 784, n. 98: One can say that the ocular condition suffered by Degas presented the following characteristics: as a young adult of twenty to thirty years of age the ocular refraction showed only myopia and weak astigmatism. He also had significant photophobia (sensitive to light) with low central visual acuity with a scotoma (a blind or dark spot in the visual field). Absent were ocular pain, metamorphoses (where a grid or series of lines would distort or not be visible); no trouble with color vision. Good peripheral vision. The overall diagnosis would be bad central vision with a scotoma. For help with the technical translation we are indebted to Rick Sanders, Department of Ophthalmology, Tulane University Medical School.

22. Brown, 1991, Box I, folder 42, Désirée to Michel Musson, November 18, 1863.

23. See Brown's essay in this catalogue.

24. Rewald in New Orleans, 117.

25. The baptismal record of 5 February 1873 was found by Victoria Cooke.

26. Garner Ranney, ed., *A Man of Pleasure— And a Man of Business: The European Travel Diaries of Duncan Farrar Kenner 1833–1834,* 1991, 49, 112. As Benfey, 1997, 268, n. 1, has shown, Kenner knew the Mussons in Paris as well.

27. Paris, Ottawa, New York, 51.

28. If the family anecdote is reliable, Madame Ducros made the excuse that Degas's portrait of her would not fit into her stateroom, and she would pick it up later—which she never did. Toledano, 1995. (I am grateful to James B. Byrnes for providing us with a copy of the manuscript.)

29. Hans Peter Mathis and Gary van Zante, eds., *New Orleans 1867: Photographs for Emperor Napoleon III* (London, forthcoming). The photographs show the cleanest and most prosperous face of the city, in keeping with the purposes of the endeavor, and very much in contrast to the city described by Vella in this book.

30. *Dance Class,* Metropolitan Museum of Art, Lemoisne 297; *Dance Class at the Opéra,* Lemoisne 298.

31. Brown, 1991, Box II, folder 46b, letter René to Estelle 17 July 1872.

32. Correspondence between James B. Byrnes and W. B. Brown of the Cunard Steamship Company. The *Scotia* was the last paddle steamer to be built for Cunard Line and is believed to have been the most powerful paddle steamer ever built. Speed was probably the factor when René had chosen to make the crossing on the *Scotia* in June that year on which voyage he struck up an acquaintance with the daughter of Pierpont Morgan who was "riche à millions." Brown, 1991, Box II, folder 45b, René to Estelle, June 18, 1872.

33. Brown, 1991, Box II, folder 49e, René to Estelle, October 6, 1872.

34. Degas's excellent cook, Clothilde, is mentioned several times in the correspondence of René, who was trying to find a French maid to bring back to New Orleans. Clothilde's dream was to go to America, but René judged her too smart, and likely to bolt for a good marriage and open her own business. It emerges in René's letters that the much-admired, and "spirituelle" Clothilde had been a laundress before working for Edgar. When the artist wrote to his confidantes, "but one Paris laundry girl, with bare arms, is worth it all for such a Parisian as I am," or "long live fine laundering in France," to his close friends was his reference generic, to art, or was Clothilde perhaps on his mind?

35. On Degas's choice not to portray the exotic, see his letters home, Appendix II, and Christopher Benfey's essay in this book.

36. The performances are announced and reviewed in the daily newspapers in great detail.

37. Rebecca R. deMuth, "Edgar Degas, Henri Rouart: Art and Industry" (M.A. thesis, unpublished, University of Pittsburgh, 1982).

38. Degas kept portraits of his Parisian family in the studio as well. He had a particular attachment for one of his father with the musician Pagans, Orsay, whether because of feelings for his father, or something that he had captured in his father's manner, or because of the success of the image.

39. Byrnes in New Orleans, fig. 1. The strips were removed before the painting was acquired by the museum.

40. See Benfey, 1997, and Vella in this book. Ampère (as in n. 5) describes it as "une certaine grâce créole."

41. Byrnes in New Orleans, 76. René's letter to Estelle, July 17, 1872, Brown, 1991, Box II, folder 46b (passage not transcribed).

42. Journal Goncourt, 1956, 967–68, as translated in McMullen, 241.

43. See Brown in this book.

44. Ibid.

45. Ibid.

46. See the correspondence in Byrnes and Cooke in this book.

47. See Paris, Ottawa, New York, 376, letter of 27 June, and correspondence between the Mussons, Achille, and Edgar in Brown, 1991.

48. Brown, 1991, Box III, folder 7a, letter from Henri to Michel Musson, 17 January 1877.

49. Copies of documents relating to the case, including the correspondence of the lawyers of Odile and Gaston Musson, are in De Gas–Musson, Box V, folders 8a, b, c.

50. Pingeot, 1991, 194, publishes the contract with Hebrard. The Mussons were not listed as heirs of René De Gas.

51. These stories were related to me by Degas's grandnieces. Nine of the bronzes were sold to Silberman Gallery in 1950. A copy of the bill of sale is in De Gas–Musson, Box V, folder 9. The tenth bronze was given to the New Orleans Museum of Art (cat. 15). Of the other nine, the location of six is known. Four bronzes are in the Art Institute of Chicago, one is in the Art Gallery of Ontario, and another is on loan to the Toledo Museum.

CHRISTOPHER BENFEY

Degas and New Orleans: Exorcizing the Exotic

TEN DAYS AT SEA ON AN ENGLISH SHIP, thirty hours in New York, four days in American trains, and—finally—New Orleans. "Oh, how far from so many things one is here!" Edgar Degas's plaint to his painter friend James Tissot on November 19, 1872, three weeks into his visit, confirms his sense of the sheer distance traveled, and the extreme remoteness of New Orleans.[1] And yet, as the native city of his mother and the adopted city of his two younger brothers, René and Achille, New Orleans was also uncannily close to Degas. It is a paradox we will encounter frequently in this analysis: that Degas in New Orleans feels both far from home and, as he once expressed it, almost one of Louisiana's children.[2] His five garrulous letters from New Orleans stand right on the divide (see Appendix II). Writing to Tissot from the offices of De Gas Brothers, he marvels at how "everything is beautiful in this world of the people." But with the next stroke of the pen, he adds, "but one Paris laundry girl, with bare arms, is worth it all for such a pronounced Parisian as I am."[3] I want to explore here Degas's complex and ambivalent response to what I will call the "exotic" appeal of New Orleans, and, more generally, to the cluster of aesthetic subjects and styles subsumed under the term *exoticism:* the charms of the "outside," the geographically remote, the unfamiliar. This will require, first, a summary of his family's long-standing valence toward the city of New Orleans, as a realm of possibility and dream. Then I will say a few things about the appeal of the exotic to Degas as a traveler and collector. And finally I will speculate on Degas's excision—or exorcism—of the exotic from his own work.

"It is the country of young men who have nerve." René De Gas's assessment of New Orleans, as he announced his intention to move there after the American Civil War came to an end in 1865, expresses the mythic allure of New Orleans as it captured the family De Gas's imagination.[4] The Louisiana branch had always been, in a sense, the "id" of the family, with the respectable banking interests in Paris and Naples functioning as the "superego." At the head of the

wilder branch of the family was Edgar Degas's maternal grandfather, the swashbuckling Germain Musson. A refugee from the French West Indian colony of Saint Domingue who made a fortune in Louisiana cotton and Mexican silver, Germain married into the prominent Rillieux family to render his riches less conspicuously *nouvelles*. He gave his children a European upbringing and education, but they were Creoles to the end—French-speaking, native-born New Orleanians. Germain's son Michel Musson returned to New Orleans and became a leading businessman in the city. (At the time of Edgar's visit in 1872, he was renting a handsome house on Esplanade, the main thoroughfare of the Creole neighborhoods below Canal Street) (fig. 17). Célestine Musson De Gas married a Frenchman, but pined in Paris for the masked balls and parties of her native New Orleans. She died when her eldest son, Edgar, was barely thirteen, thus giving New Orleans an elegiac aura in his imagination.

Edgar Degas's visit to New Orleans, the most exotic of American cities then and now, was a homecoming of sorts and a chance to come to terms with a significant part of his cultural and personal inheritance. What was originally planned as a visit of two months stretched into five and a half, as Degas, that quintessentially Parisian painter of ballerinas and thoroughbreds, began to feel increasingly at home. By the time of his visit, both of Degas's younger brothers had emigrated to New Orleans, and René—following in his grandfather's footsteps—had married into New Orleans aristocracy. The marriage wasn't much of a reach, to be sure. In 1869, René De Gas, who had worked for a brief period in Michel Musson's cotton brokerage firm, had married Musson's daughter and his own first cousin, Estelle Musson. The young and beautiful Estelle, whose first husband was killed in the Civil War, had spent the war years in France, where Edgar had sketched her portrait on at least two occasions (cats. 8, 10). Estelle's return from France brought her another tragedy: her eyes began to fail. By the time of Degas's journey to New Orleans ten years later, she was almost completely blind.

Surely a visit with René's family, who were expecting a child in December (for whom Edgar served as godfather), was a major motivation for Degas's trip to New Orleans. But there were other reasons as well. Degas had not yet settled on the subjects and styles that would occupy him for the rest of his career. His commitment to painting contemporary life was recent; he had painted his first pictures of ballet rehearsals and horse races, but was uncertain of their quality or marketability. He admired other artists (his friend Manet, for example, and Delacroix) who had found extraordinary subjects in geographically remote realms. Furthermore, Degas's service in the National Guard during the Prussian siege of Paris, and the slaughter that followed the establishment of the Commune in 1871, had left him exhausted and depressed. He was having trouble with his eyes—the result, he suspected, of the deprivation he suffered during the siege.[5]

When René visited Paris during the summer of 1872, the brothers visited the sites where Edgar had served. René, sensing perhaps his older brother's need for a change of scene, extended an invitation to accompany him back to New Orleans. Once plans were in place for departure, Degas, who knew little English, developed a passion for English words. He wandered through the streets of Paris, repeating his favorite phrases. "Edgar . . . is crazy to learn to pronounce English words," René wrote to his wife, Estelle, on July 12, 1872, "he has been repeating *turkey buzzard* for a whole week."[6] Whether he was thinking of the New Orleans–based Audubon's portraits of American birds, or he just liked the buzzing sound of the indigenous vulture's name, Degas was already trying out in his own voice the sound of the exotic realm he was about to explore.

Degas was thirty-eight when he began his five-month stay in New Orleans. He wasn't yet the famous cantankerous grouch we meet in eyewitness accounts from the 1890s. Degas in the early seventies was engaging, even chatty, and good company. A rare contemporary photograph, taken in New Orleans, shows a jaunty bearded man, sailor's cap perched on his head (fig. 1). He looks upright, a bit like the soldier he still considered himself to be, but there's a friendly, amused look in his dark eyes. Degas at thirty-eight was showing his first gray hairs, but he had barely begun the career that led to his lasting fame. Much of the work for which he is best known—the dancers, the bathers, the racehorses—was still in the future. So were the Impressionist exhibitions, in which he played such an important role. Degas's letters from New Orleans, as Douglas Druick and Peter Zegers have noted, "reveal him in crisis, intensely reviewing both his personal and professional life."[7] Degas in New Orleans was an artist in transition, assessing in middle age what he wanted to do with his life.

Despite the lively letters Degas wrote home, three soon after his arrival and two toward the end of his stay, we know little of Degas's daily life in New Orleans. Aside from the dinner parties and disappointing concerts mentioned in his letters, and his plans to visit such sights as the new ice factory, we don't

know how he amused himself. It seems unlikely that this connoisseur of the racetrack did not visit the new fairgrounds a couple of blocks up Esplanade, especially since his cousin-in-law William Bell was an official there (fig. 18). We don't know if he visited the notorious brothels of New Orleans, though he made no secret of his acquaintance with the Parisian demimonde. We can't even be certain that Degas attended Mardi Gras festivities in late February 1873, even though his brother René had been looking into insect costumes ("all ravishing, from the ladybug to the roach") for the Mistick Krewe of Comus. There was great excitement about the politically charged Mardi Gras that year, the theme of which was "The Missing Links to Darwin's Origin of Species," with President Grant and his representatives in Louisiana assigned various bestial identities (fig. 19).[8] It hardly seems likely that Degas did *not* watch the Mardi Gras parades that February, but if he did, he said nothing about it.

What we do know is that each day Degas made his way—presumably by streetcar or on foot—across the French Quarter to his brothers' firm in the commercial sector above Canal Street. His uncle's cotton brokerage was in the same neighborhood, as was the business of William Bell and his partner Fred Ogden, which provided materials for baling cotton. Then he returned from this

masculine redoubt to the feminine realm of the house on Esplanade, where he chatted with his female cousins and worked on portraits of them. "All day long I am among these dear folk," he reported, "painting and drawing, making portraits of the family."

There are persistent and continuing debates over which paintings Degas actually painted in New Orleans, and over the identities of their models. I suspect that some of these arguments never will be resolved, and that a broader approach to these interesting portraits might be more fruitful. Several of the portraits, for example, show some hesitation or blurring or obscuring of the eyes of the model— a trait that has encouraged a perhaps hasty identification of the almost blind Estelle as Degas's favorite model. But Degas himself was suffering from eye problems at the time of his arrival, and it may be that he projected his own fears onto these portraits—a mirroring of sorts.

But Degas was also painting a society, specifically the decimated Creole society of post–Civil War New Orleans. This self-styled aristocracy, always scornful of modern business practices, had already, before the war, financially lost out to the "American invasion" that followed the Louisiana Purchase of 1803. The Civil War put an end to their social status as well. Old Creole families such as the Mussons continued to speak French and to cling to the props of the ancien régime way of life. They retained the box at the French Opera, though the 1872 season was canceled for lack of money, much to Degas's disappointment. Other signs of high Creole style were the books about Marie Antoinette, the mansion on Esplanade Avenue, the black servants (former slave-owning families like the Mussons considered white servants déclassé), the visits from specialists (one of Degas's most arresting New Orleans pictures records the visit of the podiatrist to tend to a young niece's feet) (fig. 21).[9] So Degas's portraits of melancholy Creole women, all of them presumably his three cousins, have a "generic" quality as well. They are pictures of the exotic, dark-eyed Creole beauty, mentioned by all visitors to the city and praised in guidebooks, but with a tinge of anxiety and elegy.

Degas's letters from Louisiana reveal a persistent counterpoint between his admiration for American technological modernity and his nostalgia for an older, pre-modern New Orleans of eighteenth-century customs and exotic cultural contacts. He found the railroad from New York to New Orleans a steady stream of technological marvels, especially the sleeping cars: "You cannot imagine what this marvelous invention is like," he wrote Désiré Dihau on November 11.[10] He showed a family pride in his brothers' apparent success in American business practices (wishful thinking on his part), and marveled at the

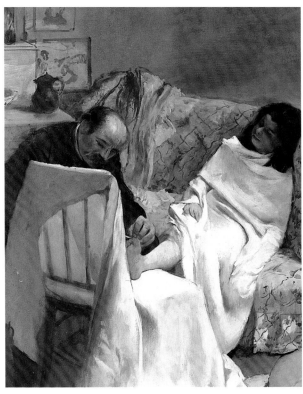

FIG. 21. Detail of fig. 98, Edgar Degas, *Le Pedicure,* 1873, essence on paper mounted on canvas, 24 × 18⅛ in. Musée d'Orsay. Lemoisne 323.

LOUISIANA ICE WORKS.

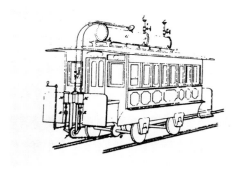

FIG. 22. *Louisiana Ice Works,* from Edwin L. Jewell, *Crescent City Illustrated.* New Orleans, 1873.

FIG. 23. Dr. Lamm, Design for a Steam Powered Streetcar, ca. 1872.

ice factory in New Orleans, designed by his Parisian friend Henri Rouart (fig. 22). He was very curious about the newly installed steam-powered tram, the ancestor of the current St. Charles line, and wrote about it to the engineer Rouart (fig. 23).[11]

At the same time he filled his letters with lists of exotic and timeless sights. To Rouart he gushed about the "beautiful, refined Indian women behind their half-opened green shutters, and the old women with their big bandanna kerchiefs going to the market . . . and the children all dressed in white and all white against black arms."[12] "Everything attracts me here," he confided to another friend, "I look at everything."

> I like nothing better than the negresses of all shades, holding in their arms little white babies, so white, against white houses with columns of fluted wood and in gardens of orange trees . . . and the fruit vendors with their shops full to bursting, and the contrast between the lively hum and bustle of the offices with this immense black animal force.[13]

In such passages, Degas was clearly listing possible subjects for paintings: "I am accumulating plans which would take ten lifetimes to carry out."[14]

But except for two paintings of those bustling offices (in which he ignored the "contrast" with the "animal force" of black workers), and a sketch of a barely decipherable black nurse and white children in a New Orleans garden, Degas as artist resolutely suppressed all this exotic imagery. Perhaps he felt that by listing it, cataloguing it so to speak, he had already acknowledged it, and thereby exorcised it. He suggested that Auguste Biard (known for such exoticizing paintings as his monumental *The Slave Trade*) and Manet might have done a better job in New Orleans. He complained that the light was too bright, the models wouldn't stand still, his sojourn in New Orleans wasn't long enough to really make sense of these materials. Degas concentrated instead on sober portraits and interiors, adding here and there a tropical splash of Louisiana flowers and plants—including of course cotton itself. But the Indian women and the orange trees and the black women of all shades—the whole exotic gumbo of New Orleans—these are conspicuously missing in Degas's New Orleans pictures.

It might be argued that Degas, especially after his conversion circa 1868 to themes of "modern life," was not drawn to exotic subjects in art. But this is emphatically not the case. The recent exhibition of Degas's private collection at The Metropolitan Museum of Art in New York made clear that Degas (who

amassed most of his collection during the 1890s) had a pronounced taste for exotica of all kinds. He bought as many feverish Moroccan sketches by Delacroix as he could get his hands on, made risky purchases of Gauguin's unfashionable South Seas fantasies, hoarded Japanese prints, and so on. And yet in his own mature work Degas resisted exotic imagery, even when, as with his trip to New Orleans, his circumstances positively cried out for it.[15]

That Degas considered New Orleans quintessentially exotic is confirmed not only by the lists of sights with which he filled his letters home, but also by an anecdote. Many years later, the dealer Ambroise Vollard reported that during a visit to his shop Degas's eye fell on a Gauguin. "Poor Gauguin, way off there on his island!" Degas sighed, "I advised him to go to New Orleans, but he decided it was too civilized. He had to have people around him with flowers on their heads and rings in their noses before he could feel at home."[16]

Actually, New Orleans may not have been exotic enough for Degas either. I have suggested in my book, *Degas in New Orleans,* some reasons why Degas may have felt uncomfortable portraying one major source of exotic images: what he called, with evident fascination, the "black world" of New Orleans. "The black world, I have not the time to explore it; there are some real treasures as regards drawing and color in these forests of ebony."[17] Degas's mother (as an article of mine was the first to reveal) had African-American cousins.[18] She was descended from the prestigious Rillieux family, but Rillieux was also a prominent name among the so-called "free people of color" of New Orleans, free blacks before the Civil War who made up a caste apart, and were

FIG. 24. *Cabbage Vendor,* 19th century, photograph. Southeastern Architectural Archive, Tulane University, New Orleans.

FIG. 25. *D. L. Kernion and the Nursemaid,* 19th century, daguerreotype. Louisiana State Museum, New Orleans.

FIG. 26. *Market,* 19th century, photograph. Southeastern Architectural Archive, Tulane University, New Orleans.

FIG. 27. Norbert Rillieux, 1885–90, photograph. Louisiana State Museum, New Orleans.

sometimes (like the Rillieux) quite successful and relatively wealthy. Vincent Rillieux Jr., Edgar Degas's great uncle, had a long-standing liaison with a free woman of color called Constance Vivant, and had several children, including the internationally famous inventor and chemical engineer Norbert Rillieux, first cousin of Degas's mother (fig. 27).

Indeed, Norbert Rillieux was easily the most distinguished of Degas's American relatives. Born in 1806 and baptized in the St. Louis Cathedral of New Orleans, he was—like many young free men of color—sent to France to be educated. His father, a wealthy engineer known for his design of a steam-operated cotton press, discovered a kindred aptitude in his son. By 1830, Norbert was an instructor in applied mechanics at École Centrale in Paris. The following year he made an extraordinary discovery, one that transformed the sugar-refining process and prompted his return to New Orleans. The traditional manner of reducing sugarcane juice for sugar production required the tedious and back-breaking toil of many slaves, who skimmed the boiling juice from one kettle to the next. Rillieux developed an ingenious apparatus, employing condensing coils that used the vapor from one vacuum chamber to evaporate the juice from a second chamber. Rillieux's cost-cutting innovation made him the Eli Whitney of the sugar industry. He found a market for his machinery in Louisiana, where his major patron was Judah P. Benjamin, the brilliant lawyer who later served as Jefferson Davis's secretary of state. It seems highly unlikely that Edgar Degas, who was fascinated with steam-powered machinery of all kinds, was unaware of Rillieux, who had a considerable reputation in both Paris and New Orleans. With such illustrious black cousins, Degas could not have painted black faces in New Orleans as mere local scenery, aspects of an exotic landscape quite foreign to himself. Nor could he entirely aestheticize blacks as mere "treasures as regards drawing and color."

But Degas's resistance to the exotic was even more pervasive than this. With an American mother and, on his father's side, numerous Italian relatives, Degas was himself something of an exotic, an olive-skinned child of Louisiana. Degas could not treat New Orleans with the necessary aesthetic detachment of, say, Delacroix in Morocco; it was not sufficiently "other" to him. It was, in fact, his "Frenchness" that this insecure Italo-American painter increasingly came to insist upon, most notoriously during the Dreyfus affair. (That Degas's brother Achille, as Victoria Cooke has recently discovered, married into a Jewish New Orleans family compounds this impression of Degas's flight from his own "exotic" identity.[19]) Preparing to leave New Orleans, in February 1873, Degas wrote to Tissot in a nationalist vein:

Remember the art of the Le Nain and all Medieval France. Our race will have something simple and bold to offer. . . . This English art that appeals so much to us often seems to be exploiting some trick. We can do better than they and be just as strong.[20]

In summary, the exotic for Degas hit a bit too close to home. It was, in Freud's terms for the "uncanny," both *unheimlich* (uncanny or strange) and too *heimlich* (in Freud's translation, "familiar"; "native, belonging to home"). "This uncanny," wrote Freud, "is in reality nothing new or foreign, but something familiar and old-established in the mind that has been estranged only by the process of repression."[21] Having lost his New Orleanian mother at a decisive time in his life (the psychoanalyzing here is unavoidable), Degas could not help but link the exotic to his own sense of loss. But to recapture that intimacy was not a simple act of travel, of "reconnecting" with the Louisiana branch of his family. It required of Degas an acknowledgment of his own "exotic" identity, and his family's connections with blacks and Jews and other "foreigners." And that acknowledgment was not, ultimately, one that Edgar Degas was prepared to make.

NOTES

Some of the ideas and arguments in this essay first appeared in different form in my article on Degas as collector, "The Exoticism of Everyday Life," *Modern Painters* (winter 1997).

1. Appendix II, letter to Tissot, 19 November 1872. See also letter to Frölich: "The ocean! How vast it is and how far I am from you . . . Borrow an atlas from your dear little daughter and take a look at the distance."

2. Ibid., letter to Rouart (". . . la Louisiane doit être respectée par tous ses enfants dont je suis à peu près un.") Michel Musson apparently agreed, calling Degas "Creole in your heart" ("créole par le coeur"). Brown, 1991, Musson to Degas, August 6, 1883, 39. Here and elsewhere, I use Brown's translations of quoted material.

3. Appendix II, letter to Tissot, 19 November 1872.

4. Brown, 1991, René De Gas to Musson, July 25, 1866, 16.

5. Valéry, 1960, 9: "Sent to Vincennes for rifle practice, he discovered that he could not see the target with his right eye. It was confirmed that this eye was almost useless, a fact which he blamed (I heard all this from his own lips) on a damp attic which for a long time had been his bedroom."

6. Brown, 1991, René De Gas to Estelle Musson De Gas, 12 July 1872, 20.

7. Douglas W. Druick and Peter Zegers, "Scientific Realism: 1873–1881," in Paris, Ottawa, New York, 197. The original photograph has disappeared.

8. For details of Mardi Gras in 1873 see Benfey, 1997, 50–58, and Reid Mitchell, *All on a Mardi Gras Day: Episodes in the History of New Orleans Carnival* (Cambridge, 1995), 65–72.

9. Brown, 1991, Degas to Michel Musson, January 1, 1864, 8. Degas reports that Musson's wife is reading a life of Marie Antoinette.

10. Appendix II, letter to Dihau.

11. One reason why New Orleanians were drawn to steam-powered streetcars was the devastating epizootic among horses in the city, culminating in December 1872. See James Guilbeau, *The Saint Charles Streetcar or The History of the New Orleans and Carrollton Railroad* (New Orleans, 1975), 50–52. On Rouart and the Louisiana Ice Works, see Brown, 1994, 122–26.

12. Appendix II, letter to Rouart.

13. Ibid., letter to Frölich.

14. Ibid.

15. See Dumas in New York, 1997.

16. Ambroise Vollard, *Degas: An Intimate Portrait*, trans. Randolph T. Weaver (New York, 1986), 48.

17. Appendix II, letter to Tissot, 18 February 1873.

18. Benfey, 1996, 25–30. Also, Benfey, 1997, chap. 7.

19. Victoria Cooke to the author, private correspondence.

20. Appendix II, letter to Tissot, 18 February 1873.

21. Freud, "The Uncanny," in *On Creativity and the Unconscious: Papers on the Psychology of Art, Literature, Love, Religion* (New York, 1958), 148.

CHRISTINA VELLA

The Country for Men with Nerve

THE MAIN THING WAS THE NEGROES. Not that one hadn't seen them in Paris now and then, along with other exotic foreigners. But in New Orleans they were everywhere, almost as commonplace as whites, except that their faces glinted in the shallow October sun. On the road out from the train station were drivers atop waiting carriages, their hands the color of the mud streets; black men standing on the levees in twos and threes; women on the stoops of cottages, "well-set Negresses," Degas called them (fig. 28), each with a child who seemed "snow white when cradled in black arms."[1] No doubt Degas had seen the Negro sharecroppers' cabins tattooed into the countryside as his train rumbled from New York into the South. But the brown bodies in New Orleans were close by, pressing all around on every street. Some of the blacks were migrants, for, just as in France, seasonal laborers gathered in the city— stevedores, grooms, warehouse workers, and wetnurses from the countryside —who came to New Orleans as soon as yellow fever subsided to rent out their backs or breasts. Others were quite at home; they were born in the city and belonged to its byways.

Except for the blacks, the New Orleans of Degas's relatives was very like a provincial town in France. Animals came and went through the business district, unnoticed and innumerable, just as in the outskirts of Paris before the recent siege. Horses added their ponderable deposits to the morass of filth and standing water in the streets, for, whereas Paris complained of a shortage of draft animals, in New Orleans there were always more horses on the streets than carts to clean up after them (fig. 29).

Degas had every reason to expect a city somewhat more like Paris, for both places had recently experienced defeat, enemy occupation, and civil war. But such similarities were superficial. In New Orleans, life went on during the long war and its aftermath, though it was a life fraught with restrictions. The city was not burned. The only bodies lying about were those of people enjoying the

FIG. 28. Louis Rousseau, *Portrait of Marie Lassus of New Orleans,* 1860, albumen print. New Orleans Museum of Art.

FIG. 29. *Carriages,* 19th century, photograph. Southeastern Architectural Archive, Tulane University, New Orleans.

shade of the magnolias in the public squares. In France, the war with Prussia had been short and hideous. The woods and villages around the capital had been destroyed in September 1870, lest they provide shelter to the advancing enemy. Those homeless villagers had retreated to Paris in carts piled high with their belongings, the children peeping out aghast between the stools and tables. The Prussians then surrounded the swollen city and waited. Food and fuel gave out in the merciless winter. Trees along the Champs-Elysées were sacrificed for firewood, then the furniture and carts were burned as well. The zoo's exotic animals were shot and eaten, as were horses, dogs, cats, and wild birds. In January 1871, five months of cold and starvation ended with surrender, followed by four more months of vicious class war—the Commune uprising, fought on the roofs and in the doorways of Paris. Entire buildings, set on fire by the insurgents, fell with their arcades into the streets. Anyone who remained in Paris during the bloody June Days might have seen some wretched Communard lying amid his entrails on the sidewalk.[2]

Degas left Paris only a year and a half after calm was restored. He arrived in New Orleans in 1872, seven years after the end of the American Civil War. And yet, much more than Paris, New Orleans was a city crippled by war and still in convalescence. In Paris, most burned-out buildings were repaired within a year; those prostitutes who had comforted the enemy were whipped and banished; theaters that had served as makeshift hospitals were again producing gaudy spectacles; and for everyone except families who had lost a man on the battlefields or barricades, life resumed its urban intensity.[3] Degas left a Paris that, despite its avenues of stumps and seedlings, was moving toward the *belle époque.* "Here we are," wrote one French journalist in a dispatch to New Orleans, "beginning the season very much in the same old way—with the old bright weather, the old sunshine, the old gay look . . . just as if there had been neither war, nor defeats, nor sieges, nor Communes, nor any such disagreeable interruption to the old life and pleasures of Paris. Just, too, as if everything in the country was 'ship-shape and Boston fashion.'"[4]

New Orleans, in contrast, never recovered its prewar position. The booming cotton port whose exports had briefly surpassed those of New York was now in mourning for the past. Any discussion, whether of public policy or private habits, might be suffused with wistful references to better times. The evident decline of New Orleans must have confused Degas, for he had been prepared by his brother for the dynamism of the New World. To his uncle Michel Musson in New Orleans, René De Gas had complained about the conservatism of life in Europe. "Old-fogeys, stingy and egotistical, that's all you see, all you meet," he wrote. New Orleans, however, was "the country of young men with nerve."[5] Perhaps Edgar was looking forward to this bracing American freshness. Instead, the shock he probably experienced was that of coming from a big French city to a smaller one—to the seeming emptiness of so-called busy streets; to the disconcerting presence of hungry freedmen going aimlessly up and down like an army perpetually on leave; to a preoccupation with the agronomy of the hinterland. Paris, for all its sanguinary lapses, remained a world capital with a population of two and a half million. New Orleans was a once-important city of less than two hundred thousand where Degas, in one of his apt phrases,

FIG. 30. Charles Nègre, *Hôtel de Ville from Nôtre Dame Cathedral, Paris*, ca. 1852, salt and paper print. New Orleans Museum of Art.

FIG. 31. Theodore Lilienthal, *Bayou St. John, New Orleans 1867: Photographs for Emperor Napoleon III*. Napoleon-Museum Arenenberg.

observed that "the perfume of the past has not quite evaporated." He had left a new metropolis for the genteel shabbiness of a place where everything, including patience, was worn out.

Degas settled in with his relatives some blocks from the Old Quarter in a neighborhood where Creoles like his uncle, in the first stage of adversity, had dwindled from more lavish uptown residences. Degas spoke practically no English, except for his well-practiced phrase, "turkey buzzard." Fortunately, he had come to the one U.S. city where he could converse in his native tongue to Americans, who were also speaking theirs. Not only did they speak French, people who never had been outside Louisiana talked of the goings-on in France as if they, too, were Parisians. *L'Abeille*, the Creoles' French newspaper, diligently reported the debates of the French Chamber of Deputies and the cases on trial in Paris courts. Alongside local shipping information and gaugings of the Mississippi River were earnest preachments on government addressed to the president of France.[6] New Orleans women read about Americans in Paris: "The American women look awfully fast, going out of banking houses with . . . an expression on their radiant and beautiful faces . . . of the pleasure of extravagance. They look so much like the men of business, these American fashionables, well able to take care of themselves and to spend all the money that is sent to them."[7] During the Civil War the Musson women had gone to Paris; but they were thrifty Creoles, not Americans. The snide admiration could not apply to them. To their own intractable southern prejudices, the Creoles added those of the native French. They criticized Bismarck with fierce borrowed nationalism, and commented on the "big and badly dressed Englishwomen" in Paris.[8] The French showed no such solidarity with the Creoles and, in fact, judged American political candidates solely on the basis of whether they had sided with France during the Franco-Prussian War or had read the *philosophes*.[9]

Degas, reaching New Orleans just before a presidential election, showed little specific interest in politics. Nevertheless, he must have heard a great deal about the black "problem," the problem not being the blacks themselves, but rather the cotton fields that they had abandoned. The Negroes, according to their envenomed former masters, never would become a dependable free labor force, as they were content to live at a subsistence level on what they could steal. Indeed, fieldhands had rarely lived above that level in their slave condition. It was therefore understandable that the black refused to labor any longer like a slave, even for a freedman's wages. Without labor, the richest land in the South was worthless. Every planter ruined for lack of hands took others with him into bankruptcy—mortgagers, creditors, agents, merchants—all of whom relied on his business. Conversations in New Orleans thus tended to come down to two subjects: cotton and blacks, that is, unharvested cotton and unemployed blacks. Otherwise, New Orleans with its overflowing privies resembled an isolated and unsanitary town in provincial France, for, away from the underground sewers that were the pride of Paris, the filth of Frenchmen and of those who only thought themselves Frenchmen was the same.

The Mussons' neighborhood was clean but rarely quiet. Crime was rampant all over New Orleans—slashings, murders, muggings, and a hundred instances of robbery, mostly unpunished. Only a few days before Degas's arrival, a fifteen-year-old servant girl living near the Mussons had thrown her newborn into a cesspool. The screaming infant was rescued by the police, who took both the baby and the mother to Charity Hospital, the usual repository for lost and found humanity. The majority of police arrests were "voluntary." On the coldest night of Degas's visit, sixty-two "homeless creatures," according to *The Daily Picayune,* "applied for and were provided with accommodations" in the jail, though without meals.[10] Stowaways regularly arriving on steamers were not arrested but were instead pronounced "sick and destitute" and taken to Charity Hospital.

The violence of New Orleans should not have alarmed Degas, for, along with revolutionaries and criminals, Paris specialized in suicides and madmen. One in every four hundred mouths in Paris was fed in an asylum such as the one where Eugène Musson, another of Degas's Creole uncles, would end his days babbling indefatigable obscenities.[11] But being a careful observer of his own health, Degas might have been disquieted by the diseases of New Orleans. Along with cargoes of bacon shoulders and soap, the ships at the levee brought in tuberculosis, plague, scabies, smallpox and, always, cholera. Forty-three people had died from cholera the week Degas arrived, despite the availability of Sasparillan Resolvent, on sale "by all respectable grocers," to cure not only cholera (in twenty minutes) but "Syphilis, Consumption, Strumotous Discharges from the Ears, Fever Sores, Scald Head, Ring Worm, Salt Rheum, Worms in the Flesh, Tumors, Cancers in the Womb, etc."[12] Paris was certainly as full of bacilli and snake oil, but the contagions of New Orleans were more proximate to Degas. Four of the children he painted while in New Orleans—his nieces and cousins—would eventually die of scarlet fever and the unremitting local plague, yellow fever.[13]

FIG. 32. *Esplanade Avenue with General Store Advertising Leeches,* 19th century, photograph. Historic New Orleans Collection.

No one took any notice of Degas's presence in the city, except his adoring family, for he was years away from being famous either in Paris or New Orleans. His cousins humored him by posing, René's wife Estelle remaining still only so long as her children did not require attention, and the children themselves being still not at all. "Our Raphael," they called him in the family, scarcely imagining that they would be remembered in the world solely because they had sat for him.

Estelle gave birth to another child while Degas was in New Orleans; Edgar was the baby's godfather. He was now surrounded by little ones, six children in all, and they made him wistful for a family of his own. They may also have gotten on his nerves, for children in good Creole homes were spoiled. At a time of high infant mortality, babies were watched over fretfully, surrounded by servants, and breast-fed until they were almost able to cook for themselves— Estelle, though pregnant, was nursing a three-year-old while she posed for Degas. The local newspapers were full of advertisements for women to sew, clean, and, quite commonly, "to nurse a child two and a half years old."[14]

FIG. 33. Theodore Lilienthal, *Steamer Great Republic, New Orleans 1867: Photographs for Emperor Napoleon III.* Napoleon-Museum Arenenberg.

The newspapers loved to report morbid incidents involving children. Even during a presidential campaign, local papers found space to report that "a lad named Eddie Swan fell from a tree in Washington Square and bruised himself pretty badly," or "Patsy Boudreau, nine years old, has been taken to the police station as homeless, while Mary Ann Grogan has been taken up on Tchoupitoulas street near Race as insane."[15]

The Daily Picayune even registered its appreciation of the rhymed obituary of a child:

> She was such a little seraph that her father, who is sheriff
> Really doesn't seem to care if he never smiles in life again.
> She has gone, we hope, to Heaven, at the early age of seven
> (Funeral starts off at eleven) where she'll never more have pain.[16]

Degas began to find the domesticity of the Musson household oppressive, or so it appears. Not entirely satisfied with the portraits he was producing of the family, he searched about for something that would inspire a major work. Nothing presented itself. He had been at first delighted by steamboats with their funnels "as high as factory chimneys" (fig. 33). He could have taken an excursion on one of the steamboats that left New Orleans daily for nearby destinations, such as Opelousas, Louisiana, or Memphis, Tennessee. Just across the levee at the foot of Esplanade, the shimmering Mississippi unrolled before him —a veritable canvas of steamships, packetboats, dockworkers, and all the exhilarating traffic of a port. But Degas's fragile eyes reacted to the glare on the water, and the river was not a subject he could easily bring indoors. He had loved his long train trip from New York, especially his sleeping car, but once ensconced with his cousins, he was not tempted by any of the Sunday pleasure trips. The Jackson and Great Northern Railroad offered, for the price of a dollar, one-day trips to such destinations as Ponchatoula and Amite, Louisiana. Degas, however, was strong on the idea that he should resist "original subjects" and "invitations to travel" in favor of scenes and themes that he knew inside out.[17]

In Paris Degas had been attracted to the ballet, as well as the circus. Though much amateur dance was performed in New Orleans in 1872, no professional ballet came to the city during that season. Circuses, however, were in town during his entire stay. The grand Barnum and Bailey played throughout the autumn, offering trapeze acts probably as accomplished as those of Paris. Degas did try out at least one of the city's diversions, opera recitals, and was disappointed—almost disgusted—with the quality of what he saw. Before the Civil War, New Orleans had been a national center for opera, ranking far ahead of New York, a position it would regain near the end of the century. But even in the 1870s, acclaimed touring groups were regularly presented in the city, along with many amateur and semiprofessional recitals. Donizetti's *Lucia di Lammermoor* had been sung in New Orleans in the spring of 1872, just as it was in Paris, though probably not as well. Signor Mario, the darling of European stages, offered his gushed-over tenor in New Orleans that season, along with uncelebrated but serious voices featured at the music academies.[18] The fall opera season was canceled, however, and Degas was unimpresed with the recitals he heard. Some of the plays offered that year at the St. Charles and Variety theaters were the same ones popular in Paris—a comedy called *Man and Wife* and dramatic versions of *Oliver Twist* and *Around the World in 80 Days,* for example. But if he complained about the music, Degas no doubt would have found the local plays truly dreadful, even at the reputable Academy of Music, which in November was presenting "a beautiful Melo-Drama, in three acts, *The Idiot Witness, or a Tale of Blood.*"[19]

What else was there to do or paint? Balls of every sort animated the nights in New Orleans, if one could reach them through the flooded winter streets. Everyone danced—except Degas, if we may take as evidence his silence concerning balls, which were a topic of daily chatter in both Paris and New Orleans. Talented with words, Degas wrote letters but only scanned the New Orleans newspapers. People eager to try "Nytrous Oxyde Gas" could have their teeth extracted free by a dentist on Dauphine Street promoting anesthesia. New Orleans was full of dentists whose chief skills were pulling troublesome teeth and fitting more troublesome false ones. Their characteristic logo, a perfect drawing of an upper plate, prefaced each of their advertisements and appeared all over the newspaper's section of "Wants" ads. So far as we know, Degas resisted the nitrous oxide; toothache was not among his several complaints.

Christmas came, moist and hot, celebrated in the city by a ball for hundreds of children. New Year's Day, for both Frenchmen and Creoles, was the traditional time for visiting friends and exchanging gifts outside the family—dictionaries were a popular present in New Orleans. In Paris, celebrations were canceled because flood waters covered most of the country. In the Musson household, too, festivities may have been curtailed that year due to the birth of Estelle's fourth baby on December 20. In any case, Christmas in both France and Louisiana was normally a quiet holiday, with many Scrooges keeping their offices open through Christmas Eve. Crime rose during the season, according to *The Daily Picayune,* which on Christmas Day thoughtfully offered the information that Japan, "having for centuries clubbed its criminals to death, is preparing to hang them, after the American style."[20]

By the time cold weather finally settled on the city, boredom had settled heavily on Degas. New Orleans, with its port, its old architecture, and its large population of maple-skinned mulattoes, was, despite its problems, a picturesque town; but Degas, convinced that "one can only love and make art out of what one is used to," seemed to be fleeing from the quaint and picturesque. He was homesick. What had charmed him when he first arrived began to irk him. "Novelty," he observed, "captivates and wearies at the same time." Degas's irritation was that of an urban man in a town preoccupied with agriculture. No crops were raised in New Orleans; but the services on which the city lived were commercial services to planters who had been floundering since the Civil War. Seven years after the end of slavery in Louisiana, the planters were still desperate for fieldhands—white, Chinese, or black hands. They even offered during harvest time to pay wages, food, and transportation to the country. However, they now finally understood that the ex-slave's conception of hell was "an everlasting cotton field."[21]

Black people fascinated Degas, but he felt intuitively that he was not the right artist to penetrate their mystique. He had observed on his arrival the contrast between "the busy, so exactly arranged offices" and the Negroes, "this immense black animal force." But he never expressly noted the connection between them. The offices represented the business end of the cotton crop—the marketing phase of the industry—exclusively in the hands of whites.

If there were no cotton, no shipments arriving from the distant plantations, then the tidy city offices of all kinds would soon empty. Current cotton prices therefore dominated the front page of every newspaper, along with secondary information about sugar, rice, and shipping. Should the impoverished cotton planter diversify, restrict his land to tenant-farming, or cut it up and try to sell it? Should a railroad be opened to Houston? What fertilizers would replenish cotton-parched land?

Degas, who once expressed pride at the way his brothers could "talk cotton," had come to realize that people in New Orleans talked of nothing else. He repeatedly expressed his exasperation with "this climate of cotton" where everyone lived "for cotton and by cotton." His frustration was reaching its peak as he was writing to friends about the artist's need to avoid "original subjects" in favor of "themes close to home . . . subjects familiar to Parisian life." But at some quite sudden point he changed, or perhaps an idea that had been developing in his subconscious emerged all at once. The subject that had wearied him for three months began to engross him. With only a few weeks left until his return to Europe, he began what he described as a major painting—a scene from his uncle's cotton office, Musson, Prestidge, & Co., Cotton Factors and Commission Merchants.

Degas's *A Cotton Office in New Orleans* is his portrait of those men who lived by and for cotton. Degas's uncle was a factor, the planter's business representative to the outside world. Under the factor system, Michel Musson or one of his partners accepted a quantity of cotton on consignment from a small farm or large plantation. He then found buyers directly or passed the cotton shipment to other commission agents in the North who would send it to overseas purchasers. Musson, Prestidge, & Co. was a fairly large company and could make all the arrangements for storing the cotton, having it inspected, classified, and insured, and repacking it for further shipment. Musson might purchase supplies for his planter clients or find loans to finance them while the crop was growing. All the factor's work was done for a commission; his success was tied to that of the growers he represented.

The cotton office dealt with ginned lint, that is, the cotton arrived from the gin already pressed into ragged bales of about 500 pounds each, bound with metal bands, and covered with several yards of jute or cotton bagging. Musson, Prestidge, & Co. no doubt had a warehouse, probably near the docks, where they stored the cotton and, with insurance, protected it against weather, fire and theft. For each bale deposited with Musson's firm, the owner received a negotiable warehouse receipt that identified the individual bale and indicated its weight. Perhaps the men in shirt-sleeves at the extreme right in *A Cotton*

FIG. 34. S. Theodore Blessing, *Picking Cotton*, 19th century, stereo photograph. Louisiana State Museum, New Orleans.

FIG. 35. *Cotton Bales at Landing,* 19th century, photograph. Southeastern Architectural Archive, Tulane University, New Orleans.

Office were engaged in some phase of re-recording these receipts—an important duty, for it was only through receipts that the cotton passed from one buyer and seller to another on its way to a final, perhaps distant, purchaser.

Because there was great variation in the quality of a shipment, each bale was classified and marked individually. Musson, Prestidge, & Co. classified the cotton lint themselves, first assessing its color, smoothness, and the amount of foreign matter contained in it, and then grading it by its more recondite qualities. Degas's uncle is in the foreground of the painting with a pile of cotton next to him. He is "pulling the staple" of the cotton, a tedious procedure, part of the classifying chore, whereby he takes one small sample after another and pulls it between his thumbs and forefingers to determine the average length of the staple, or fiber, in a particular bulk. He will thus determine if the bulk is Middling Fair, Strict Good Middling, Low Middling, Strict Good Ordinary, etc. The operation required patient, experienced hands.

The table in the middle contains samples, for the office is also a salesroom. The man standing near the center of the picture holding up a handful of cotton was in some places called a spot broker. His customer, the man nearly facing us on the other side of the table, may be a dealer or a mill buyer making a large purchase on the basis of the samples displayed. The sample table resembles a gaming table, as well it might; the cotton business was highly speculative. Degas's uncle and his partners no doubt were members of the Cotton Exchange, located in a nearby building, where cotton futures contracts were bought and sold. A contract provided for the future delivery or receipt of a stated quantity of cotton of a particular quality at a fixed price. Like stock exchange quotes, the contracts traded at the Cotton Exchange were reported in *The Daily Picayune,* the paper being read by the man in the center of the picture.[22]

Cotton offices were probably not as clean as the one Degas portrayed, for people came in and out from the streets tracking dirt and dung. Insects and more dirt entered through the windows. Light garments, such as the young man's blue pants, were easily stained by muck and algae in the roads. Moreover, as cotton had a tendency to cling to clothes, men often got into their shirt-sleeves to handle it. The cotton itself, even if it were carefully ginned, would ordinarily look dirtier than the frosty stuff of Degas's picture. In the course of the day, some of it would float to the floor and gather in corners to mingle with other debris. Degas intended the painting for a European buyer— he specifically had in mind a certain Manchester cotton merchant—someone who perhaps knew everything about cotton and nothing about New Orleans. He did not therefore include details that would have distracted a foreign viewer. In spite of his pronounced interest in Negroes, he did not paint the black porters who were surely somewhere in the office, ready to rewrap the cotton, take those samples back to storage, or bring up other packages.

Degas's aim was not, of course, a photographic representation of a cotton office, but a portrait of the American business style—intense and self-absorbed, but at the same time unself-conscious and informal. If his picture lacks a redolence of burlap, we do not miss it, for his point is not to show us cotton—the plant on the table could just as well be sugar, tea, or rice—but rather, to portray occupation. In Degas's cotton office, there seems to be a place for everyone and everyone is in his place. The reality was more awkward. Nineteenth-century commerce in both France and America lacked the standardization we now take for granted. Businessmen entering into an important contract were likely to write the document themselves, revealing their immigrant origins and recent tenancy in the English language. All advertising was disarmingly direct: "If you spend money for whiskey, beer, tobacco, and cigars," one apothecary admonished, "can't you afford to please your sick and feeble wife with a bottle of English Female Bitters?"

Europeans, unmindful of the size and diversity of America, thought of the whole continent as one modern, buzzing company, its unharnessed energy symbolized by the sight every traveling Frenchman wanted to see: Niagara Falls. The De Gas brothers, Achille and René, who left Paris to go into business across the ocean, must have also believed that capitalism in the United States, even in the cotton business, was efficient and individualistic, with a place of "men with nerve." The Creoles themselves were not deceived about their separate situation. They might read that Americans "with their businesses and banking houses, have turned rue de Scribe into one of the liveliest and most attractive streets in Paris"; but they knew where those businessmen had come from—the America of factories, traffic, and luxuries, the America that had won a war and now looked forward to the future. There was no Niagara in Louisiana, either real or symbolic. Cotton would revive as an export crop, but farther west in Texas. In New Orleans, the cotton business would remain as Degas saw it but did not paint it—harrowed with failure.

The firm of Musson, Prestidge, & Co.—the cotton office of the picture— would collapse before the painting was finished, its illustrated bustle having

FIG. 36. *Steamboat with Cotton Bales,* 19th century, photograph. Southeastern Architectural Archive, Tulane University, New Orleans.

been perhaps a fiction. As for the figures going about their business, Degas, himself a private man, keeps all their tragic secrets. The old man in front, giving his untroubled attention to the cotton and handling it so professionally—that is Degas's uncle Michel Musson who is deeply in debt. His daughter is losing her sight; his brother will lose his mind. His grandchildren will die, one after another.

The two youthful men who are not working were those Degas loved best, his brothers. Achille, the one standing idle and innocuous with his elbows on the window sill—carries a revolver. In a few years, in Paris, he will be thrashed in public by an irate husband whom he in turn will shoot.[23] The rakish one serenely scanning the news is René, emotional and mercurial. He has a new baby. His wife is the woman who will soon be blind. He will desert her and their children to run off with someone else's wife and children, and raise another unhappy brood as best he can. The other woman who will come into his life is his neighbor and is named "America." The old man whose back is to him in the picture, his father-in-law and uncle, will then turn his back on him forever.

In a literal sense, the sufficiency of these men, their focused, positive energy, and air of pleasant expectation is artificial. But of course, the figures in the picture are not literally Degas's tormented relatives; they are profound expressions of America's obsession with work. Degas's room is suffused by a mood of optimism, the windows and doors suggesting more and more activity. The real cotton office of Musson, Prestidge, & Co. was indeed an oblong place with interior windows. But by 1872, most such offices were peopled by deeply discouraged men who could no longer afford to put on either their best faces or best clothes to deal with cotton and each other. If the figures in Degas's cotton office are men with prospects—men with nerve—it is because the office is not, after all, "in New Orleans," but in a psychological space where Degas trapped a powerful but fugitive abstraction—the European idea of American enterprise.

NOTES

1. Degas's remarks about New Orleans are quoted in Loyrette, 296, my translation.

2. Degas was in Ménil-Hubert in Normandy with friends during the Commune uprising.

3. Denis, 1901, unpaginated.

4. "Letters from Paris," *The Daily Picayune*, November 11, 1872.

5. De Gas–Musson, René De Gas, London, to Michel Musson, 25 July, 1866, Box III, folder 23.

6. Degas was irritated by these "lectures on republicanism" and found the local journals wanting in discussions of French politics; however, *L'Abeille* of New Orleans contained more foreign news in 1872 than Paris's *Le Figaro*, and even included summaries of all the major articles appearing in the city's English-language papers.

7. "Letters From Paris," *The Daily Picayune*, November 11, 1872.

8. *The Daily Picayune*, September 4, November 11, 1873.

9. *Le Temps*, 20 aout 1872; the contest was between U.S. Grant and Horace Greeley, who died soon after losing the election. The French papers favored Greeley.

10. *The Daily Picayune*, December 10, 1872.

11. Not all the mouths belonged to lunatics, however, as incurables and epileptics were mixed with the insane. The women in asylums were supplied with sewing machines wherever possible. The occupation of sewing, together with the soothing mechanical hum, served to pacify the inmates. In one way New Orleans was ahead of Paris. Having fewer manufactured clothes, it had many sewing machines. Even sane women possessed them. Denis.

12. U.S. Customs House, "Excerpts from Letter Books, 1834–1912," 189–94, ms. in Louisiana State Museum; *The Daily Picayune*, September 7, 1873.

13. Estelle Musson's children René-Henri De Gas and Jeanne De Gas died of yellow fever in 1878; her son Pierre De Gas and her daughter from her first marriage, Joe Balfour, died of scarlet fever in April 1881. The epidemic of most concern in 1872 was the "horse-sickness" killing thousands of the country's eight million horses, and giving rise to gloomy prophesies of untilled southern fields and a breakdown of transportation.

14. New Orleans *Times*, November 21, 1869. *The Weekly Louisianian*, a moderate Negro paper, advertised as many toys as medicines.

15. *The Daily Picayune*, October 23, 1872; New Orleans *Times*, November 21, 1869.

16. *The Daily Picayune*, November 11, 1872.

17. On 295–97, Loyrette, quotes, without giving precise dates, a number of Degas's letters on what he considered proper subjects for his art.

18. *L'Abeille de la Nouvelle-Orléans*, 7 décembre, 1872.

19. *The Daily Picayune*, November 3, 1872.

20. *Moniteur Universel*, Paris, 26 decémbre 1872.

21. *The Daily Picayune*, August 31, 1873.

22. This was not to be the only time the artist used the device of a newspaper to give a scene verisimilitude. In Degas's *The Dance Class* (cat. 39), painted in 1879 and now in the Philadelphia Museum, a woman peruses a newspaper, ignoring the hubbub of young dance students all around her.

23. For accounts of the shooting, see *Paris Journal* and *Le Figaro*, 20 aout, *Le Temps*, 26 septembre 1875. The Paris papers commented that Achille had acquired the habit of carrying a gun while in the United States.

MARILYN R. BROWN

Franco-American Aspects of Degas's A Cotton Office in New Orleans

PAINTED IN NEW ORLEANS IN 1873 by the only French Impressionist to visit America, shown in Paris at the Second Impressionist Exhibition in 1876, and, as of 1878, the first picture by an Impressionist to enter a French museum, Degas's *A Cotton Office in New Orleans* remains a rich, if paradoxical, witness to Franco-American relations (cat. 31).[1] In this essay I explore how the specifically American aspects of the painting, which relate most obviously to its production in New Orleans, also had a bearing on its marketing, public reception, and eventual purchase in France. I begin with a look at some rather contradictory nineteenth-century French assumptions about America, and especially American business, from the point of view of Tocqueville and others. I consider how the scene Degas represented both confirmed and undermined French stereotypes about rich American businessmen. To do this, I situate the specific cotton firm depicted by Degas, as well as the manner in which he represented it, within the complicated economic context of New Orleans and its relations with France during Reconstruction. I see the artist's family, both Parisian and Creole, as providing the social mediation between the economic and personal elements of the painting. In questioning why the American aspects of the picture would *not* have appealed to the cotton manufacturer in Manchester, England, whom Degas initially had in mind as his patron, I suggest how its American content positively contributed to the painting's critical success in Paris, as well as how French stereotypes about American business may well have played a role in the painting's purchase by the museum in Pau. I argue that the painting's messages about Franco-American relations, interpreted in the context of shifting audiences and patronage, were neither stable nor static. Rather, they were fluid and sometimes contradictory.

By choosing a characteristically American topic, Degas was addressing some contradictory French assumptions and stereotypes about modernity and progress. America was seen by many nineteenth-century Frenchmen as the

FIG. 37. *Levee Loading Area with Steamship,* 19th century, photograph. Historic New Orleans Collection.

epitome of democratic capitalism: if Europe was old-fashioned, America was "new-fashioned," literally *le Nouveau monde* (the new world).[2] By Degas's day the romantic idea of America as an imagined forest primeval, an exotic and utopian myth celebrated by Chateaubriand, Girodet, Delacroix, Considérant, and others,[3] had, according to many accounts, been subsumed by notions of America as the enterprising land of infinite raw materials and universal industrial expansion.

The most brilliant nineteenth-century French analysis of American life and institutions, Tocqueville's *Democracy in America* (1835–40), had presented a more complex and equivocal assessment. On the one hand, Tocqueville described how American democracy embodied Enlightenment ideas of future progress. In this sense, Tocqueville saw America as the modern unbound self, freed from the inhibitions of European tradition. On the other hand, America clearly represented to him not only the possibilities, but also the dangers of modern democratic and capitalist progress. Thus, he saw majority rule watered down by mediocrity and the most rapid industrial and commercial expansion in the world colored by a restless and isolating philosophy of greedy and speculative individualism.[4]

Some subsequent French observers of America threw Tocqueville's aristocratic reserve and cautionary diagnoses to the wind, while others took his warnings about American lucre more to heart.[5] By the mid-nineteenth century there had emerged in France a stereotype of the ruthless American businessman pursuing not so much universal progress as personal profit. In his novel *A Man of Business* (1845), Honoré de Balzac made passing reference to a fraudulent and bankrupt French businessman who had fled to America as the only possible haven for such shady characters and dirty dealers.[6] In his travel account *Flânerie parisienne aux Etats-Unis* (1856), Alfred d'Almbert described all America as a vast department store full of get-rich-quick schemes.[7] Tocqueville's tyranny of the majority had been supplanted by the tyranny of the dollar. Meanwhile, the French stereotype of the rich "American uncle" *(l'oncle d'Amérique)* reached a comic apotheosis in Victorien Sardou's play *L'Oncle Sam,* first performed in Paris in November 1873, not long after Degas returned from visiting his own uncle in New Orleans. Sardou parodied the new industrialist "aristocracy" of *le Cinquième avenue,* in which the protagonist was presented as a self-made man, who, before he invested his millions in banks, railroads, and real estate, made his fortune, interestingly enough, in cotton.[8]

It is clear that the American topic of Degas's picture, and more specifically, a representation of what the French today call *le business,* could have elicited certain kinds of assumptions, both positive and negative, on the part of French audiences at the time. It was Degas's contradictory formal strategies, in concert with his entrepreneurial subject matter, that expressed a cultural and, apparently, a personal ambivalence about progress, and particularly American commercial progress, analogous in some respects to Tocqueville's analysis.

The compositional formulation of a social order in the painting is simultaneously undercut by autonomous gesture; and the representation of sober business activity is countermanded by signs of bored indolence. The image hovers indeterminately between portrait and genre, between human detail and commercial exchange, between private and public worlds. Such tensions are built compositionally into its pictorial structure.[9] Within the asymmetrical fictive space of the composition, there is a palpable tension between casual order and scattered dislocation. Near and far are conflated by identical rendering of blacks, whites, tans, and, to a certain degree, variations on blues in the foreground, middle ground, and background of the picture, regardless of representational subject. The cool greens and warm russet-browns of the walls and floor create a subtle complementary tension between receding void and advancing plane. The cottony white pigment that ostensibly signifies the raw material being exchanged also conjoins and somehow levels other inanimate and animate substances on one material plane, including starched shirts, crackling newspaper, jettisoned invoices, and the bleached light from a rear window. The graduated size diminution of the fourteen male figures joins with the diagonal orthogonals to organize the illusion of an off-centered spatial recession. Yet surface tension is maintained in that the virtual isocephaly of all but the foremost of these figures forms a horizontal coordinate system that counterbalances the verticals dominating the left and right edges of the canvas. The rectangular shape of an opened transom shutter at the top of the door or window forming the left-hand "frame" of the scene is echoed by the central newspaper and is deflected back to the picture plane by the rear window and the self-referential picture-within-a-picture on the right rear wall. In these ways the artist fabricates a somewhat unstable oscillation between "objectively" represented "modernity" and its random dispersion into and absorption by the surfaces of depicted "modernism."[10]

The resulting disjunctive human relations in Degas's scene are all the more peculiar because they represent members of the artist's own family, including his mother's brother Michel Musson, who checks the grade of a cotton sample in the foreground; his own brother René Degas, who casually smokes a cigarette and slouchingly reads *The Daily Picayune* (as it was then called) just off center; and his other brother Achille, who leans like a Parisian *flâneur* against a window sill on the left.[11] Musson's American son-in-law William Bell shows a handful of cotton to a customer at the sample table. Musson's French-Creole partner John E. Livaudais examines ledgers on the right, while his other partner, James S. Prestidge, talks to a customer behind René. A clerk in shirt-sleeves in the rear echoes Livaudais's gesture in the right foreground, but the remaining figures simply occupy space as they wait for undetermined reasons. (One in a bowler hat to the left of the rear clerk stares emptily at or past the cotton and another seated in the inner office stifles a sneeze.) Within Degas's dislocated space, traditional equilibrium and hierarchies as well as traditional human contact have been disrupted, and the absorbed figures occupy a privatized realm of separated activities of the kind that Tocqueville and others associated with the new economic conditions of American industrial capitalism. Shared human values seem to have been supplanted by more abstract, monetary ones. Through its "objective" modernist form, then, the *Cotton Office* seems simultaneously to affirm and criticize the modernity of its chosen American subject.

But can this rather Tocquevillean reading of *A Cotton Office* be corroborated historically? The letters Degas wrote from New Orleans, where he visited his American relations during the winter of 1872 to 1873, establish that it was the thick atmosphere of business in New Orleans that focused his own aspirations as an artist-entrepreneur. Writing on February 18, 1873, to the French artist Tissot in London, Degas, evidently impressed by his friend's fashionable success with British collectors, said he hoped to sell the *Cotton Office* through the British dealer Agnew to a rich Manchester textile manufacturer whom he called "Cottrell."[12] This and other letters written from New Orleans indicate that Degas saw a direct analogy between speculating in American business and launching his own artistic career. He bragged to Tissot: "My vanity is positively American."[13]

Information that can be recuperated about the chosen site and subject of *A Cotton Office in New Orleans* makes it clear that Degas's apparently "natural" representation was actually an artifical construction. The ramifications of subject matter in particular can be seen to suggest that the New Orleans painting contained latent messages about business that the artist did not mention in his enthusiastic letter to Tissot.

So far as the site itself is concerned, it comes as no surprise that Degas was accurate but inventive in his visual response to it. Degas's artistic practice has

long been understood as an extremely deliberate processing and reprocessing—in the privacy of his studio—of mingled borrowings from observed modern life, artistic tradition, Japanese prints, photography, and commercial illustration.[14] It is highly unlikely that he painted on location; his "studio" in this instance was probably the spare bedroom and second-floor gallery of his uncle's rented house on Esplanade Avenue. He probably painted there with the aid of drawings that are now lost.[15]

The site represented in *A Cotton Office* was the premises of Musson, Prestidge, & Co., Cotton Factors and Commission Merchants, located on the second floor, backside, of Factors' Row, number 63 Carondelet Street, at the corner of Perdido Street.[16] As the building stands today, its facade, though unfortunately not its interior, has been preserved almost in the state in which it was built in 1858 (fig. 38). In 1873, Factors' Row was at the heart of New Orleans's business and financial district, the local equivalent of Wall Street or the vicinity of the Paris Bourse (fig. 39). Not far away, at 3 Carondelet Street, was the office of De Gas Brothers (René and Achille), Cottonbuyers.[17] And close by, at 187 Gravier Street, was the New Orleans Cotton Exchange (fig. 40), which had been founded in 1871, and whose name has occasionally been confused with the title of Degas's painting.[18]

Determining the relationship between Degas's representation and the physical site of Musson, Prestidge, & Co. is made difficult by recurring interior renovations of Factors' Row. The seemingly spacious office represented by

FIG. 38. Factors' Row, 407 (formerly 63), modern photograph, Carondelet Street, New Orleans.

FIG. 39. Theodore Lilienthal, *Factors' Row*, ca. 1870, stereograph card. Historic New Orleans Collection.

FIG. 40. *New Orleans Cotton Exchange*, from Edwin L. Jewell, *Crescent City Illustrated*, New Orleans, 1873.

FIG. 41. Former Musson cotton factor's office, interior photograph taken during renovation in 1975.

Degas has been subdivided into windowless, flourescent-lit cubicles, the only memento of 1873 being the dado of the (now blocked) inner windows depicted in the left middle ground of Degas's picture. Before the most recent changes, however, the premises were photographed in varying states of renovation.

A professional photograph was taken in 1975, for an article in *The Times-Picayune* (fig. 41).[19] The photographer recalls that in attempting to approximate Degas's perspective he became acutely aware of the liberties Degas had taken with space. Even though an extremely wide-angle lens was used, it was impossible to register a width encompassing the inside shutters and transom on the left as Degas did.[20] The artist apparently stretched the space even beyond the capability of wide-angle photography. This seems to confirm an art historical argument that wide-angle effects in the work of Degas, Caillebotte, and other Impressionists actually preceded the kinds of optical effects that photography would not touch upon in a significant way until years later.[21]

In the process of constructing the wide-angle perspective of *A Cotton Office,* what other changes did Degas make in relation to the physical site (as recorded in the photograph), and what do these changes suggest about his attitude toward the represented scene? Despite obvious renovations of the site, including lowered ceilings and an enclosed stairway where the inner office once stood, the interior wall that parallels Carondelet Street, depicted separating the inner and main offices in Degas's scene, still exhibits the casings, moldings, and pulleys that allowed the windows to operate. When the 1975 photograph was taken, the dividing wall on the right, which parallels the plane of the rear wall, still contained the framed black wall-safe, which appears like a rectangular "halo" (or indeed a fireplace) behind the head of the clerk working behind John Livaudais at the ledger table on the right edge of Degas's canvas. The orthogonal system of the painting converges asymmetrically toward (if not exactly to) this vault, whose shape is echoed by the framed picture hung on the wall above it. The spatial and symbolic convergence and juxtaposition of the signs of secure money and framed art may seem an apt expression of the central concerns Degas expressed in his letter to Tissot. Yet the displacement of these important signs to the picture's very margin is, albeit typical of the artist, somehow unsettling.

The dramatically cropped and more painterly version in Harvard University's Fogg Museum (cat. 32) departs even further from resemblance to the physical site. What Degas in his letter to Tissot referred to as the "less complicated and more spontaneous" composition of this picture radically telescopes the space that, in the Pau version, exists between the cotton sample table and the gold-framed seascape.[22] As Degas moved the framed picture to the edge of the intervening wall, which looks so much like a Japanese screen, he entirely eliminated the étagère of cotton samples wrapped in brown paper, as well as the letterpress located in the Pau version just behind Livaudais's head. And due to the deletion in the Fogg version of the framed wall-safe found in the Pau composition, the parallel placement and painterly treatment of what Degas in his letter called the "sea of cotton" on the table and the depicted seascape on the wall seem to draw a comparable visual analogy between commodity and art. Later in 1876, in writing the dealer Charles Deschamps, Degas twice sarcastically referred to the New Orleans picture as "my cotton,"[23] that is, as the commodity it represented. The Fogg painting offers an adumbrated, condensed vision of rituals of American commercial transaction in a manner that situates art itself, if only marginally, as a part of the exchange.

This exploration of the physical site of *A Cotton Office* suggests that after closely observing the scene, the painter entirely recreated it on canvas. The carefully constructed imagery that resulted from Degas's process of formal manipulation presents an apparently casual scene of leisurely profitmaking. But how does this calculated representation of American capitalism compare historically with the financial conditions of the depicted firm?

A reconstruction of historical information about the financial dealings of both Michel Musson and the De Gas Brothers helps elucidate a subtext of speculation, risk, and uncertainty that underlies Degas's letters to Tissot from New Orleans as well as his painting of his uncle's cotton firm.[24] To understand how Musson's unsettled business circumstances, which directly affected the financial health of Degas's father's bank in France, inflected in the painting of *A Cotton Office in New Orleans,* it is necessary to go back to the American Civil War, the economic reverberations of which were felt for more than a generation.

Michel Musson had been involved in cotton since before the Civil War. At some point during the 1850s, he became a partner in the firm of John Watt and Company, Cotton Factors and Commission Merchants, located at 3½ Carondelet Street. Before he was forty years old, Musson had amassed a comfortable fortune by New Orleans standards, including seven slaves. By the time of the Civil War he had built himself a mansion at Third and Coliseum Streets in the Garden District, the most prestigious American sector of New Orleans.[25] During the war Musson remained in New Orleans but sent his wife and two of his daughters to France, where Edgar Degas met, entertained, and depicted them in a well-known pencil and wash drawing *(Mme Michel Musson and her Daughters Estelle and Désirée,* cat. 8).[26]

Before New Orleans fell to Union forces in 1862, Michel Musson was commissioned as a private in the Louisiana regiment of the Confederate army, and he served as a purchasing agent for the quartermaster.[27] Musson's allegiance remained staunchly Confederate after the fall of New Orleans; he evidently refused to take the oath of allegiance to the Union.[28] In lieu of military service, he now began to invest heavily in Confederate bonds, an ill-fated financial scheme that also involved his business associates, as well as René and, most astoundingly, Edgar Degas, and which was overseen by the bank owned by Auguste De Gas (Edgar's father) in Paris.

Several letters from Auguste De Gas to Michel Musson written in 1863 to 1864 (now located in the De Gas–Musson archive in the Tulane University Library) indicate how deeply the artist's father's bank was involved in supporting the Confederacy.[29] In two notable letters written in 1864, Auguste De Gas unwisely urged Musson to sell a house in New Orleans belonging to Edgar Degas (a property evidently willed to the artist by his mother or by his grandfather Germain Musson), so as to convert the proceeds into Confederate bonds.[30] Related documents from the same period indicate that Musson even at one point considered moving to Mexico to join a French-Mexican-Confederate collaboration that was envisioned, but never accomplished, by the French emperor Napoleon III.[31]

These documents establish that the Musson–De Gas loyalties and bank accounts were staunch in their support of the South. It is certain that Michel Musson's financial standing never recovered from the effects of the Civil War and its aftermath. By 1869 he found it necessary to sell his Garden District mansion and to move his family to the rented property in the French enclave on Esplanade Avenue where Edgar Degas was to visit. One source implies the move may have been necessitated by bankruptcy.[32] After the death of his cotton partner, John Watt, in 1867, Musson was on his own for a brief period and soon formed the partnership known as Musson, Prestidge, & Co., which moved by 1869 to the location at Carondelet Street subsequently depicted by Degas. Here Musson attempted to carry on his factoring business in much the same way as it had been conducted before the war, but in quite altered economic circumstances.

Since the late eighteenth century, cotton factors in port cities had occupied a conspicuous position as indispensable middlemen involved in financing and marketing the staple crop on which the southern economy most depended.[33] Engaged to buy, sell, receive, and forward goods to planters, factors received a commission, called factorage, for the credit service they provided. In the selling of raw cotton, the factor often worked in concert with a third party, the broker, an agent of the buyer, who acted as an intermediary between buyer and seller.

At the center of this system, the cotton factor was banker and bookkeeper, supplying credit to the planter. It is undoubtedly the factor's practice of keeping a set of books for the planter, recording income, expenditures, debts, and surpluses that is depicted on the right-hand side of Degas's *A Cotton Office in New Orleans.* This activity is counterweighted, in the center and on the left of the picture, by the exchange among factors, brokers, and buyers, including René and Achille De Gas. It is notable that the factoring office of the artist's American uncle functioned in some respects like his father's bank in France. And like his father's bank, his uncle's business faced financial risks and abrupt dissolution.

FIG. 42. *Ships with Bales of Cotton,* 19th century, photograph. Historic New Orleans Collection.

The Civil War did not bring an immediate end to cotton factoring, but it initiated economic changes in the system of exchange that soon made the factors in southern port cities obsolete. It was in the midst of these changing postwar conditions that René De Gas joined Musson and Watt's firm in 1865.[34] Letters he subsequently wrote from Europe in the summer of 1866 to Michel Musson in New Orleans are quite revealing of the philosophy and practice of speculation that, at times adversely, linked the Musson-Watt business in New Orleans with the De Gas family's banking firm in Paris. In a long and disjointed letter written from London on July 25, 1866, he described a loss of some $8,000 (equivalent to more than $80,000 in today's currency) from a speculation in cotton futures, a debt that was to continue to cripple the finances of the De Gas bank, not to mention René's brothers and sisters, who had provided him with capital.[35]

The involvement of the brothers De Gas in cotton was peripatetic and uneven.[36] The same held true for Musson, Prestidge, & Co., with the significant distinction that this firm's instability reached an unforeseen crisis at exactly the time Edgar Degas was painting it, probably due, most immediately, to the international financial panic of that year.[37] The dissolution and subsequent liquidation were formally announced on February 1, 1873, on page five of *The Daily Picayune,* in an article René De Gas could even be perusing as he slouches near the center of his brother's picture (fig. 43).[38] Thus, although the gist of Degas's letter to Tissot, written a little more than two weeks after the dissolution, seems to echo the former reputation of his uncle's firm, the painted detail of *The Daily Picayune* in Degas's picture can be seen as more than a nonchalant

The Daily Picayune.

DISSOLUTION—THE FIRM OF MUSSON, PRESTIDGE & CO. is this day dissolved by mutual consent, Messrs. M. Musson and Jno. E. Livaudais retiring. Our successors as below will have charge of the liquidation.
M. MUSSON,
JAS. S. PRESTIDGE,
JNO. E. LIVAUDAIS.
New Orleans, Feb. 1, 1873.

COPARTNERSHIP—THE UNDERSIGNED having formed a partnership for the purpose of doing a Cotton Factorage and General Commission Business, assume all the liabilities of the late firm of MUSSON, PRESTIDGE & CO.; will collect all debts due the same, and continue the business at No. 63 Carondelet street, under the firm name of PRESTIDGE, GRAHAM & CO.
JAS. S. PRESTIDGE,
S. L. GRAHAM,
of Pinewood, Tenn.
W. D. HARDEMAN,
of Carroll parish, La.

IN RETIRING FROM BUSINESS, I TAKE pleasure in recommending to my friends my successors Messrs. PRESTIDGE, GRAHAM & CO., and solicit in their behalf the liberal patronage heretofore bestowed upon me and my late firm.
M. MUSSON.
F1—2w

PRESTIDGE, GRAHAM & CO.—
—Successors to—
MUSSON, PRESTIDGE & CO.,
Cotton Factors and Commission Merchants,
63 Carondelet street,
James S. Prestidge,   New Orleans.
S. L. Graham,
W. D. Hardeman.   F3 '72—1y

FIG. 43. Announcement of dissolution of the Musson firm, *The Daily Picayune*, 1 February 1873, page 5. New Orleans Public Library.

bit of local color. This off-centered caveat in the general disequilibrium of the perspective might imply that the picture incorporated not only a meditation on speculation in cotton futures, but also an ironic observation on the very precariousness of such risky business. Degas's silence about the firm's dissolution in his ambitious letter to Tissot probably indicates his own uneasiness about it, especially in view of his hopes of selling the picture to a cotton manufacturer. Under the circumstances the artist could indeed have found more than a passing analogy between the cotton commodity he painted and the painted commodity he hoped to sell.

Although Musson tried subsequently to get involved in other business ventures, his fortunes as a whole did not fare well. The long obituary that appeared in *L'Abeille de la Nouvelle-Orléans* when he died in 1885 did not even mention the cotton business painted by Degas. It stressed that although Musson's name had been linked with notions of "progress, enterprise, and public utility," his fortunes had been cruelly reversed by business caprices and personal tragedy, and his successes had ended in collapse.[39] But Musson's various misfortunes were not just a matter of mismanagement or bad luck. In particular, the dissolution of his cotton business in February 1873 fits into the larger economic picture of the southern cotton trade in the rapidly changing world market during the postbellum period. One of the central problems with the southern economy during the postwar years was the decline in the world demand for American cotton at exactly the time when the historical coincidence of wartime destruction, temporarily high cotton prices, and the rise of sharecropping combined to push the region more deeply into cotton production.[40] As René De Gas and an associate pointed out in a published assessment of the New Orleanian cotton trade in the 1870s, the Franco-Prussian War (1870–71) further reduced raw cotton exports to France due to the loss of Alsatian textile factories.[41] Cotton prices meanwhile fell in inverse proportion to growth output as world demand plunged then stagnated. All of this was compounded by the depression following the international stock market crash of 1873.[42]

In the midst of the political and economic turmoil of Reconstruction, the role of cotton factors changed dramatically.[43] The progressive expansion of railroad and telegraph systems helped undermine the old factorage system by

changing the pattern of cotton movement, diverting it to inland markets from the ports, especially
New Orleans.[44] The changed market structure
resulting from the institution of cotton exchanges
meant that the old-style factoring office (such
as we see in Degas's picture), which was usually
a small family outfit dealing in spot or transit
cotton based on cotton samples on the premises,
was quickly made obsolete in the face of large-
scale speculation in cotton futures, conducted
at a rapid pace, based on the international telegraph system of cotton exchanges.[45] Whereas the
cotton factor's office was like a quiet family store,
the cotton exchange was like a frantic stock market
(fig. 44).

FIG. 44. *New Orleans Cotton Exchange,*
from *Frank Leslie's Illustrated Newspaper,*
March 24, 1883.

Meanwhile, the profound social changes wrought by the emancipation of
slaves meant that the old planter system was supplanted by the sharecropping
system in which newly freed African-American tenant farmers obtained from
inland local storekeepers the kind of credit services that planters had formerly
obtained from factors in ports.[46] In his picture Degas was pointedly focusing
on the exclusively white and masculine inhabitants of a scene of apparently
leisurely enterprise at precisely the time when their economic and racial authority was being thrown radically into question.[47]

As I have argued, Degas's painting is constructed formally to create a sense
of tension between order and dislocation. This choice of a subject precisely at
the precarious juncture of its dismantling, exactly at the tension point between
past and present, between the habitual and the new, is typical of Degas.[48]
And such aesthetic choices seem to have been grounded in the social and economic fabric of his time. Degas was even to hear echoes of the dissolution of
his uncle's cotton firm when, the following year, his father's small family bank
in France collapsed in the wake of financial panic, being outdated by such large
and anonymous new joint-stock banks as Crédit Mobilier and Crédit Lyonnais.
The pronounced financial shift during the mid-nineteenth century from private
credit to impersonal speculation, from small French-style, to larger, more
American-style businesses (whether in the cotton or banking trades), seems
to have helped mold Degas's own uneasy attitudes about commercial progress
in general and about the art business in particular. In the destabilized world
of *A Cotton Office in New Orleans,* he constructed his first major painting about
that ambivalence.

In my reading of *A Cotton Office*, I have attempted to indicate the contradictory ways in which Degas both acknowledged and undermined contemporary French notions about American business. In my concluding section, I turn briefly to the equally contradictory ways the American aspects of the painting affected its marketing, public reception, and patronage. As mentioned, Degas hoped or speculated that he would be able to sell *A Cotton Office* to a Manchester textile manufacturer. Degas probably knew about William Cottrill's large art collection from a series of illustrated articles that had appeared in *The Art Journal* in 1870 to 1872.[49] What is known about Cottrill, however, indicates that his taste in pictures did not tend toward the avant-garde and that financial instability probably caused him to sell the greater part of his art collection in the wake of the stock market crash of 1873.[50] Moreover, the chances that Degas's scene of the American cotton trade would have had an appeal in Manchester in 1873 are exceedingly slim. Before the Civil War the United States had supplied Britain with some eighty percent of its raw cotton. But during and after the American cotton famine, which resulted from the blockading of southern ports, Lancashire cotton mills suffered enormous financial losses, unemployment, and pervasive bankruptcy. After the war the British understandably turned away from the American market. But in the ensuing industrial depression in Manchester, cotton manufacturers saw the American-induced famine as a significant cause.[51] In the context of these market forces and conditions, Degas's subject of apparently leisurely profitmaking in the American cotton trade would have had little appeal for a Manchester industrialist in straitened circumstances.

Nonetheless, when *A Cotton Office* was exhibited in Paris at the Second Impressionist Exhibition in 1876, the painting received a more positive critical response than other less finished works, most especially Degas's own *Woman Ironing* (cat. 37), to whose sketchy form and working-class, female subject matter critics often compared the more slick, bourgeois, and masculine New Orleans painting.[52] *A Cotton Office* was most successful with critics from the conservative press, several of whom mentioned its typically individualistic American subject matter as part of its appeal. For example, Louis Enault, who wrote in the Bonapartist journal *Le Constitutionnel*, described the picture in rather Tocquevillean terms as "a collection of cotton merchants examining the precious commodity that is today one of the fortunes of America. It is cold, it is bourgeois; but it is seen in an exact and accurate way, and what is more, it is rendered correctly." Despite its "coldness," *A Cotton Office* was nonetheless preferred to what this critic called the "coarseness" of the laundress scene.[53] Given French loyalties to the South during the Civil War, it makes sense that the American aspects of the New Orleans painting would be less problematic in

Paris than in Manchester following the cotton famine. For conservative French critics, the apparent accuracy of *A Cotton Office* confirmed and safely naturalized middle-class and masculinist notions of the individualism of American commodity culture.

Immediately after the Paris exhibition, Degas renewed efforts to sell *A Cotton Office* in England through Charles Deschamps, an associate of the dealer Durand-Ruel.[54] But since no buyer came forward, he sought other markets for the picture, his sense of urgency no doubt increased by family money troubles and by the renewed economic depression of 1877. Through the influence of two well-connected French friends, Paul Lafond and Alphonse Cherfils, the secretary and vice-president of the Société des Amis des Arts in provincial Pau, Degas exhibited the New Orleans picture in that winter resort town in the Pyrenees in 1878.[55] It was not long afterward that Degas painted his two friends in *Les Amateurs* (fig. 45).[56] When the *Cotton Office* was exhibited in Pau, there was a critical campaign in the local press, some of the positive remarks evidently coming from the anonymous hand of Lafond.[57] The picture was subsequently purchased for the museum in Pau by a special municipal committee appointed by the mayor to distribute funds provided by the will of one Emile Noulibos. The committee was composed of the mayor, the museum curator, several businessmen and proprietors, a journalist, the founder of the local photographic society, and an artist. Since Noulibos was the scion of an old cotton and linen textile manufacturing family in Pau, it seems likely that the committee members at least partly intended the purchase of *A Cotton Office* as an homage to the

FIG. 45. Edgar Degas, *Les Amateurs*, ca. 1878–81, oil on oak panel, $10\frac{3}{4}$ × $13\frac{7}{8}$ in. Cleveland Museum of Art.

MISS DIANA VERNON DE L'OHIO.

Folle de la chasse au renard. Ne s'est jamais cassé que deux jambes et un bras,
mais tout est remis. Le cœur est intact.

FIG. 46. Bertall, "Miss Diana Vernon de
l'Ohio," illustration from *La Vie hors de
chez soi*. Paris, 1876.

textile origins of the money donated to them by their benefactor.[58] Beyond
this, the painting was likewise compatible with the newest industry in Pau:
tourism. A large foreign population dominated by wealthy British and American tourists spent the winter season in Pau each year, seeking leisurely recreation (fig. 46) and engaging in financial speculation in local industries and real
estate.[59] As French writer Albert d'Almbert had ironically explained it, France
exported its impoverished immigrants to America in search of wealth and
America exported its own richest citizens back to France to spend surplus
money.[60]

In the context of burgeoning municipal leisure industries in Pau, the museum curator, Charles Le Coeur, clearly recognized the usefulness of art. In his
various publicity campaigns for the museum, he reiterated the progressive
theme that art was basically good for tourism because it could provide an attractive amusement for wealthy foreigners.[61] As Degas's *A Cotton Office in New
Orleans* found a home in Pau, its subject matter in particular, reinforced by a
relatively conservative finish, may well have been considered appropriate for the
audience of visiting wealthy Americans. The American elements of its content
that might have proved problematic in England after the cotton famine could
remind its French audience in Pau of individualistic American entrepreneurs of
the type that had been written about by Tocqueville, and who formed a substantial part of the immediate commercial clientele. It may even have played to
popular French fantasies about the proverbial *oncle d'Amérique,* that stereotype
of unlimited wealth to which, ironically, Degas's own American uncle did not
particularly conform. In the paradoxical slippage in meanings between the
original production and eventual reception of the picture, common denomina-
tors can nonetheless be found in ideas of individualism and progress, ideas
that the French specifically connected with America. It seems likely that an
Americanized notion of entrepreneurial commerce was precisely what appealed
to Degas's French buyers, despite his own ambivalence about it.

1. This essay is based on my previous publications, including Brown, 1994, 1991, 1990, and 1980.

The title of the painting has varied. For the sake of simplicity, I have adopted the rather abbreviated title under which it is exhibited in the Musée des Beaux-Arts in Pau: *Un Bureau de coton à la Nouvelle-Orléans (A Cotton Office in New Orleans)*. See Philippe Comte, *Ville de Pau, Musée des Beaux-Arts, Catalogue raisonnée des peintures* (Pau, 1978), n.p. Degas first mentioned it in a letter to James Tissot from New Orleans on February 18, 1873, as *Intérieur d'un bureau d'acheteurs de coton à la Nlle Orléans, Cotton buyers office*. See Guerin, 1947, no. 6, 29. It was exhibited as *Portraits dans un bureau (Nouvelle Orléans)* in the Second Impressionist Exhibition in Paris in 1876. See *Catalogue de la 2e exposition de peinture . . . 11, rue Le Peletier* (Paris, 1876), no. 36, 7. It was exhibited as *Intérieur d'un bureau de coton à la Nouvelle-Orléans (Etats Unis)* in Pau in 1878. See Société des Amis des Arts de Pau, *Livret du Salon 1878* (Pau, 1878), no. 87, 31. After it was purchased by the museum in Pau the same year, its title was listed as *Intérieur d'un comptoir de Coton à la Nouvelle-Orléans (Etats Unis)*. See Société des Amis des Arts de Pau, *Catalogue des ouvrages exposés dans les salons de l'exposition au Musée de la Ville* (Pau, 1879), "Liste des ouvrages achetés à l'exposition de 1878," opposite 14. It was perhaps the term *comptoir,* with its monetary emphasis that spawned the frequent mistranslation of the title as *The Cotton Exchange at New Orleans*. See, for example, Washington, San Francisco, 1986, no. 22, 170. For reasons that will be made clear below, the latter title is a misnomer.

2. See, for example, Auguste Javary, *De l'Idée de progrès* (Paris, 1851), 267–68; Edmond About, *Le Progrès* (Paris, 1864), 56–57.

3. For French notions of America before the nineteenth century, see Gilbert Chinard, *L'Amérique et le rêve exotique dans la littérature française au XVIIe et au XVIIIe siècle* (Paris, 1911). See also Detroit Institute of Arts, *The French in America, 1520–1880* (Detroit, 1951). Chateaubriand's *Atala,* a novel of American Indian life that was incorporated into his *Le Génie du christianisme* (Paris, 1802), inspired Girodet's Salon painting *The Burial of Atala*

(1808; Paris, Louvre) and Delacroix's painting *The Natchez* (Salon 1835, New York, The Metropolitan Museum). Victor Considérant spent 1852 to 1969 in the United States, attempting to found in Texas a utopian phalanstery based on Fourier's socialist principles. See Victor Considérant, *Au Texas* (Paris, 1855) and Dr. Savardan, *Un Naufrage au Texas* (Paris, 1858).

4. Alexis de Tocqueville, *Democracy in America,* translated by George Lawrence (London, 1966), especially vol. II, 652–4, 692–5, 713–17, 795–97.

5. For the former strategy, see, for example, Michel Chevalier, *Lettres sur l'Amérique du nord* (Paris, 1838), vol. I, vi–vii; vol. II, 370–79.

6. Honoré de Balzac, *Un Homme d'affaires,* translated by William Walton (Philadelphia, 1896), 294.

7. D'Almbert, 157–63. It is worth noting that some years later a delegation studying French immigration in New Orleans took special pains to guard against illusions and stereotypes of the "promised land" by warning their readers about the harsh realities of life in Louisiana and urging them not to come without considerable capital. See Paul d'Abzac et al., *Enquête sur la navigation, l'immigration et le commerce français à la Nouvelle-Orléans en 1876* (Paris, 1876), 79–86.

8. Victorien Sardou, *L'Oncle Sam,* comédie en 4 actes en prose, au Vaudeville, 6 novembre 1873 (Paris, 1875), especially 10, 12–13. See also Charles Monselet, "Théatres: Vaudeville: *l'Oncle Sam,* comédie en quatre actes, par M. Victorien Sardou," *Le Monde illustré* (November 15, 1873), 315, for the observation that '*L'Oncle Sam* can be considered the counterpart to *l'Oncle Tom*. It's white America after black America. It's satire after elegy." See also d'Almbert, 250–51, on the "American uncle" stereotype.

9. It should be noted that a visible pentimento shortens the forward leg of the *étagère* of cotton samples in the background so as to add to the rising effect of the floor and contribute to the distinctive tipped-up, diagonal construction that numerous critics and historians have connected with both photography and Japanese prints. Studies of Degas's rather problematic relationship to photography include:

Ulrich Schumacher, "Gruppenporträt und Generbild; zur Bedeutung der Photographie für die Französische Malerei des 19 Jahrhunderts," *Giessenen Beiträge zur Kunstgeschichte,* IV (1979), 19–62, especially 48–51, on *A Cotton Office;* S. Varnedoe, "Of Surface Similarities, Deeper Disparities, First Photographs, and the Function of Form: Photography and Painting after 1839," *Arts Magazine,* LVI (September 1981), 112–15; K. Varnedoe, 1980A, 1980B; Elizabeth Anne McCauley, *A.A.E. Disdéri and the Carte de Visite Portrait Photograph* (New Haven, 1985), 125–28, 151–72; Eugenia Parry Janis, "Edgar Degas' Photographic Theater," in Centre Culturel du Marais, *Degas: Form and Space* (Paris and New York, 1984), 451–866; Carol Armstrong, "Reflections on the Mirror: Painting, Photography, and the Self-Portraits of Edgar Degas," *Representations,* no. 22 (Spring 1988), 108–41; New York, 1998. The problematic relationship between *A Cotton Office* and photographs of the same site will be considered below. For Degas's relationship to Japanese prints, see, among other accounts, Theodore Reff, "Degas, Lautrec, and Japanese Art," in Yamada Chisaburo, ed., *Japonisme in Art: An International Symposium* (Tokyo, 1980), 189–213; and Lipton, 1986, 56–62; Colta Ives, "Degas, Japanese Prints, and *Japonisme,*" in New York.

10. The literature on "modernity" and "modernism" is vast. For helpful historical and theoretical overviews, see Johanna Drucker, *Theorizing Modernism: Visual Art and the Critical Tradition* (New York, 1994); and Charles Harrison, "Modernism," in Robert S. Nelson and Richard Shiff, eds., *Critical Terms for Art History* (Chicago and London, 1996), 142–55.

11. On the idea of the *flâneur,* see Charles Baudelaire, "The Painter of Modern Life," (1859–63) in Jonathan Mayne, ed. and trans., *The Painter of Modern Life and Other Essays* (London, 1964), 9; Walter Benjamin, "The Flâneur," in Harry Sohn, trans., *Charles Baudelaire: A Lyric Poet in the Era of High Capitalism* (London, 1973), 35–66; Griselda Pollock, "Modernity and the Spaces of Femininity," in her *Vision and Difference: Femininity, Feminism and the Histories of Art* (London, 1988), 50–90.

12. Appendix II, letter to Tissot, 18 February 1873. The original is in the Bibliothèque Nationale de France, Paris, Manuscripts, NAF13005, no. 8. For a complete French transcription, see Paris, 1989, 360–62.

13. Ibid. For related letters, see Appendix II in this book.

14. See above, n. 9. On a possible source in journalistic illustration see also Albert Boime, "Thomas Nast and French Art," *The American Art Journal,* vol. 4 (Spring 1972). But one should bear in mind Degas's often-quoted statement in a letter of November 27, 1872, written from New Orleans to the artist Lorenz Frölich about the careful blending of visual elements over time so that no single one, whether illustration or photograph, took precedence over careful calculation, selection, and the conditioning of repeated exposure. See Appendix II.

15. The De Gas–Musson archive in the Tulane University Library (hereafter abbreviated D-M), Box V, folder 3, contains an undated letter from Odile Musson (daughter of Estelle Musson and René De Gas) to P. A. Lemoisne, giving information which he later incorporated into his *Degas et son oeuvre* (Paris, 1946–49), I, 74. According to Musson: "[Degas's] workshop was a large gallery shady and cool surrounded by magnolia and oak trees, secluded, so as not to be disturbed, and it was there every morning he was to be found hard at work. The *Bureau de Coton* was started and finished out there." On preparatory studies (and the lack thereof), see Jean Sutherland Boggs in Zürich, 1994, 37, n. 72.

16. See *Edwards' Annual Director to the . . . City of New Orleans for 1873* (New Orleans, 1873), 324; and Mary Louise Christovich et al., *New Orleans Architecture* II (Gretna, La., 1972), 190.

17. *Edwards',* 126. This was not the site of Degas's painting, as Guerin suggested, 18.

18. See above, n. 1.

19. *The Times-Picayune,* June 8, 1975, section 3, 6. (The article announced an exhibition of the Pau painting in New Orleans.) My thanks to Nancy Burris, head librarian of *The Times-Picayune,* for providing me with a print of the photograph. For other photographs of the site, see Brown, 1994 (as in n. 1), fig. 9, and Joseph F. Newell, *A Microcosm of Mid-Nineteenth Century New Orleans Architecture and Development as Seen in the 2300 Block of Esplanade Avenue* (M.A. thesis, Tulane University, New Orleans, 1982), fig. 117.

20. Conversation with Ron Todd, 1987.

21. K. Varnedoe, 1980A, 1980B; and Peter Galassi, "Caillebotte's Space," in *Gustave Caillebotte: A Retrospective Exhibition* (Houston, 1976), 60–73, on wide-angle effects.

22. Apendix II, letter to Tissot, 18 February 1873. Given the passing resemblance between the cropped seascape and representations of the Civil War confrontation between the *Kearsarge* and the *Alabama,* there may be a veiled comment on the stubbornly prolonged Confederate loyalties of Degas's family, or on the fortunes of the South and its cotton trade in the postbellum period. The best-known image of the *Kearsarge* and the *Alabama* was Manet's painting of 1864, which had been exhibited at the Paris Salon of 1872 (Philadelphia Museum of Art, John G. Johnson Collection). The image in the Degas is rather closer to contemporary journalistic illustrations of the event. There was a revival of interest in the Alabama and the Kearsarge when in 1871 to 1872, Britain, which had built the Alabama for the Confederacy, was found liable, in international arbitration, for over $15 million in damage that the vessel had inflicted on sixty-five Union ships before being sunk by the Kearsarge off Normandy in 1864.

23. Archives Durand-Ruel, Paris. For a complete French transcription see Paris, Ottawa, New York, 1988, 436–37. Also excerpted and translated in Denys Sutton, *Edgar Degas: Life and Work* (New York, 1986), 115–16.

24. In a letter to P. A. Lemoisne in 1933, Odile Musson, the daughter of Estelle Musson and René De Gas, noted that "the leisure aspect of the picture offers quite a contrast to the hustle and bustle of a modern cotton office, and fortunes were made and lost there just the same." See letter cited above in n. 15.

25. See S. Frederick Starr, *Southern Comfort: The Garden District of New Orleans, 1800–1900* (Cambridge, Mass., 1989), 42, 59, 200.

26. See Jean Sutherland Boggs, "'Mme. Musson and Her Two Daughters' by Edgar Degas," *The Art Quarterly,* XIX (Spring 1956), 60–4; Baumann and Karabelnik (as in n. 15), no. 80, 200–201. For letters in the De Gas–Musson papers concerning the visit, see Brown, 1990 (as in n. 1), 120–21, as well as the essay on the archive in this catalogue.

27. See Andrew B. Booth, *Records of Louisiana Confederate Soldiers and Louisiana Confederate Commands* III (New Orleans, 1920), book 1, 1115. See also the pro-Confederacy and pro-slavery tract by his brother Eugène Musson, *Letter to Napoleon III on Slavery in the Southern States, by a Creole of Louisiana* (London, 1862).

28. D-M, Box VI, folder 2.

29. Including D-M, Box I, folder 46, letter from Auguste De Gas to Michel Musson, December 22, 1863; Box I, folder 61, letter from Auguste De Gas to Michel Musson, March 17, 1864; Box II, folder 1, letter from Auguste De Gas to Michel Musson, July 1, 1864; Box II, folder 8, letter from René De Gas (in Paris) to Michel Musson, August 26, 1864; Box II, folders 10 and 13, letters from Auguste De Gas to Michel Musson, September 23, 1864, and December 22, 1864. See Brown, 1990 (as in n. 1), 123–24, as well as the essay on the archive in this catalogue.

30. D-M, Box II, folder 15 and Box II, folder 1; Brown 1990 (as cited in n. 1), 124, as well as the essay on the archive in this catalogue. Given the evident extent of the involvement of Edgar Degas's family and their finances in the Southern cause, the interpretation of his violent history painting *Scène de guerre au moyen âge* (Salon of 1865, Paris, Musée d'Orsay) as a veiled allusion to the American Civil War and *Les Malheurs de la Nlle Orléans* seems to gain an amount of credence. See Hélène Adhémar, "Edgar Degas et la 'Scène de guerre au Moyen Age,'" *Gazette des Beaux-Arts* LXX (November 1967), 295–98; Paris, Ottawa, New York, no. 45, 105–07. For an opposing position, see Richard Thomson, *Degas: The Nudes* (London, 1988), 51, 58.

31. D-M, Box II, folder 30; Brown, 1990, 123, as well as the essay on the archive in this catalogue.

32. Newell, 213, states that Musson moved to Esplanade the same year he filed for bankruptcy. I have been able to find no independent documentation pertaining to a bankruptcy at that time.

33. The single best source on the changing role of cotton factors in the South is Harold D. Woodman, *King Cotton & His Retainers:*

Financing & Marketing the Cotton Crop of the South, 1800–1925 (Lexington, 1968). See also S. S. Hall, Laws of Louisiana Relative to Cotton Factors and Commission Merchants (New Orleans, 1861); Matthew B. Hammond, The Cotton Industry: An Essay in American Economic History (New York, 1897), especially chap. 10, "The Evolution of the Cotton Market," 278–323.

34. D-M, Box II, folder 17, letter from John Watt to Désirée Musson (Michel's daughter), January 15, 1865 (written, interestingly enough, in Pau, Basses Pyrénées), mentions that her father has asked René De Gas to join him in New Orleans. Other correspondence indicates that René began formulating his idea of moving to New Orleans as early as June, 1863, during the visit of the Musson women to France during the Civil War. He reiterated the notion in many subsequent letters. His father was initially opposed, preferring him to join the Italian branch of the family bank. But Edgar supported him in the American move for financial reasons. Brown, 1990, 120, as well as the essay on the archive in this catalogue.

35. D-M, Box II, folder 23.

36. See D-M, Box II, folders 24, 48. The brothers began by trading in wines and oils, but shifted to decidedly less epicurean commodities. See Alberta Collier, "New Trace of Degas' Family," The Times-Picayune, August 15, 1965, for a display board from the steamboat Wild Wagoner (active 1864–76) featuring an advertisement for a fertilizer sold by the De Gas Brothers. The firm won a petition filed in Federal Circuit Court on January 15, 1870, charging the South Eastern Rail Road Company and its president Benjamin Laurent Millaudon [whose plantation in St. Bernard, Louisiana, Edgar Degas was to visit] for a large debt of $18,778.87 for expenses and credit damage accrued from an undelivered shipment of 1250 tons of railroad iron. Court records are in the National Archives—Fort Worth Branch, case 6052, entry 121, archives box 247, location A1700352. City directories indicate that De Gas Brothers changed location three times between 1868 and 1873. By 1874 the brothers had separated. Achille returned to France to oversee the affairs of his deceased father's failing bank and René became associated with John Leisy's cotton factoring firm between 1875 and 1878, when he abruptly left New Orleans, deserting

his wife and children. Achille assumed his brother's association with Leisy between 1879 and 1883.

37. For sparse remaining business records of the firm, Brown, 1994, 31–2.

38. The Daily Picayune, XXXVII, no. 8 (February 1, 1873), 5. The announcement stated that while the dissolved firm was being liquidated, Prestidge and some new associates would assume all the debts and liabilities of the departing Musson and Livaudais. The announcement of dissolution included a personal message from Musson: "In retiring from business, I take pleasure in recommending to my friends my successors Messrs. Prestidge, Graham & Co., and solicit in their behalf the liberal patronage heretofore bestowed upon me and my late firm." The term "retiring" seems to have been a euphemism: Musson subsequently continued a variety of business ventures and his letters make it clear that this was done out of financial need. The family history Musson sent to his brother Henri in 1881 cited Musson, Prestidge, & Co. as dissolving in February 1873 and listed his subsequent association with the New Orleans Mutual Insurance Association, 1873 to 1879 (D-M, Box IV, folder 21). The advertisement for Musson, Prestidge, & Co. usually featured up until January 27, 1873, in the New Orleans Price Current, Commercial Intelligencer and Merchants' Transcript suddenly stopped appearing as of February 1. The other local directories began as of 1874 to list Prestidge, Graham, and Company as cotton factors at 63 Carondelet Street; in fact, an advertisement for this new firm appeared on the same page in The Daily Picayune as the announcement of Musson's dissolution. Given John E. Livaudais's immediate departure from the firm, and given his depiction as being actively engaged in its business on the right side of Degas's composition, it seems unlikely that Degas's painting should be interpreted as a depiction of the new firm, even though the old one dissolved exactly while he was working on it. The picture seems, rather, an evocation of the old firm at the very time of its failure. In subsequent years, city directories listed John E. Livaudais at various addresses, and in various businesses, as both a cotton factor and bookkeeper. In a letter from Paris of April 3, 1873, Eugène Musson congratulated his brother Michel on

retiring from business, but suspected that he would find other work to do (D-M, Box II, folder 52). In a later letter of October 25, 1873, Eugène wished Michel success in starting a sulphur mining company (D-M, Box II, folder 57).

39. L'Abeille de la Nouvelle-Orléans, May 5, 1885 (D-M, Box IV, folder 48). This assessment is confirmed by Musson's letters, which, in spite of outlining projects for a business upswing, acknowledge his "tribulations," "straitened circumstances," his compagnies en désarroi, and the repeated moves he and his family had to make from one rental property to another. All of this was exacerbated by René De Gas's desertion of the now blind Estelle Musson, as well as by the death of Musson's daughter Mathilde Bell and the death by yellow and scarlet fever of several grandchildren: D-M, Box II, folder 65; Box III, folders 17, 18, 19, 20; Box IV, folders 4, 11, 13, 21. In 1877, Musson mortgaged the "Fall Back" plantation in Mississippi (inherited from the family of Estelle Musson's first husband), which was subsequently sold. Records of the mortgage are found in the succession papers of Mathilde Bell, Civil District Court for the Parish of Orleans, archives, docket 5731, filed April 6, 1882, New Orleans Public Library. Musson is quoted by Rewald in New Orleans, 31, Rewald, 1985, 43, as describing himself in 1882, as "old and partially paralyzed, without employment, poor and recently deprived of the pension which I had been receiving from the New Orleans Insurance Association since 1880." In a letter to Edgar Degas on August 6, 1883, Musson claimed, "Je n'ai rien, je gagne rien." See D-M, Box IV, folder 37. Musson died insolvent, leaving a sum of $3,666.86 inherited from his recently deceased brother Eugène, all of which was owed to Estelle Musson, who had lent him over $4,000. See the succession papers of Michel Musson, Civil District Court for the Parish of Orleans, archives, docket 24568, filed July 21, 1888, New Orleans Public Library.

40. Gavin Wright, The Political Economy of the Cotton South: Households, Markets, and Wealth in the Nineteenth Century (New York, 1978), chap. 6; Old South, New South: Revolutions in the Southern Economy Since the Civil War (New York, 1986), especially 12–13, 51, 56–57.

41. E. Allgeyer and R. De Gas, "Exportations; cotons," in Paul d'Abzac et al., *Enquête sur la navigation, l'immigration et le commerce français à la Nouvelle-Orléans en 1876* (Paris, 1876), 46. (The main point of the essay was to encourage more cotton trade with France.) On the effects of the Franco-Prussian War, see also George Ruble Woolfolk, *The Cotton Regency: The Northern Merchants and Reconstruction 1865–1880* (New York, 1958), 111. The year 1872–73 was an especially unpropitious one for southern cotton production, due to drought and heavy damage from the bollworm. See Charles A. Easton, *Reports of the Agricultural Bureau on Cotton, For Seven Years—from 1870 to 1876, Inclusive* (New York, 1877), 22–3, 75–9; James L. Watkins, *King Cotton: A Historical and Statistical Review, 1790 to 1908* (New York, 1908), 203.

42. See "Report of Mr. Consul de Fonblanque at New Orleans," *Parliamentary Papers* LXXV (1875), 435–59, quoted by Woolfolk (as in note 41), 112. On the crash of 1873 and the depression of subsequent years see: H. L. Beales, "The 'Great Depression' in Industry and Trade," *Economic History Review* V (1934), 65–75; A. E. Musson, "The Great Depression in Britain, 1873–1896: A Reappraisal," *Journal of Economic History* XIX (1959); D. J. Coppock, "The Causes of the Great Depression, 1873-1896," *Manchester School* XXIX (1961); S. B. Saul, *The Myth of the Great Depression 1873–1896* (London, 1969). Although modern research by economic historians has challenged the idea of the existence of a "Great Depression" during this period in a unified sense, there is general agreement that businessmen at the time went through unusual and worrying economic experiences that they tended to characterize as a "Great Depression." See also E. J. Hobsbawm, *The Age of Capital 1848–1875* (London, 1977), 16, 46–62. For the effect on New Orleans, see Dorothy M. Barker, "An Economic Survey of New Orleans During the Civil War and Reconstruction" (M.A. thesis, Tulane University, New Orleans, 1942), 13, 21, 53; Joe Gray Taylor, *Louisiana Reconstructed, 1863-1877* (Baton Rouge, 1974), 358–63. By 1876 it was reckoned that among the French population of Louisiana "fortunes have not been displaced, they have been destroyed." See F. Limet, "Observations générales sur la situation du commerce d'importation à la Nouvelle-Orléans," in d'Abzac et al., 1976, 14.

43. See Robert M. Davis, *The Southern Planter, the Factor and the Banker* (New Orleans, 1871), 3–15.

44. Woodman (as cited in n. 33), 176–86; 263–64; 269–94. See also Michael Wayne, *The Reshaping of Plantation Society: The Natchez District, 1860–1880* (Baton Rouge and London, 1983), chap. 6.

45. See Henry Hentz, "Cotton at $1,000 a Bale: Reminiscences of the Cotton Trade of Old," *The New York Times*, December 29, 1890, 2; Hammond (as cited in n. 33), 291–99, 301–23; Woodman (as cited in n. 33), 266–68; Taylor (as cited in n. 42), 392–400; see also C. Vann Woodward, *Origins of the New South, 1877–1913* (Baton Rouge, 1951), 185–86; *Charter, Constitution, By-laws and Rules of the New Orleans Cotton Exchange* (New Orleans, 1885); Watkins (as cited in n. 41), 38–42; James E. Boyle, *Cotton and the New Orleans Cotton Exchange: A Century of Commercial Evolution* (New York, 1934), 65–133; Audrey Imelda Sherman, "The History of the New Orleans Cotton Exchange 1871–1914" (M.A. thesis, Tulane University, New Orleans, 1934). It is significant that four of the key figures portrayed in Degas's painting were actively involved in the New Orleans Cotton Exchange at the time the artist painted it: Musson, René De Gas, Prestidge, and Bell. See Brown, 1994, 35; New Orleans Cotton Exchange Minutes, Tulane University Library, ms. 652, Sherman, 8, 15, 50, 80.

46. See above, nn. 43, 44.

47. As I argued in my book (Brown, 1994, as in n. 1, 37–42), the African-American labor that actually picked the depicted cotton is noticeably absent from this scene of black-suited white men, and yet it is indexed by the very presence of the raw commodity, by the painted whiteness of what Degas referred to (in the letter to Tissot cited in n. 12) as "the precious material" for sale. Tactile traces of the literal work of the artist's hand in painting the cotton thus supplant reference to more latent or invisible forms of manual labor in the very sign of the product of that labor. In Appendix II, letter to Frölich, Degas pointedly described "the contrast of the busy and so positively appointed offices with this immense black animal force." His visual separation of the two was not unrelated to the racial attitudes of

his family, and, most specifically, their participation in the White League, something I discovered in the family papers in the Tulane University Library (see Brown, 1990, 124–25, as well as the essay on the archive in this catalogue). Michel Musson and William Bell, both of whom are depicted in the *Cotton Office*, were active participants and even leaders in the White League, including the famous or infamous battle of Liberty Place in 1874. (Musson presided over the mass gathering of the White League that preceded the battle of Liberty Place.) In research more recent than mine, Christopher Benfey has revealed the fact that Degas's mother's first cousin Norbert Rillieux, an important inventor of a sugar-refining process, was a free man of color. See Benfey, 1997, chap. 7, and his related work, Benfey, 1996. Benfey asserts (chap. 9) that despite this evidence of miscegenation in the artist's own family, and despite his uncle's participation in the "Unification Movement," which was an attempt to bring about cooperation between white and black businessmen, Degas's *Cotton Office*, painted fully a year before the battle of Liberty Place, can be read as a sinister conspiracy of the White League to plot racial violence. Whether or not one completely accepts this reading, it is clear that Degas chose to depict a scene of white cotton factors at an exceedingly precarious historical moment.

48. Lipton, 45, 73–74, has discussed in particular his choice of racetrack and ballet subjects as examples of a penchant for topics that focused on the fissures between an old world of class privilege and a new world of social uncertainty.

49. My thanks to Julian Treuherz, Keeper of Fine Art, City Art Gallery, Manchester for this reference: "Visits to Private Galleries. The Collection of W. Cottrill, Esq., Singleton House, Higher Broughton, Manchester," *The Art Journal*, new series, IX (1870), 68–70; "Selected Pictures. From the Pictures in the Collection of W. Cottrill, Esq., Higher Broughton," ibid., X (1871), 36, 72, 80; XI (1872), 68, 92.

50. Christie, Manson, & Woods, *Catalogue of the Highly Important Collection of Modern Pictures and Water-Colour Drawings of William Cottrill, Esq., Who Has Disposed of His Residence, Singleton House, Higher Broughton, Manchester* (London, 1873). The sale was announced in

The Manchester Guardian, April 19, 1873, 11, "Sales by Auction." See also Brown, 1994, 54–58.

51. See Brown, 1994, 43–54. In 1870, before the stock market crash of 1873, the president of the Manchester Chamber of Commerce cited the American cotton famine and the increase in American cotton prices during and after the Civil War as a major, if not the sole, cause of what he termed the "disasters" suffered by the overextended Manchester cotton manufacturing industry. He listed nearly 145 firms as having failed in 1869 alone. He described many mill owners as being forced into emigration while cotton "operatives" were driven into destitution. See J. M. Bennett, *The Condition of the Cotton Trade in Lancashire and the Operation of the Anglo-French Treaty of 1860* (Manchester, 1870), 3–39. See also William E. A. Axon, *Annals of Manchester: A Chronological Record from the Earliest Times to the End of 1885* (Manchester, 1886), 274–301; William O. Henderson, *The Lancashire Cotton Famine 1861–1865* (New York, 1969); Douglas Anthony Farnie, *The English Cotton Industry and the World Market 1815–1896* (Oxford, 1979), 135–70. During and immediately following the Civil War, trading relations between Britain and America had been strained by both the cotton famine and the international arbitration lasting until 1872 over the British-built Confederate ship Alabama. See Max Belloff, "Great Britain and the American Civil War," *History* XXVII (1952), 40–8; Arthur Redford and B. W. Clapp, *Manchester Merchants and Foreign Trade, II. 1850–1939* (Manchester, 1956), 12–20, 90–9.

52. See Brown, 1994, chap. 2, for a complete analysis of the criticism in 1876.

53. Louis Enault, "Mouvement artistique: L'Exposition des intransigeants dans la galerie Durand-Ruelle [sic]," *Le Constitutionnel,* (April 10, 1876), 2: "M. Edgard [sic] Degas est peut-être un des plus intransigeants de cette intransigeante compagnie. Il faudrait vraiment que je me sentisse coupable d'un bien grand crime pour consentir à garder sous mes yeux pendant vingt-quatre heures ces deux blanchisseuses, dont l'une appuye avec tant de lourdeur et de gaucherie sur son fer, tandis que l'autre bâille ignoblement, en étirant ses bras, avec un geste atrocement canaille. M. Degas qui n'a pas crainte de lasser la patience

du public, n'expose pas moins de vingt toiles, à peu près de la même valeur, et dans la composition desquelles il semble avoir obéi aux mêmes préoccupations malheureuses. C'est le réalisme dans ce qu'il a de plus triste et de plus fâcheux. Je fais cependant une exception pour le tableau portant ce titre au moins bizarre: *Portrait* [sic] *dans un bureau.* Le tableau ainsi désigné, ou déguisé, n'est autre chose qu'une collection de marchands de cotons examinant la précieuse denrée qui est aujourd'hui une des fortunes de l'Amérique. C'est froid, c'est bourgeois; mais c'est vu d'une façon exacte et juste, et de plus c'est correctement rendu." Excerpts translated in Washington, San Francisco, 171; and Armstrong, 1991, 29.

54. See Brown, 1994, 83–84.

55. Ibid., chap. 3, for a complete analysis of the exhibition and subsequent purchase, especially 93–4 on Lafond and Cherfils.

56. Ibid., 109–10.

57. Ibid., 99–102. For the reviews in question see Anonymous [Paul Lafond?], "Exposition des Amis des Arts," *Journal des étrangers,* (February 9, 1878, 2; February 16, 1878), 1–2.

58. See Brown, 1988, and Brown, 1994, 102–14, for archival sources in Pau and identification of the committee members. Chantal Georgel, "En 1878, le musée de Pau achetait un Degas," in Musée d'Orsay, *La Jeunesse des musées: Les musées de France au XIXe siècle* (Paris, 1994), 251–52, incorrectly gives the museum curator, Charles Le Coeur, sole credit for the purchase.

59. Bertall [Charles-Albert d'Arnoux], *La Vie hors de chez soi* (Paris, 1876), 214–59. For more of the same, see Guide-Joanne, *Pau et ses environs* (Paris, 1912), 14–17; Pierre Tucoo-Chala, et al., *Pau, ville anglaise: du Romantisme à la Belle époque* (Pau, 1978), 14; Brown, 1994, 87–88.

60. As in n. 7, 45: "Singulier contraste! Tandis que les enfants de notre sol s'expatrient douloureusement pour aller chercher la fortune au nouveau monde, les Américains viennent chez nous dépenser le superflu de leur argent. Nous leur envoyons nos pauvres, ils nous expédient leurs plus riches citoyens, et cependant,—voyez comme ils sont entendus en affaires!—c'est encore eux que gagnent au change!"

61. Charles Le Coeur, *De la fondation d'une Société des Amis des Arts à Pau* (Pau, 1863), extract from the *Mémorial des Basses-Pyrénées* (March 1863), reprinted in Charles Le Coeur, *Les Institutions artistiques de la ville de Pau (1863–1880)* (Pau, 1880), 129–42, especially 131: "Pour rendre le séjour de Pau agréable aux étrangers, il faut, dit-on chaque jour, leur offrir des distractions attrayantes. Mais quelle plus attrayante distraction peut leur être offerte qu'une exposition publique de tableaux et d'objets d'art, appelés de tous les points de la France?"

MARILYN R. BROWN

A Tale of Two Families: The De Gas–Musson Correspondence at Tulane University

IN WHAT READS RATHER LIKE A BIBLICAL "BEGAT," the De Gas–Musson Papers were formally placed on loan in the Special Collections of Tulane University Library in 1973, through the generosity of the late Mrs. Edmund B. Martin, née Dora Odile Musson, daughter of Gaston Edgar Achille Musson (fig. 47), who was, in turn, the son of René De Gas (cats. 2, 3) and Estelle Musson (cat. 28), the brother and cousin, respectively, of the famous French Impressionist artist Edgar Degas (cat. 1). The papers were later donated to the library in 1991 by the children of Dora Musson. The collection consists of six boxes divided into folders containing some 437 letters and documents in French and English dating from 1834 to 1950. Prior to my own work on the archive, selected excerpts of a few of the letters had already been published, including some, but not all, of those that refer to Edgar Degas himself. These excerpts helped illuminate Degas's family relationships and the basic chronology of his biography. The remainder of the archive contains considerably more information of interest, not only to Degas scholars, but also to historians of the society, politics, and economics of the American South and of Franco-American relations.

The content of many of the letters and documents is quite mundane, in fact, often quite delightfully so, including the various letters from children relating activities like catching lightning bugs. It is not my aim here to provide a complete overview of the collection; that kind of coverage can be found elsewhere in the annotated inventory I prepared in 1991 for the Tulane University Library, which includes selected transcriptions, translations, and summaries of each document.[1] My purpose here is to give an idea of the flavor of the archive by selecting and mentioning some of the documents that seem to me the most worthy of attention with specific respect to the painter Degas, his work, and his social formation as exemplified by his relations with his New Orleans family. I should emphasize that although the artist himself may be the raison d'être for

FIG. 47. Caranon, *Gaston De Gas Musson,* ca. 1876, cabinet portrait, New Orleans. Collection of Edmund Martin.

FIG. 48. *La Sainte Bible,* Paris, 1846, Musson family Bible with genealogy of the family. Collection of Edmund Martin.

FIG. 49. Washburn, *Michel Musson,* ca. 1876, cabinet portrait, New Orleans. Collection of Edmund Martin.

the existence of the collection, his presence in it is rather ancillary (however significant), and the papers taken as a whole constitute a family archive more than an artistic one in the strictest sense. As such, they are a valuable source of historical materials relating both directly and indirectly to Edgar Degas, his family, and the complicated and conflicted times in which they lived.

A few examples can suffice at this point to give a sense of the scope of the archive. There is one letter in the collection from the period of Reconstruction recounting some of the activities in European exile of the remarkable Judah P. Benjamin, the so-called Jewish Confederate, who had been born in South Carolina, married a New Orleanian, had risen to power in Louisiana politics, and served as Attorney General, Secretary of War, and Secretary of State of the Confederacy. He had escaped to England to avoid imprisonment, went to law school in his middle age, and became a Queen's Counsel and leading international lawyer. Aside from this brief mention of a famous person (in addition to the artist himself), there are some fascinating letters from Ellen Shields, daughter of Major Gabriel B. Shields of Natchez, in which she presents a woman's educated perspective on the economics, politics, and various health crises of the Reconstruction and post-Reconstruction periods. There are also numerous letters from Degas's cousin Estelle Musson that are virtually illegible, scrawled, despite her near blindness, in overlaid perpendicular configurations on translucent paper.[2]

The main protagonists mentioned in the archive include: Michel Musson (fig. 49), Degas's uncle in New Orleans (brother of the artist's mother, Célestine Musson), who collected the family papers and methodically kept letterpress copies of much of his own correspondence; Musson's wife, Odile Longer; and their children Désirée (referred to variously as Didi, Didy, Dy, Tantetine) (cat. 7), Mathilde (Mouche) [Bell] (cats. 25, 26), and Estelle (Tell) [Balfour De Gas] (cats. 27, 28). The New Orleans branch often corresponded with the artist's family in Paris, including his father, Auguste De Gas (fig. 59); his brothers René and Achille; and his sisters Marguerite [Fevre] (cat. 4), and Thérèse [Morbilli] (cats. 5, 6). Michel Musson also frequently wrote to and heard from his own brothers, Henri and Eugène, who were also in France (fig. 50).[3]

Aside from the various letters in the archive mentioning the artist, other related topics of interest touched upon in the papers include: the considerable involvement of the De Gas–Musson clan (including Edgar) in an ill-fated scheme of investing in Confederate bonds during the American Civil War; family political attitudes about the Civil War, Reconstruction, racial strife, and Franco-American relations during the period; the family's pattern of speculation, as well as the lack of wisdom of its business dealings—most notably René De Gas's considerable loss in speculating cotton futures in 1866, which created a large debt that was to plague the family bank during the economic crises of the 1870s; the liquidation of the De Gas family bank in Paris and Naples (beginning in 1873); René De Gas's desertion of his wife and children in New Orleans (in 1878); and the descent into insanity of Edgar's uncle Eugène Musson—which began in the mid-1870s and led to an increasingly ruptured exchange between an angry Michel Musson and a cold Edgar Degas in 1883 to 1884.

Two letters from the artist himself are found in the collection. Both are addressed to his uncle Michel Musson and give news of the visit of the Musson women to France during the American Civil War. The first letter, written from Paris on *mercredi* 24 (Wednesday), is badly deteriorated and in places illegible. The date is torn away, but this is clearly the letter from June 24, 1863, partly quoted by Lemoisne, in which Edgar gives news of the Musson women's arrival in France. He also touches upon the topic of photography and portraiture and mentions the political campaign in Mexico of the French emperor Napoleon III in relation to the American Civil War:

> My dear uncle, your family arrived here last Thursday 18 June and is now completely ours. Things couldn't be better, or simpler. Accept all my warm regards. Your photograph is definitely you, although it conveys less of the air of [illegible] humor of which René has frequently spoken, an air that I can scarcely find [in the photograph]. Our aunt Odile is walking very well and I admit that, judging from the portrait we have of her, I expected her to be less spry. Didy is really her first mate. As for Estelle, poor little woman, it's hard to look at her without thinking that her face has flashed before the eyes of a dying man [her late husband]. Please give our warm regards to the pleasant and

FIG. 50. Catherine Longchamps, *Portrait of Henri and Eugène Musson*, ca. 1835, chalk and wash, believed destroyed.

pretty Mathilde whose young boy [illegible] cared for by Negresses [?] is known and admired by everyone. Our Thérèse has not been here for five weeks. How I would have liked to have seen her fussed over as I am now by our aunt and cousins.

At 7 o'clock the day before yesterday a loud ring of the door-bell announced to us the arrival of M. Philippe Beauregard . . . the mischievousness was already what one would have expected. He came in the evening to see our aunt. The various stories recounted to us keep us abreast of what is happening over there. Uncle Eugène [Musson] . . . [illegible] secretly announces that we have a good hand in Mexico and [swears?] to you that the Emperor [Napoleon III] is giving a political or [illegible] turn of the screw to the rest of your enemies.

He ends dutifully by sending his affection.[4]

The second letter from the artist is scrawled inconspicuously on the back of a long letter to Michel Musson from Didi Musson in Bourg, written over the course of several days, December 25, 1863 through January 1, 1864. On December 31, Didi mentions the arrival in Bourg of Edgar and that he has already made a drawing *(croquis)* of Mme (Odile) Musson reading to a dozing Tell (Estelle). Didi also reports that Mme Musson has some pain in her hand. Edgar's note, written, presumably, on January 1, 1864, is badly deteriorated:

You know, my dear uncle, that I'm writing you just two steps away from your dear wife. I arrived here yesterday and will leave day after tomorrow. The life of [illegible . . .] absolutely for your poor family. There would be still very little [to report] except for a little indisposition on the part of my aunt. As for the cold, [the women] have good, well-heated lodgings. That indisposition shouldn't alarm you. Her right hand ails a bit [and she's] treating it with opium.

She's reading the life of Marie Antoinette near the mantelpiece, on which is sitting that elephant about which you know. Didi writes at the same table where I am. [Virtually illegible sentence about Estelle and her daughter completing the picture.]

Goodbye[,] I send my love as your nephew and almost as your son. A thousand things to Mathilde. Take care. E. De Gas.[5]

Although the scene the artist describes in this letter may bring to mind his drawing *Mme Michel Musson and Her Daughters Estelle and Désirée* (cat. 8), that work was evidently completed on a later visit to Bourg in 1865. As we shall see, the familial warmth of this letter's closing would cool by the 1880s.

Some fifty-two other letters in the collection, of which approximately a dozen have been published in excerpt form, refer directly to Edgar Degas and the development of his artistic career. Several letters from 1861 to 1863 describe his attempts to get his career off the ground. René De Gas wrote Michel Musson from Paris on January 17, 1861, primarily to discuss the American Civil War and strategies of how to *battre les Yankees* and mentioned: "Edgar is so absorbed by his painting that he writes no one in spite of our remonstrances. That doesn't keep him from thinking of you often and very much wanting to see you. When will his wishes, which are also ours, be realized? . . . The violin lessons proceed, but very slowly. It's atrociously difficult. Edgar is learning it too."[6] Auguste De Gas was cautious about his son's artistic career in letters to Michel Musson of November 21, 1861, and March 6, 1863, respectively: "Our Raphael is always working, but hasn't yet produced anything accomplished; meanwhile the years go by."[7] And, "What can I say about Edgar? We are waiting impatiently for the opening of the exhibition. I myself have good reason to believe he will not finish in time; he will scarcely have prepared what needs to be done."[8] A joint letter to Michel Musson from René and Marguerite De Gas in Paris, October 13 and 16, 1861, expressed concern about the Yankee campaign against New Orleans and mentioned that "Edgar has just come back from a three-week trip in Normandy and works hard at his painting."[9] Later, on March 6, 1863, René reiterated to Musson his brother's single-minded pursuit of painting: "As for Edgar, . . . He works furiously, and thinks of only one thing, his painting. He works so hard that he does not take time out to enjoy himself."[10]

In the same letter, René acknowledged the upcoming visit of his aunt, Mme Odile Musson, to France; and several subsequent letters recount Edgar's interaction with his aunt and two cousins (Désirée and the recently widowed Estelle, as well as Estelle's baby daughter Joe Balfour).[11] Henri Musson wrote his brother Michel from Avallon on April 7, 1863, saying that although he himself would not be able to spend much time with the visitors from Paris, they would be attended by René, Marguerite, and Edgar.[12] Didi [Désirée] Musson wrote her father on June 24, 1863 (the same day the artist wrote his uncle in New Orleans to report the safe arrival of the Musson women), from Paris, where René and Edgar had shown them the sights: "Edgar, whom we were told was so brusque, is full of consideration and kindness."[13] René wrote to Michel Musson from Aix-les-Bains on August 12, 1863, that he and Edgar would endeavor to spend New Year's day with the Musson women in Bourg-en-Bresse.[14] By this time, René himself was formulating plans of emigrating to New Orleans to join his uncle's firm; and according to a letter from Didi of November 18, 1863, Edgar was the only one who encouraged René in the venture and did so with a view to his brother's independence from the limitations of a career in his father's bank, specifically the branch in Naples:

> Mother requests me to say to Papa that he should pay attention to the manner in which he writes to René on the subject of his departure for America; René is a charming boy, full of intelligence, ambition, and heart. He has only one idea, and that is to leave his father's banking firm to go to work and live with us; he says if he stays in Paris, or if he goes to Naples [to work for the branch of the family bank there], he will be *50 years old,* earning *30 francs* a month; this revolts him. He would rather be a success at age 30, be his own master in all things; and make a fortune from life . . . However ardent to attain his goal, he will have to talk and reason a lot before obtaining the consent of his father . . . Edgar is the only one who encourages René, because he knows all that he suffers from his position, one with perhaps no future.[15]

As yet oblivious of René's plans, his father, Auguste, wrote to Michel Musson from Paris on December 22, 1863, giving news of the calming effects of the stay in Bourg on the Musson women and saying that Edgar would soon visit them: "In a few days Edgar will be with his Aunt and his cousins and you only have to leave it to him, he won't fail to cheer them up."[16] Marguerite De Gas wrote Michel Musson from Paris on December 31, 1863, telling him of her recent visit in Bourg-en-Bresse with her aunt and cousins from New Orleans and mentioned that Edgar had just left to do the same: "Edgar left from here yesterday to go spend the new year holidays with them and he is so gay that he will amuse and entertain them a bit. He took with him a lot of pencils and paper to draw Didi's hands in all positions, because it is rare to find so pretty a model."[17]

On the same day, Estelle Musson wrote her father from Bourg, mentioning that Edgar had arrived.[18] It was at this time that Edgar wrote the previously quoted note to his New Orleans uncle assuring him of the continued well-being of his wife and daughters in France. On February 3, 1864, Estelle again wrote her father and mentioned sketches Edgar made of the baby [Joe Balfour] (cat. 9).[19] Edgar evidently made at least two trips to Bourg in early 1864, because René wrote Michel Musson from Paris on January 6, 1864, noting that "Edgar has just spent five days in Bourg,"[20] and Didi wrote Michel from Bourg on February 11, 1864, mentioning that "Edgar gave us his week."[21] Back in Paris, Edgar was again hard at work on his art, as attested to by a letter to Michel from René on April 22, 1864: "Edgar still works enormously without seeming to. What ferments in that head is frightening. For my part, I think and am even convinced that he has not only talent but even genius, only will he be able to express what he feels? That's the question."[22] Later that summer, René De Gas wrote Michel Musson from Paris on August 26, 1864, to tell him that Edgar had supported him in presenting their father with René's wishes to go to New Orleans (rather than entering the branch of the family banking firm in Naples, which Auguste would have preferred): "Edgar who knows the family said it well when he told me that if I want to become something I must completely detach myself with respect to advantage and depend on them only with respect to affection. He is distressed to see me go because we love each other a lot but he understands that I will find my life over there rather than here."[23]

By December, the artist was planning another trip to see the Musson women, as Didi wrote Michel from Bourg on December 15, 1864: "We hope to see Edgar at the first of the year. We always see these good friends with happiness."[24] She wrote again on January 5, 1865, to recount Edgar's arrival while they were at mass:

> We were waiting for Edgar who didn't arrive. We had lost all hope of seeing him when he arrived this morning around nine o'clock loaded up to his neck. Mother and I were still at mass, he came down and as soon as mass was over he came and tapped mother on the shoulder. I was on the very front row of chairs, I didn't see anything of all that and was quite surprised on returning home to find master Edgar in mother's room all busy unloading a little trunk full of bonbons, toys, etc. . . . Edgar made several sketches of little Joe, but he wasn't content with them, it was impossible to make her hold still for more than five minutes.[25]

She went on to mention having a photographer take pictures (fig. 51), something that, perhaps, has a bearing on Degas's drawing *Mme Michel Musson and Her Daughters Estelle and Désirée,* which is inscribed January 6, 1865.[26]

After the Musson women returned to the United States and René De Gas settled in New Orleans, news of Edgar Degas continued to reach Michel Musson in New Orleans. On February 16, 1869, Achille De Gas wrote his uncle to report on family business—which he obviously took to include both the import-export firm he had set up with René in New Orleans and Edgar's burgeoning artistic career. He drew a parallel between the two and seemed to see an analogy with his uncle's cotton business as well:

> René must have told you that our business is in good shape and that we are all in hopes of having finally found the road to fortune. . . . You

probably knew that I spent around a fortnight in Belgium for our business . . . Edgar came with me to Brussels. He met M. Van Praet, minister of the king, who bought one of his pictures, and it was on view in the Galerie, one of the most famous in Europe, which gave him a certain pleasure, as you can well imagine, and finally gave him some confidence in himself and his talent, which is real. He sold two others during his stay in Brussels and a well-known picture dealer, [Arthur] Stevens [brother of the painter Alfred], offered him a contract at the rate of twelve thousand francs a year. There he is, decidedly launched, and I think you'll learn that with pleasure, he has certainly merited it, given the time he has worked like a Negro and with so little profit up till now. But this career of painter is by far the most difficult there is, and it takes so much time to establish a reputation; and once there, on the other hand, you're all alone. We, and to a lesser degree you, are beginning to float gold bonds, one might say, that the luck of the De Gas is moving from the state of myth to that of reality after having undergone like certain stars a slightly too prolonged total eclipse.

I hope, my dear uncle that your business has continued to go well this year. I see that cotton still maintains high prices, which shouldn't grieve you excessively.[27]

The next news of Edgar was reported to New Orleans by René, who (after his marriage to Estelle in 1869) had returned to Europe on business in 1872. A letter to Estelle from Paris on June 26, 1872, described, among other things, how Edgar met him at the station and was advancing in his art:

At the station I found Edgar who has matured, some white hairs sprinkling his beard; he is also stouter and more fit. I dined at his place with my Father and we went to Marguerite's after dinner. . . . Marguerite is plump & good-looking. Her husband [Henri-Gabriel Fèvre, an architect] is Mr. Stuffy Bourgeois incarnate, self-important and stupid like all self-styled successful people. Edgar is really doing some charming things. He has a portrait of Mme Camus in profile in a garnet red velvet dress, seated in a brown armchair against a pink background which, for me, is purely a masterpiece. His drawing is something ravishing. Unfortunately he has very weak eyes, he is forced to take the greatest precautions. I have lunch at his place every day. He has a good cook and a charming bachelor's apartment. . . .

Yesterday I dined at Edgar's with Pagans who sings with guitar accompaniment. Achille will give you some details on him.[28]

In another letter to Estelle from Paris on June 28, 1872, René gave more news of Edgar: "Edgar thinks me an American, & I also feel completely foreign. . . . Edgar comes to get me for dinner . . . turkey buzzard (Edgar repeats this word every two minutes.)"[29] René had more to report along the same lines in his next letter to Estelle from Paris on July 12, 1872: "Edgar with whom I lunch every day tells me to send his love to you all, his eyes are weak and he has to take the greatest precautions. He is still the same, but is crazy to learn to pronounce English words, he has been repeating *turkey buzzard* for a whole week."[30] As René's next letter to Estelle from Paris on July 17, 1872, makes clear, Edgar's continuing ironic attempts to speak like an American evidently helped inspire in him the notion of coming to the States for a visit when René returned in mid- to late October (fig. 52):

Edgar has got it into his head to come with me and to stay with us for a couple of months. I couldn't ask for anything better. He contemplates all sorts of things about the natives and never stops asking questions about you all. I decidedly think that I'll bring him back. His eyes are better, but he has to spare them and you know how he is. Just now, he makes small pictures, which is what tires his eyes the most. He is doing a dance rehearsal which is charming. As soon as the picture is finished, I'll have a large photograph taken of it. I have lunch every day with him. He has a cook named Clothilde who does admirably. Her dream is to come to America, but she's too intelligent a girl not to drop us after too little time, to marry a rich man and set up a cook-shop for herself. That's what holds me back, otherwise I would think of sending her over. . . . After dinner I go with Edgar to the Champs-Elysées, from there to the Café-chantant to hear idiotic songs, like the song of the guildsman mason and other absurd foolishness. . . . Prepare yourselves to give a

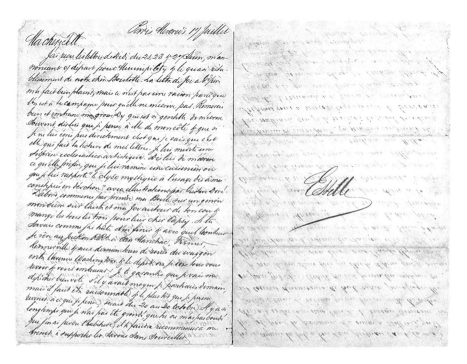

FIG. 52. Letter to Estelle Musson from René De Gas, July 17, 1872, De Gas–Musson Papers, ms. 226. Special Collections, Tulane University, New Orleans.

fitting reception to the Grrrreat Artist, he asks in this regard that you refrain from coming to meet him at the station with Colored Band, militia company, firemen, clergy, etc.[31]

Writing his stepdaughter Joe Balfour from Le Havre on July 25, 1872, René said he would return to Paris the last week of September "to get Edgar who wants to come with me to kiss you all."[32]

In a letter to Estelle from Liverpool on August 7, 1872, René thanked her for sending him locks of their children's hair, which delighted the family in Paris, most notably Edgar: "Naturally I showed them in Paris. Edgar found the blond hair of my little man so pretty."[33] A slightly later letter to Estelle from Paris on August 20, 1872, recounted how René was continuing to inquire after hiring a maid for them [see above, letter of July 17, 1872] and in doing so, revealed that Edgar's housekeeper Clothilde was a former laundress—something that perhaps sheds some light on the artist's interest in that subject matter:

> I had a good one at hand, Edgar's, but she is much too astute. It's true that she knows how to sew [and] launder admirably, having been a laundress, and cooks till you lick your fingers. She badgers me to take her, but she is too shrewd, & I'm afraid would drop us quickly to find something better elsewhere. . . . Edgar charges me to kiss you all.[34]

In two letters to Estelle from Paris in September, however, René indicated that Edgar was now hesitating about making the trip to New Orleans. On September 14, 1872, he reported: "Edgar is undecided, I don't believe he's coming & that might be best for him."[35] On September 25, 1872, he reiterated this and suggested that worry about his eyesight was causing Edgar's indecision: "I told you I believe we shouldn't count on Edgar. He wants to come, but I haven't pushed him to; if the trip harmed his eyes, I wouldn't want to have myself to blame for it."[36] Given the probability that Edgar would not come, he also asked Estelle to send photographs of the children for Edgar to see.

But either the artist cast caution to the wind at the last moment or else he and René had been plotting a surprise visit all along, because in a letter to Michel Musson on October 19, 1872, Eugène Musson described from Paris the brothers' departure for America:

> Before you get this letter, our travellers departed on the 'Scotia' will have given you the unedited details of the freshest news of the family and of our poor France. But having a week's advance over this letter, will they arrive before it? That would be a bet to make. From here I see the one shooting like the devil towards his little wife and children,

and his business; the other, doubtlessly full of good will and of the desire to get there, but stopped at each step by the thousand and one things that he has seen in that big America, so different from this old Europe (not as young and not as old as they always say). He will tell you all about it when he gets to you. He will do well to be there. But he will do even better when he comes back to us after a long *flâne* [dawdle] in the South, West, and North. He will make his father die laughing with his tales of one thing and another, his sketches, notes, and anecdotes, that Edgar![37]

With René back in New Orleans, Michel Musson continued to receive news of Edgar from Eugène Musson and Achille De Gas in Paris. On April 3, 1873, Eugène wrote to describe Edgar's return from his voyage to America:

> Edgar came back to us enchanted by his voyage, enchanted to have done so many things new to him, but especially enchanted to have made the acquaintance of all his good relatives in America. He is, as you say, an amiable boy [he was thirty-nine at the time] who, moreover, will become a very great painter if God preserves his sight and makes him a little less feather-brained.[38]

FIG. 53. *Mathilde Musson Bell*, ca. 1864, photograph. Collection of Adelaide Wisdom Benjamin.

Later, on July 6, 1873, he again mentioned Edgar, saying that he had gone to London, presumably on business: "Edgar is leaving for *Londres* or for London 'as these English try to call it.'"[39] Achille likewise sent Michel Edgar's best wishes for health and prosperity in September 1874;[40] but on December 4 of the same year, he mentioned that Edgar was having continuing difficulties with his eyes: "Edgar continually complains about his eyes, which keep him from working as much as he'd like."[41]

Aside from a mention by the traveling businessman René in a letter to Estelle from Rouen on July 6, 1876, that he had spent the night in Paris with Edgar,[42] most of the remainder of references to the artist come in letters written to Michel Musson from his brother Henri from Paris and Normandy between 1877 and Henri's death in 1883. Two of the letters, written on January 17 and May 16, 1877, mention Edgar in relation to the liquidation of the De Gas family bank, discussed below. Correspondence from 1878 to 1881 sets forth Edgar's position on René's desertion of, and subsequent divorce from, Estelle. As we shall see, there are references in several of these letters to a portrait of the now deceased Mathilde Musson Bell (fig. 53), which Degas seemed to have promised to his New Orleans relatives as an appeasement, however inadequate, for René's behavior.

Besides letters with specific mention of the artist himself, another document of interest in relation to the social status of the artist's family is a photocopy of the history of the coat of arms of the Famille De Gas, taken from the Archives Générales de la Noblesse de France in Paris on June 30, 1863, claiming origins in thirteenth-century Languedoc. The original is in the exhibition (fig. 4). Recent studies of Degas indicate that Achille De Gas commissioned the fraudulent family tree and that the family's origins were, despite fluctuations in name, solidly middle class.[43]

Other letters and documents, a few of which mention the artist himself, are quite revealing of his family's political, economic, and racial attitudes during the American Civil War and Reconstruction. Several letters written during the war to Michel Musson from Auguste De Gas in Paris express the artist's father's concern about the events and politics of the Civil War and the allegiances of France and England relative to the South.[44] A family biography clearly establishes Musson's staunch allegiance to the Confederacy, in whose army he served.[45] After New Orleans fell to Union forces, he, like many other Confederates, considered moving to Mexico. Several letters in the collection attest to this, and a hand-copied, unsigned article from the early 1860s, "La France, Le Méxique, et les Etats Confédérés," gives a rationale. In view of the French campaign in Mexico, the article argues for a French-Mexican-Confederate collaboration for the purposes of regenerating the transatlantic commerce that had been disrupted by the blockade of southern ports. It says that since France must count on southern raw materials for its factories (as opposed to the English reliance on India), it is to the commercial advantage of France to support a separate Confederate nation.[46] Musson's contemplation of emigration fitted into a larger Franco-Southern myth of setting up a "new Virginia" in Mexico, composed of ex-Confederate colonists and former slave apprentices. Napoleon III and his foreign minister had even written a secret position paper in 1863, proposing the reorganization of the United States and Mexico into a "hyphenated confederation" similar to that in Germany. But with the end of the Civil War, and under U.S. pressure, the French government withdrew support from its Mexican puppet emperor Maximilian in 1867, and the dream of a Mexican "new Virginia" ended abruptly.[47]

In lieu of active military service after the fall of New Orleans in 1862, Musson embarked on a scheme of financially supporting the Confederacy through investing in Confederate bonds. Letters in the collection establish that he enlisted the participation of the De Gas bank in Paris and, most astoundingly, Edgar Degas, in this venture—evidently both out of loyalty to the Southern cause and in the ill-advised hope of financial gain. In the same letter to Michel Musson from Paris on December 22, 1863, in which Auguste De Gas mentioned Edgar's upcoming visit to his aunts in Bourg, he reported that Eugène Musson was occupied with preparing a brochure about the endangered cotton business and he discussed the fluctuations in mutual investments in Confederate bonds:

He wants, I think, to expose how vain the efforts are to search the Mississipi [*sic*] valley for the growing of cotton. There is something that strikes the spirits even more in this moment and makes them condemn this American war. India and Egypt are not and will never be consumers; it is thus necessary always to continue the drainage of cash! Impossible, it must stop at a given moment. Now Europe for better or worse, wants this war to end, and (Europe) seems to me to be disposed to cheapen its sympathies for the South for as little as these sympathies might prolong it [the war]. Bragg's retreat after his victory has discouraged the most fervent. Since that moment, we have seen the Confederate cotton funds fall from 68 to 30. The buyers[?] of 8% Richmond bonds have disappeared. There are some of those titles [bonds] here that would go at 40% and no buyers. I didn't answer your October letter sooner, always hoping for something more feasible, but, on the contrary, it has gone from bad to worse. I regret to see this feeler from M. Lüling. This dispatch of $20,000, which were presumably bought at 16% with exchange at 3/50, would make parity at 11¼ at 5 fr. per $, if I could [manage it]. If the rate is securely 20% and 5 fr. per $, there would still be a good margin, but I repeat, no one interested. It is obvious that if things change, I'll hurry to write you about it.[48]

Auguste wrote again on March 17, 1864, sending accounting figures from yields on Confederate bonds, including $1,000 for Musson's business partner John Watt and the same amount for Musson, placed on his credit at the De Gas bank. He continued:

If these Bonds cost you 16% exchange at 3.15 in other words 504 f.[rancs] the margin is even prettier. Mummy has others of which he wants to sell 21. I doubt that I'll succeed, but the rate today is fairly firm at 19. You have to make sure the stamp is well visible on the Bonds otherwise it's a cause for rejection and I would be obliged to send you back the titles [bonds] without being able to sell them at any price.[49]

Letters to and from Paris and New Orleans between René De Gas and his uncle in 1864 likewise mentioned the fluctuation of Confederate bonds and the receipt by Auguste De Gas of some $5,000 in five bonds from Michel.[50]

Two letters to Michel Musson from Auguste De Gas alluded further to the yield of bonds for Musson and Watt and authorized Musson to sell a house in New Orleans belonging to Edgar Degas so as to convert the proceeds into Confederate bonds. On July 1, 1864, he wrote: "For my part I approve of your idea of seizing the moment of a panic in greenbacks to find a price of $28,000 to $29,000 for the *maison de passage* and a proportional price for Edgar's house. Then immediately convert the greenbacks into Conf. Bonds."[51] He proceeded to speculate about the effects of news from New York on the market and discussed rates for greenbacks and Confederate bonds in relation to the victory of General Lee. In another letter from Paris [1864], he again urged Musson to sell the house belonging to Edgar, and to convert the proceeds into Confederate bonds. The property was evidently willed to the artist by his grandfather (Germain Musson and/or his mother Célestine Musson):

> The Bonds have gone down in the meantime to 14, due to precipitate sales made by an agent[?] in London. The price next rose to 16½ at ¾ and that's the rate today. You wrote to René to ask me if I authorized you to sell Edgar's house and convert the proceeds into Confederate Bonds. But I'm sure I authorize you and Edgar too. And do it, I beg you, as fast as possible to profit from this desire to convert credit paper into property and to obtain from these faint-hearted[?] some conditions that probably won't be found ever again; because it seems that these properties willed to us by your father are struck with a curse; one must get rid of them. I will regret it if you missed the score while waiting for my response. And aren't there some interested individuals who will pay us in Bonds for the *maison de passage*? If only I could recover the pitiful $28,000 it cost me. Work on it my dear friend and if you have a proposition answer me about it.[52]

Other letters to Michel Musson from Auguste and René De Gas in Paris, on August 5 and 26, 1864, respectively, discussed fluctuations of *le Cotton Loan* (probably a reference to the Southern Cotton Loan floated in early 1863 through the French firm Erlanger). Auguste said that in spite of the depression of bonds, *le Cotton Loan* had maintained stability and risen from 76 to 78½. He reported that the English were now buying from both the North and the South, not trusting the outcome of peace.[53] But René noted that the value of bonds had gone down, even though *le Cotton Loan* had reached 79½ in London.[54] A letter to Michel from Henri Musson in Paris, August 12, 1864, struck a further note of warning, expressing concern about Michel's plan to turn greenbacks into Confederate bonds. Henri was apparently worried about the involvement and safety of his own investments, as well as those of other family members.[55] Considerable family funds were presumably lost in these various ventures.

Many of the letters reveal family racial attitudes, which however typical of a particular class, were strongly held and vehemently acted upon, especially during the turmoil of the Civil War and Reconstruction. In a letter to Michel Musson from Bourg on January 20, 1864, Didi Musson expressed alarm over newspaper reports of blacks hanging thirty white officers and soldiers; and on October 23, 1863, she mentioned reading about the decision of the [Confederate] government to arm blacks—something "we would have never believed."[56] The previously mentioned article in Musson's possession entitled "La France, Le Méxique, et les Etats Confédérés" tried to rationalize slavery by accusing the North of exploiting freed blacks as cannon fodder and argued for a more gradual emancipation.[57] The family's racial attitudes seem to have been rooted in part in antebellum economics. In writing Musson from Paris to discuss bonds on December 22, 1864, Auguste De Gas also recounted a conversation in Paris with (John) Watt (Musson's business partner), who feared he would lose financially, no matter whether the North or South won, because of the abolition of black slavery: "But the cultivation of cotton, the liberty of the Negroes, will bring general destitution. Given the impossibility of planning to set his *maison de commerce* on its feet again, M. [Watt] says he will lose everything for good. Each of us must look after his and his family's well-being as best he can."[58] When René De Gas wrote Musson from Paris on August 10, 1866, to describe the founding of the De Gas Brothers import-export company, he also mentioned an incident of racial street fighting [known as the New Orleans "massacre"], but he seemed to assess it quite coldly, in financial terms, pondering what effect it might have on business: "I saw in the newspapers that the Negroes had been injured in a meeting of the radical party & that 31 of them had lost the sweet light of day, that the state of siege had been proclaimed then raised & I see today that it has been proclaimed again. Where are we going then. Gold should rise because the 5.20s are falling here."[59] Yet in another letter, written to Estelle Musson from Liverpool on August 10, 1872, René spoke of a New Orleanian who had moved to England with his mulatto son, who was attending school near Bristol and was well accepted because "prejudices about color don't exist in England."[60]

As racial and political agitation in New Orleans increased during Reconstruction,[61] however, the family's racial attitudes evidently became more hardened and eventually turned into action. In a letter to Michel Musson from Achille De Gas in Paris, September 1874, in which he mentioned the liquidation of the De Gas bank, he also discussed the *tyrannie des radicaux* (tyranny of the radicals) in New Orleans where President Grant had sent in troops to support Governor Kellogg. He compared the situation to the Paris Commune of 1871.[62] On September 14, 1874, Michel Musson was chosen to preside at a huge gathering of the White League (euphemistically referred to by Rewald as the "Citizens' League"), a Klan-like paramilitary organization that wanted to oust Radical Republican rule from Louisiana once and for all. Musson's son-in-law William A. Bell (who appears in Degas's *A Cotton Office* as the figure at the table showing a handful of cotton to a client) was treasurer of the organization at the time. Following the mass meeting occurred the so-called battle of Liberty Place, involving some eight thousand men, evidently the largest insurrection ever carried out against an American state. In 1874, Kellogg's government was only temporarily displaced; but Musson's pride in his participation in the event is confirmed by a family biography compiled in 1947. The family's racial attitudes are especially significant in light of Christopher Benfey's recent revelation of the fact that Degas's mother's first cousin Norbert Rillieux, an important inventor of a sugar-refining process, was a free man of color then living in exile in France.[63]

Meanwhile, the family's business ventures fared poorly in New Orleans during Reconstruction, in the wake of presumed losses from investments in Confederate bonds. Letters and documents in the Tulane collection attest to financial developments and problems on both sides of the Atlantic at this time. Michel Musson's finances were already considerably strained by the expenses of the Musson women in France during the Civil War.[64] And like most cotton factors, he and his partner John Watt were uncertain whether their business would survive the war and emancipation.[65] It was during the unsettled period of war and Reconstruction that René De Gas, upon making the acquaintance of his aunt and cousins in Bourg, decided to quit his apprenticeship with his father's bank and join Musson and Watt's cotton firm in New Orleans. A letter from René to Musson, written from Bourg on September 2, 1863, acknowledges his uncle's permission for René to join him in America.[66] As mentioned previously, René was supported by his brother Edgar in his decision;[67] and René's letters (as well as those of his cousins) to Michel Musson during 1863 to 1866 attested to his own enthusiasm in the venture, despite his father's opposition.[68]

But the letters René sent to Michel Musson in preparation for his departure for New Orleans added a note of disjointed panic as they described the complications and perils of banking on cotton futures while trying to begin a wine importing business.[69] He wrote Musson from Paris in July 1866, to report that his father still did not understand his decision to leave and that in dining with Edgar, René had somehow thought of jumping out the window. Going on to mention that he and Edgar had visited their sister Marguerite after dinner, René did not elaborate on his seemingly suicidal thoughts.[70] But the apparent reason for them surfaced in another letter to his uncle on July 25, 1866, from the Hotel Tavistock in London, in which he recounted at length a disastrous speculation in cotton futures—one that endangered the fortune of his brothers and sisters, presumably including Edgar, who had provided him with capital. (The debt he incurred, amounting to some $8,000—equivalent to more than $80,000 in today's currency—would weaken his father's bank and continue to plague the family during the liquidation of the bank in the 1870s.)[71] Despite this damaging loss, René's next letter to his uncle in New Orleans, written from Paris on August 10, 1866, continued to elaborate plans for an export-import company to be founded in league with his uncle Henri Musson in France and his brother Achille, who was coming to join him in New Orleans.[72]

After he had moved to New Orleans and married Estelle Musson, René De Gas frequently wrote to her from various business trips to Europe. Letters from August 1872 indicate that he followed busy itineraries taking him to England, Belgium, France, Germany, and Switzerland, where he did business with one Reinhart, evidently his agent there (and an ancestor of the famous collectors of Winterthur).[73] But a letter from Henri to Michel Musson, written on August 22, 1872, expressed worries about the wine business, especially because De Gas Brothers had drawn off too much money to New Orleans. He hoped that, as a cotton factor and commission merchant, Michel would be able to give them the commissions for French products purchased for his client planters, so as to make the best of their common interests. But Henri was not hopeful that fortune would smile.[74]

By this time, Michel Musson had entered a partnership with John E. Livaudais and James S. Prestidge, in the cotton factoring firm that Edgar Degas would in 1873 depict in *A Cotton Office in New Orleans* (cat. 31). (Livaudais stands at the ledger table on the right and Prestidge talks to a customer just behind René De Gas, who reads *The Daily Picayune*.) This was the business alluded to by Achille De Gas in his letter of February 16, 1869, to Michel Musson, cited above, in which Achille seemed to draw a hopeful analogy between the progress of the family businesses and the launching of Edgar's artistic career.[75] Yet there is evidence that all was not well in the cotton business in New Orleans in general and in Musson's business in particular. A letter written to Michel

Musson from René De Gas in New Orleans on March 13, 1873, mentions the closing of Frank Minor's cotton business because of a lack of payment on a large quantity of cotton[76]—this coming just after the dissolution of Musson, Prestidge, & Co. in February 1873. This latter event, which has considerable significance in relation to Degas's representation of his uncle's office at exactly the time of the dissolution, is revealed in an unpublished history of the Musson family compiled and sent by Michel Musson to Henri Musson on July 27, 1881, listing thirty-three domestic and commercial addresses associated with the family in New Orleans between 1803 and 1881.[77] Musson's financial situation continued to deteriorate after 1873, as he became involved in other business ventures, including insurance and sulphur mining, but without much success.[78]

The situation was compounded by the liquidation (beginning in 1874) and failure (in 1876) of the De Gas family bank, following the death of Auguste De Gas in Naples in February 1874. Several letters in the Tulane University collection describe the liquidation and the straitened circumstances in which Edgar Degas and his relations were forced to live as a result. The first mention of the liquidation came in the letter of September 1874 mentioned earlier, in which Achille De Gas wrote Michel Musson about the "tyranny of the radicals" in New Orleans. He also requested papers relating to the succession of Germain Musson in connection with the liquidation of the family bank.[79] Achille mentioned his father's will and asked for related information in a slightly later letter of December 3, 1874, the same letter in which he described the worsening of Edgar's eyesight, as mentioned earlier.[80] More elaborate descriptions of the De Gas liquidation began to reach Michel Musson in late 1875, in letters from his brother Henri in Paris. On December 10, 1875, Henri wrote:

> You know from René of the closing of his brother's firm [his late father's bank]. Named liquidator in a friendly capacity, I hope, if I am allowed, to arrange to pay 25% on account and 25% in five years. You must urge René to make honorable arrangements with his family, so as to help them by quarterly remittances to fulfill the promises that will be made. He owes an enormous debt and aside from the amount necessary for the upkeep of the family, he must pay what he owes to Leysy [John Leisy, his business associate in New Orleans]. I am counting on you to have a very serious conversation with him.[81]

Later, on January 17, 1877, Henri described the situation in greater detail, including the large outstanding debt from René's speculation in cotton futures, which had been covered by the bank in 1866, but which René still neglected to repay—something that was causing Edgar and other family members to take the strictest economic measures to save the family honor:

My friend, you know the heavy, as well as quite arduous task of liquidating A. Degas & Cie. I have succeeded with what I found on hand in the till, with the help of Edgar and Fèvre, to give 30% on the 50% promised to the creditors to make up for its failure. I had 5% to pay at the end of December and I will have as much at the end of next June. I was counting on René who has sent me nothing. How can I do it? Am I going to let an edifice that was held up with so much effort tumble down? The day when that happens, and it is soon, they will find out about everything versus René and they will destroy his financial standing, which was otherwise well on its way. An example. Besides the liquidation of the A. Degas Firm of Paris, The Bank of Antwerp presses Achille and the guarantors [Edgar] Degas and Fèvre for 40,000 francs. This week the business comes to the docket. The outcome is not doubtful. Armed, the Bank is selling the furniture of Fèvre and Edgar; unsatisfied by 3 or 4 thousand francs, it is attacking René. I submitted to him the bill for our necessities, while his brother Edgar and one brother-in-law Fèvre are hard at it, and for what doesn't concern them. He thinks he's safe, he's wrong. If he lets things get worse, he will be a victim in his turn. He knows what he had due at the end of December, the business of the Bank of Antwerp, what we have due at the end of next June, the monetary sacrifices made by Edgar and Fèvre. He has contented himself with writing Achille at the end of three months of silence that he sent nothing at the end of December and that if cotton stays in the doldrums, he won't be able to do anything in June. I can't allow this careless behavior. In Paris, I see Edgar depriving himself of everything, living on as little as possible. The seven Fèvre children are dressed in rags. They only eat what is necessary. It is a matter of honor. René much more than they should cut back. His conscience demands it. I speak to you gravely of a very grave subject and I beg you likewise to talk with him.

My friend, you personally now owe 7,500 francs to Achille. That is to say to his liquidation. As liquidator I ask you for an explanation. If you can answer yes, can you pay in one lump sum or do you want fixed intervals? Answer me immediately. In the midst of this mess, I want to make one last effort. Obviously I'm not the one who'll prosecute you.

If the creditors put me with my back against the wall, I will resign. But the judicial liquidation will take place and roughly, by legal means. . . . I read in the newspapers about the terrible crisis which is hanging over you. How will you get out of it? From here it seems quite dark.[82]

On May 16, 1877, Henri sent Michel official notification of the liquidation of Degas & Cie, requested Michel to discuss an insurance document with René, who had not answered his letter, and asked when Michel would pay another note. He described Edgar's situation further: "Tracked down by the Bank of Antwerp, Fèvre and Edgar pay monthly installments with great difficulty."[83] During 1878 to 1880, Henri continued to discuss René's debt and disregard for his family and asked Michel to confront René with the matter.[84]

But by this time, René De Gas had deserted Estelle Musson and their children for a New Orleanian neighbor, an action that caused a tremendous rupture in family relations across the Atlantic. Many of the letters and documents in the Tulane collection recount the course of events and Edgar Degas's stance upon them. Estelle Musson had in 1862 married Joseph Davis Balfour, a nephew of Jefferson Davis, but had soon become a war widow after bearing him one child.[85] When the Musson women visited France during the Civil War (and were depicted, as mentioned previously, by Edgar Degas), René De Gas wrote his uncle in New Orleans several letters that make it clear he was quite smitten by Estelle. On June 24, 1863, he wrote from Paris:

FIG. 54. Watch belonging to Estelle Musson. Double Case Hunter Pocket Watch and Key, 18 karat gold, ca. 1855–70. Collection of Hugh Miller.

I can't tell you with what happiness we have made Estelle's acquaintance. She inspires so much sympathy, she has so much sweetness in her sadness that she made us all become attached to her in an instant. . . . One sees that the depth of her character is gaiety; because in the midst of her suffering she has hints of a wit that loves to laugh; & we notice each day a favorable progress.[86]

Various other letters from Bourg recount how René took long walks with Estelle, who surprised him with her stamina.[87] His acquaintance with her seemed to solidify his decision to move to New Orleans. After they were married in 1869, René faithfully and affectionately wrote Estelle and their children from his business trips in Europe during the 1870s.[88] Estelle, who had contracted ophthalmia in 1866, meanwhile lost the vision in her left eye in 1868 and that of her right in 1875[89]—a condition with which Edgar Degas had considerable sympathy, as indicated by his sensitive portraits of his cousin.

Family letters from the mid-1870s, including one by René, mention Mme

Léonce Olivier, née America Durrive,[90] the neighbor for whom René was to desert Estelle in 1878. Later letters bitterly recount how René left on April 23, 1878, and married Mme Olivier on May 3 in Cleveland. The couple subsequently traveled to Europe and returned to New York.[91] In several letters written in the wake of these events, Henri Musson and Achille De Gas attempted to justify Edgar Degas's silence on the matter to the deeply offended New Orleans relations. On May or June 5, 1878, Henri Musson wrote his brother Michel from Paris, claiming that Achille was keeping the desertion secret from Edgar and the rest of the family.[92] But on July 29, 1878, Henri assured Michel:

> I have seen Edgar since my return. He is everything you could want him to be, absolutely attached to your wishes. M. René has not tried to see him. He would have shown him the door. Marguerite shares Edgar's sentiments. . . . their hearts are entirely yours. Blot out of your mind the impressions that have mistakenly assumed a place there.[93]

On August 15, 1878, Achille De Gas wrote Didi Musson from New York, likewise assuring her: "My uncle Henri, Edgar, Marguerite charged me on my departure from Paris to kiss you all on their behalf & in particular that dear Estelle" (fig. 55).[94]

Estelle successfully sued for divorce and child support, changed her name and that of her children to Musson, and meanwhile was grieved by the deaths of her daughter Jeanne De Gas (who was Edgar Degas's godchild) of yellow fever in October 1878 and of her son Pierre De Gas and her daughter Joe Balfour of scarlet fever in April 1881.[95] Henri Musson wrote his brother Michel from Paris on November 9, 1878, saying that he had communicated to Edgar and his sister Marguerite the news of Jeanne's death and details of Estelle's child support.[96] As Michel Musson's anger at René De Gas continued unabated, he railed in one letter of August 20, 1879, that he would shoot his former son-in-law on sight should he ever return to New Orleans.[97] Meanwhile he deeply resented the continuing silence of Edgar and Marguerite on their brother's behavior. On December 4, 1879, he wrote his brother Henri:

> You have of course discovered the real reason for the silence of Edgar & Marguerite regarding Estelle—their repugnance to call their brother by the name he deserves. It will have to suffice for us to know that

FIG. 55. Washburn, *Estelle (standing) and Désirée (seated) Musson*, ca. 1879, cabinet portrait, New Orleans. Collection of Edmund Martin.

their heart is open to the unfortunate one and her children and closed to the guilty one. But we renew our request to Edgar for the portrait of our dear Mathilde of whom we have only sketches in black pencil and a photograph taken in 1862.[98]

Edgar Degas's silence and Michel Musson's request to receive the artist's portrait of the late Mathilde Bell (Musson's daughter, who had died in September 1878) continued to be discussed in letters between Michel and his brother Henri. Henri wrote Michel on September 29, 1879, to say that René De Gas had a new baby in New York and was himself in France but that Edgar refused to see him:

> I know that neither Edgar nor his sister wishes to see him . . . Edgar & Marguerite have their hearts opened to Estelle and closed to René, this I affirm to you, they have told me ten times to write it to you. Now why haven't they written. Is it an invincible repugnance which prevents them from calling their brother a scoundrel? I transmitted to Edgar your desire to have the portrait of Mathilde. He said it was sent by Achille who ought to be in New Orleans the first of September. I haven't seen these people since July 19. On my return I'll go seek out Edgar.[99]

On January 12, 1880, Henri wrote, "I reminded Edgar of his promise to send you his study of Mathilde. He told me that he was going to do it. He sends you his love."[100] He wrote again in 1880: "Edgar keeps answering yes and doesn't send the portrait. I won't let him off the hook. It's not bad will, but the impossibility of finding time to harmonize [the color]."[101] And again on June 27, 1881:

> Edgar asked me to send his best to you. The decent boy [he was forty-seven at the time], because he has a very delicate and intelligent nature, is reluctant to write you. He is so ashamed of the machinations of his brothers [this reference probably including the involvement of Achille in a shooting incident at the Paris Bourse in 1875] that he is afraid you will confuse him with them—it's obviously a mistaken view in his mind, which I told him in every way. In any event, doubt not that he loves, respects, pities you and is completely on our side. He has never seen M. René again and doesn't plan to do so. He told me everything a good and noble heart can manage to feel, asking me to transmit it to you.[102]

On July 31, 1881, Michel sent Henri a history of the Musson family in New Orleans, along with photographs of the family (Didi, Estelle, and her surviving children, Gaston and Odile), and requested him to share them with Edgar:

> Show these portraits to Edgar and give him this letter as well as the outline and historical account of the family. What you tell me *of him* and *from him* is a quite sensitive proof to us of his attachment and sympathy for us. His elite nature should make him take vengeance for our side; if it grieves him to write us, and we hope that is the case, *have him sign and date* (in place of a letter) a sketch of *you*. . . .

Michel went on to mention portraits by other hands and photographs he possessed in New Orleans of Eugène Musson and Maurice de Rochefort (their nephew); but he had none of Henri or Célestine (Edgar's late mother, Michel's sister) and asked of Edgar: "Won't Edgar give me the pleasure of filling my collection? That would be so grateful of him and I would be so proud to have something else from him besides the oil or pencil sketch of our late lamented Mathilde."[103] It is unknown whether the sketch of Henri was accomplished or whether the portrait of Mathilde was sent.

Edgar Degas and his uncle Michel Musson finally did communicate again, but with unfortunate, estranging results. On July 16, 1883, Edgar evidently wrote his uncle to inform him of the death of his brother Henri Musson in Normandy on July 12.[104] On August 6, 1883, Michel responded at length. Besides reclaiming his nephew as a *créole* and calling the rest of the De Gas clan Italian cads,[105] Musson requested news about the care of his remaining brother in France, Eugène Musson, likewise Edgar's maternal uncle. A Chevalier of the Legion of Honor, Eugène had since 1876 been committed to the insane asylum at Charenton. This measure had been deemed necessary after a sequence of events in which he had squandered much of his fortune in high living and had affronted Edgar and others with private obscenities and offensive public behavior.[106] In a long letter about the liquidation of the De Gas bank, Henri Musson had recounted on January 17, 1877, how he had had Eugène committed in February 1876, after an especially troublesome incident in which Eugène had laid siege to the *Hôtel des affaires étrangers* (the foreign affairs office) in Paris, the police had been brought in, and Edgar's friend Dr. Camus had been called into consultation.[107] Doctors deemed Eugène incurable and placed him in isolation.

But Edgar Degas's only response to Michel Musson's request for help with Eugène was apparently silence. On November 6, 1883, having heard nothing from his nephew, Michel wrote Edgar a second, this time bristling, letter:

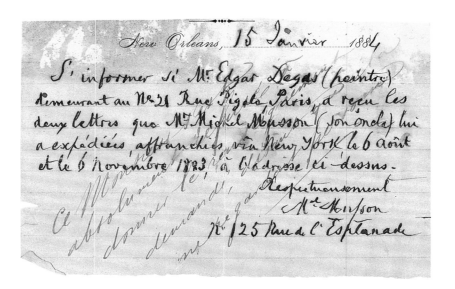

FIG. 56. Telegram to Edgar Degas from Michel Musson with response in red ink, January 25, 1884, De Gas–Musson Papers, ms. 226. Special Collections, Tulane University.

My dear Edgar

Not a word from you nor from Anna [Henri Musson's stepdaughter], since your letter of July 16, announcing to me the death of my brother Henri. There is a big wrong between us; so that it not be blamed on me, I am sending you, enclosed, the copy of my response of August 6 (21 rue Pigalle Paris). With the same sentiments for you and the same wishes concerning the poor afflicted one, your uncle & friend. M[ichel] Musson.

P.S. By court decree and notarized act, I have just *adopted* my grandchildren Odile and Gaston (Degas) who henceforth will bear my name—I ask you to take note of it.[108]

Still receiving no reply, the beleaguered but persistent Musson sent a telegram on January 15, 1884, to Degas's studio in Paris: "Wishes to know whether M. Edgar Degas (painter) residing at no. 21 Rue Pigalle, Paris, has received the two letters that M. Musson (his uncle) sent him, stamped via New York, August 6 and November 6, 1883, to the above address. Respectfully, M[ichel] Musson, no. 125 Rue de l'Esplanade."[109] The telegram was returned with a short and withering response in red ink: "This gentleman absolutely refused to give the requested information, saying that it concerned no one" (fig. 56).[110] Given Musson's agitated mental state in the wake of repeated family tragedies, the histrionic and accusatory tone of his letters seems to have put Degas in an impossible position. The New Orleans family received no further communication from the artist, and for the two remaining years of his life, Michel Musson was evidently reduced to overseeing the care of his invalid brother by mail.[111]

In 1900, Edgar Degas was furious that the curator of the museum in Pau, France, which had in 1878 bought his painting *A Cotton Office in New Orleans,* sent it without his permission for exhibition at the World's Fair in Paris.[112] By this time the picture evidently contained too many reminders of family ruptures across the Atlantic. Later in life, the increasingly reclusive and cantankerous artist reportedly lambasted the modern intrusion of the telephone. To the degree that the remarkable letters in the De Gas–Musson collection would not have been written had telecommunications been invented earlier, one may see his point in a different light.

NOTES

Reprinted, in a different form, with permission from *The Art Bulletin*. I would like to thank Elaine Koss, deputy director of the College Art Association of America, for generous permission to publish here versions of articles that first appeared (without English translations) as Brown, 1990, and "Two New Degas Letters in New Orleans," *The Art Bulletin* LXXIII, no. 2 (June 1991), 313–14.

1. Brown, 1991. The De Gas–Musson papers are ms. 226 in Special Collections of the Tulane University Library. Unless otherwise indicated, family letters are in French. Selected excerpts were published by Lemoisne, 1946–49, 41, 63, 70–73, 81. These derived primarily from excerpts sent in correspondence in 1933 to 1937, between Odile Musson (daughter of René De Gas and Estelle Musson) and Monsieur and Madame Paul-André Lemoisne in France. For this correspondence, see Box V, folders 3–7. More excerpts were published by Rewald in New Orleans, 1965, 40–41; Byrnes in New Orleans, 1965, 46–52; Paris, Ottawa, New York, 1988, 54–57, 59–60, 118, 181, 214, 215. I cited and quoted Brown, 1994, chaps. 1 and 3. Before the archive was catalogued, a typed, partial inventory of the papers from the period 1843 to 1874 was prepared by James B. Byrnes. This guide does not correspond to the current cataloguing system of the collection. Its summaries, occasional transcriptions and translations, while incomplete, are quite helpful. It should be noted that the spelling of "Degas" varies in the archive, with the artist's father and brothers usually, though not consistently, referred to as "De Gas" and the artist himself as "Degas." I have followed this example in my own spellings. The translations I provide in the text are, unless otherwise specified, my own. In the notes I have literally transcribed the occasionally awkward or faulty French, which is often characterized by idiosyncratic or idiomatic locutions, as well as touches of *franglais*.

2. Box II, folder 57a; see also E. N. Evans, *Judah P. Benjamin: The Jewish Confederate* (New York, 1988); Box III, folders 6, 7f, 13d, 15a for Ellen Shields; Estelle Musson's letters are found primarily in Boxes I and II, before her vision completely deteriorated.

3. For a helpful family tree, see Rewald in New Orleans, 28–29, as well as this catalogue. For

the presence of free people of color in the family tree, see Benfey, 1997, chap. 7; Benfey, 1996, 25–30. See Rewald and Byrnes in New Orleans; and Paris, Ottawa, New York, nos. 111–16, for Degas's various depictions of his New Orleans relatives. See also Boggs, 1956, Brown (below, n. 77), and Benfey, 1997.

4. "Mon cher oncle, votre famille est arrivée ici jeudi passé 18 Juin et elle est maintenant tout à fait la nôtre. On ne peut être ni meilleure, ni plus simple. . . . Acceptez toutes mes amitiés biens vives. Votre photographie est bien vous, à ce qu'il parait moins cet air de [illegible] humeur dont René a tant parlé, air, du reste, que je ne pensais guère retrouver. Notre tante Odile marche fort bien, je vous avouerai que je la croyais moins alerte la jugeant sur le portrait que nous avions d'elle. Didy est tout à fait son second. Quant à Estelle, pauvre petite femme, on ne peut la regarder sans penser que cette tête a voltigé devant les yeux d'un mourant. Vous direz bien des choses aimables à la bonne et jolie Mathilde dont le garçon sur [illegible] portier de négresses est connu et admiré par tout le monde. Notre Thérèse n'est plus ici depuis cinq semaines. Que j'aurais voulu la voir caressée comme je suis par notre tante et nos cousines.

A 7 heures du soir avant hier un fort coup de sonnette nous annonçait l'arrivée de M. Philippe Beauregard . . . les polissonneries étaient déjà telles qu'on pouvait s'y attendre. Il est venu dans la soirée voir notre tante. Avec les récits des uns et des autres nous sommes maintenant à peu près au courant de ce qui se passe là-bas. L'Oncle Eugène . . . [illegible] de crier sourdement qu'il y a trop beau jeu avec Mexique et vous [jure?] que l'Empereur ne donne un tour de vis politique ou [illegible] au reste de vos ennemis."

Box II, folder 3, partially quoted by Lemoisne, 1946–49, 73, from whom my transcription differs slightly. Philippe Beauregard was the grandson of Mme Elina de Vezin Ducros, a New Orleanian who had visited the De Gas family in Paris during the late 1850s. Mme Ducros and her daughter, Mme Benjamin Laurent Millaudon (whose previous marriage had been to the late Gabriel Toutant Beauregard) belonged to Creole families that were friendly with the Mussons. See Byrnes in New Orleans, 61, and Lemoisne, II, 1946–49, nos. 41–44.

5. "Vous savez, mon cher oncle, que c'est à deux pas de votre chère femme que je vous écris. Je suis ici depuis hier et je pars après demain. La vie de [illegible . . .] absolument pour votre pauvre famille. Cela serait encore peu de chose sans un peu d'indisposition pour ma tante. Pour le froid, elles sont bien logées et bien chauffées. Cette indisposition ne doit pas vous effrayer. Elle souffre de la [sa?] main droite [et elle?] y met de l'opium.

Elle lit la vie de Marie Antoinette près de la haute cheminée sur laquelle repose cet éléphant que vous savez. Didi écrit sur la table où je suis. Estelle . . . sa fille a sa bonne [illegible] . . . tableau.

Adieu[,] je vous embrasse comme votre neveu et même un peu comme votre fils. Mille choses à Mathilde. Portez vous bien. E. De Gas." Box I, folder 47.

6. "Edgar est tellement absorbé par sa peinture qu'il n'écrit à personne malgré nos représentations. Ça ne l'empêche pas de penser souvent à vous et de désirer vivement vous voir. Quand ses voeux, qui son les nôtres, se réaliseront-ils? . . . Le violon va toujours, mais bien lentement. C'est atrocient difficile. Edgar l'apprend aussi." Box I, folder 27b, excerpted in Paris, Ottawa, New York, 54.

7. "Notre Raphaël travaille toujours mais n'a encore rien produit d'achevé, cependant les années passent." Box I, folder 27d. (Edgar was twenty-seven at the time.) Excerpted in Lemoisne, 1946–49, 41.

8. "Que dire d'Edgar, nous attendons impatiemment le jour où s'ouvrira l'exposition des peintures. Pour ma part, j'ai tout lieu de croire qu'il ne sera pas à temps, il n'aura point se dressé ce qu'il faut." Box I, folder 33a, excerpted in Paris, Ottawa, New York, 55.

9. "Edgar revient d'un voyage de 3 semaines en Normandie, il pioche ferme sa peinture." Box I, folder 27e, excerpted in Paris, Ottawa, New York, 54.

10. "Quant à Edgar, vous ne le connaissez pas encore. Il travaille avec furie, et ne pense qu'à une chose, à sa peinture. Il ne se donne pas le temps de s'amuser tant il travaille." Box I, folder 33b, excerpted in Lemoisne, 1946–49, 41.

11. Lemoisne, 1946–49, 73, quotes a letter from Edgar Degas to Michel Musson of June 18,

1863, giving news of the arrival of the Mussons in France. This letter is not in the De Gas–Musson collection. See also Byrnes in New Orleans, 46–8. Numerous letters from the Musson women in France, 1863–65, are found in Box I, folder 34 through Box II, folder 19.

12. Box I, folder 33c.

13. "Edgard [sic] qu'on nous avait dit si brusque, est rempli d'attention et d'amabilité." Box I, folder 34d, cited in Lemoisne, 1946–49, 73.

14. Box I, folder 35.

15. "Mère me charge de dire à Papa qu'il ait à faire bien attention de la manière qu'il écrit à René, au sujet de son départ pour l'Amérique; René est un charmant garçon, plein d'intelligence, d'ambition, et de coeur. Il n'a qu'une idée, c'est de quitter la maison de Banque de son Père pour aller travailler et vivre avec nous; il dit s'il reste à Paris, ou s'il va à Naples, il atteindra *50 ans*, gagnant *30 francs* par mois; ceci le révolte. Il veut au contraire arriver à 30 ans, être son maître en tout[e] chose; et sur la voie de faire fortune . . . Mais ardent d'atteindre son but, il aura à beaucoup parler[,] raisonner avant d'obtenir le consentement de son père . . . Edgar est le seul qui encourage René, car il sait tout ce qu'il souffre de sa position peut-être sans avenir." Box I, folder 42; the last point (about Edgar) cited in Paris, Ottawa, New York, 55.

16. "Dans quelques jours Edgar sera auprès de sa Tante et de ses cousines et il n'y a qu'à le laisser faire, il ne manquera de les egayer." Box I, folder 46.

17. "Edgar est parti d'ici avant-hier pour aller passer avec elles les fêtes du jour de l'an, et il est si gai qu'il les amusera et les distraiera un peu. Il a emporté force crayons et papier pour dessiner les mains de Didy dans toutes les formes, car il est rare de trouver un aussi joli modèle." Box I, folder 49, quoted by Lemoisne, 1946–49, 73.

18. Box I, folder 48.

19. Box I, folder 53.

20. "Edgar vient d'aller passer cinq jours à Bourg." Box I, folder 54.

21. "Edgar nous a donné sa semaine." Box I, folder 55.

22. "Edgar travaille toujours énormément sans en avoir l'air. Ce qui fermente dans cette tête est effrayant. Pour ma part je crois et suis même

convaincu qu'il a non seulement du talent mais même du génie, seulement exprimera-t-il ce qu'il sent? That's the question." Box I, folder 60, excerpted in Lemoisne, 1946–49, 41; Byrnes in New Orleans, 48; and Paris, Ottawa, New York, 55.

23. "Edgar qui connait la famille m'a bien dit que si je voulais arriver à quelque chose il fallait me détacher complètement sous le rapport de l'intérêt & m'en dépendre que sous le rapport de l'affection. Il est affligé de me voir partir car nous nous aimons beaucoup mais se rend bien compte que je trouverai mon existence plutôt là-bas qu'ici." Box II, folder 8. Auguste himself wrote Michel on September 23, 1864 [1863?] and sent "Tendres amitiés d'Edgar et René." See Box II, folder 10.

24. "Nous avons espoir de voir Edgar au premier de l'année. C'est toujours avec bonheur que nous voyons ces chers amis." Box II, folder 12f. See also her letter of December 22, 1864, Box II, folder 14a, in which she hopes Edgar's visit will do their ailing mother some good.

25. ". . . Nous attendions Edgar qui n'arrivait pas. Nous avions perdu tout espoir de le voir lorsqu'à près de neuf heures ce matin il est arrivé chargé jusqu'au cou. Mère et moi étions encore à la Messe, il descendit et aussitôt la messe finie il vint frapper mère sur l'épaule. Je me trouvais tout à fait au premier rang de chaises, je ne vis rien de tout cela et fut bien étonnée en rentrant de trouver maître Edgar dans la chambre de mère et tout occupé à défaire une petite malle pleine de bonbons, etc., joujoux. . . . Edgar a fait plusieurs esquisses de la petite Joe, mais il n'en est pas content, c'est une impossibilité de la faire rester en place plus de cinq minutes." Box II, folder 16, excerpted by Lemoisne, 1946–49, 74, incorrectly dated 1864; see also Byrnes in New Orleans, 52.

26. For the drawing see Boggs, 1956.

27. "René a du vous dire que nos affaires étaient en bon chemin et que nous avons tous bien d'espérer avoir enfin trouvé la route de la fortune. . . . Vous avez su [lu?] probablement que j'avais été passer environ 15 jours en Belgique pour nos affaires . . . Edgar est venu avec moi à Bruxelles. Il a fait connaissance avec M. Van Praet, ministre du roi, qui avait acheté un de ses tableaux, et il s'est vu dans la Galerie, une des plus célèbres de l'Europe, cela lui a fait un certain plaisir, comme bien vous pensez,

et lui a donné enfin quelque confiance en lui et son talent qui est réel. Il en a vendu deux autres pendant son séjour à Bruxelles et un marchand de tableaux très connu, Stevens, lui a proposé un contrat à raison de douze mille francs par an. Décidément le voilà lancé, et je pense que vous apprendrez cela avec plaisir, il l'a bien mérité depuis le temps qu'il travaille comme un nègre et avec si peu de profit jusqu'alors. Mais cette carrière de peintre est bien la plus difficile qui existe, et que de temps il faut pour établir la réputation; une fois là, par exemple, cela va tout seul. Vous peu que nous aussi, nous nous mettions à assurer des flots d'or[,] on pourra dire[,] que la chance des De Gas avance de l'état de mythe à celui de réalité après avoir subi comme certaines étoiles une éclipse totale un peu trop prolongée. J'espère, mon cher oncle que vos affaires de cette année ont continué à bien marcher. Je vois que le coton se maintient toujours dans les hauts prix, cela ne doit pas vous faire trop de peine." Box II, folder 29, partially excerpted in Lemoisne, 1946–49, 63. Lemoisne noted (233, n. 71) that Edgar Degas evidently did not accept the contract with Stevens.

28. "A la gare j'ai trouvé Edgar qui a mûri, quelques poils blancs tachent sa barbe; il est aussi plus gras et plus posé. J'ai dîné chez lui avec mon Père et nous avons été chez Marguerite après le dîner. . . . Marguerite est grasse & a bonne mine. Son mari est Joseph Prudhomme incarné, suffisant & bête comme tous les gens soi-disant arrivés. Edgar fait réellement des choses charmantes. Il a un portrait de Mme Camus de profil avec une robe de velours grenat, assise dans un fauteuil brun et se détachant sur un fond rose qui, pour moi, est purement un chef d'oeuvre. Son dessin est quelque chose de ravissant. Malheureusement il a les yeux très faibles, il est forcé de prendre les plus grands ménagements. Je déjeune chez lui tous les jours. Il a une bonne cuisinière et un charmant appartement de garçon. . . . Hier j'ai dîné chez Edgar avec Pagans qui chante avec accompagnement de guitare. Achille te donnera des détails sur lui." Box II, folder 45c, partially excerpted in Lemoisne, 1946–49, 70. See Degas's *Portrait of Mme Camus in Red*, 1870 (National Gallery of Art, Washington), and cf. his paintings of *Lorenzo Pagans and Auguste Degas*, ca. 1871–72 (Musée d'Orsay, Paris, and later versions, L 257 and 346). See

also Box II, folder 45d in reference to a musical evening at the De Gas residence.

29. "Edgar me trouve d'un américain, & je me trouve aussi tout à fait étranger. . . . Edgar vient me chercher pour dîner . . . turkey buzzard (Edgar repète ce mot toutes les deux minutes)." Box II, folder 45d, partially excerpted (and wrongly dated) in Lemoisne, 1946–49, 70.

30. "Edgar avec qui je déjeune tous les jours me dit de vous embrasser tous, ses yeux sont faibles et il lui faut les plus grands ménagements. Il est toujours le même, mais a la rage de vouloir prononcer des mots anglais, il a répété *turkey buzzard* pendant une semaine." Box II, folder 46a, excerpted in Lemoisne, 1946–49, 71, and Paris, Ottawa, New York, 60.

31. "Edgar s'est mis dans la tête de venir avec moi et de rester avec nous environ deux mois. Je ne demande pas mieux. Il médite [*sic:* me dit?] toutes sortes de charges sur les natifs et ne tarit pas de questions sur vous tous. Je crois décidément que je le ramènerai. Ses yeux vont mieux, mais il faut qu'il les ménage et tu sais comme il est. C'est justement maintenant, qu'il fait de petits tableaux, c'est-à-dire ce qui lui fatigue le plus la vue. Il fait une répétition de danse qui est charmante. Aussitôt le tableau fini, j'en ferai faire une grande photographie. Je déjeune tous les jours avec lui. Il a une cuisinière nommée Clothilde qui fait admirablement. Son rêve est de venir en Amérique, mais c'est une fille trop intelligente pour ne pas nous lâcher après fort peu de temps, faire une riche marriage et s'installer gargotière pour son compte. C'est ce qui la retient, sans ça je penserais à [te] l'expédier. . . . Après dîner je vais avec Edgar aux Champs-Elysées, de là au Café-chantant entendre des chansons d'idiots, telles que la chanson du compagnon maçon et autres bêtises absurdes. . . . Nous allons quelquefois[,] quand Edgar est en train[,] dîner à la campagne et revoir les endroits mémorables du siège. . . . Allons adieu . . . embrasse un milliard de fois chacun de nos enfants, ça fera un emprunt de trois milliards que je te rendrai capital & intérêts. Préparez-vous à recevoir dignement le Grrrrand Artiste, il demande à ce qu'on ne vienne pas avec Brun[?] Band, compagnie de milice, pompiers, clergé, etc." Box II, folder 46b, partially excerpted in Lemoisne, 1946–49, 71. Cf. Degas's *Dance Class*, 1871 (The Metro-

politan Museum, New York) and his later café-concert scenes.

32. "[P]our prendre Edgar qui veut venir avec moi pour vous embrasser tous." Box II, folder 46d.

33. "Je les ai naturellement montrées à Paris. Edgar a trouvé les cheveux blonds de mon homme si jolis." Box II, folder 47b.

34. "J'en ai bien une sous la main, c'est celle d'Edgar[,] mais elle est beaucoup trop Spirituelle. Il est vrai qu'elle sait coudre, blanchir admirablement, ayant été blanchisseuse & fait la cuisine à s'en lécher les doigts. Elle me tracasse pour que je l'emmene, mais elle est trop spirituelle, & je crains nous lâcherait bien vite pour gagner davantage ailleurs. . . . Edgar me charge de vous embrasser tous." Box II, folder 47d. Gail Feigenbaum suggests to me that Degas's well-known mention in a letter written to Tissot on November 19, 1872, of a Parisian "blanchisseuse de fin, bras nus" as being preferable to all the sights of New Orleans should be seen in light of Clothilde's former occupation. That letter is in the Bibliothèque Nationale de France, Paris, Manuscripts NAF 13005, no. 5. See Paris, 1989, 359.

35. "Edgar est indécis, je ne crois pas qu'il vienne & ça vaudra peut-être mieux pour lui." Box II, folder 49c.

36. "Je t'ai dit je crois qu'il ne faillait pas compter sur Edgar. Il a envie de venir, mais je n'ai pas l'y pousser [*sic*], si le voyage lui faisait mal aux yeux je ne voudrais pas avoir à me le reprocher." Box II, folder 49d.

37. "Nos voyageurs partis par le 'Scotia' devançant la présente vous auront donné les détails inédits des nouvelles toutes fraîches de la famille et de notre pauvre France. Mais quoique ayant une semaine d'avance arriveront-ils avant elle? Ce serait un pari à faire. Je vois d'ici l'un tirant comme un grand diable pour aller vers sa petite femme et ses enfants, à ses affaires, l'autre, plein de bonne volonté sans doute et de bon désir d'arriver, mais arrêté à chaque pas par les mille et une choses qu'il a vues dans cette grande Amérique si différente de cette vieille Europe (pas toute jeune et pas toute vieille qu'on veut bien le dire toutefois). En aura-t-il à vous raconter quand il vous arrivera! Il fera bon d'être là. Mais il fera encore meilleur quand il nous reviendra après une longue flâne au Sud, à l'Ouest, au Nord. Ce qu'il aura à

raconter, du coq-à-l'âne, de croquis, de notes et d'anecdotes fera mourir de rire son père, cet Edgar!" Box II, folder 50, excerpted by Lemoisne, 1946–49, 71–2.

38. "Edgar nous est revenu enchanté de son voyage, enchanté d'avoir fait si de choses nouvelles pour lui, mais enchanté surtout d'avoir fait connaissance avec tous ses bons parents d'Amérique. C'est, comme tu dis, un aimable garçon et qui de plus deviendra un très grand peintre si Dieu lui conserve la vue et lui met un peu plus de plomb dans la tête." Box II, folder 52b, excerpted in Lemoisne, 1946–49, 81.

39. "Edgar part pour Londres ou pour London 'comme ces Anglais s'intentent [*sic*] à l'appeler'." Box II, folder 55. See Guerin, 1947, 33–35, 41–42, nos. 7, 8, 14, for Degas's (undated) letters to Tissot about the trip.

40. Box II, folder 63.

41. "Edgar se plaint toujours de ses yeux, ce qui l'empêche de travailler autant qu'il le voudrait." Box II, folder 66.

42. Box III, folder 5b.

43. Box IV, folder 3. See McMullen, 1984, 8–9, on the "spontaneous ennoblement" of the Degas family during the July Monarchy. Edgar Degas's paternal great grandfather was a *boulanger*. See also Sigwalt, 1988, and Loyrette, 1991, 678, n. 1.

44. See, for example, Box I, folder 27c, June 17, 1861.

45. Box VI, folder 2, biographical sketch of Michel Musson by L. V. Huber, based on an interview with Gaston Musson (son of René De Gas and Estelle Musson) and his son Michel, June 9, 1947. See also Andrew B. Booth, *Records of Louisiana Confederate Soldiers and Louisiana Confederate Commands* III (New Orleans, 1920), book 1, 1115. Musson served as a private in Company D of the Orleans Guards, in the Louisiana regiment of the Confederate army and served as a purchasing agent for the quartermaster. After the war, he reportedly refused to take the oath of reallegiance to the Union.

46. The hand copied article is in Box II, folder 30. See also Box I, folder 54, and Box II, 8, letters to Michel Musson from René De Gas in Paris, January 6, 1864, and August 26, 1864; Box II, folder 13, letter to Michel Musson from Auguste De Gas in Paris, December 22,

1864; Box II, folder 17, letter to Didi Musson from John Watt (Michel Musson's business partner) in Pau, January 15, 1865.

47. See K. A. Hanna, "The Role of the South in the French Intervention in Mexico," *Journal of Southern History* XX (1954): 3–21; L. M. Case and W. F. Spencer, *The United States and France: Civil War Diplomacy* (Philadelphia, 1970), 595–96; J.-B. Duroselle, *La France et les Etats-Unis: des origines à nos jours* (Paris, 1976), 61–64; J. L. Roark, *Masters Without Slaves: Southern Planters in the Civil War and Reconstruction* (New York, 1977), 124–31.

48. "Il [Eugène] veut, je crois, faire voir sur ses doigts combien sont vains les efforts pour chercher aussi la vallée du Mississipi [*sic*] pour la culture du coton. Il y a q[uel]que chose qui frappe encore plus les esprits en ce moment et les porte à maudire cette guerre américaine. L'Inde et l'Egypte ne sont et [ne] seront jamais des consommateurs, il faudrait donc pour toujours continuer le drainage des espèces! Impossible, il faut qu'il cesse à un moment donné. Or l'Europe pour *fas et nefas* veut la fin de cette guerre, et elle me semble (l'Europe) disposée à faire bon marché de ses sympathies pour le Sud pour peu que ces sympathies dussent la prolonger. La retraite de Bragg après sa victoire a découragé les plus ferven[t]s. Depuis ce moment, nous avons vu les fonds Confédérés coton de 68 tombés à 30. Les acheteurs[?] de Bonds [illegible] 8% Richmond ont disparu. Il y a de ces titres ici qu'on donnerait à 40% et pas d'acheteurs. Je n'ai pas répondu plus tôt à ta lettre d'Octobre esperant toujours q[uel]que chose de plus faisable, mais cela n'a été au contraire du mal en pis. Je vois [illegible] à regret ce ballon d'essai de M. Lüling. Cet envoi de $20,000, qui on supposait achetés à 16% avec change à 3/50 faisaient la parité de 11¼ à 5 fr. le $, si je pouvais. Si le cours a 20% et 5 fr. le $ à coup sûr, il y aurait encore une belle marge, mais je repète point d'amateurs. Il est évident que si les choses viennent à changer je m'empresserai de t'en écrire." Box I, folder 46.

49. "Si ces Bonds vous coutent 16% chg. à 3.15 soit f 504 la marge est encore bien jolie. Mummy en a d'autres qu'il veut vendre 21. Je doute que j [y] réussirai, mais le cours aujourd'hui est assez ferme à 19. Il faut faire bien attention que le *stamp* [ou] le timbre [illegible] soit bien visible sur les Bonds autrement c'est une cause de rejeter et je serais

obligé de te renvoyer les titres sans pouvoir les vendre à aucun prix." Box I, folder 61. He wrote with more news about the yield of bonds on March 25, May 13, and June 10, 1864 (Box I, folders 63, 69, and 72).

50. Box I, folder 68, letter to Michel Musson from René De Gas, May 13, 1864; Box I, folder 71, letter from Michel Musson to René De Gas, June 9, 1864.

51. "Pour mon compte j'approuve ton idée de saisir le moment d'une panique des greenbacks pour trouver un prix de 28/m au 29/m de la maison de passage et un prix proportionnel de la maison d'Edgar. Convertir ensuite et immédiatement les greenbacks en Conf. Bonds." Box II, folder 1c; noted by Byrnes in New Orleans, 48–50 (without mention of Edgar's house).

52. "Les Bonds ont baissé depuis à 14, suite de ventes précipitées faites à Londres par un disposeur[?]. Le prix s'est ensuite relevé à 16½ à ¾ et c'est le cours d'aujourd'hui. Tu as écrit à René de me demander si je t'autorisais à vendre la maison d'Edgar et convertir le produit en Bonds Confédérés. Mais je crois bien que je t'y autorise et Edgar aussi. Et fais le, je t'en prie, au plus vite pour profiter de ce désir de convertir en propriétés le papier de crédit et obtenir de ces peureux[?] des conditions qui probablement ne se retrouveront jamais plus; car il semble que ces propriétés que nous a leguées ton père sont frappés de malédiction; il faut s'en débarrasser. Je regretterai que pour attendre ma réponse tu eusse manqué le coche. Et la maison du passage n'y a-t-il pas d'amateurs qui nous paieraient en Bonds? Si je pouvais récupérer mes pauvres $28,000 qu'elle me coûte! Occupes t'en mon cher ami et si tu as une proposition réponds m'en [*sic*]." Box II, folder 15b. The date on this letter has been torn off; Byrnes in New Orleans, 50, lists it as (April?) 22, 1864, but it seems to be written after the related letter of July 1, 1864 in Box II, folder 1c, cited in preceding note.

53. Box II, folder 3. For further discussion of bonds, see Box II, folder 13, letter to Michel Musson from Auguste De Gas in Paris, December 22, 1864.

54. Box II, folder 8.

55. Box II, folder 5. Henri thought he and the Rocheforts (their brother-in-law and his son) should be consulted.

56. Box I, folders 51 and 38d.

57. As cited in n. 46.

58. "Mais la culture du coton, la liberté des nègres, amènera la misère générale. Impossible de plus songer à relever sa maison de commerce, M. perdra à tout jamais dit il. Il faut que chacun de nous avise à pourvoir à son existence et à celle de sa famille." Box II, folder 13.

59. "J'ai vu par les journaux que les nègres avaient été endommagés [*sic*] dans un meeting du parti radical & que 31 d'entre eux avaient perdu la douce lumière du jour, que l'état de siège avait été proclamé puis levé & je vois aujourd'hui qu'il a été de nouveau proclamé. Où allons nous donc. L'or doit monter car les 5.20 baissent ici." Box II, folder 24.

60. "les préjugés sur la couleur n'existent pas en Angleterre." Box II, folder 47d. (This, I suspect, would have been news to the Asians and West Indians in England at the time.)

61. For further comments on the *cataclysmes radicaux*, rumors of violence, *tribulations politiques*, "politico-madness," and fears of bloodshed during Reconstruction, also see Box II, folders 48, 57a, 65; Box III, folders 6 and 13d.

62. Box II, folder 63.

63. Box VI, folder 2, biographical sketch of Michel Musson, cited above, n. 45. For Musson and Bell's involvement in the White League and battle of Liberty Place, see J. S. Kendall, *History of New Orleans* I (Chicago and New York, 1922), 360, 363; and S. O. Landry, *The Battle of Liberty Place: The Overthrow of Carpetbag Rule in New Orleans—September 14, 1874* (New Orleans, 1955), 85, 141. See also Benfey, 1997, chaps. 7, 9, 10. Benfey also discusses Michel Musson's paradoxical participation in the "Unification" movement. The racial mix in Degas's family tree was independently discovered, though not published, by James B. Byrnes in the 1960s.

64. See Box I, folder 38e.

65. See above, n. 58.

66. Box I, folder 36d.

67. See above, nn. 15, 23.

68. See Box I, folders 32b, 34c and f, 42, 54, 56, 57, 68, 71; Box II, folders 1a and c, 2a and e, 8, 17, and 18a.

69. A letter to Michel Musson from Henri Musson in Paris, August 3, 1866, said he was

trying to interest René in the wine business. See Box II, folder 2e.

70. Box II, folder 22.

71. Box II, folder 23.

72. Box II, folder 24. He ended this letter with the mention of the New Orleans "massacre" cited above.

73. Box II, folders 47c and 49a, letters of August 10 and 29, 1872, respectively. See also Rewald in New Orleans, 45, n. 20. For other letters with mention of René De Gas's business dealings, see Box II, folder 63 and Box III, folder 5a and b.

74. Box II, folder 48.

75. See above, n. 27.

76. Box II, folder 52a.

77. Box IV, folder 21. Edgar Degas left New Orleans in mid-March, 1873. I discuss the dissolution of Michel Musson's own cotton firm on February 1, 1873, in relation to Degas's representation of it in *A Cotton Office in New Orleans,* 1873 (Musée des Beaux-Arts, Pau) in Brown, 1994, chap. 1; Brown, 1988; and Brown in this book.

78. For other letters and documents mentioning his *compagnies en désarroi,* debts, legal battles, legal fees, "straitened circumstances," and declining fortunes, see Box III, folders 19, 20, 26, 31; Box IV, folders 1b and c, 2a 4, 7a, 9, 10, 19, 20, 26c, 32, 33, and 36. Achille De Gas sued Michel Musson for a debt of $1,051.85 (with 8 percent interest for two years) in U.S. Circuit Court on April 19, 1879 (National Archives—Fort Worth Branch, case 8738). Henri Musson and his nephew Maurice de Rochefort sued René De Gas in Civil District Court in New Orleans, March 5–21, 1881, over delinquent property taxes (docket 2531, Civil District Court archives, New Orleans Public Library).

79. Box II, folder 63. He also mentioned that René had joined (John) Leisy's (cotton) firm. This marked the definitive end of De Gas Frères, which had dissolved for all intents and purposes when Achille returned to France to oversee the family bank. See also Box II, folder 65, November 6, 1874, in which Michel Musson sent Achille the requested figures, specifically the division of the proceeds of $111,573 from the sale in 1851 of Germain Musson's properties at Canal and Royal Streets.

80. Box II, folder 66.

81. "Tu sais par René la suspension de la maison de son frère. Nommé liquidant à l'aimable j'espère, si l'on me le permet, arriver à 25% comptant et 25% d.[ans] 5 ans. Il faut que tu pousse René à prendre des arrangements honorable avec sa famille pour qu'il l'aide par des envois trimestriels à acquitter les engagements qu'on[?] va prendre. Il doit enormément et en dehors de ce prix[?] nécessaire à l'entretien de la famille il doit fais [*sic?*] ses bénéfices chez Leysy. Je compte sur toi pour une conversation très sérieuse avec lui." Box III, folder 1a, translated in part by Rewald in New Orleans, from whom my transcription differs slightly. Byrnes's typescript notes another letter from Henri to Michel Musson of October 16, 1875, mentioning René De Gas's large debts, the liquidation of De Gas Frères, and Eugène Musson's brain fever. Rewald in New Orleans, quotes from another letter of August 31, 1876, from Achille De Gas to Michel Musson, in which Achille described the complete failure of the De Gas Bank—blaming it, in large part, on René De Gas's large outstanding debt (see Box II, folder 23, cited above, n. 71), which he was unable to pay because of other financial obligations to Mrs. Leisy (wife of his partner) and Mr. Puech (his agent). Achille described how he, Edgar, and Marguerite were obliged to live on a bare subsistence in order to cover the debts. Neither of these letters is found in the De Gas–Musson Papers at Tulane.

82. "Mon ami, tu sais la lourde tâche, bien pénible aussi, de la liquidation d'A. Degas & Cie. Je suis parvenu avec ce que j'ai trouvé en caisse, avec le secours d'Edgar et de Fèvre, de donner aux créanciers 30% sur les 50% à eux promis pour combler[?] sa faillite. J'avais 5% à payer fin Xbre [décembre] et j'en ai autant à fin juin prochain. Je comptais sur René qui ne m'a rien envoyé. Comment puis je faire? Vais-je laisser crouler un édifice étayé avec tant de peine. Le jour où cela arrivera et il est prochain, on se retrouvera contre René tout se sait et on ira détruire sa situation en voie de formation. Un exemple. En dehors de la liquidation de la Maison A. Degas de Paris. *La Banque d'Anvers* pressait Achille et les cautions Degas et Fèvre pour 40,000 F. L'affaire vient cette semaine au rôle. L'issue n'est pas douteuse. Armée, la Bque fait vendre les meubles de Fèvre et d'Edgar; inassouvie par 3 ou 4m fr., elle attaque René. Je lui ai soumis la note de

nos *nécessités,* pendant que son frère Edgar et 1 b.[eau] frère Fèvre sont sur la brèche, eux pour cela ne regardait pas, il se croit à l'abri, il se trompe. S'il laisse les choses s'aggraver, il en sera à son tour victime. Il savait nos échéances de fin Xbre, l'affaire de la Banque d'Anvers, nos échéances de fin Juin prochain, les sacrifices d'argent faits par Edgar et Fèvre, il se contente au bout de trois mois de silence d'écrire à Achille qu'il ne fait rien envoyer le fin Xbre et que si le coton reste dans le Marasme, il ne pourra rien en juin. Je ne puis admettre cette légèreté d'allures. Je vois à Paris, Edgar se priver de tout, vivre du moins possible. Les 7 enfants de Fèvre vétus de trous. Ils prennent seulement leur nécessaire. L'honneur est engagé. René doit bien mieux qu'eux encore s'astreindre. Sa conscience l'exige. Je te parle gravement d'un sujet très grave et je te prie d'en causer de même avec lui. Mon ami, maintenant personnellement tu dois 7,500 fr. à Achille. C'est à dire à sa liquidation. Comme liquidateur je te demande explication. Si oui peux-tu t'acquitter en une fois ou veux-tu des termes fixés. Réponds moi de suite. Dans l'inextricable je veux cependant essayer d'un dernier effort. Evidemment ce ne sera pas moi qui vous poursuivrai les uns et les autres. Mis au pied du mur par les créanciers, je donnerai ma démission. Mais la liquidation judicaire se fera et sans ménagements par les voies de droit. . . . Je lis dans les journaux la terrible crise que vous incombe. Comment en sortirez vous? D'ici cela semble bien sombre." Box III, folder 7a, portions translated by Rewald in New Orleans.

83. "Fèvre et Edgar traqués par la Banque d'Anvers, paient avec la plus grande peine par des versements mensuels." Box III, folder 7e, translated (undated) by Rewald in New Orleans.

84. See Box III, folder 13c, February 28, 1878; Box IV, folders 7c and d (1880).

85. Documents with a bearing on the marriage and upon Balfour's military career in the army of Victor Emmanuel and in the Confederate army include Box I, folders 26a, 27a, 29, 33c and d. On January 17, 1862, René De Gas wrote to Estelle Musson Balfour, expressing the hope that she and Mr. Balfour could come for a visit to France. See Box I, folder 28c.

86. "Je ne vous dirai pas avec quel bonheur nous avons fait la connaissance d'Estelle. Elle

inspire tant de sympathie, elle a tant de douceur dans sa tristesse qu'elle nous a tous attachés à elle en un instant. . . . J'espère de bons résultats pour Estelle de ce voyage; on voit que le fond de son caractère est le gaieté; car au milieu de sa douleur elle a des pointes qui dénotent un esprit aimant à rire; & nous constatons chaque jour un progrès favorable." Box I, folder 34c.

87. Box I, folders 34f and 35; see also Box II, folder 9a.

88. Box II, folders 45, 46, 47, 49; Box III, folders 3 and 5.

89. See Box II, folder 48; Box III, folder 6.

90. See Box II, folders 52a and 64.

91. See Box III, folders 13f and 19.

92. Box III, folder 13e: "Le silence d'Edgar et de Maguerite vient certainement de ce que je ne leur ai rien dit." See also Box III, folders 14b and c. In June 1878, Henri wrote, "Je m'attendais à une visite d'Edgar et d'Achille. Je ne l'ai pas reçue. Je pense qu'ils t'auront écrit, te chargeant de toutes leurs affections pour notre Estelle."

93. "J'ai vu Edgar depuis mon retour. Il est tant [tout?] que tu peux désirer qu'il soit absolument attaché à vos voeux. M. René n'a pas essayé de le voir. Il l'aurait mis à la porte. Marguerite partage les sentiments d'Edgar . . . Ils ont la coeur et l'âme entièrement vôtres. Effacez de votre esprit les impressions qui y ont pris place à tort." Box III, folder 14d.

94. "Mon oncle Henri, Edgar, Marguerite m'ont chargé à mon départ de Paris de vous embrasser tous de leur part & en particulier cette chère Estelle." Box III, folder 15, unpublished. See also Box III, folders 16a and b: "Si mes soeurs ne vous ont pas écrit, c'est qu'elles ignorent ce qui s'est passé et que mon oncle Henri, Edgar & moi avions jugé sage de leur épargner le chagrin que cette catastrophe leur causera dès qu'elles l'apprendront."

95. See Box III, folders 17g, 18a and c, 19, 20, 23, 25, 31, 38; Box IV, folders 2, 4, 5, 11, 13, 39, and 40.

96. Box III, folder 25: "J'ai communiqué à Edgar et à Marguerite le contenu de ta lettre."

97. Box III, folder 34.

98. "Tu as sans doute trouvé la vraie raison du mutisme d'Edgar & Marguerite envers Estelle —leur répugnance à qualifier leur frère du titre qu'il mérite. Qu'il nous suffise donc de savoir que leur coeur est ouvert à la malheureuse et ses enfants et fermé au coupable. Mais nous renouvelons encore notre demande à Edgar du portrait de notre chère Mathilde dont nous n'avons que nos [ses?] croquis au crayon noir et une photographie prise en 1862." Box III, folder 38. The mentioned portrait of Mathilde Bell was perhaps related to L 305, 318, 319, or the drawing in Chicago reproduced by Byrnes in New Orleans, pl. VII.

99. " Je sais que ni Edgar ni sa soeur ne veulent le voir . . . Edgar & Marguerite ont le coeur ouvert pour Estelle et fermé à René, ceci je le t'affirme, ils m'ont dit dix fois de te l'écrire. Maintenant pourquoi n'ont ils pas écrit. Est-ce une répugnance invincible qui les empêche d'appeler gredin leur frère? J'ai transmis à Edgar ton desir d'avoir le portrait de Mathilde. Il l'a dit envoyé par Achille qui doit être à N. Orléans 1er s[eptem]bre. Je n'ai pas vu [plus?] ce monde depuis le 19 juillet. A mon retour j'irai chercher Edgar." Box III, folder 39.

100. "J'ai rappelé à Edgar sa promesse de t'envoyer son étude de Mathilde. Il m'a dit qu'il allait le faire. Il t'embrasse." Box IV, folder 2a.

101. "Edgar répond toujours oui et n'envoie pas le portrait. Je ne lui laisserai pas. Il n'y a pas mauvaise volonté mais impossible de trouver le temps de l'harmoniser." Box IV, folder 7d.

102. "Edgar m'a chargé des meilleures choses pour vous tous. Le brave garçon, car c'est une bonne délicate et intelligente nature, répugne à vous écrire. Il est tellement honteux des agissements de ses frères qu'il craint que vous ne le confondiez avec eux—c'est évidemment une fausse vue de son esprit, je lui ai dit sur tous les tons. Dans tous les cas, sachez à n'en pas douter qu'il vous aime, vous respecte, vous plaint et s'est rangé complètement de notre bord. Il n'a jamais revu M. René et ne compte pas le revoir. Il m'a dit tout ce qu'un coeur bien fait peut trouver de senti[?] et d'elevé en me priant de vous le transmettre." Box IV, folder 20.

103. "Fais voir à Edgar ces portraits et communique à lui cette lettre ainsi que les plans et l'historique de famille. Ce que tu me dis *de lui* et *de sa part* nous est une preuve bien sensible de son attachement et de sa sympathie pour nous. Sa nature d'élite devait le porter à se venger de notre côté; s'il lui coûte de nous écrire, et bien nous l'espérons; *mais qu'il signe et date* (en place d'une lettre) un croquis de *toi*. . . . Est-ce qu'Edgar ne se fera pas de mon plaisir de remplir ma collection? De lui ça serait si reconnaissant et je serais si fier d'avoir de lui quelque chose de plus que l'ébauche ou croquis fait de notre regrettée Mathilde." Box IV, folder 22. See also Box IV, folder 21, for the family history (as mentioned above).

104. The letter from Edgar Degas is not in the De Gas–Musson collection.

105. Box IV, folder 37: "My dear Edgar, I received day before yesterday your letter of July 16. My brother Henri died the 12th!! His wife is quite ill. Anna her daughter tries to keep her alive and you, the *only* loyal one, you are going to rejoin them soon to console them. *This is good Edgar.* Everything that you just told me is written with your heart's blood diluted by your real and bitter tears. Ah! my friend, how I have also wept—even though at my age, and given how much I have already wept, the stream is nearly dried up. Having been so *martyrized* for four months, to die *after all.* Patient, heroic Christian that he was, I nonetheless understand his wranglings with Death when *She* came to pluck him away from those he loved so much. Now everything is said. 'Rest in peace,' *alone,* in that little corner of Normandy, [and] why not there, instead of in Paris among a disunited family? I'm waiting now for the letter Anna should write me, dictated by my poor sister-in-law, to transmit to me Henri's last wishes or desires. Already in his last letter of the 10th [*sic*] he told me: 'I suffer, I endure, dyspeptic; we'll see. In any event I embrace you and ask you to shoulder being devoted to my wife as to me.

P.S. In about a week I'll see more clearly in the cloud of my thought.' Alas! two days later he expired, and I wrote to him again on the 25th!

But if I lose a brother I gain a nephew— Prodigal son who comes back to me after having suffered much, I open my arms and bless you! You are indeed that Edgar whom we always loved, the cherished son of my sister Célestine, the favorite of my daughters. Like the four of them you are creole in your heart; by birth and outlook you are indeed French; but you are not like them . . . Italian cads.

Poor boy, shorn lamb, you also have not been spared!—I know from Henri that you and Fèvre have thrown yourselves into the breach for the honor of the signature A. Degas & Co., 'that you live on as little as possible and that the 7 children were dressed in rags,' but I don't know their conduct toward you *since* their return to Europe with wife and children. You tell me enough to make me see the rough picture, but you lash them in such a light manner[?] and your palette is loaded so little, that I have to guess or invent the details.

But let's set aside these indignities for the moment, and let me talk to you of our poor brother and uncle Eugène! Henri's death deprives him of the supervision and interest that my brother exercised up to a certain point—A Mr. Hans Olivier was in 1876 named judicial administrator and was charged with the 25,000 francs the liquidation of Eugène's business netted. If M. Olivier invested the sum in a life annuity there will be enough for the decent upkeep of the patient (3,000 francs a year) until his death; but if the capital is consumed, the poor man will soon fall into government care. I have nothing, I make nothing, I can't remedy the situation! All I have left is to beg you to inquire about the financial *status* of the subject in Charenton as well as Paris, and to inform and calm me, I hope. *Poor Eugène, may you die!*

Tell me also what has become of a certain Mr. Degas who was spoken about in the *Revue des Deux Mondes* on page 481 of Volume 33, 2nd installment, May 15, 1879. I leave to Didi the sweet duty of good memories and affectionate reconciliations. I embrace you with all my heart, dear Edgar. Your uncle and friend M[ichel] Musson."

("Mon cher Edgar, J'ai reçu avant hier ta lettre du 16 juillet. Mon frère Henri est mort le 12!! Sa femme est bien malade. Anna sa fille cherche à la rattacher à la vie et toi le *seul* dévoué, tu vas bientôt les rejoindre pour les consoler. *C'est bien Edgar.* Tout ce que tu viens me raconter est écrit avec le sang de ton cœur dilué [sic] par tes larmes vraies et amères. Ah! mon ami, que j'ai pleuré aussi—quoique à mon age et que j'ai déjà tant pleuré, la source est presque tarie.

Avoir été tant *martyrisé* depuis 4 mois, pour mourir *après tout.* Quelque chrétien patient, héroïque qu'il fut, je comprends ses tiraillements avec la Mort lorsqu'elle est venue l'arracher à *Elle*, à ceux qu'il aimait tant.

Maintenant tout est dit. "Requiescat in pace," *solitairement,* dans ce petit coin de Normandie, pourquoi pas là, aussi bien qu'à Paris parmi une famille désunie?

J'attends maintenant la lettre qu'Anna doit m'écrire, sous la dictée de ma pauvre belle sœur, pour me transmettre les suprêmes volontés ou désirs d'Henri. Déjà dans sa dernière lettre du 10 [sic] il me disait: "Je souffre, j'endure dyspeptique; nous allons bien voir. Dans tous les cas je t'embrasse et te demande attache ma femme comme moi sur le dos. P.S. Dans 8 jours je verrai plus clair dans le nuage de ma pensée." Hélas! deux jours plus tard il expirait, et moi je lui écrivais encore le 25!

Mais si je perds un frère, je retrouve un neveu—Enfant prodigue qui me reviens après avoir beaucoup souffert, je t'ouvre mes bras et te bénis! Tu es bien *cet* Edgar que nous aimions toujours, le fils cheri de ma sœur Célestine, le préféré de mes filles. Comme elles quatres tu es *créole* par le cœur; de naissance et d'esprit tu es bien français; mais tu n'est pas, comme *eux* . . . lazzarroni.

Pauvre garçon, brebis à tondre, toi aussi on ne t'as pas épargné!—Je savais par Henri que toi et Fèvre vous vous étiez jetés dans la brèche pour l'honneur de la signature A. Degas & Cie, "que vous viviez du moins possible et que les 7 enfan[t]s étaient vêtus de trous," mais j'ignorais leur conduite envers toi depuis leur rentrée en Europe avec femme & enfants. Tu m'en dis suffisamment pour me fair voir la chose en gros, mais tu les cingles d'une manière[?] si légère et ta palette est si peu chargée, qu'il me faut deviner ou inventer les détails.

Mais écartons ces indignes pour le moment, et laisse moi t'entretenir de notre pauvre frère et oncle Eugène! La mort d'Henri le prive du contrôle et de l'intérêt qu'exercait mon frère jusqu'à un certain point—Un Mr. Hans Olivier fut nommé en 1876 administrateur judiciaire et fut chargé des F25,000 que netta la liquidation des affaires d'Eugène. Si M. Olivier a placé cette somme en viager il y aura de quoi pourvoir à l'entretien convenable du malade (F3000 par an) jusqu'à sa fin; mais si le capital est mangé, le malheureux va bientôt tomber à la charge du Gouvernement. Je n'ai rien, je ne gagne rien, je ne puis pas y rémédier! Il me reste à te prier de t'enquérir du *status* financier du 'sujet' tant à Charenton qu'à Paris, et de me renseigner et tranquiliser, je l'espère. *Pauvre Eugène, puisse-tu mourir!*

Dis moi aussi qu'est devenu un certain Mr Degas dont s'est entretenu la Revue des deux Mondes à la page 481 du Tome 33me,

2de Livraison, 15 mai 1879.89 Je laisse à Didi la douce tâche des bons souvenirs et des affectueux rapprochements. Je t'embrasse de tout cœur, cher Edgar. Ton oncle et ami Mel Musson.")

The review in question had given Degas only qualified praise while panning the Impressionists in general: G. Lafenestre, "Les Expositions d'Art: Les Indépendants et les aquarellistes," *Revue des Deux Mondes* XXXIII (May 15, 1879): 481.

106. See Box I, folder 46; Box II, folders 29, 41, 43, 50, 52b, 55, and 57; Box III, folder 1a.

107. Box III, folder 7a. See also Box III, folders 7e, 13c, 25, 39; Box IV, folders 2a, 7d, 20, 26e, and 28.

108. "Mon cher Edgar

Pas un mot de toi ni d'Anna, depuis ta lettre du 16 juillet, m'annonçant la mort de mon frère Henri. Il y a un *gros* tort entre nous; pour qu'il ne me soit imputable, je t'envoie, ci-joint, la copie de ma réponse du 6 août (21 rue Pigalle Paris). Avec les mêmes sentiments pour toi et les mêmes vœux pour le pauvre affligé, ton oncle & ami. Mel Musson

P.S. Par décret de Cour et note notarié, je viens *d'adopter* mes petits enfants Odile et Gaston (Degas) qui dorénavant porteront mon (n.b.) nom—Je te prie d'en prendre note."

Box IV, folder 41. The change of name might have been an especially sore point for the artist since Gaston's full name had been Edgar Achille Gaston De Gas. Records of Michel Musson's adoption of Estelle's children are located in docket 9482, October 3, 1883, Civil District Court for the Parish of Orleans, archives, New Orleans Public Library.

109. "S'informer si Mr Edgar (peintre) demeurant au no 21 Rue Pigalle, Paris, a reçu les deux lettres que Mr Michel Musson (son oncle) lui a expédiées, affranchies via New York le 6 août et le 6 novembre 1883, à l'adresse ci-dessus. Respectueusement, Mel Musson, no 125 Rue de l'Esplanade." Box IV, folder 43a.

110. "Ce Monsieur s'est absolument refusé à donner le renseignment demandé, disant que cela ne regardait personne." Box IV, folder 43b.

111. See Box IV, folders 44, 45, 46a, b, and c.

112. See Brown, 1994, 121.

New Orleans and the Work of Degas

JEAN SUTHERLAND BOGGS

PREFATORY ACKNOWLEDGMENTS

This section concentrates on the works by Degas that have some relationship with New Orleans. Most of these are in the exhibition and reproduced in color.[1] Details of their histories are given in a separate section beginning on page 108.

In the text that follows this two-part preface, each work is considered and its relationship to New Orleans examined. There has not been the time or opportunity to undertake the technical examination that a conservator might make; but, otherwise, all the considerations an object suggests, as well as related archival material, have been pursued. This provides an understanding of the object's place in the work and life of this French artist who, because of his New Orleans–born mother who died when he was an adolescent, spent five months in New Orleans from October 1872 to March 1873 before returning to Paris where he would exhibit in the First Impressionist Exhibition in 1874.

The archival material has been particularly important in the organization of the exhibition and in the preparation of this section, largely due to the deposit at Tulane University of papers by the family of Mrs. Edmund B. Martin, a granddaughter of the artist's younger brother, René.[2] These were catalogued by Marilyn R. Brown, the author of "A Tale of Two Families: The De Gas–Musson Correspondence at Tulane University" in this publication.[3] Her work has inspired other research here and abroad,[4] some of it for this show by Victoria Cooke, the associate curator for the exhibition, who has indefatigably explored the resources of the Catholic Archdiocese and historic houses in New Orleans.

The contribution of more traditional publications must be acknowledged, in particular those of a tenacious quartet—Paul-André Lemoisne, John Rewald, James B. Byrnes, and Henri Loyrette—working at different times, quite independently. Lemoisne, who began his work with a visit to the artist in 1895 and pursued it with correspondence he and his wife conducted with the family's descendants in New Orleans, which is to be found in the Tulane archives, published his four-volume *catalogue raisonné,* which also includes a biography and certain archival records in the notes, from 1946 to 1949.[5] Rewald, the historian of Impressionism, who visited New Orleans to conduct his research, consulted surviving members of the family of René De Gas, and published an article in the *Gazette des Beaux-Arts* in 1945.[6] Byrnes, as director of the Isaac Delgado Museum (now the New Orleans Museum of Art) organized the exhibition and was principal author of the catalogue of *Edgar Degas: His Family and Friends in New Orleans* in 1965, for which he uncovered certain hitherto unknown documents and photographs, an encouragement of others to follow his example.[7] The fourth, Loyrette, director of the Musée d'Orsay in Paris, in 1992 published by far the most thoroughly documented biography of Degas, using a great deal of hitherto unpublished material.[8]

Preface: The Father of the Painter

Since the exhibition and this publication concentrate upon Degas and his relationship to his mother's birthplace and, although admittedly less on his relationship to his mother, who died when he was thirteen, than to her family and their friends, it nevertheless almost ignores the existence of his father—Auguste De Gas—who did not die until after Degas returned from his famous visit to New Orleans. There is actually little evidence of any sentimental attachment to his mother on the part of Degas and very little opportunity in those first thirteen years for her to have influenced his future career.[9] On the other hand, there is every evidence that the painter was close to his father. (This does not exclude, however, the importance of New Orleans to the artist.)

Auguste shared certain things in common with his wife's eldest brother, Michel Musson, who would eventually become the gentleman looking over his spectacles as he feels cotton in the foreground of *A Cotton Office in New Orleans.* Both were the first sons in fairly large families—and both chose as adults to separate themselves from those families. Auguste, whose father was a Frenchman who lived most of his life in Naples and his mother Italian, chose to leave the rest of his family in Naples to set up a branch of his father's bank in Paris and in the process to be the first in his family to divide his name into the more snobbishly acceptable "De Gas." His reasons for leaving Naples were probably a desire for independence, particularly from his successful, domineering, outspoken father and a feeling that Paris would offer him more of the cultural pleasures he enjoyed than Naples could. After the death of Michel Musson's mother, the rest of his family—his father, two brothers, and two sisters—elected to stay in France to where their father had brought his children for their education. Michel was the only one to have felt himself American enough to return to New Orleans. There could have been an irony for Auguste De Gas in all of this because he seems to have exchanged one family for another. After he and Célestine married they lived in the same house as her father, and by the time the painter's brother Achille was born, they were living in the same house as his new sister-in-law and her husband, the comte and comtesse de Rochefort, which could have been the basis for the eventual rift between the Rochefort and the Degas families.[10] (Some sixty years later, before the painter's sister Marguerite Fevre died in Buenos Aires in 1895, she expressed a wish to be buried in the Degas vault in Montmartre cemetery in Paris. There was no space since their Musson aunt, the comtesse de Rochefort, without any blood relationship to the Degas family, had been buried there as a courtesy in 1857; so Degas arranged with her only child, Henri de Rochefort, to have her body moved elsewhere so that Marguerite's could join her family. When his aunt's body was removed, as Degas described it, "Bartholomé and I went to the exhumation. Her son didn't even come. He is a skunk whom I never see any more.")[11]

It is possible that Degas's father was temperamental and irascible, but it is more likely that, since he was demonstrably not a good businessman and inevitably listened to (and acted upon) the worst possible advice with disastrous results, he must have felt increasingly inadequate when compared with the memory of his own father. This could not have improved his temperament. Although Auguste De Gas may not have actually been abused by the Mussons, he was certainly often misled by them, as his father had predicted, but he does not seem to have born grudges against the family.[12] In fact, he encouraged his children to be hospitable to their aunt Odile Musson and their cousins Estelle and Désirée when they came to France in 1863 and stayed until 1865, the last year we have any record of his correspondence with Michel Musson. Auguste may always have enjoyed the Creole manners of the Mussons, which would have seemed relaxed and pleasing compared with the stiff formality of his Neapolitan relatives.

There was a paternal side to Degas's father. He took his role as single parent seriously, getting Achille out of a bad scrape in the Marines, worrying about René's future, and finally supporting René's desire to try New Orleans, even lending him far too much money from the bank to do so.[13] It could not have been easy without a wife to have married off his daughters, but he did it satisfactorily. Desperately as he wanted Edgar to be his partner and successor in the bank, during the long period of Edgar's education, Auguste encouraged his son's greater interests in the visual arts and music.

FIG 57. Edgar Degas, *Lorenzo Pagans and Auguste De Gas,* c. 1871–72, oil on canvas, 21¼ × 15¾ in. Musée d'Orsay, Paris. Lemoisne 256.

Auguste's indulgence of Degas's love of music and the theater is difficult to document because with a Neapolitan father it seemed such a natural part of his life. But it is interesting that when it came to painting a portrait of his father, which he did only three times, Degas chose the same circumstances—his father listening to the guitarist and tenor (at the Opéra) Lorenzo Pagans (fig. 57).[14] Pagans normally sang at the Opéra but he also seemed to enjoy entertaining at informal gatherings of friends.[15] In these paintings Degas showed him in a room in a somewhat untidy apartment or house, which from the presence of the grand piano and the gilt-framed pictures apparently belonged to someone devoted to the arts—perhaps Degas's father's own on the rue Mondovi between the Place de la Concorde and the Place Vendome. The rather romantically handsome performer appears to dominate while Degas *père* sits with his shoulders bent, his mustaches drooping, and his fingers interlocking as he listens to Pagans. In the second version, which is larger, the position of the father is much the same but Pagans had changed so that he is almost in profile but still the more commanding figure. It is possible that this was posthumous, painted by Degas after the death of his father in 1874, perhaps even when we know Pagans was posing for him in 1882.[16] And then there is a third that was certainly painted, not only after the death of the father, but after the death of Pagans, who died young in 1883. In style and handling, this square canvas belongs with Degas's works about 1895, a pious reminder of the pathos of his father—so long dead—and the beauty of Pagans, who in the painting no longer performs. The existence of the three paintings and the fact that the first, the one reproduced here, was kept by Degas in his bedroom "above the small iron bedstead" are signs of the filial piety Degas felt for his father—even if his image became increasingly remote with time.[17]

From these portraits of Auguste De Gas with Pagans, we would be prepared for a role that the father would play as a listener. But as Lemoisne made clear in quoting from letters Auguste wrote Edgar, which are otherwise unpublished, he was actively engaged in the development of his son's career. Much as he regretted that Degas did not persist with the study of law, once he enrolled in the École de Droit at his father's request, or that he did not stay with the official education of an artist once he was accepted at the École des Beaux-Arts, Auguste did make it possible for Degas to complete his self-education with remarkably little interference, even from his Italian family, when Degas chose to work on his own in Rome (and eventually Florence) for some three years. Auguste had revealed his own interest in works of art in buying some, including two pastels attributed to Quentin de la Tour and a painting by Perronneau.[18] He had already taken his son to important collections like that of Dr. Louis

La Caze, who in 1869 bequeathed his great *Bathsheba* by Rembrandt to the Louvre, or that of the father of Paul Valpinçon, who owned remarkable works by Ingres and introduced the young Edgar Degas to this artist, who was the living painter Auguste admired most, or to amateur artists like Grégoire Soutzo, a discriminating collector of prints as well as a respectable printmaker whose advice Degas appreciated.

When Degas did leave the family nest, Auguste pursued him with advice by mail. He suggested what Degas should see in Italy, since he believed that a basic part of the education of an artist should come from examining the work of Old Masters. In one letter he characteristically wrote, "I am indeed glad that you have been studying Giorgione. Your color, although true, needs to be warmed a little."[19] He admitted—and accepted—differences in taste, for example his son's admiration of Delacroix with which he did not agree, but there was also a level that he found unacceptable, for example the school of painting at Lyon headed by Hippolyte Flandrin and Louis Lamothe. In writing to his son on 11 November 1858 he congratulated him, "You have rid yourself of that flabby and trivial drawing style of Flandrin and Lamothe and that dull grey color."[20] Having come to terms with this transformation of the future banker and lawyer into a painter, Auguste followed Degas's work critically and undoubtedly encouraged the youngest of his children, René, to do so. Edgar's émigré uncles, Henri and Eugène, also became part of this family assessment of his talents—grudging at first, enthusiastic finally. And very early, Auguste, with surprising perspicacity, warned his son, "The question of earning your living in this world is serious, imperative, even overwhelming."[21] But it could not have been easy to have had such an unexpected and fundamentally unassuming genius in the family nest.

When Degas returned from Italy, he and his father continued to be close, even when Degas found a studio outside his father's home. Characteristically the painter wrote his first letter to his father upon arriving in America at New York.[22] Degas's father was, however, not prospering. On one trip to Italy when he sold his interest in the Degas family bank in Naples to his brothers, he fell ill in Turin and Degas had to come to his rescue. Eventually Auguste did continue to Naples, where he died in 1874 and was buried in the family mausoleum in the Naples cemetery, which is marked by the unequivocal letters—DEGAS—which he had succeeded in changing to De Gas for his heirs in France (aside from the painter who came to reject it). Auguste died essentially bankrupt. Even when his movable effects were inventoried, they were worth something less than 5,000 francs, to be divided evenly among his five children.[23] But he had given each of them encouragement in turn—perhaps most to the painter who ironically was spelling his name the more unpretentious Degas.

1. It was not possible to borrow certain works because of the terms of their gift to a public museum. A few works have not been found.

2. Mrs. Martin was born Dora Odile Musson, the daughter of Gaston Edgar Achille Musson, the son of the painter's brother René De Gas and their cousin Estelle Musson De Gas. When René deserted Estelle and her children, her father Michel Musson adopted the children who consequently used Musson as their last name rather than De Gas.

3. Brown, 1991.

4. For example, Harvey Buchanan of Case Western Reserve University in discovering the marriage record of 3 May 1878 of René De Gas and America Durrive at the Cuyahoga County Archives (Ohio) and the baptism of the painter in the Protestant Reformed Church in Paris at the Société de l'Histoire de Protestantisme français, Paris.

5. Lemoisne, 1946–49, new edition (New York, 1984).

6. Rewald in New Orleans, 1965.

7. Byrnes in New Orleans.

8. Loyrette, 1991.

9. For the best assessment of Degas's relationship to his mother (along with his father) see McMullen, 1984, 18–22; also Boggs in Paris, 1989, 35–45.

10. Lemoisne I, 1946–49, 8.

11. Halévy, 1964, 70.

12. Raimondi, 1958, letters of René-Hilaire Degas in 1835 to his wife in Paris, 105, 107, 108–9.

13. Brown, 1991, Box II, folder 23.

14. The three paintings of Pagans and the father of Degas are L 256, Musée d'Orsay, ca. 1869–72; L 257, 1882 ?, Museum of Fine Arts, Boston; L 345, ca. 1895, on exhibition at the Museum of Fine Arts, Boston.

15. For example, at the Manet Salon; see Rouart, 1981, 81.

16. Although in Boggs, 1962, I suggested that L 345 might have been painted in 1882 when Degas wrote to Bartholomé on 5 August, "Monday morning portrait sitting with Pagans before he leaves for Spain" (Guerin, 1947), I now believe that Degas must have painted L 257 then and L 345 in the 1890s.

17. Paul Poujaud in Guerin, 233–34.

18. Ives in New York, 1997, nos. 753 and 921.

19. Lemoisne I, 1946–49, 30.

20. Ibid.

21. Ibid.

22. Fevre, 1949, 30–31.

23. Notarized record in a private collection. See Pantazzi in Paris, Ottawa, New York, 1988, 212 for 4 April 1874.

JEAN SUTHERLAND BOGGS

Catalogue

The De Gas Family in Paris,
ca. 1832–72

FIG. 58. Anonymous miniaturist, *Célestine De Gas,* ca. 1832–34. Location unknown.

FIG. 59. Anonymous miniaturist, *Auguste De Gas,* ca. 1832–34. Location unknown.

THE DE GAS FAMILY IN PARIS came into being with the accidental meeting of a young man and young woman across rented garden walls in the part of Paris known as La Nouvelle Athènes and more prosaically as the ninth arrondissement.[1] The painter's father was born Agostino (in French, Auguste) Degas in Naples to a father, René-Hilaire Degas, who was born in Orléans in France to a family of bakers[2] but, because of the French Revolution and subsequent adventures, ended up as a man of property in Naples.[3] That property included the vast Palazzo Degas (formerly the Palazzo Pignatelli) near the Gesù Nuovo. As a wife, he took a young woman from Livorno, Giovanna Teresa Aurora Freppa. Of their seven surviving children he managed to marry his four daughters to titled members of the minor aristocracy in Naples and one son to a wife from a slightly more distinguished background. Two sons did not marry. The eldest son, the painter's father, was the only one to leave Naples; Auguste opened a small branch of his father's bank in Paris and changed the spelling of his last name to the more distinguished De Gas. (The painter was the only one of his children to revert to the original spelling, which he did before he reached forty.)

Something of the complexity of that background is revealed in the baptism of that couple's first child, the painter known as Edgar Degas.[4] His godfather was his American grandfather Germain Musson, described on the birth certificate[5] as a resident of Paris—although he had not long before finished the commercial building in New Orleans that would be known as "Musson's Fort" (fig. 60).[6] The other godparent was Auguste's twenty-year-old Neapolitan sister, Laure Degas, whom Degas would make famous as the baroness Bellelli in his great painting, *The Bellelli Family,* now at the Musée d'Orsay. Although it has long been known that when the painter attended the Lycée Louis-le-Grand, it was noticed that there was no record of his baptism or confirmation,[7] it had not been realized that he might have been baptized a Protestant, probably as a concession to his American grandfather of Huguenot descent. The marriage of the young couple on 14 July 1832 had, after all, taken place at the Roman Catholic Church of Notre-Dame-de-Lorette.[8]

Degas's other grandfather, René-Hilaire, might have seemed too far from Paris to have had much influence on the rearing of his grandson, and to some degree that must have been the case. But he was sufficiently attracted by the idea of little Edgar to have sent his wife to inspect the boy when he was a year

FIG. 60. Moody's Department Store on Canal (in Musson's Fort) from Edwin L. Jewell, *Crescent City Illustrated*, New Orleans, 1873. Historic New Orleans Collection.

FIG. 61. Edgar Degas, *René-Hilaire Degas*, 1857, oil on canvas, $20\frac{7}{8} \times 16\frac{1}{8}$ in. Musée d'Orsay. Lemoisne 27.

old. He wrote to her in Paris asking about his daughter-in-law and "the little monkey, Edgar . . . What does he do? Has he teeth? Does he walk a little?— because he is a year old. Is he strong?"[9] Before Edgar was two years old this grandfather was already afraid of the demands for investments or loans being made upon him by the American family into which Auguste had married. He wrote then somewhat prophetically to his wife in Paris, "They have no idea . . . of the work that was the price we paid for what we possess. They would like to avoid it and become Rothschilds in one blow."[10] Although both families would suffer from the wars and depressions the rest of the nineteenth century would bring, René-Hilaire was correct in his hesitations about the acumen of the American family, which would destroy the small De Gas bank in Paris and most of the interests of the family in America as well, a subject Marilyn R. Brown of Tulane University has examined and published most thoroughly.[11]

When Degas was twenty-three and visiting his grandfather in Naples, he painted a small portrait of him that conveys the authority and probity of René-Hilaire (fig. 61).[12]

1. For general information about the life of Degas, well documented with footnotes and indexed, see Loyrette, 1991.

2. Sigwalt, 1988.

3. For the Italian background, see Raimondi, 1958; Boggs, 1963.

4. Harvey Buchanan has found the record of the baptism of the painter on 21 August 1834 in the *Nouveau Régistre de Baptêmes de l'Église Réformée de Paris* at the Société de l'Histoire du Protestantisme français, 54 rue des Saints Pères, Paris.

5. For the birth certificate (as against the baptismal certificate) of 18 July 1834, see Lemoisne I, 1946–49, 225, n. 6.

6. Built between 1825 and 1837, New Orleans Architecture Series, vol. II.

7. Lemoisne I, 1946–49, 226, n. 10, quotes from the record of the painter's admission to the Lycée Louis-le-Grand, "n'a pas fait son première communion."

8. Lemoisne I, 1946–49, 225, n. 5.

9. Raimondi, 92, letter of 28 May 1835.

10. Ibid., 107, letter of 9 December 1835.

11. Brown, 1994.

12. L 27, Musée d'Orsay, Paris.

1. Self-Portrait in a Soft Hat

1857–58
Oil on paper mounted on canvas
10¼ × 7½ inches (26 × 19 cm)
Sterling and Francine Clark Art Institute,
Williamstown, Massachusetts (Inv. Acc. 544)
Lemoisne 37

LIKE MANY YOUNG ARTISTS Degas was often his own model. The histories (or provenances) of the resulting self-portraits, whether in oil, pencil, or etching, do not indicate, however, whether any were sent to members of his family, his father's in Naples or his mother's in New Orleans.[1] When the family of his maternal uncle Michel Musson did appear in France in 1863, they seem to have been genuinely moved by the friendliness of Edgar Degas as if it were unexpected. As Désirée Musson put it to her father in a letter of 24 June 1863, "Edgard [sic] whom we had been told was so brusque, was full of consideration and kindness."[2] The wariness of their expectations may have been because the painter's father had the reputation, even in his Neapolitan family, of having a difficult character, which they may have expected his eldest son to have inherited. But it also could have been because they had found their cousin or nephew to be far less remote than they had believed from some portrait of himself.

It was probably five years before the arrival in France of his aunt Odile Musson and her daughters Désirée and Estelle that Degas painted this tiny self-portrait. He was then living in Italy, largely centered in Rome, a period during which he came to know his father's family. It is true that his mother's sister Anne Eugénie Musson, comtesse de Rochefort (fig. 5), unexpectedly lived in Florence, at least from 1851 until her death there in 1857,[3] but there is more evidence of antagonism than of affection between the Rochefort and Degas families, into which the two New Orleans–born sisters, Eugénie and Célestine Musson, had married. In actual fact Degas lived pretty much on his own in Rome, paying dutiful trips to his grandfather René-Hilaire Degas in Naples and his aunt and godmother Laure Bellelli in Florence. The independence of those years turned Edgar Degas into an artist much more effectively than his sporadic training in Paris had done.

To us this might seem a traditional self-portrait. But if we examine the clothes, we find it is more daring. Although Degas wears a conventional soft hat, the edge of its brim is uneven as if it were frayed. The rose scarf is an exquisite piece of painting but indicates unexpectedly fragile stuff. The dark could be a sweater rather than a vest. Over it is the whitish, roughly painted material that must have been a smock. These clothes and perhaps the fringe of a beard declare this obviously cerebral youth to be somewhat improbably a working man, a painter. And he lifts his head—his eyes at the angle the use of a mirror for self-portraits required—looking at us (and possibly once at his New Orleans relatives) with gravity, dignity, and some sadness.

1. Of the painted self-portraits catalogued by Lemoisne, 1946–49, or Brame and Reff, 1984—L 2, 3, 4, 5, 11, 12, 13, 14, 31, 32, 37, 51, 103, 104, 105, 116 and B/R 28, 29, 30—only L 103 and 104 were in the Ventes. L 5, 14, 32 and B/R 30 are said to have been in his studio at the time of his death and are therefore presumably stamped Atelier and were therefore never given or sold. It is more probable that the remaining thirteen were gifts to friends or members of his family rather than sales.

2. Brown, 1991, Box I, folder 34d.

3. Ibid., folders 14, 18, 23.

FIG. 62. Edgar Degas, *René De Gas,* 1855, oil on canvas, 36¼ × 28¾ in. Smith College Museum of Art, Northampton. Lemoisne 6.

1. Loyrette, 1991, 17, 680, n. 32; Reff, Nb. 6 [1856], 1, as "Mme Adèle Loyé." She accompanied Thérèse and Marguerite to Naples in March 1860, Loyrette, 192.

WHEN HIS NEW ORLEANS–BORN MOTHER, Célestine Musson De Gas, died in Paris in 1847, Edgar Degas, then thirteen, was the eldest of five children, while the youngest, René, was only two. We do not know what domestic arrangements were made at the time, although it is often suggested that one of the two Musson uncles, probably Henri, acted as a tutor. In 1847 Edgar had already been at boarding school for two years, and presumably Achille would follow him when he reached eleven; in 1845 this second son was nine. A nurse was probably hired, if one did not already exist, for the two girls, Thérèse, seven, and Marguerite, five. This would have been in addition to the maid Adèle Loÿe who was with them for some years.[1] The situation of the youngest child, the motherless two-year-old René, must have been particularly appealing then; and, from the number of drawings and paintings Degas made of him later, it seems that he would respond as an artist at least to that appeal.

In 1855, the year this younger brother was ten and the year before Edgar was to leave for Italy, the artist dated a drawing he used for his largest painting of René, which is now in the Smith College Museum of Art (fig. 62). The small painting of René's head and shoulders in the exhibition must have been part of the same exercise. Both the painting and its interpretation of René are admittedly more tentative than in Smith's portrait, in which Degas's handling hardened handsomely in the manner of Italian Mannerist artists like Bronzino. Here the hair is not as thick. The eyebrows disappear. The pupils of the eyes follow us anxiously. And the mouth is opened, leaving the face more exposed than in Smith's version. René even seems rather frail, whereas from Smith's painting we are led to believe that he could sturdily protect himself.

In this painting René is too delicate and tender to make us want to confront his future. It is more charitable to consider the insecurity of his background beginning with the death of his mother when he could scarcely walk and talk. That insecurity must have been increased by their father Auguste De Gas's moving his family's residence six times between 1845 and 1852, when René was nine. (These moves were at least confined to the sixth and ninth arrondissements in Paris.) It was natural therefore that René should have romanticized the background of his dead mother and felt strongly drawn to the idea of New Orleans.

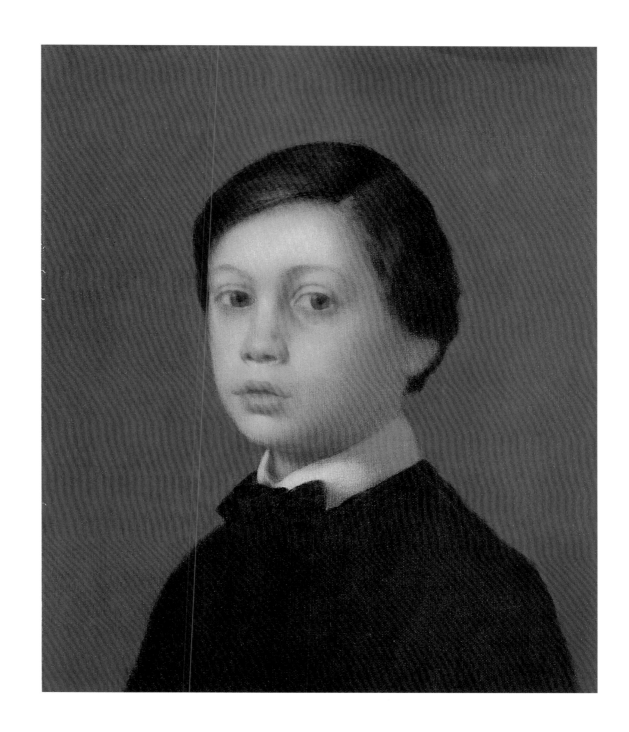

2. *Portrait of René De Gas*

1855
Oil on canvas
$15\frac{1}{2} \times 12\frac{5}{8}$ inches (39 × 30 cm)
National Gallery of Art, Washington, D.C.,
Collection of Mr. and Mrs. Paul Mellon, (995.47.8(PA))
Lemoisne 7

3. René De Gas, The Artist's Brother

ca. 1861
Etching
10 × 6⅛ inches (8.8 × 7.2 cm)
New Orleans Museum of Art, Museum Purchase through
the Ella West Freeman Foundation Matching Fund (69.14)

ABOUT SIX YEARS AFTER having painted and drawn his other portraits of René in 1855, Degas made this tiny softground etching of his head. For most of those intervening years, Edgar had been separated from the younger brother by two trips to Italy—the first the long stay from July 1856 to April 1859, the second his return in the spring of 1860. On the one occasion during those years when we know that René with his two sisters visited the family in Naples, in September 1859, Degas was back in Paris.[1] Although the years they were separated can be reasonably well documented in the life of the painter, not too surprisingly we know almost nothing of what was happening to René. He did pass his examinations in 1861,[2] but we do not even know whether he followed his two brothers to the Lycée Louis-le-Grand. Those years, which were so important to Edgar in his evolution as an artist, must have been just as important for René in his progress through adolescence from ages eleven to fifteen. It is assumed that he was about sixteen when Degas made this etching.

Degas rarely kept the letters sent to him by members of his family or his friends. This was true of those of René, who was a good correspondent with members of the family and, in particular, with their New Orleans relatives. He often showed a proud concern for his brother as an artist. In fact in 1863 he wrote to his uncle Michel Musson in New Orleans of Edgar, "He works furiously and thinks only of his painting."[3] And in 1864, "On my part I believe and am even convinced that he is a genius."[4] That realization of his brother's promise must have grown with Edgar's return to Paris in 1860.

René was also increasingly drawn to—even obsessed with—their American family. When his aunt Odile Musson with two of her daughters and her infant granddaughter, arrived in France to escape the Civil War in New Orleans, René wrote to his uncle Michel of his aunt, "When one is near her, one feels oneself loved, so that for me, who never had a mother to caress me, I am doubly happy to be coddled in this way."[5] At the same time René was attracted by his pretty

Eau forte d Edgard Degas
(portrait de Rem Delus) offert
par le mien Etirond delus n son
vieux Camarade Rem Liffey.
22.1.21

twenty-year-old cousin Estelle, recently widowed by the war. The outcome of the Mussons' two years in France was that René, who did not want to work with his De Gas uncles in Naples and had been disappointed in working with his father in Paris, accompanied his aunt, two cousins, and Estelle's baby to New Orleans in 1865. In 1866 he was joined by his brother Achille in a business venture there. In 1869 René married his pretty cousin Estelle, two years his senior, in spite of the objections of both their families and the knowledge that since 1866 she had been slowly (but inevitably) going blind.

When Edgar made this etching, René may already have been psychologically prepared for the meeting with his mother's relatives, the Mussons, and his move to America, but this would still be in his future. The artist, working with softground etching, which suggests the immediacy of a drawing, described the coarsening of his brother's features since 1855, particularly in the nose and the contours of his face. With that coarsening went a greater energy, partly conveyed by the activity of the collars around his neck but most strongly realized by the exuberant curls of his hair, which are no longer disciplined by scissors and a brush. The axial, confrontational position of the head gives this energy a source in the latent passion of the large black eyes, crowned by mobile brows and underlined by bold shadows. The passion is hesitantly rather than fully realized in the sensual, slightly opened lips. It is easy to understand how over the next few years René would rebel, leave home, and succumb to the charms of his slightly older, tragic first cousin, Estelle Musson Balfour.

The inscription on the etching in the collection of the New Orleans Museum of Art states that it was in the collection of Edmond De Gas, a son of René by his second wife, America Durrive.

1. Loyrette, 1991, 156, 709, n. 12, from an otherwise unpublished letter to Degas from Edmondo Morbilli, 30 July 1859.

2. Brown, 1991, Box I, folder 27d.

3. Ibid., folder 33b, from 6 March 1863.

4. Ibid., folder 66, from 22 April 1864.

5. De Gas–Musson, Box, I, folder 66; for the quotation from this letter of 22 April 1864 from René to Michel Musson, see Loyrette, 289, 730, n. 141.

4. *Marguerite De Gas*

1860–62
Etching and drypoint, 5th state, 4th proof
$4\frac{7}{8} \times 4\frac{1}{4}$ inches (12.5 × 11 cm)
Museum of Fine Arts, Boston, Katherine E. Bullard
Fund in Memory of Francis Bullard (1973.2)

MARGUERITE DE GAS was the younger of the painter's two sisters and, like the other, never visited New Orleans. She was nevertheless friendly with their Musson cousins, Désirée and Estelle, who were in France from 1863 to 1865, and on one occasion stayed with them for two months at Bourg-en-Bresse, where they had settled, breaking that stay with two or three weeks in Switzerland with Désirée.[1] Marguerite's father apparently used her to carry on some of the family correspondence with New Orleans, even before she had met the recipients.[2] Although she never went to Louisiana, she did end up in the Western Hemisphere, moving with her husband and children to Buenos Aires in 1889 and dying there in 1895. It was her body that was returned to France and buried in the De Gas family vault, replacing the body of their New Orleans–born aunt, the comtesse de Rochefort.[3]

When the Mussons were in France, they found the De Gas family in something of a quandary after having married the older sister Thérèse to a Neapolitan first cousin, Edmondo Morbilli, whom her father described as, "a young Neapolitan, with little money twenty-six years old, and deeply in love."[4] On 28 January 1864 Désirée wrote from France to her father in New Orleans about Marguerite's difficulty in finding a husband as satisfactory as Thérèse's Edmondo.[5] By June 1865 Marguerite had nevertheless married—the only one of the De Gas siblings with the courage to do so outside the family circle. She also had her own friends, one of them Louise Bréguet, the future wife of a school friend of Degas, Ludovic Halévy. The Halévy's son Daniel wrote later, "Marguerite was his sister; a charming woman, a great friend of my mother's, an excellent musician. She used to sing old Italian songs for her brother."[6] Certainly Degas retained the fondest memories of Marguerite.

In marrying Marguerite, Henri Fevre, a Beaux-Arts architect who exhibited his designs in the annual Salon, assumed greater responsibilities than he could ever originally have imagined. First, they were to have seven surviving children,

not so improbable then. Second, when Degas's father died leaving his estate, the bank, and his children essentially bankrupt, Henri Fevre joined the artist in paying off a large debt over some years to the Bank of Antwerp. The artist's brother René never pretended to be able to help and the other, Achille, soon gave up. René even had the gall to describe Fevre as "Her husband is Mr. Joseph Prudhomme incarnate, conceited & stupid like all self-proclaimed parvenus."[7] Word of the hardships of the Fevre family reached New Orleans when Michel Musson's brother Henri, who lived in France, wrote to Michel on 17 January 1877, "The seven Fevre children are clothed in rags. They eat only what is necessary. Honor is involved."[8] Twelve years later, with their debt of honor paid, the Fevres moved to Buenos Aires, hoping to make their fortune.

This etching was made, however, when Marguerite was, at the most, twenty. Her features have a delicacy we find in all of Degas's few portraits of her, including a painting of her not long after her marriage (fig. 63), wearing a more flattering but still protective bonnet. Even there, although she is charming, she is also serious if not as much as in this earlier etching. In some ways her etched face appears pinched against the richness of her accessories, a bonnet with flowers under the brim, a large, dashing bow, and a magnificently rich fur muff. In their catalogue of Degas's prints Reed and Shapiro have pointed out that this etching reveals the influences of specific works by Rembrandt, Ingres and Delacroix, which are, however, fused into a highly refined image of unrequited longing.[9]

Although the Fevres had sacrificed so much to the financial irresponsibility of the De Gas family, it is good to know that sometime in the twelve years between the death of Marguerite and the death of the artist, Edgar's friend the American painter Mary Cassatt persuaded the children of Marguerite, who had returned to France, to make all the right moves with the artist that resulted in Degas dividing his estate between his brother René and the heirs of Marguerite (instead of leaving it only to René as he had previously intended).[10] As a result the surviving five of the Fevre children were compensated as they would not have otherwise been for the unselfishness of their father.

FIG. 63. Edgar Degas, *Marguerite De Gas,* 1868, oil on canvas, 90 × 7⅛ in. Private collection. Lemoisne 185.

1. Brown, 1991, Box II, folders 2c, 2d, 2e, 6b, n. 49.
2. Ibid., Box I, folder 27e, 28c, n. 49.
3. Halévy, 1964, 70.
4. Brown, 1991, Box I, folder 33.
5. Ibid., folder 52.
6. Halévy, 69.
7. Brown, 1991, Box II, folder 45c.
8. Ibid., folder 7a.
9. Boston, Philadelphia, 1984, no. 14.
10. Loyrette, 1991, 665–66; Nancy Mowll Mathews, ed., *Cassatt and her Circle: Selected Letters* (New York, 1984), 328, Cassatt to Havemeyer, 2 October 1917.

5. Thérèse De Gas

ca. 1855
Black crayon with graphite on paper
$12\frac{5}{8} \times 11\frac{1}{8}$ inches (32 × 26.4 cm)
Museum of Fine Arts, Boston, Julia Knight Fox Fund (31.434)

DEGAS COULD NOT HELP having a particular affection for his elder sister Thérèse. She may not have been the most amusing member of the family, but even as an erratically trained artist, he would have realized that her features recalled the great classical tradition in painting, going back certainly to Roman frescos, glorified by Raphael in the sixteenth century, and resurrected in the nineteenth by his idol Ingres. Having Thérèse around the house for Degas must have been a little like having a juvenile Mme d'Haussonville, even if the spirit within the shell would not presumably have been as challenging. Late in his life when he was collecting works of art, he visited the two daughters of Mme d'Haussonville separately in the hope of buying one of the two magnificent portraits painted of her by Ingres—the standing figure against a magenta wall now in the National Gallery of Art, Washington, D.C., and the seated figure in the sumptuous dress now in the National Gallery, London. He was unable to buy the paintings, but he did acquire some studies for both works.[1]

It is unlikely that Thérèse, even at the age of about fifteen, which she would have been when her brother made this drawing of her, ever fantasized about being a Parisian hostess in the tradition of Mme d'Haussonville. She was too forthright, too sensible, her mind, like the oval of her head, too unyielding. On the other hand, just as René was drawn like a magnet to New Orleans, Thérèse was attracted to Naples. In a sense this happened at birth because she was born in the Palazzo Degas in that city, her American mother spoiled by her father-in-law René-Hilaire Degas and entertained by her young sisters-in-law.[2] Whenever Thérèse turned up in Naples, for example five years later with René and her sister Marguerite in 1860, she probably sought a mate among the male members of that extended family. In the end she was successful.

1. New York, 1997, vol. 1, 26.
2. Boggs, 1963, 275.

6. *Portrait of Mme Edmondo Morbilli, née Thérèse De Gas*

1865
Oil on canvas
$15\frac{1}{4} \times 11\frac{3}{8}$ inches (39 × 29 cm)
Collection of Walter Feilchenfeldt, Zürich
Lemoisne 132

WHEREAS DEGAS SAW his younger sister, Marguerite, as delicately formed, her features essentially linear, he found the head of his other sister, Thérèse, to be bolder and more sculptural, its oval classically inviolate. Marguerite appears to reach out to the external world, even if she is hesitant about its very modernity; but, Thérèse withdraws into her own thoughts, which, as suggested by the sunken dark eyes and the faint petulance of the lower lip, are troubled. She also holds her head upward slightly, raising her brows and lifting her chin so that we are made aware of a natural pride, which Degas emphasized further by placing her off-center to the left and up on the canvas. He used a monochromatic brown paint to emphasize the classical simplicity of her head. Thérèse is made to appear as if she would endure illness or tragedy nobly.

In 1863 at the age of twenty-three, Thérèse married one of the sons of their father's sister, Rose Adelaide Degas Morbilli, Duchessa di Sant Angelo; he was Edmondo Morbilli, who was four years older. His family had been ennobled in 1526 and given the title of Duke of San Angelo à Frosolone in 1730,[1] but it was impoverished to a point that René-Hilaire Degas, the grandfather, had to contribute to its support. As a child of six at the time of Thérèse's birth, Degas had enjoyed the companionship of his Morbilli cousins; and, when he paid visits to Naples between 1856 and 1860, he made formal portrait drawings of the three young men and their mother.[2]

After Edmondo Morbilli and Thérèse De Gas married, she was soon pregnant. Her visiting American aunt Odile Musson was immediately worried about her; Désirée Musson wrote to her father, "Thérèse is still very unwell and Mother thinks she is in a very critical position and entertains great fears for the period of delivery."[3] Degas was probably particularly concerned with her both before and after the loss of the child and made some remarkable portraits of her in the mid-sixties, including two with her husband. In one unfinished oil painting in the National Gallery of Art, Washington, D.C., she is still pregnant whereas in the large masterpiece in the Museum of Fine Arts, Boston, she has lost the child and sits protected by her Jove-like husband.

Removed as she was in Naples, Thérèse did occasionally visit Paris and sometimes thought of her relatives in America. She and her husband tried to intervene in the painter's relationship with René after he had deserted his blind wife, Estelle, and their children to elope with a neighbor to Cleveland and then to Paris. Edgar had refused to speak to René for several years, while the Morbillis tried to argue that the artist was being unreasonable and uncharitable. When Thérèse was in Paris in 1881, René asked her to persuade her husband to come there to bring about a reconciliation between the two brothers. Edmondo refused, saying that it was because the painter had "given such proof of lack of understanding that I despair of being able to use reason to persuade him."[4] In the same year Henri Musson from France was assuring his brother Michel in New Orleans of Degas's faithfulness (in supporting the cause of Estelle, whom René had deserted), "He [Edgar Degas] has never seen M. René again and he does not intend to do so."[5] By then the gap that had always existed between the American and Italian members of the Degas family had widened. Two years later Michel Musson, who was a broken and dying man, wrote to Degas, "you are créole at heart; by birth and spirit you are indeed French . . . you are not like *them . . . lazzaroni*."[6] Degas was trapped between the two camps but may have pleased Thérèse and her husband when he became reconciled with René in 1887.

Thérèse and her husband did have a few years of a certain affluence at the Palazzo Degas when they acted as guardians of two children of an uncle and aunt who had died by 1870, but eventually they quarreled with their charges and had to move to humbler rented apartments in Naples. After the death of Edmondo in 1893, Thérèse continued to live in the same circumstances but now with Edgar's support. She apparently kept herself occupied embroidering small rugs or throws, which she would often send to her brother. On 5 January 1902 he would write that one had arrived and his housekeeper Zoë had spread it on his bed. He added, "It is too pretty for me . . . its pretty green background with the veil of pink across the lace. When I think of all this work for an old bear like me, I feel guilty."[7]

1. See Loyrette, 1991, 691, n. 14.

2. Baroness Morbilli: L 50; Alfredo Morbilli: IV: 102.c; III: 93; Adelchi Morbilli: III: 91; III: 93; IV: 102.a.

3. Brown, 1991, Box I, folio 41.

4. Boggs, 1963, 276.

5. Brown, 1991, Box IV, folder 20.

6. Ibid., folder 37.

7. Pantazzi, 1988, 128.

The Musson Family in Europe, 1857–65

GERMAIN MUSSON, THE FATHER of the painter's mother, was, like Edgar's paternal grandfather, René-Hilaire Degas, an adventurer and an entrepreneur. He had been born in Cap Francis on the island of Saint Domingue (now Haiti) in 1787, apparently the descendant of French Huguenot watchmakers traced back to Pierre I Musson (1631–1709), a member of the Reformed Church in La Charité-sur-Loire in France.[1] The lives of both the artist's grandfathers were cut off from their antecedents by revolutions. Whereas with René-Hilaire Degas it was the French Revolution that had driven him abroad and left scars that, according to family tradition, made him unwilling to cross the Place de la Concorde on the few occasions he ever returned to Paris,[2] with Germain Musson it was the revolution in Saint Domingue that freed this country from France and liberated its slaves. On arriving in New Orleans, he did not seem to possess any family or any traditions aside from a possibly token Protestantism. McMullen, however, suggests that he had come to New Orleans "clearly with some capital."

Although a Protestant, Musson managed to marry into one of the more distinguished and more liberal of New Orleans families, the Rillieux, who were Catholic and headed by Don Vincent Rillieux, who died ten years before the Mussons' marriage.[3] Musson's wife was Céleste Rillieux, who was sixteen—he was twenty-three—when they married in St. Louis Cathedral in New Orleans on 8 September 1810. Their five children were also baptized at the same Cathedral.[4] As Christopher Benfey has shown, it was his wife's first cousin, a reputedly brilliant engineer, Vincent Rillieux, who had contracted the equivalent of a common-law marriage with a free woman of color.[5] One of their sons, officially a quadroon, Norbert Rillieux, born the year before the Musson-Rillieux marriage, rivalled his father in his reputation in France and Louisiana as an inventor (fig. 27). The ties of Musson and his five children to the Rillieux family may have been weakened with the early death of his wife in 1819 when she was twenty-five and he still only thirty-two.

Germain Musson must have believed his five children should be educated in Europe and, toward that end, seems to have spent considerable time in Paris himself. We do not know the details of the education of his children but the eldest, Michel, was enrolled for two semesters at the University of Göttingen from 1828 to 1829 and even engaged in a ritual duel in which neither combatant was injured.[6] Germain managed to marry his two daughters in France, the painter's mother, Célestine, to Auguste De Gas in 1832 and her sister Anne Eugénie to a comte de Rochefort, presumably by 1838 when her husband was a witness for the birth certificate for the painter's brother Achille.[7] Probably conscious of the possibility of missing his daughters when he would return to New Orleans, Musson had a portrait in chalk and wash made of them in charming Empire dress by the Swiss artist Catherine Longchamps in 1835, the year after Edgar was born (fig. 5). It may have been at the same time that he had a double portrait painted of his two younger sons—Eugène, who would have been eighteen in 1835, and Henri (fig. 50).[8] Eugène, who wrote a pamphlet about slavery, never married and finally died in the mad house at Charenton.[9] Henri—about whom Michel's eldest daughter, Désirée, wrote to her father, "What a pity that a man with such a good heart should not have been more successful in life"[10]—revealed both compassion and common sense in his letters that have survived. But it was only Michel who returned to live in New Orleans.

Even though Germain Musson's own heart may often have been drawn to France, he seems to have prospered from shipping cotton to New England and using ice and eventually granite as a ballast for his returning ships. We have difficulty now in figuring out exactly where he spent his time from the death of his wife in New Orleans in 1819 to his own death prospecting for silver in Mexico in 1853. He must have been in Paris for the courtship of the painter's mother by Auguste De Gas in 1831 leading up to the wedding in 1832. He may have been there as early as 1828 when Michel was at Göttingen, and he was certainly there for the baptism of Edgar in 1834. His real money-making may have been accomplished before 1828 and to have been given physical form in New Orleans by the commercial building he had constructed of the New England granite he used as the ballast for his ships after they emptied their cargos of cotton (fig. 62). There is some disagreement about the dating of this building—but none about the assertiveness of its architecture against the other buildings of New Orleans. Henry Hobson Richardson is said to have been strongly influenced by its architecture as he grew up in New Orleans, with the "fort" diagonally across Canal Street from both his father's house and office.[11] Consequently, Germain Musson influenced another great artist beside the fortunes of his grandson.

The survival of correspondence is such an accidental thing that it must be an error to put too much weight upon it over 150 years later. But there is evidence that Germain Musson was not universally beloved. The painter's Neapolitan grandfather was often exasperated with Musson for trying to persuade him to give his eldest son, the painter's father, Auguste, more than his share of the Degas fortune. On 9 December 1835 he wrote, "Mr Musson has written me a letter with regard to Auguste which I cannot describe because my pen refuses to put it on paper. I cannot imagine what reasons Auguste has given him for overwhelming me with unjust reproaches, of abandoning him, of keeping his money, etc."[12] Another is in a gossipy letter in the correspondence of a quite different family in which a nephew on a visit to New Orleans in 1833 describes for his uncle, "a most magnificent soirée" given by M. Hermann for 350 persons, for which fireworks were planned but did not materialize because of the weather. He told his uncle, "it was no doubt the finest party that had ever been given here, his commodious house, splendid furniture . . . making it as agreeable as it could possibly have been made." By contrast, he points out that "M. Musson has also been giving two parties since he is here, but does not seem to become very popular here in spite of his soirées—the fact is, that his present good circumstances have given him a sort of arrogance, which his former circumstances will by no means admit. He has thus broken with many of his former friends, who do not stand equally high in point of fortune."[13] There is probably enough truth in both documents to suggest M. Musson's social ambitions and his capacity to irritate those people he knew. Curiously, his greatest claim to fame was to be in the hands of his infant grandson.

Germain Musson died in 1853 when Degas was emerging from his lycée. Although Degas seemed to have disliked his aunt Eugénie de Rochefort, he did seem to feel some responsibility and presumably also some affection for his two Musson uncles Eugène and Henri who lived largely in France. But the real head of the Mussons after the death of Germain was his eldest son, Michel, who had returned to New Orleans, entered into the cotton exchange, married an amiable wife and produced three surviving daughters, all of whom enter into the fortunes of Edgar Degas in relation to New Orleans. When Michel sent his wife, two of his daughters, and a grandchild to France during the summer of 1863, his brothers were unable to look after them,[14] and it fell to the De Gas family to be attentive to them during the two years they spent in France.

1. Francis Roux-Devillas, "Les Musson, ascendants maternels d'Edgar Degas," *Cahiers du Centre de Généalogie Protestante*, no. 4 (4th trimester, 1983): 339–47.

2. Fevre, 1949, 21.

3. Mrs. Thomas Nelson Carter Bruns, compiler, *Louisiana Portraits*, Historical Activities Committee of The National Society of The Colonial Dames of America in the State of Louisiana, 1975, 222.

4. Records examined by Victoria Cooke.

5. Benfey, 1997, 124–33.

6. "Louisiana Students in German Universities in the Nineteenth Century," *Genealogical Review* (Baton Rouge, La., June 1967).

7. Lemoisne I, 1946–49, 225, n. 7.

8. Presumed destroyed.

9. Eugène Musson, *Letter to Napoleon III on Slavery in the Southern States by a Creole of Louisiana* (London, 1862); Brown, 1991, Box III, folder 7a.

10. Brown, 1991, Box II, folder 41.

11. Reference provided by the late John Coolidge.

12. Raimondi, 1958, 9 December 1835, 107.

13. Letter of Carl Cohn to his uncle, 7 March 1833, Historic New Orleans Collection. The reference was provided by Mary Strickland and Victoria Cooke.

14. Brown, 1991, Box I, folder 33c, Henri Musson writes his brother Michel that he will be unable to look after Michel's family when they arrive in France in the summer of 1863 but that Edgar, Marguerite, and René De Gas will.

7. *Désirée Musson*

ca. 1857
Pencil on paper
$10\frac{3}{8} \times 8\frac{7}{8}$ inches (26.6 × 22.75 cm)
Collection of Mrs. T. Ham, Virginia

THERE IS A NATURAL DESIRE to attach unidentified portraits by Degas to particular people whom he knew and might have painted or drawn. In this respect the very brevity of his relationship with New Orleans—either as a visitor or host—and its distance from Paris makes this exercise particularly tempting. Disappointingly, however, often the style of these works indicates that it is improbable that Degas could have executed these portraits at any time he could have seen the sitters. On the other hand, this can also be a challenge to anyone as indefatigable as James B. Byrnes, the former director of the New Orleans Museum of Art, who organized the exhibition *Edgar Degas: His Family and Friends in New Orleans* in 1965. He knew this drawing of a young woman—bred to be dignified, slightly troubled, only barely adult—and believed it could be Désirée,[1] the eldest of the children of Michel Musson.

We know that in 1863, when Désirée was already twenty-five and Estelle twenty, Désirée went to France with her mother, her sister Estelle, and Estelle's baby to escape the miseries of Union-occupied New Orleans during the Civil War.[2] If the question of age can be forgotten and this head compared with the watercolor Degas made of these two Musson cousins with their mother two years later (cat. 8), some justification can be found for the hypothesis that this is a portrait of either of these two Musson sisters. The style of her hair, parted in the center and pulled into a chignon behind her ear, is consistent with the hair of all three women and particularly close to that of the seated Estelle. In addition there is some similarity in the features, particularly in the slitted almond-shaped eyes weighted down by heavy eyelids and set back well under faintly quizzical brows. Although the mouths are not as visible in the watercolor, it is not impossible, particularly in a happier moment for the Mussons than exile in France would have been, that they too would have an incipient cupid's bow for an upper lip. As a result it does not seem irresponsible to consider some relationship between the drawing and these cousins of Degas.

FIG. 64. *Estelle Musson*, photograph of a drawing, ca. 1860. Collection of Marie Estelle Moyer.

FIG. 65. Edgar Degas, *Giovanna and Giulia Bellelli*, ca. 1865–66, pencil, 11 × 7⅞ in. Museum Boymans-van Beuningen, Rotterdam.

There are still some difficulties to overcome. One is that this young girl appears younger and more naïve than even Estelle would have been when they arrived in France in 1863. In the pencil drawing there is still baby fat from the cheek bones to her chin, and the expression is faintly disdainful, suggesting inexperience rather than complacency. Neither Désirée nor Estelle could have looked this young after 1863. Byrnes also publishes a photograph of a drawing of Estelle (fig. 64) for which he proposes a date of about 1860 when she would have been seventeen.[3] This rather matronly image is, however, more probably 1862, not long before her husband was killed and her daughter born, and is therefore quite close to the watercolor he did of the three at Bourg-en-Bresse. It nevertheless shows an encouragingly strong family resemblance to this drawing in the exhibition.

There is still another hurdle. By the time of the arrival of the Mussons in France, Degas was already in the process of giving up the style of this drawing, where everything is in low relief, with little indication of color and few dark accents. This way of seeing and drawing belongs to the period of his beautiful studies of Italian cousins—the two Bellelli girls, for the large painting *The Bellelli Family* and, in particular, for the slightly later painting *The Bellelli Sisters*[4]— and not to the more animated style he was developing between 1863 and 1865. (A preparatory drawing of his two Bellelli cousins [fig. 65], about 1860 when they were about ten, shows how aware he was by then of the coarsening physically and the hardening psychologically of little girls as they matured.)

But Byrnes found his answer and defense in the archives given by various descendants of the Musson family to Tulane University. In a letter of 1863 to his uncle Michel Musson, describing the arrival of the uncle's family in Paris, René

De Gas wrote a sentence so short that it is easily overlooked, "Didi [one of the many family nicknames of Désirée] is indeed better looking than she was in 1857."[5] We might question René's capacity to judge the appearance of Désirée in 1863 when he was only sixteen, but we become even more skeptical about his judgment in 1857 when he was twelve. Of course he was probably parroting his elders; but he must at least have been certain that he had seen Désirée then, presumably in Paris. But in 1857 the artist was in Italy. The other possibility is that at the age of nineteen Désirée Musson had come to Europe with very close and enduring friends of the Musson family in New Orleans, Mme Ducros and her son-in-law and daughter, M. and Mme Millaudon, and her Beauregard grandchildren, the children of Mme Millaudon's first marriage (see "New Orleans Friends Visiting Europe" in this catalogue section). We know that Degas made portraits of Mme Ducros, the Millaudon husband and wife, and the Beauregard twin girls and shipped them from Italy to his father in France so that they had arrived by 13 August 1858,[6] so that it is not impossible that he made this drawing as well and that it is nineteen-year-old Désirée feeling alone in a foreign land.

1. In Byrnes in New Orleans, 1965, see 53, caption for pl. XI, as *Madame Estelle Musson,* with notes: "Boggs, in letter, "Désirée Musson (?), Byrnes, "Désirée Musson, ca. 1857 (?)."

2. Ibid., 46, 96, n. 16, suggests that Désirée had already been in Europe in 1857.

3. Ibid., 40, fig. 12.

4. Laure, baroness Bellelli, the painter's paternal aunt and godmother, had two daughters whom Degas painted and drew frequently at their apartment in Florence between 1856 and 1862; in 1862, when he probably painted *The Bellelli Sisters* (L 126, Los Angeles County Museum of Art), for which fig. 65 was a study, Giovanna was thirteen and Giulia eleven.

5. De Gas–Musson, Box I, folder 34c, letter of 24 June 1863.

6. See Lemoisne, 1946–49, no. 41, for excerpts from a letter of 13 August 1858 from Auguste De Gas to the painter, describing his response to the works that had been shipped from Italy.

8. *Mme Michel Musson and Her Daughters Estelle and Désirée*

1865
Watercolor with touches of charcoal and brush and red chalk wash, heightened with touches of white gouache, over graphite on cream wove paper
$13\frac{5}{8} \times 10\frac{3}{8}$ (34.8 × 26.6 cm)
The Art Institute of Chicago, Margaret Day Blake Collection (1949.20)
Lemoisne supp. 43

AFTER DEGAS'S DEATH IN 1917, his own works were inventoried for sale and some withdrawn for the heirs—his brother René and the children of his sister Marguerite. Certain works were clearly retained because of sentimental family associations.[1] This was true of the watercolor drawing of the three Musson women from New Orleans at Bourg-en-Bresse in January 1865: the painter's aunt by marriage Mme Michel Musson, born Odile Longer in New Orleans, her daughter Désirée (standing), and her daughter Estelle Balfour (seated), who had recently been widowed in the Civil War. After the death of Degas, René, long remarried with a second family of children, was not apt to have been anxious to be reminded—by the sadness of the seated Estelle Balfour—of the pain that he had inflicted upon her by marrying then deserting her and their children. Instead it was chosen by one of Marguerite's sons, Henri Fevre, who may have selected it because he remembered his mother in exile in Buenos Aires, talking about the arrival in France of their New Orleans aunt and her two daughters and the melancholy they experienced so far from their American roots. Marguerite had always expressed a special sympathy and affection for these Mussons.

The Mussons had come to France to escape the Union occupation of New Orleans and had gone to Bourg-en-Bresse in Burgundy because a physician had recommended the locale as a restorative for Mme Musson's health.[2] For a group portrait of the three women, Degas chose an expressive range of browns to gray and black washes, which he used over a delicate pencil drawing. In hue it is not unlike the portrait of the head of his sister Thérèse (cat. 6) in a more opaque oil paint on canvas. The selection of the watercolor for this portrait was probably made because the medium and papers were easier to carry on a train or coach than oil paints, canvas, and an easel for the four hundred kilometers from Paris to Bourg-en-Bresse. Accepting the practicality of the decision, the very translucency of the watercolor, its fluidity, the emotional nuances it can suggest were exploited by Degas to convey the pathos of his aunt and two

cousins, each isolated psychologically and physically but gathered together in the intimacy of a strange room in which they are interlopers like the books piled untidily on the flamboyantly carved mantelpiece. Instead of the single, unyielding impression of Thérèse De Gas, we are confronted with a similar sadness but greater variety in the expression of it as the three women pose for their nephew or cousin.

A significant figure in the Musson group is not unexpectedly the mother (fig. 51). The De Gas children—Edgar, Thérèse, Marguerite, René, if not Achille, who was largely abroad as a naval ensign—welcomed her as a replacement for their own mother.[3] To some degree, as we read the letters exchanged between France and New Orleans, she played that role, worrying about Thérèse's pregnancy,[4] advising her husband through a letter from Désirée about how to respond to René, whom she described as "a charming boy, full of intelligence, ambition, and heart," in his eagerness to go to America.[5] They in turn worried about her health, for example the hand that hurt so much it had to be treated with opium, and assured their uncle, "As for the cold, they are well housed and well heated,"[6] and shared Désirée's hope that Edgar's visit would restore her spirits.[7] Perhaps because none of her blood ran in the artist's veins, no one has been very curious about her own background. We gather that her French-born father and New Orleans–born mother[8] lived in a beautiful house on Esplanade in New Orleans with their many children and were known for their hospitality. It is a shock to discover that she was born in New Orleans as late as 1819,[9] only fifteen years before Edgar. In the watercolor of her with her daughters at Bourg-en-Bresse, she was therefore only forty-six. Although it had been intended originally to send only Désirée and the pregnant Estelle to France, it was decided that their mother should accompany them because of her health.[10] And after she returned to New Orleans there were efforts to find cures for her, even in New York.[11] But she died of Bright's disease on 31 August 1871.[12] It may be sentimental to suggest it, but her absence might have been a factor in the later unhappy history of her husband, children, and even grandchildren.

With her death, the nearest thing to a substitute for the mother the Mussons would find is another figure in this watercolor, the standing Désirée, the eldest child of her generation. Even with her mother living while they were at Bourg-en-Bresse, she assumed many responsibilities, corresponding with their father, worrying about money,[13] even teaching English to supplement their income.[14] Since she was twenty-five when she arrived in France, it was probably already expected that she would remain a spinster and be the backbone in many respects of her family. There were two compliments that the De Gas family paid Désirée in the surviving correspondence. One was on the beauty of her hands. Although nothing is ever said to suggest any vanity on her part, we notice that in the watercolor she has slightly puffed white sleeves that protrude from her gray dress and draw attention to her hands and that her right hand is self-consciously placed on the mantelpiece. After all Marguerite De Gas wrote to her uncle Michel, Désirée's father, at the end of 1863 about Edgar's proposed visit to Bourg-en-Bresse for the new year that, "he is bringing lots of pencils and paper to draw the hands of Didy [the family name for Désirée] in every position because it is rare to find such a pretty model."[15]

The second compliment paid to Désirée is more difficult to assess. Edgar made it in writing to his uncle Michel on 25 June 1863 of her in relation to her mother, "Didi [Désirée] est tout à fait son second," which as translated into English can have a double entendre, either applicable to Désirée and his aunt Odile—one that she was another version of her mother, the other that she served her as a lieutenant.[16] As her mother's successor she saw her family through the mother's death; the desertion of Estelle and her children by René in 1878[17]; the death the same year of her other sister, Mathilde Musson Bell, who had remained in New Orleans when the other women in the family went to France; the protection of at least the Catholicism of Mathilde's four surviving children with a Protestant father[18]; the adoption of Estelle's children by their grandfather Michel Musson in 1883[19]; the breakdown of their father followed by his death in 1885.[20] She even continued as a companion to Estelle. During these years there is at least some expression of independence in her demand for a separate income.[21] When she died in 1902, an obituary probably prepared by a friend or family member read: "In the death of Miss Désirée Musson one of the best known and most beloved figures in Creole circles has passed away, Miss Musson, in her more than three-score years, crowned with a wealth of snow-white hair, still bore evidence of a soft and winning girlhood of long ago. She was distinctly a type of the old regime and the popularity that she enjoyed as a belle in the beautiful home of her father, years ago, she sustained as only a kind and noble nature can to the end in her venerable years. She was particularly a friend and counselor to the young who often gathered at her home on Esplanade Avenue. Miss Musson's mother was one of the numerous Longer sisters, prominent at the time."[22] So to the end Désirée was still a little in her mother's shadow.

1. For the inventorying of the collection and the sales see New York, 1997.

2. Brown, 1991, Box I, folder 35.

3. Loyrette, 1991, 289, 730, n. 141.

4. Brown, 1991, Box I, folder 41.

5. Ibid., folder 42.

6. Ibid., folder 47.

7. Ibid., folder 14.

8. According to Bruns, 1975, the mother of Odile Longer was born Marie Mannette de Buys (ca. 1792–1886), daughter of Gaspar Melchior de Buys and Eulalie le Jan, who married Pierre Victor Amédée Longer (ca. 1785–1841) of Rouen, France. A portrait of her by Jean J. Vaudechamp of 1836 was in the collection of Harry McCall, New Orleans.

9. St. Louis Cathedral Baptismal Record.

10. Brown, 1991, Box I, folders 33a, b.

11. Ibid., folder 28.

12. Ibid., Box II, folder 33a.

13. Ibid., Box I, folders 34e, 37; Box II, folder 12f.

14. Ibid., folder 70.

15. Ibid., folder 49.

16. Ibid., Box II, folder 31.

17. Ibid., folders 15b, 16.

18. Ibid., folder 30i; Box IV, folder 23e.

19. Ibid., folders 39, 40, 41.

20. Ibid., folder 48.

21. Ibid., folder 47.

22. This text was found by Victoria Cooke in the family papers and is probably a draft obituary that does not seem to have been printed in a New Orleans newspaper.

9. Four Studies of a Baby's Head (Joe Balfour ?)
ca. 1864
Pencil on white, light wove paper
$12\frac{5}{8} \times 8\frac{1}{2}$ inches (4.5 × 3.3 cm)
The Minneapolis Institute of Arts,
The John de Laittre Fund (25.33)

IN THE WATERCOLOR of the Mussons at Bourg-en-Bresse (cat. 8) one member of this family group is absent—Estelle Musson Balfour's baby, Joe [Josephine], born three weeks after her father's death on 4 October 1862, and not baptised until 19 May 1863. As a baby of seven months, she had been brought by her mother, her grandmother and her aunt Désirée from New Orleans to France—arriving in New York on 4 June 1863 and at Southampton in England by the 16th of the same month. She was in Paris by the 24th. Very soon the Mussons moved to the more tranquil setting of Bourg-en-Bresse in Burgundy, where this baby must have provided a welcomed diversion to the mournful sobriety of the three women in exile.

Degas paid two trips to Bourg-en-Bresse to celebrate the holiday of the Epiphany on 6 January in both 1864 and 1865. It was more probably on the first trip that he would have made such drawings of the baby girl at fourteen months. In addition, although we cannot be certain that this infant is Joe Balfour, it is likely to come from the time when her aunt Désirée wrote to New Orleans, "Edgar has made several sketches of little Joe, but he is not happy with them. It is impossible to make her be still for more than five minutes."[1] That very unpredictable movement would have been part of her appeal to the artist. Degas drew this baby, whether or not she is Joe Balfour, with a snubbed nose, richly long eyelashes and tousled hair as if she were sleeping innocently in the upper two drawings and only in the lower two suggested the independent action involved in holding her head upright. Although she is not very active in these sketches, Degas placed the four views of her head on the page in a way that implies change. We can understand Edgar's frustration but also his pleasure in the sense of the baby's character emerging miraculously from her very helplessness in her defenseless sleep. Her vulnerability is emphasized by the apparent weight of her cranium, and the fragility of the back of her neck needed to support it. In the second drawing from the top, the eyelashes and eyebrows are romantically darkened as if to suggest dreaming, even in infancy. He drew her very tenderly, as if she represented hope in that house of mourning.

The Tulane archives record that on 31 August 1864 Joe at almost two learned to say, "Bonjour René De Gas" to her future stepfather.[2]

1. Brown, 1991, Box II, folder 16, letter of 5 January 1865.
2. Ibid., folder 9.

10. *Estelle Musson Balfour*

1865
Oil on canvas
$10\frac{1}{2} \times 8\frac{1}{2}$ inches (26.9 × 21.8 cm)
Walters Art Gallery, Baltimore (Inv. 3110)
Lemoisne supp. 40

THIS SMALL PAINTING OF ESTELLE against a barren clump of trees might easily have been painted by Degas very soon after he returned from Bourg-en-Bresse in January 1865. The trees are as he could have remembered them in the surrounding wintry countryside where they could have appeared visually responsive to the unrelieved sadness of Estelle's face. In this canvas there is none of the histrionic appeal for sympathy of Chicago's watercolor of her with her mother and sister (cat. 8) or of the pencil drawing of her seated in an armchair alone, reaching out for support (cat. 11). She does not confront us, even turning away and looking downward, her eyes deeply shadowed and lowered as if they were seeing nothing at all. Her withdrawn chin, the thinness and tightness of her upper lip, as well as the untidy strands of hair, suggest that she is very near tears. When compared with the unhappy face of Thérèse De Gas Morbilli (cat. 6), her features appear cramped rather than expansive. She has lost any sense of her own self-worth, to have given herself over humbly to despair. Degas probably had explained and forgiven this in writing to her father shortly after their arrival in France, "As for Estelle, poor little woman, one cannot look at her without thinking that that face filled the eyes of a dying man."[1]

Estelle must have discouraged the efforts of her family. We do not have any evidence that she had found consolation for the death of her young husband in the birth of their daughter, nor any comfort from the companionship of her mother and sister, nor readiness to take pleasure in the visits of the members of the Degas family with their gifts, for example Edgar's "toys, bon bons, marrons glacées etc," intended to captivate her.[2] Her depression must have been absolute and difficult to penetrate.

Presumably to René in his very youth—by now almost twenty—and his naiveté, it was a challenge that he was to sustain. After all, he accompanied her with her mother and sister back to New Orleans in 1865, persuaded his brother Achille to join him to start an importing business in 1866 and, in spite of the

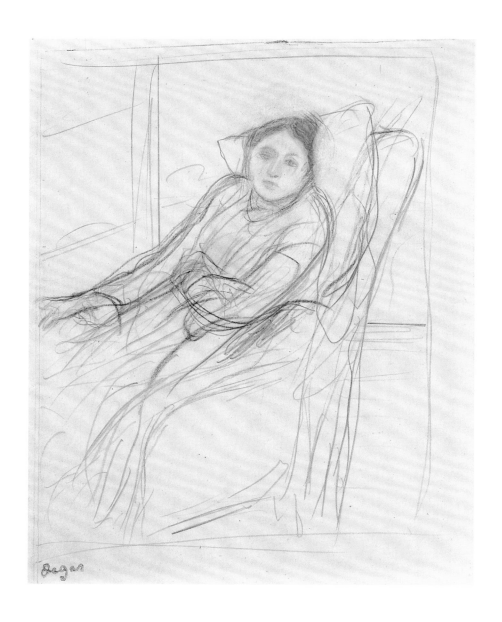

11. *Young Woman in an Armchair*
(drawing of Estelle Musson Balfour)
ca. 1865
Pencil and pastel
$9\frac{3}{8} \times 7\frac{5}{8}$ inches (24 × 19.5 cm)
Private Collection, The Bahamas

fact that Estelle was beginning to lose her eyesight and against the advice of those who were older and wiser, married her in 1869.

It is curious that Henry Walters, the son of the Baltimore collector upon whose collections the Walters Art Gallery is based, in adding to that collection after his father's death, should have bought this painting from Mary Cassatt in 1903.[3] This artist friend of Degas may have known the subject and sold it because it made her particularly indignant with René De Gas, a man she very much disliked, who, in deserting Estelle, left his wife to confront such misery alone again. She may even have believed it appropriate that it should go to America.

In painting the three Musson women formally arranged as a daguerreotype on that New Year's visit to Bourg-en-Bresse in January 1865, Degas also almost inevitably made some informal sketches.[4] One is this drawing of Estelle, who, instead of crouching on a stool as she does in the other work, huddles against an armchair, supported and protected by its back and generous pillow. She is less valiant here but her position and the dark smudges for her eyes make her appealing. Even the looseness and repetitions of the pencil strokes are tearful.

René De Gas, who was eighteen when he first met Estelle, immediately felt tenderly toward his young cousin. On 4 June 1863 he wrote to her father, his uncle Michel: "I can't tell you with what happiness we have made Estelle's acquaintance. She inspires so much sympathy, she has so much sweetness in her sadness that she made us all become attached to her in an instant . . . I hope for some good results for Estelle from this trip; one sees that the depth of her character is gaiety; in the midst of her sorrow she gives hints of a wit loving to laugh; & we notice each day a favorable progress."[5] Unfortunately the sorrows were so deep that the gaiety was probably hardly exposed during Estelle's two years in France. Nevertheless, from this drawing of her a year and a half after René wrote this to her uncle, we can see that Degas shared his brother's compassion for this young cousin who reaches out for his and our sympathy.

There is one possible happier interpretation of her outstretched arm—that it is directed toward the toddler, her daughter Joe.

1. Lemoisne I, 1946–49, 73; Brown, 1991, Box II, folder 31.

2. Brown, 1991, Box II, folder 16

3. *A Selection of Nineteenth-Century Paintings, The Walters Art Gallery, Baltimore* (Baltimore, 1965), no. 22, based on the entry in George A. Lucas, *The Diary of an American Art Agent in Paris, 1857–1909,* ed. Lilian M. C. Randall (Princeton, 1979), 913, 20 April 1903; 914, 22 April 1903.

4. There is also somewhere a tiny drawing of the head of Mme Musson that was owned by John Rewald.

5. Brown, 1991, Box I, folder 34d.

New Orleans Friends Visiting Europe

THE MUSSONS WERE NOT the only Americans to cross the Atlantic and pay their respects to the De Gas family in Italy or Paris. Paul-André Lemoisne (1875–1964), a curator of graphic arts at the Bibliothèque Nationale in Paris, in his pursuit of the artist's background, was able to read and quote from some letters the artist's father had written to Edgar when his son was living in Italy between 1856 and 1859.[1] In a letter of 13 August 1858, the father was unembarrassed about giving his gifted son advice. He was enchanted with Edgar's drawing of two little girls, Gabrielle and Angèle Beauregard (born 1848), the twin daughters of Mme Benjamin Laurent Millaudon (1826–1912) by her late husband, a cousin of an important Civil War general, Pierre Gustave Toutant Beauregard, all from New Orleans. The drawing, which the artist's father specifically mentioned, is not believed to have survived in any form—but there is a photograph of a painting of the twins (fig. 66) which is otherwise, however, almost equally unknown.[2] In the same letter De Gas *père* with characteristic frankness wrote that on the other hand he was not satisfied with the three portraits of M. and Mme Millaudon and Mme Millaudon's mother Mme Ducros (1808–96)—the stepfather, mother, and grandmother of the Beauregard twins. Lemoisne, who had actually paid a visit to Degas in 1895, had published the first—small—monograph on the artist in 1912, and spent much of his lifetime accumulating and organizing material on the artist and his works, which would be published after the Second World War as the only *catalogue raisonné* of the paintings of Degas,[3] was, like all of us, eager to find material that could be related to New Orleans. In the 1930s he and his wife carried on a correspondence with the descendants of René De Gas and Estelle Musson, which today is part of the Tulane University archives.[4]

FIG. 66. Edgar Degas, *Gabrielle and Angèle Beauregard*, 1857–59, oil on canvas, 8 × 10⅝ in. Location unknown. Lemoisne 45.

Naturally Lemoisne wanted to find the portraits that hadn't satisfied the artist's father. His solution was that the husband and wife—"M. et Mdm M." in the letter—were in the painting *Portraits* (L 41, fig. 67), now at the Hermitage Museum, Saint Petersburg, where it is called *Interior with Two Figures*.[5] He dated the work about 1857 to 1859, a decade before Degas would paint his other very different domestic drama, *The Interior* (L 348, Philadelphia Museum of Art). Lemoisne's error—because it *was* a mistake—was that he ignored the group of notebooks given to the Bibliothèque Nationale de France by the artist's brother René when Lemoisne was already its curator of graphic arts and would be the author of an article in the *Gazette des Beaux-Arts* of 1921 welcom-

ing the gift.[6] Although he essentially disregarded the contents of those notebooks, he did give a reference for a compositional study, Reff notebook 23, page 34 (fig. 68),[7] for *Interior with Two Figures* without investigating any evidence for dating it. There is also a study for the impatient gentleman at the right in Reff notebook 22, page 119 (fig. 69), which Lemoisne neglected. The chronological spread of the drawings in these two notebooks according to their careful cataloguer, Professor Theodore Reff of Columbia University, could not be greater than 1867 to 1874. It is reasonable to assume that about 1868 is the date for these drawings and the painting.

It is still not impossible that Lemoisne was correct about the identification of the sitters in *Interior with Two Figures*—and only wrong about the dates. The Ducros/Beauregard/Millaudon clan seem to have been close friends of the Mussons over a long period of time. We first hear of them when they visited the De Gas family in Italy and Paris in the late 1850s and obviously encouraged the young artist by sitting for him in Rome. On 4 November 1858 M. Millaudon sent a long letter to Edgar, suggesting a particular intimacy with the family since he seems to have known that the painter's brother Achille had barely escaped expulsion from the navy as a midshipman in July of that year "for unruliness and insubordination"[8]; Millaudon wrote the artist that his stepson Philippe Beauregard was becoming very close to René De Gas, but more significant, he added reassuringly, "I have seen your brother Achille who is in good shape now and gives the impression of being a solid fellow."[9] Our next record seems to be when Mme Millaudon's son by her first marriage, Philippe Beauregard (he could have been sixteen), visited the Mussons at the De Gas apartment as soon as they arrived in Paris from New Orleans in 1863, suggesting on his part an assurance of welcome from the Mussons as well as his concern for their welfare. As Degas described it to his uncle Michel, "At 7.00 in the

FIG. 67. Degas, *Interior with Two Figures*, ca. 1869, oil on canvas, $23\frac{1}{4} \times 28\frac{3}{4}$ in. State Hermitage museum, St. Petersburg, Russia. Lemoisne 41.

FIG. 68. Edgar Degas, Notebook 23, page 34. Bibliothèque Nationale de France, Paris.

FIG. 69. Edgar Degas, Notebook 22, page 119. Bibliothèque Nationale de France, Paris.

evening the day before yesterday a loud ring of the door-bell announced the arrival of M. Philippe Beauregard . . . the mischievousness was already what one would have expected."[10] He was actually not a stranger to Degas, to whom René had written on 5 September 1859, "And you painted the portrait of Master Philippe, not without difficulty, I'm sure."[11] On 13 March 1873, about the time that Degas left New Orleans, René wrote to Michel Musson, for some years his father-in-law and now widowed, "The Millaudons have come to dinner."[12] On 6 September of the same year he wrote again that Désirée was not well and that Mme Millaudon has been coming over every evening.[13] These occasions are just after the painter's visit to New Orleans and suggest that he would have met the Ducros/Beauregard/Millaudon family with some frequency there. On the other hand, considering the amount of work he did in New Orleans, painting portraits of members of his family in what he considered impossible conditions,[14] it is unlikely that he would have painted Mme Millaudon or her children then—but he might have done so in Paris in the 1860s.

To agree that there is *any* possibility that Mme Millaudon was painted in the canvas that is now in Saint Petersburg, we have to make the assumption that the Ducros/Beauregard/Millaudon clan went to France more than for the one extended stay in the late fifties and could have posed for Degas about 1868.[15] The presence of Philippe Beauregard in Paris in 1863 makes it seem possible. Roulhac Toledano, married to a descendant of one of the Beauregard twins, has pointed out in an unpublished manuscript that in 1867 or 1868 the father of Laurent Millaudon died, leaving $2,000,000, a gigantic sum then, which would have made it possible for the Millaudons to have been in Europe in the late sixties.[16] The second assumption has to be that when the painting was accessible at all to the public, at the second sale in December 1918 of the artist's own works after his death[17] or after that in the collection of the dentist Dr. Georges Viau[18] someone who would have known the sitters—and it is difficult to think that this could have been anyone but René De Gas who was living in Paris and did not die until 1921—could absentmindedly have identified Mme Millaudon. Perhaps someone else—even M. Lemoisne—might have overheard this remark but did not remember its source.

James B. Byrnes in his catalogue for the 1965 Degas exhibition in New Orleans reproduced photographs of the Ducros/Beaugregard/Millaudon family. At one point he placed a photograph of about 1895 of four women on the steps of the house in the Millaudon plantation (fig. 70), with the woman at the left identified as a Beauregard twin with her daughter in front of her, their grand-

mother or great-grandmother, Mme Ducros, in the center, and their mother or grandmother, Mme Millaudon, at the right (figs. 70, 71).[19] In that 1965 catalogue the photograph faces an oil sketch (fig. 72) for *Interior with Two Figures*.[20] Although Mme Millaudon must have been about seventy in the photograph, she is so startlingly like the oil sketch in the position of her head and the formations of her eyes, as well as in the largeness of her ears that it is difficult to argue that Mme Millaudon could not have posed for the figure in the painting, particularly if she had been in France in the late sixties. Byrnes suggested Mme Ducros as the model, but the same photograph of her (fig. 73)—admittedly in her nineties—shows a thin, skeletal face with a very long nose and an angular, sprightly manner, which is very unlike her more lethargic and sensual daughter. There is still one problem, however, in identifying this figure as Mme Millaudon. There is a pencil drawing for the standing female figure,[21] which unfortunately shows a much harsher, even brutalized face, but it must have been based upon another model whom Degas decided should be replaced by someone softer and more refined like Mme Millaudon for the oil on canvas.

If we return to *Interior with Two Figures,* we must admit that it is more genre than portraiture. Mme Millaudon, if it is she, acts the part of the prettily dressed but aggrieved woman who seems to withdraw into a cocoon as she stands in the exotic Parisian drawing room well apart from the irritated gentleman looking out the window. One thing that is fairly certain is that the male figure is not her second husband, Laurent Millaudon. The irascible man seems younger and might have been posed by Philippe Beauregard, her son by her

FIG. 70. *Four Generations of the Ducros Family on the porch of the Millaudon Plantation,* ca. 1895. Mme Ducros, center: her daughter, Mme Millaudon at right; granddaughter Angèle Beauregard Hall Chiapella, and great-granddaughter Lulu Hall, seated on steps. Courtesy of James B. Byrnes.

FIG. 71. Mme Millaudon, detail of fig. 70.

FIG. 72. Edgar Degas, *Debout en Manteau Noir (Mme Ducros),* 1858, oil on canvas, 13 × 9½ in. Musée Marmottan. Lemoisne 43.

FIG. 73. Mme Elina de Vezin Ducros, detail of fig. 70.

first marriage, then just into his twenties, but, since the scene is pure fiction and not portraiture, it could have been any friend of Degas.

It seems appropriate here to record a further connection between Degas and M. Millaudon, who had sent him that comforting letter about his brothers in 1858. Christopher Benfey, who has explored Degas's American connections in New Orleans in his *Degas in New Orleans*,[22] has described Millaudon as a sound, established businessman. He wrote of "the financier Laurent Millaudon, the major developer of the new town of Carrollton (upriver from the residential Garden District) and the head of the suburban railroad into New Orleans,"[23] who probably showed the tramway design by Émile Lamm to Degas. This would be when Degas visited New Orleans the winter of 1872 to 1873 and wrote enthusiastically about the tram to his great friend Henri Rouart.[24] But Benfey for the first time points out another more surprising connection between Degas and Millaudon, which they may never have confessed to each other. M. Millaudon early became a patron of Norbert Rillieux, Degas's distinguished second cousin who was an inventor and a "quadroon."[25] The footsteps of Rillieux and the painter rarely overlapped,[26] but the painter could not have easily ignored the prominence of this man with his maternal grandmother's last name.

1. Lemoisne I, 1946–49, 19; Loyrette, 1991, 133, n. 233.

2. L 45, where it states that they are daughters (rather than granddaughters as they were) of Mme Ducros; their mother is Mme Millaudon. The painting has not been in a public sale or exhibition in recent years.

3. Lemoisne, 1912; Lemoisne, 1946–49.

4. Brown, 1991, Box V, folders 3a, 4–7.

5. Albert Kostenevich, *Hidden Treasures Revealed* (New York, 1995), no. 14: 60–63, calls it *Interior with Two Figures* and dates it ca. 1869.

6. Lemoisne, 1921.

7. All references to Degas's notebooks in the Bibliothèque Nationale de France, Paris, are designated by the numbers used in Reff, 1976.

8. Loyrette in Paris, Ottawa, New York, 1988, no. 4, 64.

9. Loyrette, 1991, 702, n. 283.

10. Brown, 1991, Box II, folder 31.

11. Paris, Ottawa, New York, 53, from an otherwise unpublished letter.

12. Brown, 1991, Box II, folder 52a.

13. Ibid., folder 56.

14. Appendix II, letter to Frölich.

15. Byrnes in New Orleans, 65–66, brings up the possibility of another trip in the sixties.

16. Toledano, 1995, courtesy of the author, with thanks to James B. Byrnes, who conveyed the information.

17. Vente II, no. 13, 13 December 1918.

18. Dr. Viau's collection was a great one, particularly strong in the work of Degas. He was encouraged by Vollard, who was often his dealer, and seems to have enjoyed showing his collection to interested visitors. The first sale of his collection after his death was at Drouot in Paris, 11 December 1942.

19. Byrnes in New Orleans, 66, figs. 32, 34 [*sic*].

20. Ibid., 67, pl. XIX.

21. Vente IV, 100.b, collection Mr. and Mrs. E. V. Thaw (or Morgan Library).

22. Benfey, 1997, 124–34.

23. Ibid., 87.

24. Appendix II, letter to Rouart.

25. Benfey, 1997. 131.

26. There was a significant age difference between the two men. Norbert Rillieux was twenty-eight when Degas was born in Paris, one year after Rillieux had returned to New Orleans from his studies, teaching and research in France. It is not known when Rillieux went back to France to stay, but it was probably about the time that Degas was settling back into Paris after his period in Italy, probably too preoccupied to have thought of this cousin. Rillieux was not in New Orleans, of course, for Degas's one visit during the winter of 1872 to 1873. After that both were living and working in Paris until the death of Rillieux in 1894. So far the name of Norbert Rillieux has not been found in any of Degas's notebooks or correspondence.

12. *Marie Lucie Millaudon*

1865–69
Black chalk
$9\frac{3}{4} \times 7$ inches (25 × 18 cm)
Museum Boymans-van Beuningen, Rotterdam
(Cat. No. F II 218)

THIS DRAWING IS A STUDY for a painting (fig. 74, L 45, owner unknown) that Lemoisne dated incorrectly as 1857 to 1859 and identified, as he had the woman in *Interior with Two Figures* (fig. 67, L 41), as Mme Millaudon of New Orleans. Again there is no doubt that his date is wrong. Quite aside from the question of the style of the artist's work, the coiffure and dress provide clues that the painting—there is less such evidence in the drawing—must come from the second half of the 1860s. Her hair, with the chignon raised higher in the painting than in the drawing, and her dress with its fitted top, loose sleeves, and full skirt gathered beneath a wide belt, which emphasizes her small waist, can be found in paintings by other artists working between 1865 and 1870, like Monet and Tissot.[1] Particularly characteristic of that period is the cut of the armholes low over the shoulders and emphasized by some ornament, here a fringe. Degas, who did not lack a sense of fashion, was never, however, sufficiently prophetic in such matters to have painted or drawn her hair and dress about ten years before a style was introduced.

Even if Degas could not have produced the drawing in the exhibition when the Millaudons visited Italy about a decade earlier, there is still the question of whether this could be the matron from New Orleans on a later trip. Our only objective evidence for Mme Millaudon's appearance is the photograph of her (at the right) with her mother, one daughter and a granddaughter on the steps of the house at the family plantation in the 1890s (fig. 70). When we compare the drawing with her head in the photograph, we can detect certain similarities, particularly in the thinness of the hair back from the forehead, the expressive brows, straight nose, and a mouth that might have become thinner and severer with the years. One difficulty is that the angle from which we look at her is not the same. The other is that, whereas Mme Millaudon in the photograph acknowledges us graciously in the inclination of her head and her steady gaze, the woman in both the earlier painting and drawing turns away and seems absorbed in something within herself. We do not know enough about Mme Millaudon to be certain whether she was capable of such a range in expression.

Whether this woman is Mme Millaudon or not, she is an important part of Degas's pantheon of contemporary women, usually his friends or acquaintances, whom he drew immaculately, sensitively, and with great respect for their difference in the period after the Mussons returned to New Orleans in 1865 and before he visited them in 1872.

FIG. 74. Edgar Degas, *Mme Millaudon*, 1857–59, oil on canvas, 23⅝ × 18⅛ in. Location unknown. Lemoisne 44.

1. For example, Monet, *Femmes au jardin*, 1866–67; *Portrait de Mme Gaudibert*, 1868; Tissot, *Jeune femme en veste rouge*, 1864; all Musée d'Orsay, Paris.

IT WAS SUGGESTED BY JAMES B. BYRNES that this might be Mme Millaudon or Mme Ducros.[1] This painting was catalogued by Lemoisne, with no attempt to identify the sitter, as 1867 to 1872, not a period we associate with New Orleans. Reff in turn, in cataloguing the two notebooks in which there are preliminary studies, one of which he dates 1867 to 1868 and the other 1867 to 1874, does not indicate any American associations. The implication we must draw from Reff's dating is that the studies for this painting fall between 1867 and 1868, the dates common to both notebooks.

It appears that Byrnes was persuaded to consider identifying this painting with Mme Millaudon or her mother, Mme Ducros, during the artist's New Orleans stay, by Agnes Mongan, the late distinguished curator of drawings and later director of the Fogg Art Museum at Harvard University. As he puts it, she "recalled the suggestion of one of her graduate students that *Portrait de femme* . . . might be connected with the artist's stay in Louisiana."[2] Clearly, Byrnes was attracted by the possibility of its being the painting of Mme Ducros, "perhaps as a variant or another version of the 'Portrait of Madame Ducros' which Lemoisne and the Millaudon descendants mention as having been left in Louisiana and subsequently lost."[3] What Lemoisne wrote was, "Degas executed whether at this moment [their Italian visit during his Italian stay] or during his visit to Louisiana a portrait of Mme Ducros seated, holding a fan, which was kept for a long time in the family and then lost after the death of Mme Millaudon [1912]."[4] Tempting as it is to believe that this is the work because of the fan, it could not have been the painting purported to have been left with the Ducros or Millaudon families because it was in Degas's studio at the time of his death. Another explanation is offered by Roulhac Toledano, married to a descendant of one of the Beauregard twins. She wrote, "When Degas showed Marie Lucie Ducros her portrait that we consider today so handsome, she looked at it, secretly shuddered and waved her hand to say, "Mon cher Edgar, charmante, but we have not space in the stateroom. We'll collect the painting in Paris on our next voyage,"—but, of course, they never did.[5]

The suggestion that the woman might be Mme Ducros is not, however, without interest. If we look back to the two photographs of her that Byrnes published in the 1965 catalogue (figs. 75, 76),[6] we discover that, absurdly far as they are apart in time—some thirty years—there are similarities in the structure of their heads. This resemblance is stronger in one of the notebook drawings

13. *Portrait of a Woman (Possibly Mme Ducros)*
ca. 1867–69
Oil on handkerchief linen canvas
$23\frac{3}{8} \times 19\frac{1}{2}$ inches (60 × 50 cm)
Private collection, on anonymous extended loan
to the Portland Art Museum, Portland, Maine
Lemoisne 174

FIG. 75. Mme Elina de Vezin Ducros, 1895, photograph.

FIG. 76. Mme Elina Ducros, detail of fig. 70.

(fig. 77) than in the painting itself. Both Mme Ducros in the photograph and the anonymous young woman in the notebook have long faces, moderately high foreheads framed with centrally parted hair, narrow but keen eyes, a straight and much elongated nose, thin lips, which are faintly smugly omniscient, and an extended and pointed jaw. It does not seem absolutely impossible that the three notebook drawings and the painting were based upon Mme Ducros, if only remembered rather than seen.

There is, however, one great difference between these three drawings and one painting and Mme Ducros as we have come to know her from the photograph. In spite of her enormous age in the photograph we feel an energy running through her body and a lively intelligence assessing us with her alert eyes and body. By contrast the woman in the most mundanely descriptive of the notebook drawings (fig. 77) is lethargic, her head bent from weariness, and her shoulders sloped. In the drawing of her arms with her fan (fig. 78), her hands are almost inert. She is certainly not as lively as Mme Ducros—nor as dignified as the woman who might be her daughter, Mme Millaudon (fig. 74, L 44). This passivity, this listlessness, this lack of animation could have been an affectation among young people of her time. It may, however, have gone too far when it comes to a casualness that could only be described as untidiness in the way she wears the blouse of her dress and lets it hang open and loose around her neck.

The two pencil drawings in notebook 22 seem to be highly observant studies of an actual woman. On the other hand, the tiny drawing in the other notebook (fig. 79) shows the composition of the final painting taking form. First, the woman is placed in a setting, and we have a hint of a chair from its arm and a window behind her head by its frame. She holds a fan we have seen in one of the other drawings, her hair and bonnet are piled higher at the back of her

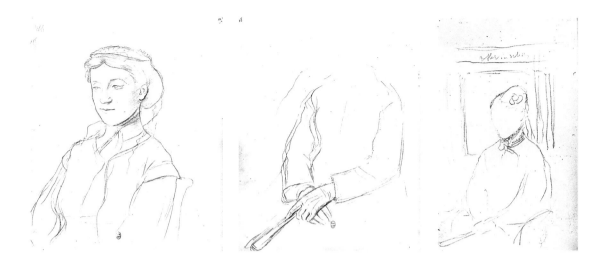

head, and her neck is made particularly conspicuous by a ribbon that repeats the shape and color of the collar of her jacket. As he worked on the canvas Degas carried this ornamentation further by adding the long ribbon tying her bonnet, a white flower on that bonnet, decorative stripes on her jacket, and, in particular, the landscape through the window. On the whole his handling is so thin, so abbreviated, and so calligraphic that much of the modeling in the pencil notebook drawing is lost and something faintly exotic and oriental remains. She is illusive, enigmatic, and mysterious, with the wisp of a smile. Her bone structure may suggest Mme Ducros but this personality does not.

FIG. 77. Edgar Degas, Notebook 22, page 107. Bibliothèque Nationale de France, Paris.

FIG. 78. Edgar Degas, Notebook 22, page 108. Bibliothèque Nationale de France, Paris.

FIG. 79. Edgar Degas, Notebook 21, page 18v. Bibliothèque Nationale de France, Paris.

1. New Orleans, 1965.
2. Byrnes in New Orleans, 70.
3. Ibid., 71.
4. Lemoisne I, 1946–49, 19.
5. Toledano, 1995.
6. Byrnes in New Orleans, 66, figs. 32, 34 [*sic*].

Degas on the Eve of New Orleans

THE THREE YEARS before Degas accompanied his brother René to his recently adopted home in New Orleans were unsettled. His father's apartment on the rue Mondovi had gradually been deserted, first by Thérèse for marriage to their cousin in Naples in 1863, then by Marguerite in 1865 for her husband, who was fortunately to continue living in Paris for more than twenty years, and by René who that same year returned with the Musson family to New Orleans, followed by Achille the next year to join his brother in business there. In June 1869 René had confirmed his intention of remaining in Louisiana by marrying another cousin of theirs, Estelle Musson Balfour. Even Degas by then had his own studio (and even his own maid). On 3 June 1871 the father Auguste De Gas wrote to his daughter Thérèse in Naples that her sister Marguerite and her children were at Deauville while Marguerite's husband had remained in Paris, and that Achille, although theoretically living in New Orleans, was doing business in Belgium.[1] This breaking down of the De Gas family unit anticipated greater divisions still that would follow Degas's visit to New Orleans.

These three years from 1869 to 1872 were a mixture of setbacks and achievements. On a personal level for Degas it was a period in which he was establishing himself with the people he found most challenging or most supportive. He seems to have derived a great deal of pleasure and strength from the evenings he spent with the Morisots, the Manets, Puvis de Chavannes, and Fantin-Latour, as well as with friends he had made over the years for other reasons than their interests in the arts like the Valpinçons, the Halévys, and the Rouarts. In 1870 he exhibited at the Salons, a portrait of Mme Camus, which René had found very beautiful when he had visited his brother's studio on a trip from New Orleans in 26 June 1872. He described her seated in a red velvet dress as "an absolute masterpiece. His drawing is ravishing."[2] Although this, along with a pastel of the head of Paule Gobillard-Morisot, a sister of Berthe Morisot, were his last submissions to the Salons, Degas was laying the ground with a network of other artists, critics, dealers, and collectors to be able to encourage and participate in the first exhibition of the group, which would be known as the Impressionists in 1874.

Those three years also contained the threats of the invasion of France by Bismarck's Prussia, the unwise response of a declaration of war against Prussia by Napoleon III on 19 July 1870, the defeat of the French under Napoleon III at Sedan on 2 September, the declaration of the Third Republic two days later, followed by the humiliation of the city of Paris, the establishment of the Commune on 18 March 1871 and its suppression, and the imposition of unreasonably heavy reparations on the French. It had been a short war, but its effects were devastating. Degas had volunteered for the National Guard in 1870, shortly after the defeat at Sedan and the creation of the Third Republic, and was posted under an old friend Henri Rouart (fig. 80).[3] On 7 March 1872 Edgar's brother Achille arrived from New Orleans to join the navy on the Loire.[4] Very shortly after, the war seemed to sputter to an end. Degas was able to seek peace on the estate of his friends the Valpinçons in the center of Normandy. He returned to Paris on 1 June 1871.

The reality of the Siege of Paris was terrible. Degas tended to joke about it. On 18 October 1870 Mme Morisot, the mother of Berthe, wrote from Paris, where she most courageously stayed, "M. Degas has joined the artillery, and, by his own account, has not yet heard a cannon go off. He is looking for an opportunity to hear that sound because he wants to know whether he can endure the detonation of his guns."[5] Manet was much more forthright in writing to his wife Suzanne. In September it was, "Paris has a military spirit now that is astonishing. Military exercises take place in the streets."[6] A few days later it was prophetically, "I dread very much, to be honest, the situation in which Paris will find itself cut off from all communication with the outside world. I would prefer a siege with its dangers."[7] In fact, the inhabitants of the city became dependent on balloons and passenger pigeons for any mail. Not long after, Manet told his wife, "Everyone is a soldier now."[8] By 8 January Mme Morisot was writing, "The bombardment never stops. It is a sound that reverberates in your head night and day; it would make you feverish if you were not already in that state . . . Yet the bombs do not do much harm—all told there are not many dead and but few wounded, and so far there is little destruction."[9] By June she was recording the damage, "Going down by boat, I saw the remains of the Cour des Comptes, of the Hôtel de la Légion d'Honneur, of the Orsay barracks, of a part of the Tuileries. The poor Louvre has been nicked by projectiles."[10] By this time some who had deserted Paris were returning. Manet left early in the New Year,[11] Degas late in the spring to rest in Normandy, but both returned so that Mme Morisot could report in June, "Tiburce [her son and Berthe's brother] has met two Communards, at this moment when they are all being shot . . . Manet and Degas."[12]

FIG. 80. Edgar Degas, *Portrait of Henri Rouart*, 1871, oil on canvas, $10\frac{5}{8} \times 8\frac{3}{4}$ in. Musée Marmottan. Lemoisne 293.

Degas suffered as everyone else suffered—from lack of food, the cold, the sound of guns, from the army itself, from the death of a good friend,[13] and from that isolation that Manet had feared. But he had over a year to recover before he set forth for New Orleans. And in that time he could enjoy his family and friends and begin to work once more, that work in large part a celebration of things that during the siege he undoubtedly discovered how much he loved: the Opéra orchestra, its dancers on the stage or in class, the racetrack, or his friends. Interestingly, nothing of the Siege of Paris appears in his work, except in two unconventional portraits.[14] René, on that trip from New Orleans that would end with Degas joining him when he returned, wrote to his wife in June 1872, "At the station I found Edgar had matured, some touches of white in his beard. He is also fatter and more composed."[15] It was this Edgar who would visit America.

1. Loyrette in Paris, Ottawa, New York, 1988, 59, from an unpublished letter.

2. Brown, 1991, Box II, folder 45c.

3. Lemoisne I, 1946–49, 67–68.

4. Loyrette, 1991, 261, from a letter of Alfred Niaudet, 7 March 1871.

5. Rouart, 56.

6. Édouard Manet, *Lettres du siège de Paris,* (Paris, 1996), 40.

7. Manet, 46.

8. Ibid., 51.

9. Rouart, 57.

10. Ibid., 73.

11. Manet, 97.

12. Rouart, 73.

13. Ibid., 56.

14. L 287, *Jeantaud, Linet, and Lainé,* dated March 1871, Musée d'Orsay; L 288, *Rabbi Astruc and General Mellinet,* 1871, City of Gérardmer.

15. Brown, 1991, Box II, folder 45c.

THE OPÉRA ORCHESTRA, 1869–72

IN THE YEARS JUST BEFORE DEGAS set out for America, he became infatuated with the dance. In investigating dancers as a subject in his paintings and drawings, he never excluded other themes; but he did persist with the dance for the remaining thirty-five years of his working life. The dancers tantalizingly first appeared in his paintings on the stage of an opera house with an orchestra or spectators in the pit below. He may have been comically inspired, as he occasionally was, by one of Honoré Daumier's lithographs, in this case *Croquis Musicaux* of 1852 called, *Orchestra Musicians during a Performance of a Tragedy* (fig. 81). With his *The Orchestra of the Opéra* (fig. 82), however, he replaced Daumier's apathetic and indeed even sleeping musicians—one yawning hugely—with more individualized men who are earnest and alert. And instead of the two tragedians in classical dress, he gives us a glimpse of the pretty tutus and pale pink–stockinged legs of a bevy of ballerinas. In both Daumier's lithograph and Degas's painting, the top of the image cuts off the heads and shoulders of the performers as decisively as a stage curtain would have done.[1]

Almost immediately after having finished *The Orchestra of the Opéra,* Degas painted *Orchestra Musicians* (fig. 83), which is similar—a glimpse of an orchestra, part of the stage, and a few dancers. In this canvas—just a little taller—he closed in on the musicians so that we see only the backs of the heads of three

FIG. 81. Honoré Daumier, *Orchestra Musicians during a Performance of a Tragedy,* 1852, lithograph, $10\frac{3}{8} \times 8\frac{1}{2}$ in.

FIG. 82. Edgar Degas, *The Orchestra of the Opéra,* 1870, oil on canvas, $22\frac{1}{4} \times 18\frac{1}{4}$ in. Musée d'Orsay. Lemoisne 186.

FIG. 83. Edgar Degas, *Orchestra Musicians,* ca. 1870–71, worked 1874–76, oil on canvas, $27\frac{1}{8}$ × $19\frac{1}{4}$ in. Stadtische Galerie im Stadel-schen Kunstinstitut, Frankfurt. Lemoisne 295.

FIG. 84. Edgar Degas, *The Ballet of Robert le Diable,* 1871, oil on canvas, 26 × $21\frac{3}{8}$ in. The Metropolitan Museum of Art, New York, H. O. Havemeyer Collection. Lemoisne 294.

and nothing of their distinguishing features. He also expanded the space given to the dancers on the stage by freeing their heads and their bodices against the trees painted on the scenery behind. Since everything is subordinated to the small dancer floodlit as she curtsies on the right of the stage, it appears to be a more unified work. In January 1872, Durand-Ruel, who would eventually become Degas's principal dealer, bought a third variation on this basic theme from the artist (fig. 84), one of the first three works he bought from Degas. It is again about the same size but recording the performance of a ballet in an actual opera, *Robert le Diable,* by Meyerbeer in which the ghosts of dead nuns rise and dance in the spirit of their true (and sensual) characters. The orchestra in *The Ballet of Robert le Diable* is replaced by a male audience that is distracted by attractions—not nuns—that were to be found in the hall but not on the stage.

By the time Degas arrived in New Orleans, he had already painted the dance in theaters in relation to an orchestra or an audience. As an artist he was still admittedly working within the terms of the conventional opera house but, as we know from a letter René De Gas wrote to his wife Estelle in New Orleans, as a man he was already exploring the more popular theater, which René found offensive. As he wrote to Estelle, they would go to "the café-chantant to listen to idiotic songs . . . and other absurd nonsense."[2] It would only be after his return from New Orleans that Degas would record both the

FIG. 85. *Robert le Diable,* album of sheet music belonging to Estelle Musson. Earl K. Long Library, University of New Orleans.

audiences and the performers in this form of theater that—unlike his brother René—he savored.

On 11 November 1872, not long after arriving in New Orleans, Edgar Degas wrote to "Monsieur D. Dihau/à l'Opéra/rue Drouot/ France/Paris/My dear Dihau, thank-you for your good letter. It is the first."[3] It was not strange that Degas from the distance of New Orleans, where he was feeling particularly deprived of the kind of performance the Paris Opéra house provided, should have thought of his friend Désiré Dihau in terms of the address where he worked as first bassoon-ist with the orchestra rather than in the apartment on the rue de Laval he was sharing with his pretty sister Marie Dihau,[4] much admired by Degas (and the artist's father)[5] and painted by Degas twice.[6] Degas peppered his letter with references to people they knew in common—ballerinas like Rita Sangalli, Gard the stage manager of the dance at the Opéra, and even an obscure painter like Piot-Normand.[7] Behind this letter was Degas's familiarity with Dihau and his world, to which he had been introduced when he painted this heterogeneous group, dominated by the bassoonist. Loyrette argues, "It is not a group por-trait . . . but a portrait of an individual within a group."[8] That love of the official music of the National Opera House must have been encouraged in Degas by his Neapolitan-born father, whom Degas painted three times listening to one of his favorite performers, the guitarist and tenor, Lorenzo Pagans.[9] Pagans is actually to be found very far back in *The Orchestra of the Opéra,* to the right of the harp and diagonally below the box in which the composer Chabrier is sit-ting. We are told that Henri de Toulouse-Lautrec, a distant cousin of the Dihaus, who also drew Désiré very much in the manner of Degas (if leading a bear on a chain through the streets of Paris rather than playing in the orchestra), used to bring his drunken friends back to the Dihau apartment. There he would take them to this painting hanging beside a portrait by Degas of Marie Dihau at the piano and say, "Kneel down, you fools, kneel down before the greatest painter of them all!"[10]

14. Musicians in the Orchestra,
Portrait of Désiré Dihau

1870
Oil on canvas
19¼ × 23½ inches (49.3 × 59.3 cm)
Fine Arts Museums of San Francisco,
Mildred Anna Williams Collection (1952.69)
Lemoisne 187

Degas painted another image of Dihau with the Paris Opéra orchestra, which is called *Musicians in the Orchestra* (cat. 14) and which is the same size although composed horizontally instead of vertically. This must have been a work painted for his own pleasure rather than as a tour de force and a masterpiece, which the other work undoubtedly is. In this version Degas worked very thinly with paint, and almost monochromatically, so that the effect is of a drawing rather than a finished oil. Dihau is even more obviously the focus of the work since his features are the only ones visible, but he is placed off center to the left so that this is not too apparent. The ungainly back of the player of the double-bass, Achille Henri Victor Gouffé (born 1805), is large and expressive but does not distract us from the small neat image of Dihau puffing out his cheeks above his walrus mustache as he blows into his bassoon. Behind Dihau and Gouffé, the orchestra seems to have dissolved into a vibrating abstraction in which diagonal strokes, perhaps representing bows or horns, provide a repetitive pattern like spears going into battle. There is no dance in this painting (except in the movements of Degas's brush). The stage appears to be occupied by cliffs—solid, impenetrable, indomitable. All the animation is in the two figures and the suggeston of music. We can understand how Degas would have missed the rhythms, the crescendos, the very noise when he found himself deprived of the music of the Paris Opéra in New Orleans and wrote to Henri Rouart on 5 December 1872, "The lack of *any* opera is a real tribulation."[11]

1. Loyrette in Paris, Ottawa, New York, 1988, no. 97, 102, on the basis of a study of the X-radiograph of the work believes that Degas had begun with a larger canvas and "had deliberately cut the sides and top of the canvas . . . and thus altered the framing of the scene."

2. Brown, 1991, Box II, folder 46b.

3. Appendix II, letter to Dihau.

4. Marie joined Désiré on rue de Laval immediately after the Franco-Prussian War.

5. Lemoisne I, 1946–49, 59, based on conversations he and Marcel Guérin had with Mlle Dihau.

6. L 172, Metropolitan Museum of Art; L 263, Musée d'Orsay.

7. Among those mentioned were Rita Sangalli, a dancer born in Milan in 1840; Gard, of whom Loyrette, 1991, 241, was unable to find any record in the Opéra archives; the painter Alexandre Piot-Normand (1830–1902).

8. Loyrette in Paris, Ottawa, New York, no. 97, 162.

9. L 256, Orsay; L 257, Museum of Fine Arts, Boston; L 345, 1895, Private Collection.

10. Oral tradition: Marie Dihau to Paul J. Saschs to author

11. Appendix II, letter to Rouart.

A DANCE CLASS,
1871

WHEN RENÉ DE GAS WAS REPORTING from Paris by letter to his wife Estelle in New Orleans in July 1872, inevitably out of his concern for her own blindness, he mentioned his artist brother's problems with his eyes. With a characteristic optimism, which in this case had some validity, he reported that Edgar's eyes were better but that perversely, "he is painting small pictures, exactly those that would tire his eyes the most." He added, "He is making a rehearsal of the dance which is charming. When he is finished I shall take a large photograph of it."[1] It is probable that René saw a dance class rather than a rehearsal and that it was slightly more than twelve by eighteen inches and is now in the Musée d'Orsay (fig. 86). Such works by Degas— miniatures of young dancers, charmingly dressed in tutus—were salable even then. And a month after René wrote Estelle, this was bought along with *The Orchestra of the Opéra* (fig. 82) by the dealer, Paul Durand-Ruel (1831–1922), who ultimately after an intervening period of an economic depression was to become Degas's principal dealer for most of his life.[2]

FIG. 86. Edgar Degas, *Dance Class at the Opéra*, 1871, oil on canvas, 12⅝ × 18⅛ in. Musée d'Orsay, Paris. Lemoisne 298.

It is not just because the canvas is small that it seems a miniature. It appears even smaller because there is so much within that surface—a ballet master[3] standing with his left hand raised to provide guidance to the young dancers; a seated male violinist to make the music on a pocket violin to accompany them; eleven young girls in tutus within the room; and at least three others reflected in the arched mirror on the far wall.

Although Désiré Dihau provided Degas with an entrée to the world of the orchestra at the Opéra, Degas may not have had the same kind of entrée to the classes and rehearsals of the dance in this period after the war and before he went to New Orleans. He did, of course, know some dancers. In fact, his submission to the Salon in 1868 was *Mlle Fiocre in the Ballet La Source*. Eugénie Fiocre was one of the favorite dancers of the Second Empire and actually sat for Degas[4] for the large painting, now in Brooklyn, which shows her seated beside a small horse and two other dancers, reflected in water on the stage— a moment of rest in a rehearsal for which a pink ballet slipper cast aside on the floor provides the clue. The dress performance for *La Source* was such a triumphant occasion that Verdi, the great Italian composer of operas, and Ingres, the great French painter, worshipped by Degas, were both in attendance.[5] It may have been the combination of the glamour of its opening and the exhibition of a painting from it in rehearsal by Degas at the Salon that made Manet write Fantin-Latour in that year, 1868, quoting Duranty, "Degas is on his way to becoming the painter of high life."[6]

In fact, Degas was to divert his path from any consideration of "High Life," but he continued to meet dancers under humbler circumstances such as "Mlle" d'Hugues [probably Hughes], whose name he inscribed on a drawing (fig. 87) for the little dancer at the left of this painting or Rita Sangalli,[7] whom he mentioned in one of his letters from New Orleans, or Josephine Gaujelin, whose portrait he had painted and exhibited in the Salon of 1869 and of whom he was to make a drawing of her as a dancer and inscribe it, in part, "formerly dancer at the Opéra"[8] or Thérèse Mallot, who was probably a mistress of his brother Achille.[9] After his return from New Orleans, he was even more naturally included in the life of the Opéra if only through his friendships with men like Ludovic Halévy, the nephew of the composer of a popular nineteenth-century opera, *La Juive,* and himself the co-author of the libretto for Bizet's *Carmen,*[10] and the vicomte Lepic, a designer of stage sets and costumes for the Opéra whose mistress was the dancer and mime, Marie Sanlaville.[11] Before leaving for New Orleans, Degas may have adored the dance world of the Opéra but he was still somewhat outside it.

At this moment in his work, in composing a group of figures within a room, Degas used many of the conventions of Japanese birds-eye perspective, looking down at the figures who seem to have been distributed in a box with views of two walls, a glimpse of the ceiling, and a good view of the floor. In some ways, although not as boldly conceived or executed on the whole, this anticipates *A Cotton Office in New Orleans.* One could easily imagine Degas having counted the eleven dancers in the room plus the three reflected as he would count the "15 individuals"[12] in *A Cotton Office* in his second letter to Tissot from New Orleans. Although there are not the same telling social juxtapositions that Marilyn R. Brown has analyzed so tellingly in her essay in this book, "A Cotton Office in New Orleans," we can imagine Degas already plotting the location of the dancers and two men as if they were pieces of chess on a board. But the result is, of course, much more passive and harmonious.

FIG. 87. Edgar Degas, *Dancer Standing,* study for *Dance Class at the Opéra,* 1871, essence and pencil on pink paper, $10\frac{5}{8} \times 8\frac{1}{4}$ in. Collection of Thomas Gibson, London. Lemoisne 300.

When Degas went to New Orleans he did not forget this *Dance Class at the Opéra;* Durand-Ruel had bought it from him in August 1872 and was to sell it in London in the following December. In November Degas had written Tissot from New Orleans, "What impression did my dance picture make on you, on you and the others. Were you able to help selling it?"[13] It makes it also quite apparent that Degas was by no means indifferent to money and to selling his work at this critical moment in his life and career.

1. Brown, 1991, Box II, folder 46b.

2. See Pantazzi in Paris, Ottawa, New York, 212, for 14 June 1873, Durand-Ruel's last purchase from Degas for some years, and 219, for 27 December 1880, for his next. The source is the Journal, Durand-Ruel Archives.

3. The ballet master is Louis Mérante (1828–87), Loyrette in Paris, Ottawa, New York, no. 107, 176.

4. See Loyrette in Paris, Ottawa, New York, no. 77, 134, figs. 71, 72, 73 for drawings for which Fiocre posed in August 1867.

5. See Ann Dumas, *Degas' Mlle Fiocre in Context* (Brooklyn Museum, 1988), for the fullest account of the significance of this work.

6. Moreau-Nélaton, 1926, I, 103. This is suggested by Loyrette in Paris, Ottawa, New York, no. 77, 136.

7. Appendix II, letter to Dihau.

8. L 165, *Mme Gaujelin,* dated 1867, Salon of 1869, Isabella Stewart Gardner Museum, Boston; preparatory drawing, III: 156(1), Boymans Museum, Amsterdam (F II:169).

9. For the an account of this relationship as it was published in *Temps,* see Loyrette, 1991, 320–23. When Mlle Mallot married Victor-Georges Legrand in 1874, she had had a child by Achille De Gas, for whom he provided some support. Also see McMullen, 250–51, who published the story first and reports that the child had died. The incident became public in the summer of 1875 when Legrand approached Achille in front of the Bourse and began to beat him with a cane; Achille pulled out a revolver and shot wildly, grazing the skin of Legrand's face with two shots. Legrand was sentenced to one month in prison and Achille to six, although Achille's later was considerably reduced. In his letter from New Orleans to Désiré Dihau (Appendix II), Degas wrote, "Mlle Malot vient de répondre ici à une lettre de René."

10. For Ludovic Halévy and his relationship to the dance and to Degas, see Henri Loyrette et al., *Entre le théâtre et l'histoire. La famille Halévy (1760–1960)* (Paris, 1996), 136–93.

11. For Ludovic Lepic and his relationship to the dance and to Degas see Harvey Buchanan, *Edgar Degas and Ludovic Lepic: An Impressionist Friendship* (Cleveland, 1997).

12. Appendix II, letter to Dihau.

13. Appendix II, letter to Tissot, 18 February 1873.

HORSES AND PEOPLE

ANY INTEREST THAT DEGAS might have had in horses is strangely undocumented aside from the paintings, drawings, and waxes he made himself. Undoubtedly he lived in a world in which this animal was indispensable, and we know that he traveled in coaches and simpler conveyances pulled by them. But there is no evidence that he ever owned a horse or, aside from his own assertion in 1895, that he ever rode one.[1] It was long after Degas returned from New Orleans, in 1890, before a horse assumed any personality at all in accounts of his life. This was when he and his friend, the sculptor Albert Bartholomé, rented a carriage and a white horse they were to call M. Plomer, which they used to visit a friend in Burgundy. On this rather long voyage Degas sent daily postcards to his friends the Halévys,[2] analyzing the character of the horse with an absorption that suggests that twenty years before when he was in New Orleans Degas would have known very little about this animal in the flesh.[3]

The horses Degas drew, painted, or modeled were undoubtedly influenced by his everyday observations of this animal, but they seem to have had their foundation in his study of other works of art.[4] He had made drawings from plaster casts of the Parthenon frieze when he was a student at the École des Beaux-Arts or a visitor in Lyon, and other drawings after battle or religious paintings by Florentine masters of the fifteenth century, or after the mounts of great rulers in more baroque paintings and sculpture when he was educating himself in Italy between 1856 and 1859. Even later in Paris he would make drawings after the horses in the contemporty history painting *Napoleon III at the Battle of Solférino* by Meisonnier.[5] But these images of horses drawn from the art of the past or the present were fused with Degas's more intimate observation of the animal on the streets of Paris, in the countryside, or at the track.

The fact that when Degas was in New Orleans for those few months from October 1872 to March 1873, he seems to have ignored this animal is probably not too significant in his whole career. In that highly unsettled period of Reconstruction it is not too surprising that any suggestions of his having visited plantations from the city are purely hypothetical. Within the city, as Christina Vella records in her essay "The Country for Men with Nerve," horses were plentiful, which could have been disastrous for the health of its inhabitants. As she puts it, "whereas Paris complained of a shortage of draft animals, in New Orleans there were always more horses on the streets than carts to clean after them."[6] Christopher Benfey in his essay in this book, "Degas and New Orleans:

Exorcizing the Exotic," informs us further that, "One reason why New Orleanians were drawn to steam-powered streetcars was the devastating epidemic among horses in the city, culminating in December 1872,"[7] when Degas, after all, was in the city. This can have been one reason Degas seems to have been more attracted by the development of other methods of transportation in America such as the Pullman train or the steam-powered streetcar.

But there was still another possible venue for the horse in New Orleans—and that was at a racetrack. We are told that there was a busy one not too far from the rented Musson mansion. During his stay in New Orleans Edgar Degas must have been given ample opportunity to get to know his cousins Mathilde and William Bell, although it is unlikely he never would have met either before. This should have been significant for his study of horses at the track in New Orleans since Bell was an official of that track;[8] but there is no evidence that Degas went near it.

When faced with these blanks in our knowledge of the artist's response to his mother's native city, we regret that he either never used notebooks here for those intimate jottings he was accustomed to make with words or drawings, or that, if he did, they have been destroyed or, more hopefully, lay somewhere forgotten, where they might someday be discovered.[9] We cannot forget that most of the group of his notebooks in the Bibliothèque Nationale in Paris were given by René when he was still living.[10] It is only too possible that just as René cut out certain—actually, only a few—passages from the notebooks he did give, he might have decided that certain notebooks were too intimate to give at all. (As some compensation to us for this lack of notebooks, largely because Degas missed his friends in Paris and London, he wrote some of his most revealing letters from New Orleans.)[11]

But to return to Paris (and excursions into the rest of France and even another country or two) in the years from, let us say, 1869, to his departure for America in 1872, Degas did make informal studies of horses pulling carts or grazing in his notebooks or in individual drawings. He developed these into paintings, among which the most appealing may be domestic gatherings on horseback or in carriages. The supreme example is *At the Races in the Countryside* (cat. 18). But in addition, with an eye toward the English market which he hoped would provide a solution for his own looming financial predicaments, Degas turned to the racetrack for subjects the English were known to enjoy and he miscalculated might buy.[12]

The racetracks around Paris or in Normandy, where he visited frequently, provided Degas with an opportunity to study the horses in an artificial, man-made situation with great dramatic possibilities. Again almost the only evidence we have for the attendance of Degas at a racetrack is his own work. He did, late in life, tell Paul Valéry about an incident on a trip he took to a suburban track by train, which makes it clear that he used the railroad to reach provincial tracks, that he largely went alone and that he never gambled.[13] Degas was sufficiently sociable that we assume that he must have had friends and relatives who shared his enthusiasm for the track, but the evidence is pretty slim. It is easy to convince oneself that his brother Achille must have gone to the track, if only because Degas is believed to have used him as the model for the fallen jockey in *Scene from the Steeplechase: The Fallen Jockey,* which he exhibited at the Salon of 1866.[14] Achille also had an erratic temperament, which could have made him a gambler at the track; and certainly, as Degas was to draw him (cat. 17), he was the typical *flâneur* at the races. Men like Paul Valpinçon, Degas's friend since their school days at the Lycèe Louis-le-Grand and the owner of an estate in Normandy near the great horse-breeding establishment at Haras-le-Pin, or Ludovic Lepic, that breeder of dogs, should have been his natural companions at the races. But strangely enough, the only person confirmed as such is Èdouard Manet. The fascination with the track for Degas must have been, however, in the anticipation of the performance itself and not, as it was for Manet, because his fellow visitors had their own attractions. (This does not mean that as an artist Degas was indifferent to these crowds.)

Degas may not have given any expression in New Orleans to his interest in the horse—but he had already revealed it in his paintings and sculpture before he left for America.

1. Thiébault-Sisson, originally in *Le Temps,* 23 May 1921, 3, trans. into English but misdated as 1897 instead of 1895, 1984–85, Paris, Marais, *Degas Form and Space,* 179.

2. Guerin, 1947, nos. 143–64.

3. This is not to imply that Degas did not eat horsemeat during the Siege of Paris. Manet, who was in the same unit and often his companion, wrote to his wife, "We eat only horsemeat when we can get it." Moreau-Nélaton, 1926, 124.

4. See Boggs in Washington, San Francisco, 1998, 16–22.

5. Reff, Nb. 22: 123, 127. The painting is in the Musée d'Orsay, Paris.

6. Vella, in this book, 33.

7. Benfey, in this book, n. 11.

8. Ibid., 10.

9. It is possible that one of our contemporaries might be tempted to produce a notebook as was done when the author published "Degas Notebooks at the Bibliothèque Nationale," *Burlington* (May, June and July 1958). Jean-Marie Lhôte published "Discours imprononçable quoique méthodique à propos d'un épisode mal connu de la jeunesse de Degas," as the whole issue of *Bizarre* (4th trimester, 1962). Unlike the original carnets, there was more text than illustrations.

10. Lemoisne, 1921.

11. Appendix II, letters to Dihau; Tissot, 19 November 1872; Frölich.

12. See Ronald Pickvance, "Introduction," in *Degas' Racing World* (New York, 1968), n.p.; Richard Kendall, *Degas Landscapes,* (New Haven, 1993), 66–68. Degas made his interest in the English market abundantly clear in his letters to Tissot: see Guerin, nos. 7, 8, 12, and Appendix II.

13. Valéry, 1960, 72.

14. See Boggs in Washington, San Francisco, 52–58. The original suggestion that the fallen jockey was posed by Achille was Lemoisne I, 1946–49, 40.

15. *Walking Horse*

early 1870s
Bronze
$5\frac{1}{4} \times 2 \times 10\frac{3}{4}$ inches ($31.4 \times 5.1 \times 27.5$ cm)
New Orleans Museum of Art, Gift of the Musson Family (50.4)

OF ALL DEGAS'S FORMS OF WORK, including his interpretations in monotype of the activities of Parisian brothels, the most intensely private may have been his innocent modeling in wax. It is true that, since none of his efforts but the famous *Fourteen-Year Old Dancer* were very large, he seemed to enjoy showing these statuettes to his friends, picking up a piece in his hands like this *Walking Horse* (cat. 15) and playing with the movements its shadows would cast upon a wall.[1] On the other hand, he made no attempt whatsoever to exhibit or sell any of these sculptures in wax except *Fourteen-Year Old Dancer,* which he promised for the Impressionist exhibition of 1880 and did actually show—if a little late—in 1881.[2] He experimented with the casting of some of the works in plaster,[3] but he resisted this being done in bronze. As he explained it, there was a "tremendous responsibility in leaving anything behind in bronze—the medium is for eternity."[4] Reproduction would also destroy the privacy of his enjoyment of their creation.

The result was that his studio was covered with decaying waxes, their fancifully contrived armatures often exposed.[5] His heirs, his brother René and the children of his sister Marguerite Fevre, were seldom in agreement but all listened to Albert Bartholomé, Degas's sculptor friend who had accompanied him into Burgundy in the carriage drawn by the horse they christened M. Plomer and who had given Degas advice at difficult moments in his career about any casting he had attempted.[6] In the end, with Bartholomé as a spectator, the heirs courageously signed a contract on 13 May 1918 for the casting with the A. A. Hébrard Foundry, with Albino Palazzolo named as the master founder.[7] The quality of the bronze casts—posthumous since Degas was at least four years dead when they were finished in 1921—is extraordinarily fine as was demonstrated recently in the exhibition at the National Gallery of Art, *Degas at the Races,* where an original wax from the collection of Mr. and Mrs. Paul Mellon, a bronze cast of the same horse from the master set or *modèle* from the Norton

Simon Museum and a cast from the set that was marked HER.D. and set aside for the heirs, also owned by Mr. and Mrs. Mellon, were exhibited side by side.[8] All three are highly refined in tooling and surface. They are also beautiful in color, although the wax admittedly has a depth and luminosity that cannot be duplicated exactly in bronze. Nevertheless, even Degas might have been prepared to face immortality with these casts.

Although we have reasonably precise information about the dating of casting, we know absolutely nothing concrete about the dating of the original waxes. It is generally assumed that one of the earliest is related to Degas's painting exhibited at the Salon of 1868, *Mlle Fiocre in the Ballet La Source,* the small horse leaning over to drink from the pool.[9] On the basis of x-rays of the armatures of the waxes, it is believed that the earlier works have the heavier, more contrived armatures, almost always handmade. The wax of the *Walking Horse* is believed to be early, about 1872, which makes the bronze cast relevant to the work of Degas just before he left for America.

In some respects the *Walking Horse* is a humble animal, its head a little gauche, its contours angular rather than fluid, its tail far from an elegant brush, the movement of its legs tentative but not apologetic. It seems to combine that liveliness in the legs with a mute determination conveyed in the head, accentuated by the blunted ears and supported by the tail, that can remind us of the small dancers Degas was drawing but perhaps not as yet modeling. The application of the surface of the wax on the torso and head is willful and arbitrary but catches the light so that the bronze statue is an awkward but precious object. In the wax, the support—like a growing organic thing in the middle of his body—was the kind of frank statement of buttressing that Degas made with his original waxes.[10] *Walking Horse* is not a classical work but appealing in its very imperfections, a record of the young and unformed, like so many of Degas's studies of young dancers.

We do not seem to know the basis for the distribution of the set of bronzes, HER.D., put aside for Degas's heirs. In terms of New Orleans, the situation was further complicated because René would have been the original heir of half the estate; it was only with his death in 1921, the year the bronze-casting was finished, that his French children, Maurice, Edmond and Odette De Gas, first discovered the existence of their American half-brother, Edgar Achille Gaston, and their half-sister Odile, both known as Musson rather than De Gas.

Apparently after a lawsuit, René's estate was evenly divided among his five children.[11] The New Orleans heirs sold nine bronzes in 1950 to the New York dealer Silberman;[12] of these, four were purchased by the Art Institute of Chicago. The only one known to have remained with this family was this horse, which was given to the New Orleans Museum of Art in 1950 by the Musson family.[13]

1. Walter Sickert, "Degas," *Burlington* XXXI, no. 176 (November 1917): 185.

2. Washington, San Francisco, 1986.

3. Richard Kendall, "Who said anything about Rodin?" *Apollo* CXLII, no. 402 (August 1995): 72–77.

4. Vollard, 1924, 12.

5. Louisine Havemeyer, *Sixteen to Sixty* (New York, 1964), 247.

6. For the particularly difficult casting of a bust of Hortense Valpinçon (Pingeot 78), see Guerin, 1947, nos. 62, 69, 70, 72, 73, 74, 75 (to Bartholomé).

7. Pingeot, 1991, 25–28.

8. Washington, nos. 117, 126, and 128.

9. Pingeot, no. 42. See Barbour and Sturman in Washington, 183 and 184, fig. 3 of x-radiograph.

10. For the ingenuity of Degas's armatures, the frankness with which they were exposed when the sculpture was in its original state, see the illustrations between 153–90 in Pingeot. These photographs were taken soon after Degas's death and were part of the Hébrard archives, which are now part of the Durand-Ruel Archives.

11. For the lawsuit, see De Gas–Musson, Box V, folders 2, 8a, b, c. The details of the actual division of the works in the set "HER.D." have not been found.

12. Brown, 1991, Box V, folder 9, agreement of sale of nine bronzes owned by Gaston De Gas Musson and other New Orleans relatives to the Silberman Galleries, New York.

13. In the collection of the New Orleans Museum of Art there is another bronze, *Dancer Putting on Her Stocking* (Pingeot, 14), which is marked HER.D. and was bought by the museum at auction at Park-Bernet, New York, 1 March 1972. Under any circumstances the work is much too late to be a legitimate consideration of the subject, "Degas and New Orleans," and the provenance seems to be French and therefore part of the settlement of the French heirs.

16. *At the Races*

1868–72
Oil on panel
$17\frac{7}{8} \times 15\frac{1}{8}$ inches (46 × 38.8 cm)
Collection of Weil Brothers, Montgomery, Alabama
Lemoisne 184

IN THE PERIOD JUST BEFORE DEGAS left for New Orleans, he painted four racetrack scenes of great beauty and extraordinary clarity. Two of these, Washington's *Before the Race* (L 317) and Yale's *The False Start* (L 258) were bought by Paul Durand-Ruel in 1872, the first he acquired from the artist, the second from a collector who already had possessed the acumen to have bought it.[1] Orsay's *Racehorses before the Stands* (L 262) was bought by the great baritone and collector Jean-Baptiste Faure in 1873 or 1874 and therefore after Degas's return from America. On the other hand, the fourth, Boston's charming *Racehorse at Longchamp* (L 334) was not sold or exhibited until 1900, perhaps because Degas did not want to part from it. Nevertheless, the fortunes of the three out of four would quite appropriately have led Degas to believe that there was a market for his racetrack scenes. On the other hand, none of them justified his interest in an English market for such works; there is no English provenance to be found for any of them.

The small vertical painting *At the Races* (cat. 16), generally accepted as painted between 1868 and 1872, represents a departure from the four presumably slightly earlier, horizontal racetrack paintings. For one thing Degas was seeking stock figures, like the two horses and riders at the right, which might need to be refined but still could be used again. There is also what would become a dramatic necessity, the single escaping or balking horse, which we see here in a silhouette of his tail and hind legs. Although the title of the work in itself suggests a track, behind the humble chorus of horses and riders, that track is reduced to a rough and bushy field with a surprising glimpse of water or a blue meadow and a cloudy sky. The real interest in the work comes in the two spectators in the foreground, isolated from any crowd by the two white posts at the left. Presumably they were the reason for the choice of a vertical canvas.

These spectators stand out because of the very sophistication and urbane character of their dress against the rustic background. They had been developed

17. Achille De Gas

1868–72
Oil on wash paper
$14\frac{1}{2} \times 9\frac{1}{8}$ inches (37.7 × 23.5 cm)
The Minneapolis Institute of Arts,
Bequest of Putnam Dana McMillan
(cat. no. 61.36.8)
Lemoisne 307

from a more natural study Degas had made a few years before of his friend, the great painter Edouard Manet (fig. 88). That drawing of Manet shows him to be stockier and more energetic than Achille De Gas, who is supposed to have posed for the figure used in this painting. Manet's suit is rumpled but his hat just as high, a thumb stuck cheekily out of his pocket as he looks through a monocle we do not see at an almost invisible drawing of a young woman looking directly at us through her lorgnette. Achille, as he was developed in the drawing from Minneapolis (cat. 17), is an appropriate companion for her—urbane, fashionably dressed, supremely self-confident, and most publicly admiring her attractions. Although isolated from the crowd they are almost regal in their indifference to it. In thinking ahead from this to the work of Degas in New Orleans we realize how separated—even cloistered—the sexes are in Degas's American painting. Degas would deliberately ignore the kind of relationship that not much earlier in Paris he had been ready to emphasize here.

One of the chief interests of the painting may have been Degas's own difficulties with it. Obviously he repainted it several times, scraping off paint and repainting it. As Pickvance put it in the catalogue for the remarkable exhibition he organized for the Edinburgh Festival in 1979, *Degas 1879,* "after completing it in 1868, Degas repeatedly returned to it, altering the positions of the horses, obliterating one of the spectators and drastically changing the landscape. (Only a recent cleaning has restored the original composition.)"[2] Degas was in a quandary because he liked the daring isolation of the pair—possibly, perhaps eventually, lovers—against the modest, muted, faceless background of horses and riders in a field. He had been trying to combine daring with discretion. But eventually discretion won—perhaps after he had returned from New Orleans—and he painted out the woman with the lorgnette.[3] It was only with a cleaning of the panel in 1950 that this woman of dubious virtue was once more exposed.

1. Durand-Ruel bought it from the Reitlinger collection on 4 April 1872.

2. Ronald Pickvance, *Degas 1879* (Edinburgh, National Gallery of Scotland, 1979), 9.

3. In the catalogue by Pickvance for Martigny, *Degas,* 1993, there is a photograph of the painting before 1950 with the woman removed (by Degas), 31.

FIG. 88. Edgar Degas, *Manet at the Races,* 1868–70, graphite on light brown paper, 12⅝ × 9⅝ in. The Metropolitan Museum of Art, New York.

18. *At the Races in the Countryside*

1869
Oil on canvas
14$\frac{3}{8}$ × 22 inches (36.5 × 55.9 cm)
The Museum of Fine Arts, Boston, 1931 Purchase Fund (26.790)
Lemoisne 281

THERE IS NO DIRECT CONNECTION BETWEEN *At the Races in the Countryside* and New Orleans. Paul Valpinçon, who sits by the dog looking down at his infant son, was one of Degas's oldest friends, perhaps even before Valpinçon went to the Lycée Louis-le-Grand in 1846.[1] Although his family had bought a château in Normandy, Ménil-Hubert near Orne, early in the nineteenth century,[2] they also lived in Paris. Valpinçon had the virtue—particularly to young Degas—of a father who was a collector and owned the great painting by Ingres called after him *The Valpinçon Bather,* which has been in the Louvre since 1879. M. Valpinçon even provided the young Degas with an introduction to Ingres, whom he visited in his studio.[3] Like many of the friends of Degas who had limited ambitions as artists, Valpinçon was an amateur who exhibited at least once in the Salon. He was also probably a sympathetic observer of his friend's work. Indeed, Degas painted portraits of all the members of Paul Valpinçon's family.[4]

Although they had been friends for some years, it seems to have been 1860 before Edgar visited his friend at his country home in Normandy, which Degas recorded with fervor in the largest of his notebooks in the Bibliothèque Nationale de France.[5] They took one long walk through the countryside, which Degas compared to the English landscape, which he had not as yet actually seen. They stopped to admire the horses pouring out of the breeding stables at Haras-le-Pin. Degas was also enchanted by the people invited into the hospitable chateau, who seemed to reflect the characters in *Tom Jones,* which Degas was reading at the time. Although he had already celebrated the engagement of Valpinçon and his fiancé with an Ingresque drawing of the couple,[6] he continued to feel himself more intimately involved in the life of the Valpinçon family and continued to do so after the death of his contemporaries as a guest of their daughter Hortense Fourchy. Over this long friendship the Valpinçons probably met Achille and René and would have heard of the visitors from New

Orleans or Degas's own expedition to America. But the only real link seems to have been his concern when he was in New Orleans for the fate of *At the Races in the Countryside,* which he had sold to Durand-Ruel before he left and which this dealer would sell to Faure after his return. He asked Tissot in one of his letters from there, "the one of the family at the races, what is happening to that?"[7]

It would be typical of the sociable Valpinçons if this were painted at the farm of a neighbor rather than on their own land. It could even be at the simple track at nearby Argentan.[8] Topographically it is rather flat with continuous fields of what looks to be impeccable grass back to gentle hills with some outcroppings of stone and a few trees like elms. The sky is vast, a thin layer of clouds subduing the possible brilliance of the sun. This was the period in which Degas was painting landscapes on the coast near Ètretat and Villers-sur-Mer and visiting Manet who was similarly engaged at Boulogne-sur-Mer.[9] Our interest in this quiet landscape is in the activity of horses and riders against it— the steeplechase in the distance, the few spectators on horseback or in carriages. Without any conflicts, it is a scene of absolute bliss, made more dashing by the surprising framing of the image that cuts through one horse and carriage, as well as the head of another horse in the foreground.

The center of the painting is, however, the nest of the carriage with a very large and limp baby lying on the lap of his wetnurse as she feeds him.[10] A dignified man in black hat, grey suit, and reddish beard looks proudly down at what we assume to be his son, born in early 1869; the father seems to resemble other portraits of Paul Valpinçon.[11] It is possible that someone other than Mme Valpinçon may have posed for the mother, who has a more piquant face than we would expect, partly hidden by the dark veil of the hat placed jauntily on top of her head. The nurse's hat, although pretty, is a conventional, traditional bonnet. Joining Paul Valpinçon in the assessment of the infant is the family dog. It is an enchanting scene on an enchanting day. Degas, who had gone to Ménil-Hubert in the spring of 1871 to recover from the Franco-Prussian War, must have been very grateful for such natural and domestic joy, which he might have remembered at moments in New Orleans.

1. Loyrette, 1991, 681, n. 44, quotes from Archives of Lycée Louis-le-Grand for Paul Valpinçon.

2. Pierre-Jean Penault, "Monsieur Degas à la compagne," *Le Pays d'Ange* (June 1990), no. 6: 5.

3. Valéry, 1960, 34–36.

4. Of Mme Valpinçon, L 125; formerly called *Woman with Chrysanthemums;* of Paul Valpinçon, L 99, Minneapolis Institute of Arts; L 197, private collection; of their daughter Hortense, L 206, Minneapolis Institute of Arts; of their baby son Henri, L 270, private collection, Paris.

5. Reff, Nb. 18.

6. Pierpont Morgan Library, New York.

7. Appendix II, letter to Tissot, 19 November 1872.

8. Loyrette in Paris, Ottawa, New York, 1988, 157 suggested Argentan as the site.

9. Reff, Nb. 23:58–59; Lemoisne I, 1946–49, 68.

10. Boggs in Paris, 1989, 37.

11. In particular L 99, Minneapolis Institute of Arts.

The Artist's Voyage to America, October 1872

19. Notebook 25
1869–73
$7\frac{3}{8} \times 4\frac{3}{4}$ inches (18.7 × 12.3 cm)
Bibliothèque Nationale de France,
Paris

ON 12 OCTOBER 1872, escorted by his younger brother René, Edgar Degas—a painter, a veteran of the recent Franco-Prussian War, a Parisian of thirty-eight years—set out from Liverpool to visit his mother's birthplace in New Orleans for the first time. In boarding the *Scotia,* the last paddle steamer to be built for the Cunard Lines,[1] as one of its 249 passengers, Degas carried with him a small memorandum book (cat. 19). All his life as an artist he had been carrying such notebooks,[2] some admittedly larger, where he jotted down notes, more often in images than in words. In this case he had picked up one in his Paris studio, which he had already used—for two paintings of horses at pasture,[3] for a genre painting called *Pouting* now in The Metropolitan Museum of Art, New York,[4] and for a third, *The Orchestra of the Opéra* (fig. 82), which centered around his friend, the bassoonist, Désiré Dihau, to whom he would write his first letter from New Orleans.[5] There is also a reminder of the *Dance Class at the Opéra* (fig. 86), the painting he had just finished and sold, in his having written the name and address of the model for the principal dancer (at the left) as "E. d'Hugues, 93 rue du Bac," on page A. But more than 130 pages were left bare—ready for his impressions of the voyage.

Degas used one page of the notebook to record the distances the boat had covered—beginning, "Scotia left 12 October 1872 at 4 o'clock from Liverpool / from Queenstown the 13 at 20 hours / Monday the 14th noon—174 [kilometers]"—until he gave up after a week.[6] He did report, however, to his father the day after he landed in New York on 23 October, "Crossing on board an English ship is sad. It has been dull for me because I could not profit from some of the conversations René engaged in, dumb as I am [in English]." He described New York more sympathetically, "Enormous city, enormous activity. Much closer in physiognomy and appearance to us than to the English."[7] Degas was not always consistent in his antipathies. Although he was clearly uncomfortable on an English ship and uneasy at entering a world where English was spoken, he very much admired the work of certain English contemporary painters.[8] He liked the

Page 161
   Sketch of a man leaning to the left and holding
   a rope with his left hand, 1872

Page 162
    Sketch of a man standing on the deck of a ship
    and drawing on his cape, seen from behind, 1872

Page 163
    Two sketches. (left) A man in profile, bust-length,
    with whiskers and a cap, with a note to the right;
    (right) A bearded man's head, 1872

Page 164
    Sketch of a man holding his arms out at his sides,
seen from behind, with water and sea gulls behind
him, 1872

Page 165
    Sketch of a man with his hands on his hips and
his head in profile, 1872

Page 167
Two sketches of cormorants, 1872

Page 169
Five sketches of white pelicans, 1872

Page 170
    Four sketches of a man, 1872

Page 171
    Four sketches of passengers on board the
    Scotia, 1872

artists when he knew them,[9] and throughout his life was always particularly welcoming to English artists and writers who wanted to visit his studio.[10]

On board the *Scotia* he found a fellow passenger he could caricature to vent his displeasure and discomfort with the English within the confines of the *Scotia*. The man was tall, ungainly, with a bristling beard, large nose and ears, and he dressed in a deer-stalker's cap, wore a very high collar that could almost be celluloid, and a rather more distinguished overcoat that—as the result of his exercises on deck—flared outward at the hem. He provided humorous silhouettes, particularly in his hat, collar, and neck from behind. On the page that faced his unfinished record of the *Scotia's* itinerary Degas drew this passenger in a grandiose position—his elbows jutting outward, his hands on his hips, his left leg bent at the knee and lifted on some support—as he looks defiantly out to sea. On another presumably stormier day, Degas showed him twisting something like a blanket over his shoulders for warmth and on the facing page grasping a rope for support on the open deck. The reduction of these absurdities to paper should have restored Degas's humor.

Degas seems to have turned the notebook around and, ignoring what he had drawn or written already, worked from the back in the opposite direction, making his first drawing of the Englishman on page 171 and the last on page 161. Before the first of these drawings he squiggled a few numbers on page 175, wrote out a list of some of the clothes he was taking on page 174, drew a mounted trainer on two pages, pages 173 to 172, obviously when the ship stopped on land, most probably at Queenstown (now Cobh) in Ireland at the entrance to Cork. The figures—presumably all of one bearded Irishman on the back of a humble steed—are rustic and furtive. From these he went on to the first two pages of studies of the Englishman and then somewhat uncharacteristically into three pages of birds, pages 169, 168, 167. One page is of charmingly spirited white pelicans drawn back into space—the first pair standing on the ground, the second swimming, and a third in isolation, possibly on the water. On one page there are two simple drawings of cormorants, the bird common to the north Atlantic—one swimming as innocently as a duck, the other standing on the ground and stretching out its beak. On the other page the drawings of seven cormorants are more varied in activity and in size (from baby birds to adults and smaller in the distance and larger closer to us). One near the invisible horizon floats with the equanimity of a swan. Degas could not resist jotting down the briefest of color notes on these birds, which are renowned for their shining black feathers—indicating "red" or "red head" or "white touches."

Much as he may have enjoyed these exercises with birds—which were probably seen when the *Scotia* was still near the shore of Ireland—Degas did not persist. He went back in the next five pages to his English gentleman.

The real quandary with this notebook and—indeed with the way Degas would work in New Orleans—is why he dropped the two practices in which he had engaged in this notebook, the one of purely informal sketching of whatever attracted his eye, the other of what he had done already in this notebook earlier (working in the opposite direction) in making studies of details and compositions that could be used in exhibitable works. When he finished with the English gentleman cavorting on deck, Degas simply gave up the notebook, leaving a substantial part of it—117 pages of 176—blank.

This continues as a quandary for the five months Degas lived (and worked) in New Orleans. There are almost no sketches or drawings for the paintings and pastels he did there and no evidence of the kind of preliminary exploration we might expect to find in a notebook, particularly for something as complicated as *A Cotton Office in New Orleans* (cat. 31).

1. W. B. Brown, Agent for the Cunard Lines Ltd., wrote James B. Byrnes, director of the Isaac Delgado Museum, now the New Orleans Museum of Art, on 12 April 1965 that the 3,871 ton *Scotia,* which had been built in 1862 and was "the last paddle steamer to be built for Cunard Line and is believed to be the most powerful paddle steamer ever built. Her length was 379 feet and her service speed was 14 knots."

2. See Reff, 1976.

3. Pp. 7 ?, 11 ?, 41, 42, studies for L 289, *Horses in a Meadow,* signed, "Edgar Degas 71," National Gallery of Art, Washington; 3, 5, 13, studies for L 291, *Two Horses in a Pasture,* owner unknown.

4. Pp. 36, 37, 39, studies for L 335, *Pouting,* Metropolitan Museum of Art, New York.

5. Pp. 28, 29, 31 33, 35, studies for L 186, *Orchestra of the Opéra,* Musée d'Orsay, Paris.

6. P. 166.

7. Fevre, 1949, 30–31.

8. Reff, Nb. 21, 31V, 31, 30, records Degas's interest in the English paintings in the World's Fair in Paris in 1867.

9. Appendix II, letter to Tissot, 19 November 1872, sends regards to Legros and Whistler and asks Tissot to tell Millais he was sorry to have missed the opportunity of meeting him and to "tell him of my appreciation for him." See also Theodore Reff, "The Butterfly and the Old Ox," in *Degas. The Artist's Mind* (New York, 1976), 15–36.

10. For an English artist's response, see Sickert, 1917, 183–91. Sickert, who was thirteen when Degas returned from New Orleans, met the French artist when Whistler sent him with a letter of introduction in 1883 but began to know him better at a gathering of writers and artists around the Halévys at Dieppe in 1885. Degas recorded this agreeable company in a pastel now in the Rhode Island School of Design Museum (L 824), in which he gave Sickert a prominent role. It was probably during this summer that Degas had talked of his stay in New Orleans and inspired Sickert to make the drawing, then or later, to which the title is given, *Degas in New Orleans* (fig. 106), which shows the painter in a smock with a palette and brushes, incongruous in a setting that is more sumptuous than the interiors Degas himself had painted in Louisiana.

Invalids and New Orleans

IT HAS BECOME USUAL TO BELIEVE that any woman painted or drawn by Degas who is ill or melancholy is one of his New Orleans cousins or was living in New Orleans itself. One reason for this is that, although none are dated, the paintings and drawings of these invalids seem to fall chronologically not too long before the First Impressionist Exhibition in 1874, which makes it convenient to place them between Degas's arrival in New Orleans in October 1872 and his departure the following March. Another reason is the suspicion that after the death of his mother when he was thirteen Degas, already for two years a boarder in a male school, the Lycée Louis-le-Grand, grew up in a masculine world—with a father; two brothers; two Musson uncles, who were then bachelors and living in France; several Degas uncles, who visited from Naples —and that he was therefore protected as a youth and young man from female tribulations, and was consequently fascinated with them in his maturity.[1] To counter this argument, except for the more than three years between 1856 and 1860 he spent in Italy, Degas did consider his father's apartment his home, where his two sisters and that rather presumptuous maid, Adèle Loÿe, lived. Just when his sisters Thérèse and Marguerite were ready to leave the family, there was the visitation of his New Orleans aunt and her two daughters and granddaughter. It may actually have been with the marriage of Thérèse in 1863 and that of Marguerite and the departure of the three Musson women for New Orleans in 1865, that Degas found he missed the daily companionship of women and wanted to understand their eccentricities. He also had substitutes for sisters and cousins in models, some of whom, like Emma Dobigny, he found sympathetic. Under any circumstances he wanted to record women when they needed or gave physical comfort.

The Musson women may have made Degas particularly aware of illness. During their stay in France they lived in Bourg-en-Bresse out of concern for the health of their mother. And it is quite clear that Estelle was suffering from serious depression. A year after their return to New Orleans, Estelle began to go blind, and six years later their mother died of Bright's disease.[2] As the painter approached New Orleans in 1872, there was some question whether he and René might be delayed because of an outbreak of yellow fever there.[3] They seem to have escaped the fever, but Estelle by then was, of course, married to René and incurably almost blind; in addition, she was pregnant with her fourth child—Degas's godchild—and was trying to hide this fact from her neighbors.[4] The third Musson sister, Mathilde Musson Bell, who did not go to France, gave birth to a child (one of six) earlier in 1872, and she might have been otherwise unwell since, after the artist's return to France she died five years later at the age of thirty-seven.[5] The associations of female invalidism with New Orleans consequently seem inevitable.

1. The author first proposed this in Zürich, 1994–95, 28.
2. Brown, 1991, Box II, folders 28, 33–49.
3. Appendix II, letter to Dihau.
4. Appendix II, letter to Rouart. The baby was expected ten days later.
5. Brown, 1991, Box III, folder 17.

20. *Head of a Woman*

1855–65
Graphite on pale pink paper
$11\frac{3}{8} \times 9\frac{3}{8}$ inches (29.1 × 20 cm)
Private Collection, on anonymous loan to
Portland Museum of Art, Maine

AT THE TIME OF THE 1965 EXHIBITION of Degas in New Orleans, this drawing was believed to be identifiable as a study of Estelle Musson Balfour about 1865, and therefore at the time of the watercolor (cat. 8) Degas had painted of her with her mother and her sister Désirée at Bourg-en-Bresse in 1865.[1] Today we are less confident that this is the explanation for this unhappy and almost histrionically compelling head, with the hair cut so roughly that only illness would seem to explain it. If it is only illness that justifies that untidy hair, the loose and petulant lower lip, and the unfocused eyes, it would have to be a much earlier drawing than 1865. The soft modeling of the flesh and the exaggerated shadow cast by the nose are consistent with Degas's drawings as a student, certainly before he returned from Italy in 1858.

There are ways in which this disturbing face suggests copies Degas made of earlier paintings like *The Preaching of St. Stephen* by Carpaccio in a French museum.[2] Although his drawing of the full figure of St. Stephen is always correctly identified, another drawing of the head alone was described as *Head of a Woman* in a recent sales catalogue.[3] This drawing possesses something of the sexual ambivalence as well as the sacrifice of personal identity to be found in many pictures of saints and martyrs. With his range of experience as a copyist in French and Italian churches and museums, Degas may have seen the same qualities in the faces of his contemporaries—normally women—whose misery could be explained by illness. Such studies may have prepared the way for his understanding of the Mussons later. Illness could be an expression of their own particular martyrdoms.

1. Byrnes in New Orleans, 1965, 54, pl. XVII.
2. Musée des Beaux-Arts, Rouen. See Loyrette in Rome, 1984, no. 2.
3. Sotheby's, New York, 26 February 1990, no. 8.

21. The Invalid (La Malade)

1868–73
Oil on canvas
25⅝ × 18½ inches (65 × 47 cm)
Collection of John Loeb, New York
Lemoisne 316

IN A NOTEBOOK DEGAS is believed to have used between 1868 and 1872, and therefore before he went to New Orleans, there is one cursory drawing of a young woman (fig. 89) who might be sitting and is leaning with her head against the back of a chair or a chaise longue. Reff, in cataloging the notebook, recognized that it was close to Degas's most poignant painting of an invalid, *The Invalid* (cat. 21). He was, however, somewhat embarrassed by the discovery and suggested that it is "possibly a study for *The Invalid* (Lemoisne 316), although the latter was supposedly painted in New Orleans and there is no evidence that this notebook was used there."[1] In the publication of a two-volume monograph on Degas immediately after his death, a good friend of Degas's, Paul Lafond, reproduced the painting.[2] Although it was shown in two early exhibitions of his work in Paris in 1923 and 1931,[3] lent in the first case by Degas's friend Henri Lerolle and in the second by Lerolle's widow, no hint of any connection with New Orleans was proposed. Lemoisne seems to have been the first to make the association by putting "Désirée Musson?" after the title in his *catalogue raisonné* of the artist's work published from 1946 to 1949.[4]

This drawing related to *The Invalid* is succeeded in the notebook by much more exact and tauter studies for works of the sixties like the portrait of Mme Gaujelin Degas exhibited in the Salon of 1869[5] or the portrait of Mme Burtin,[6] but with this drawing there was an abrupt change in subject matter and style. The subjects were more casual, informal, and usually, if not here, involving groups of figures— most frequently young girls in loose, belted dresses—in movement (fig. 90). Those movements, although they do indicate activity, have something of the languor of *The Invalid*. One could imagine that the setting had altered with this change in pace in the notebook, but the evidence of certain details suggests that the change was to the country house at Ménil-Hubert in Normandy of Degas's friends, the Valpinçons, rather than to New Orleans.[7]

FIG. 89. Edgar Degas, Notebook 22, page 45. Bibliothèque Nationale de France, Paris.

FIG. 90. Edgar Degas, Notebook 22, pages 114–15. Bibliothèque Nationale de France, Paris.

FIG. 91. Edgar Degas, Notebook 22, page 46. Bibliothèque Nationale de France, Paris.

1. Reff, Nb. 22, 45.

2. Lafond, 1918–19, II, reproduced facing 14.

3. 1924 Paris, Galerie Georges Petit, *Exposition Edgar Degas*, 12 April–22 May, no. 38; and 1931 Paris, Musée de l'Orangerie, *Degas Portraitiste*, 19 July–1 October, no. 54.

4. Lemoisne, 1946–49, no. 316.

5. Ibid., no. 165, Isabella Stewart Gardner Museum, Boston.

6. Ibid., no. 108, Virginia Museum of Fine Arts, Richmond.

7. See cat. 18, *At the Races in the Countryside*.

8. Reff, Nb. 22, 37, 41.

The only way to validate Lemoisne's hypothesis that *The Invalid* was painted in New Orleans is to concede that Degas might have taken another drawing of the same composition with him, or a canvas with the figure roughly brushed in, or that he had memorized the drawing so that in New Orleans he had no difficulty developing it. Even if he began with a drawing possibly made as much as five years before he went to New Orleans, he finished with paint and brush with the same kind of freedom he was achieving in the Fogg's version of the *Cotton Merchants in New Orleans* (cat. 32), which he painted there in early 1873.

The notebook in which the preliminary drawing exists has studies for some of Degas's most sensitive hands—in the portraits, for example, of Mme Burtin,[8] —but not unhappily for the hand on which this invalid leans her cheek. The delicate, long fingers are as limp as petals of a flower, somehow expressing their helplessness in not offering her consolation and giving very little support. The fingers of her right hand hang equally inadequately in the lower left corner of the painting. The white shift she wears glows beautifully but is shapeless. The black cape offers protection and conveys her sorrow. The thin brown veil that creeps from under the hood is another expression of inadequacy. (The cape, the veil, the shape of the dress are very much like the garments worn by the female figures [fig. 91] in the notebook, which contains the study for the position of her body.)

The focus of the painting is, however, the oval head with magnificent black eyes, the lids red and swollen, the mouth slightly and apathetically opened, the teeth visible, the skin of her cheek apparently faintly bruised—but from tears, not blows. Some hair falls down over her forehead as an expression of her absolute helplessness. We do not know whether she is suffering from illness— a physical malady—or is the victim of some tragedy. But we do know that her spirit has almost been destroyed.

If there is any question as to which of the Musson sisters this is, it is more likely to be Estelle than Désirée, whose face remained indomitably round.

21b. Young Woman Seated in a Garden

ca. 1868–73
Oil on canvas
13 × 16½ inches (33 × 42 cm)
Private Collection, New York
Lemoisne 315

SOMEWHAT IN THE SPIRIT of the drawing of young girls, which succeeded the original idea for *The Invalid* in the earlier notebook (fig. 89), is *Young Woman Seated in a Garden* to which Lemoisne added a line, "Probablement Désirée Musson à la Novelle-Orléans," in the entry for it in his catalogue (cat. 21b).[1]

She is as relaxed as the figure in *The Invalid* and as informally dressed as the girls in the notebook, but she lies back on the chaise with a certain contentment as if the rest had eased the pain, possibly in an ear. The white scarf or bandage around her head makes a decorative headdress. She is lethargically indulging herself out of doors and may actually appreciate the plots of flowers behind her. There is a sexual confidence in her bearing and the expression of her eyebrows, eyes, and mouth that do not suggest Désirée. She could more easily be the sister who did not go to France, Mathilde Musson Bell. A photograph shows that she had the same fine black hair, eyes, and brows (fig. 93). In any case the pain of *Young Woman Seated in a Garden* seems to be a passing affair, and we are free to take pleasure in the sight of a pretty young woman drowsing in a garden.

1. Lemoisne, 1946–49, no. 315, private collection.

FIG. 93. Mathilde Musson Bell, detail of fig. 128, ca. 1864. Collection of Adelaide Wisdom Benjamin.

22. *The Nurse (La Garde-Malade)*

1872–73
Oil on canvas
13 × 16½ inches (90 × 71 cm)
Private Collection, courtesy of Walter Feilchenfeldt
Lemoisne 314

FIG. 94. *Mathilde Musson Bell*, ca. 1864, photograph. Collection of Adelaide Wisdom Benjamin.

OF THESE FOUR PAINTINGS of invalids we are examining here, only *The Nurse* makes us believe that it *must* have been painted in New Orleans. Admittedly, the seated woman—the nurse—does not seem inevitably Creole as she sits with her arms folded, the lining of her hood framing her face, and the hem of her white nightgown revealed under her robe. Her appearance and even her bored impatience are international. On the other hand, since we know René had had a frustrating time in France hunting a nursemaid on the trip in which he brought Edgar back to New Orleans—even with the help of his father and the painter himself[1] and since this nurse is not black, it seems relatively safe to assume that this is the role Désirée would have played in the household in an emergency. Lemoisne does not fail to make this identification and indeed enlarges upon it proposing, "Probablement étude de Désirée Musson viveillant un de ses petits-neveux à la Nouvelle Orléans."[2] Her position does suggest patience overseeing the illness of a child rather than involvement in a more dramatic event like the birth of Estelle's child in December.

A photograph of the profile of Mathilde Musson Bell (fig. 94) has persuaded Victoria Cooke to suggest that it was Mathilde rather than Désirée who was the model. The contour of her hairline, the long slope of her nose, the withdrawn chin, as well as the probability that she, as a mother of three living children and the aunt of two (with another expected), was as often in this position as Désirée would have been; so this is a convincing proposal.

It is the architecture and the relationships of the spaces that persuade us that it is New Orleans—the very high ceilings, French windows, a suggestion that draperies are protecting the interior from light rather than exposing it. This space is provocative with the rapid recession across the nurse to the window in the back corner and, above all, with so much space given over in the foreground to a temptingly comfortable and empty bed with sheets of a frothy whiteness. Is it the bed the nurse has deserted for her patient? Or does it have some more sinister meaning? Whatever Degas intended with the setting, the nucleus of the work—the nurse—remains constant even if her lips are pursed and a piece of hair has escaped over her forehead. She is the symbol of family continuity.

1. Brown, 1991, Box II, folders 49d, e.
2. Lemoisne, 1946–49, no. 314.

23. *Woman with Bandage*

1872–73
Oil on canvas
$12\frac{5}{8} \times 9\frac{1}{2}$ inches (32 × 24 cm)
The Detroit Institute of Art, Bequest of
Robert H. Tannahill (70.168)
Lemoisne 275

HERE WE HAVE A THIRD INVALID (since the one in *The Nurse* is invisible), and she is positively saucy and smiling. The rather scraggly brown hair of the young woman is tucked under a plain bonnet and the huge white bandage over her left eye. Her costume and coiffure are simple enough to suggest that she is either a domestic or a modest housewife; nevertheless, she is placed beside a coffeemaker and a proper cup and saucer. Her folded arms and slightly crooked smile convey her jaunty courage. Because the eye that is not bandaged is red and swollen, it is obviously correct to think that she has a serious problem with her eyes, which would apply to the recently blind Estelle. However, although Estelle's face seemed round when she was at Bourg-en-Bresse, photographs of her in the seventies show that she had become quite gaunt, perhaps because of illnesses and childbearing. In fact, Estelle must have been closer to the physiognomy of the woman in *The Invalid* (cat. 21) than this. It is as if Degas had decided to pull the woman in *The Nurse* (cat. 22) out from the shadows into the light and, in addition to the sun, to give her courage, humor, and an indomitable spirit, in part conveyed by the red on her enchantingly *retroussé* nose. The small painting is the kind of gem to recall the work of Vermeer, an artist Degas very much admired but seldom challenged.

The Artist in New Orleans, October 1872–March 1873

DEGAS AND THE THREE MUSSON SISTERS IN NEW ORLEANS, 1872–73

WHEN DEGAS WENT TO NEW ORLEANS in October 1872, he found himself living in the same house (with three different households) with the three daughters of Michel Musson, his first cousins. The three were Désirée Musson (1838–1902), Mathilde Musson Bell (1841–78), and Estelle Musson De Gas (1843–1909). He probably met Désirée for the first time if she visited Italy in the late 1850s[1] and saw her in any case when she came with Estelle— who had been recently widowed—their mother, and Estelle's baby daughter to France to escape the Civil War in 1863.[2] After their return to New Orleans, Estelle had married the painter's brother René. There was no certain occasion on which Degas could have met the third sister, Mathilde Bell, before his arrival in October 1872.[3] He was a guest in the mansion Michel Musson had rented on Esplanade, living with his uncle and Désirée on the ground floor. The second floor was divided into two apartments, with the Bells in one and the family of René De Gas in the other. This arrangement gave Degas a chance to know these three sisters as intimately as he would have known his own. In addition, there would have been considerable pressure upon him to paint their portraits. As he wrote his friend, the Danish painter Lorentz Frölich, "It is true that I am not working very much but on some difficult things. Family portraits, near enough to the taste of the family, in impossible light, everything upset, with the models full of affection but a little shameless, taking you less seriously because you are their nephew or cousin."[4]

Degas took the portraits he painted or drew back with him to France. Only one painting and one drawing of these were sold in his lifetime. They were the *Woman with a Vase of Flowers* (cat. 27), which Degas's friend the engraver Michel Manzi bought and sold to the great collector Isaac de Camondo in 1894, who gave it to the Louvre in 1914. The pastel drawing (fig. 95) was bought by Édmond Taigny and made its way through the Havemeyer Collection into The Metropolitan Museum of Art, New York, by 1929.[5] The others were only known through the exhibitions and catalogues of the contents of the artist's studio after his death in 1917. By then all three sisters were dead. Their father, who in extended mourning for his middle daughter Mathilde Bell continued to plead with Degas to send him the pastel he had made of Mathilde,

FIG. 95. Edgar Degas, *The Artist's Cousin, probably Mrs. William Bell*, 1872–73, charcoal and pastel on cardboard, 25 × 22⅞ in. The Metropolitan Museum of Art, H. O. Havemeyer Collection. Lemoisne 319.

had died in 1885. As a result, with the single exception of the painter's youngest brother, René, who had married Estelle in 1869 and deserted her nine years later, no one was in a position to help with the identification of the portraits Degas made in New Orleans that could have been of any of these three women. Consequently, even here their identification is on rather treacherous ground.

1. Boggs in this book, 126–29.
2. Ibid., 130–32.
3. Feigenbaum in this book, n. 20.
4. Appendix II, letter to Frölich.
5. Gretchen Wold in Alice Cooney Frelinghuysen et al., *Splendid Legacy, The Havemeyer Collection* (New York, 1993), no. 204, 327.

PORTRAITS OF MATHILDE MUSSON BELL

THE SINGLE PORTRAIT of any of the three Musson sisters in which the identity of the sitter seems to be secure by common consent [1] and also by some external documentation is the pastel *Woman Seated on a Balcony* (cat. 24), which is almost certainly Mathilde Musson Bell. There is a preparatory drawing for it (cat. 25), which Degas inscribed in the lower right, "Nouvelle Orléans 72/Degas" so that there is no question about the location and date of either. It would have been natural of Degas in coming to New Orleans and meeting this cousin for the first time to have made her the object of one of his first portraits there.

When Mathilde died sadly young—age thirty-seven—in September 1878, her father, who was already distraught because of the desertion of Estelle by his nephew René De Gas in April, received a letter of 29 September 1879 from his brother Henri in France saying, "I transmitted to Edgar your desire to have the portrait of Mathilde. He said it was sent by Achille who ought to be in New Orleans the first of September." [2] In December Michel wrote to Henri, "Once more we renewed our request to Edgar for the portrait of our dear Mathilde of whom we have only sketches in black pencil and a photograph taken in 1862." [3] Henri wrote Michel in January 1880, "I reminded Edgar of his promise to send you his study of Mathilde, He told me that he was going to do so." [4] Later in the year in a letter with the date now obscured, Henri wrote Michel, "Edgar keeps answering yes and doesn't send the portrait. I won't let him off the hook. It's not bad will, but the impossibility of finding time to harmonize [the color]." [5] In July 1881 Michel still persisted with Henri as the intermediary, "I would be so proud to have something else from him besides the oil or pencil sketch of our late lamented Mathilde." [6] We can sympathize with both uncle and nephew: the uncle distraught by the desertion of Estelle by his nephew and his perception of the need to adopt her children; both seriously worried about money in part, at least, because Michel had persuaded the French family to invest in Confederate bonds; [7] the painter desperate because he was finding it impossible to meet his obligations to supply certain works of art to the baritone and collector,

24. *Woman Seated on a Balcony*

1872
Pastel
24$\frac{3}{8}$ × 29$\frac{7}{8}$ inches (62.5 × 76.5 cm)
Ordrupgaard, Copenhagen, Denmark
Lemoisne 318

25. *Mathilde Musson Bell*

1872
Pencil and yellow chalk on paper
12½ × 9½ inches (31 × 24 cm)
Collection of Carol Selle, New York

Jean-Baptiste Faure;[8] and both men humiliated by the actions of René. Against those passions it is almost impossible to judge the depth of their affection for Mathilde. And it is even more difficult to get any sense of Mathilde herself aside from Degas's portraits of her and perhaps even from his variations on those portraits.

We are told that Mathilde was the third child of Michel and Odile Musson, but when she was almost eight her brother, born between Désirée and Mathilde, died at the age of nine. She lost two other brothers and a sister before she turned twenty. At twenty-one Mathilde married William Bell, English-speaking and a Protestant, and gave birth to a son who died two years later, just after her mother and two sisters returned from France in 1865. By the time Degas visited New Orleans, she had a daughter and two sons who survived and would have another daughter who lived and a son who did not. Degas wrote to Tissot on 19 November, "To make a cousin sit for you who is feeding an imp of two months is quite hard work."[9] But other than a reference given by Christopher Benfey to her relief work,[10] we know very little of Mathilde.

The assumption that the pastel at Odrupgaard is a portrait of her is based on two facts. Two photographs of her (figs. 93, 94) survive but neither support nor deny the assumption. One assumption is that the pastel is clearly unfinished, which would explain Degas's unwillingness to send it before it was clarified and unified—not normally an impossibility if he had not been otherwise so much preoccupied. The other is that her bearing—her neck stretched slightly upward under the black ribbon, her head tilted both graciously and attentively, her eyebrows raised and her lips slightly pursed with a pleasure that is politely restrained—shows a desire to please and gives her considerable charm, more than there is in any of his portraits of Estelle Musson. That Degas worked toward this effect is apparent in a preparatory drawing, dated 1872, in pencil with a few decorative touches of color (cat. 25), the yellow on the hair wishful thinking because the hair of all three cousins seems to have been resolutely dark when they were young. Two places in which we can see the increasing refinement that makes Mathilde in the final pastel such an understated seductress are in her shoulders and the back of her neck, where the contours have been changed.

This young woman in the pastel, with the large tropical fan[11] wears a dress that is faintly, shimmeringly mauve with orange ribbons. This is set off by the understated green foliage we see beyond the ornate cast-iron veranda typical of New Orleans houses in the nineteenth century. In the late seventies and early eighties, in spite of the irritating pleas of his uncle, Degas may have decided

26. Mathilde Musson Bell

1872
Pastel on beige paper
$25\frac{3}{8} \times 11\frac{5}{8}$ inches (66 × 49 cm)
Göteborgs Konstmuseum, Göteborg, Sweden
Lemoisne supp. 65

that he didn't want to shatter the fragility, the very allusiveness of the impression given of Mathilde in the pastel, which is enhanced by the theatrical artificiality of the architecture in the background.

Degas did two other things with the face of Mathilde Bell. In one magnificent drawing (fig. 95), which was sold during his lifetime and is now in The Metropolitan Museum as part of the Havemeyer Collection, he made this variation on her portrait more authoritative and commanding than mildly flirtatious. He lifted her head up and back on a longer and barer neck, added height to her forehead and lengthened her chin, and subdued her eyebrows so that she appears more elegant and aristocratic. He also deepened her eyes so that she is more withdrawn. Any allusions this head might make to the eighteenth century are reinforced by the second rough, incomplete mask of her face, as Quentin de la Tour might have drawn it, to emphasize the distinction of the other head on the page.[12]

Lemoisne in his catalogue of the works of Degas with color, wonders whether it was The Metropolitan's drawing with pastel or Ordrupgaard's fuller pastel that made Degas write in November 1872, "I have just spoiled a large pastel with a certain mortification."[13] It is more probably Göteborgs's pastel (cat. 26) that is in the supplement to Lemoisne's catalogue and in which the features and even the body have been coarsened and made clumsy. This is the second [*Variations on a*] *Portrait of Mathilde Musson Bell* in which the shoulders, for example, hump forward and the tie of her black ribbon escapes against her shoulder as if it were a wayward lock of hair. This wanton effect is emphasized by her worried expression. Everything is exaggerated by the strength of the contrast between the light pastels and the paper, which has been burned brown with the years. Degas had been seeking something quite different from the refinement of the other pastels—but one could understand his mortification in realizing that ultimately in this expressive work he had been suggesting that Mathilde Bell was unhappy, immature, and giddy, perhaps not unrelated to his reading of Fielding's *Tom Jones* a little over a decade before.[14]

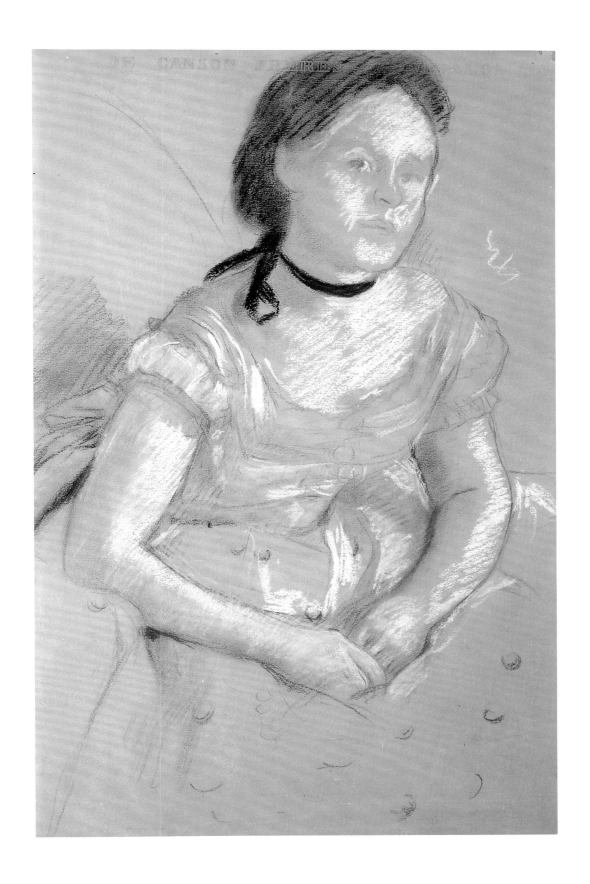

The two variations upon the original portraits of Mathilde Musson had ranged from refined elevation to something close to bawdy crudity. Whether there had been anything in this cousin of the two extremes he had fantasized with charcoal and pastel when thinking of Mathilde Bell, Degas himself was capable of exploring that range of possibilities, independently of the sitter.

1. Lemoisne 318, 319 in his postwar *catalogue raisonné* still clung to the identification of cat. 24 and fig. 95 as Estelle Musson De Gas. Boggs in Saint Louis, 1967, no. 68, 108, 110, identified cat. 25 as Mathilde Musson Bell because "her eyes are too animated to be her sister"; Brame and Reff, in their supplement to Lemoisne's catalogue, BR no. 65, have not only identified this pastel but also L 318, L 319 and cat. 25 as Mathilde Musson Bell; Rewald, 1985, 32, 33 and figs. 12 and 13, identified cat. 24 and cat. 25 as Mathilde Bell ?; Mikael Wivel, *Degas in Time* (Copenhagen, 1994), 23 identifies the woman in the pastel (cat. 24) as "more probably Mathilde Musson Bell than Estelle Musson Degas"; Felix Baumann and Marianne Karabelnik in Zürich, 1994–95, no. 113, 343, color plate p. 201 as Mathilde Musson Bell.

2. Brown, 1991, Box III, folder 39.

3. Ibid., folder 38.

4. Ibid., Box IV, folder 2.

5. Ibid., folder 6d.

6. Ibid., folder 22. There may have been a certain hypocrisy in this letter of 31 July 1881 since in a letter to Degas on 12 July 1883, he makes a detailed reference to a critical assessment of his work in the *Revue de deux mondes* of 15 May 1879 (Brown, 1991, Box IV, folder 37) and could not have been ignorant of his nephew's growing fame.

7. For the most reliable references, see Brown, "Franco-American Aspects of Degas, *A Cotton Office in New Orleans*," in this book, nn. 29, 30, p. 62.

8. For the most succinct account of Degas's difficulties with Faure, see Pantazzi in Paris, Ottawa, New York, 1988, 221–23.

9. Appendix II, letter to Tissot, 19 November 1872.

10. Benfey, 1997, 192, writes, "Mathilde Bell joined in relief efforts for the families of the dead and the wounded." In n. 45 under "Mardi Gras," he refers to Stuart Omer Landry, *The Battle of Liberty Place* (New Orleans, 1955), 222.

11. Maheux in Boggs and Maheux, 1992, no. 5, 48, describes it as an embroidery hoop, but it is in fact a palmetto fan.

12. Boggs in Boggs and Maheux, 10–11.

13. Lemoisne 318. Appendix II, letter to Tissot, 27 November 1872.

14. Reff, Nb. 18, 161, "En ce moment je lis Tom Jones."

PORTRAITS OF ESTELLE MUSSON DE GAS

WHEREAS DEGAS HAD NOT REALLY KNOWN Mathilde Bell and therefore tried to understand her better by expanding on the possibilities in her character from his own imagination, her sister Estelle was not only more familiar because she was his sister-in-law but also because he had known her and drawn and painted her more than once during her stay in France almost a decade earlier. What he had seen and painted then was the inevitable melancholy of a young woman who had just been widowed and afterward given birth to a baby and was living in exile with her mother and a sister in what must have seemed a foreign land. In New Orleans, on the other hand, she had been married for four years to Degas's brother René, had given birth to two of his children (Pierre and Odile) and was expecting a third. Her daughter by her first marriage, Josephine (Joe) Balfour, was now ten. Estelle was pursued by tragedy and, in spite of being in a situation we would like to be able to describe as domestic bliss, she was facing the prospect of total blindness. Because Degas was always worried about this possibility himself, this made him particularly sympathetic to Estelle.

It is curious, nevertheless, in reviewing the artist's letters from New Orleans the extent to which he emphasized Estelle's blindness. To Désiré Dihau he wrote, "My poor Estelle, the wife of René is blind as you know. She manages it in an unprecedented manner, hardly needing help in the house. She recalls the rooms and the location of the furniture so that she never bumps into anything. And there is no hope!"[1] To Tissot he wrote that she is "an excellent wife who scarcely seems blind, although she is, almost without hope."[2] To Henri Rouart he wrote that she is blind "but overcomes this misfortune" and later commented that "the lack of Opera is a real deprivation for Estelle who is a musician and counts upon it."[3] To counter this emphasis on her blindness, he usually mentions that she is pregnant with a child for whom he will be the godfather and is attempting to hide her pregnancy outside the family.

Degas did paint one portrait of Estelle pregnant (fig. 96), which is in the National Gallery of Art in Washington, D.C., from which it cannot be lent

27. *Woman with a Vase of Flowers*

1872–73
Oil on canvas
$25\frac{5}{8} \times 13\frac{3}{8}$ inches (65 × 34 cm)
Musée d'Orsay, Paris (RF 1983)
Lemoisne 305

because of the terms of the bequest of its donor, Chester Dale. Although the painting is in oil and larger than the paper used for the pastel of Mathilde (cat. 24), now in Ordrupgaard, it also has a horizontal format and is intended to please. Estelle, like Mathilde, sits with her charming muslin skirt spread about her, which also conceals her pregnancy. Although the painting is in oil and the canvas larger than the paper used for the pastel of Mathilde, its effect is more intimate. Estelle sits in a room without the vistas to the external world of Mathilde's balcony. Estelle's room's soft pink walls and white chaise both protect and flatter her. She sits formally, sedately, with her hands folded, like a good child or even a doll. These virtues are also found in comparing her dress with that of Mathilde in the pastel. Although the fabric of the dress, as in the drawing of Mathilde (cat. 25), is covered with large dots like coins showered by a generous Zeus, Estelle's dress, perhaps because of her pregnancy, is of a much more conservative cut—the sleeves long and fully covering her arms, the V of her neck equally modest. And there is nothing of the conquettishness of Mathilde as Estelle looks away from us, as removed as she was (if not remotely as tragically so) as in the head Degas had painted of her (cat. 10) at Bourg-en-Bresse seven years before. As Loyrette describes it (although he does not agree with all the conclusions here), "Estelle's soft gaze, darkened with blindness,"[4] keeps her apart. The slight mobility in the eyebrows and mouth do indicate some uncertainty and a slight yearning which are not, however, focused upon us.

In the next painting accepted here as Estelle and called somewhat evasively *Woman with a Vase of Flowers* (cat. 27), we seem to face a contradiction in the vertical strain of the composition against the repose of the National Gallery painting—the dramatic intensity of the forms closing in and around the women's body. The tension in that body is revealed in the fingers of her right hand and the drama in the face. Could it possibly be the same woman?

If we can forget the question of pregnancy, we should consider the heads in both paintings, assuming that they are the shells for a superb actress. Could

FIG. 96. Edgar Degas, *Madame René De Gas*, 1872–73, oil on canvas, 28¾ × 36¼ in. Chester Dale Collection. National Gallery of Art, Washington, D.C.

they then possibly be the same? The eyebrows are both wide and prominent, the eyes narrow, the nose long, the lips thin but expressive. If we compare the head of the National Gallery painting with Degas's representations of Estelle at Bourg-en-Bresse (cat. 10), it seems that the young woman in that painting must be Estelle. On the other hand if we turn to a family photograph of Estelle with Désirée (fig. 55) about 1879 (the year after René left her), the length of the head and the nose, the very blackness of the small eyes, the narrow lips are close to the Musée d'Orsay's *Woman with a Vase of Flowers*. These differences may not have been impossible for an actress to reconcile.

Degas, in his love of the theater and his affection for Estelle, turned her into a very great actress indeed. Instead of the docile, tender, accommodating young matron in Washington's painting, we have a genuinely tragic figure hemmed in by the fates and straining like a panther against such a destiny. In her pinkish beige dress and pale skin, she is made commanding and attractive, but she is surrounded by more assertive colors—the greenish blue of the wall, the purplish blue of the vase, the deep red of the flowers—that seem to mock her inability to experience their intensity. The leaves are equally challenging and dangerous. Consolation is offered in the velour of the chair and possibly even in the scent of the flower. Nevertheless, her entrapment in her own blindness is further emphasized by the dramatic shadow her head casts on the wall and particularly by those sensitive fingers pressed against the back of the chair and played off against her deeply shadowed eyes. The tension of her other hand is offered release in the empty gloves cast aside on the table. Her head with its harsh features and somewhat untidy hair, as if it were the wing of a raven, suggests the erosion that is taking place from within—weighing down her brows, casting black smudges under her eyes, attempting a smile with her lips. Degas's ultimate expressive touch is one that Picasso would have admired—the isolation of Estelle's right eye by a passage of light against the shadow so that there could be no question of her blindness and perhaps even her compensatory dramatic powers. It is a complex and bewildering painting that René identified as his former wife.[5]

With the largest canvas we know Degas to have used in New Orleans, he began another portrait of Estelle (cat. 28), in which the panther inside her was subdued and she appears contentedly domestic, "the excellent wife" as Degas had described her to Tissot. Of the three portraits of her in New Orleans by

28. Portrait of Mme René De Gas,
née Estelle Musson

1872–73
Oil on canvas
39⅜ × 54 inches (102 × 138 cm)
New Orleans Museum of Art: Museum Purchase
through Public Subscription (65.1)
Lemoisne 306

Degas, she is the most naturally pregnant in this painting. She wears a flattering black dress with white sleeves framing her hands and a white ruff around her neck and down her bodice, meeting a pink camellia in a bouquet, which directs our eyes gently toward her womb. She also balances her cumbersome body as if its very girth were foreign to her. Her blindness is suggested by that shadowed face. Its attention does not seem directed toward the delicate action of her right hand as it places a gladiola in a tall vase of flowers. The blindness is there—just as the pregnancy is, framed by the leaves, vase, and flowers—but it is more irreversible. What is painted most sensually is what she would understand from her own sense of touch and smell. The wall is indefinite, its plane unclear because it would not matter to her, the window a symbol, viewless rather than a reality, but the flowers are very much alive, as they are torn apart on the tabletop or inserted into vases by those deft fingers. Although it is probable that Degas intended to continue to develop this painting and added canvas to do so, when removed from Estelle after his return to Paris, he may never have felt the same urgency to complete it (see bottom fig. on page 15). But it is a major work in the New Orleans Museum of Art, standing for Degas's growing admiration for Estelle.

The domestic side of Estelle is important here, but there is something of the actress as well in the thick black hair and the reddened lips. Degas also lengthened her face and, in particular, her chin. This does not make it improbable that Estelle could have been the model for *The Invalid* (cat. 21), whose features are similar. Degas makes us believe that Estelle could also have played that role.

1. Appendix II, letter to Dihau.

2. Ibid., letter to Tissot, 19 November 1872.

3. Ibid., letter to Rouart.

4. Loyrette in Paris, Ottawa, New York, 1988, no. 112, 182.

5. Lemoisne told the author. See Boggs in Berkeley, 1962, 93, n. 82.

DÉSIRÉE MUSSON

IN THE SPECULATION about which of these women was painted or drawn by Degas in New Orleans, Désirée Musson has been a favorite candidate. One reason for this is probably romantic—to assume an attraction between Degas and Désirée because there had been a tradition of cousins marrying in both the Degas and Musson families and because, after all, she was an appropriate four years younger than he. But there does not seem to be evidence of any particular familiarity.

It has been speculated that Désirée could have been the model for the *Woman with a Vase of Flowers* (cat. 27) or for the painting in the New Orleans Museum of Art believed to be Estelle Musson De Gas (cat. 28). She has also been considered to be the figure in *The Invalid* (cat. 21) and more probably *The Nurse* (cat. 22), but there is not enough evidence to confirm these speculations. Important as she was in the life of the Musson family in New Orleans, there is no evidence that she had the same importance in the paintings by Degas on his only trip to America.[1]

1. Loyrette considers the possibilities of Désirée as the model in certain New Orleans works sympathetically in Paris, Ottawa, New York, 1988, no. 112, 182; no. 114, 184.

THE CHILDREN IN
NEW ORLEANS

IN VISITING NEW ORLEANS Degas, at the age of thirty-eight, was tempted by the charms of family life. This makes it seem that suggestions of some consideration of a marriage between Désirée and Degas may be justified— and that Degas may even have contemplated it himself. In our earliest letter from America, Degas began his description to Désiré Dihau of the reception he (and René) received from the New Orleans family at the railroad station when they arrived, with—"What a good thing a family is!"[1] To Henri Rouart, the very model of a *paterfamilias,* he confessed, "I am thirsting for order.—I do not even regard a good woman as the enemy of this new method of existence.— A few children for me of my own, is that excessive too? No. . . . It is the right moment, just right."[2] He echoed the same sentiment to Tissot, "A good family; it is really a good thing to have good children," but he may have revealed the superficiality of these sentiments when he added, "to be free of the need of being gallant."[3] It is possible that that need to be gallant was becoming oppressive and, because of his genuine love of children, marriage offered some form of escape.

Degas did have nieces and nephews by his sister Marguerite in Paris and he showed an affection for them in drawings like one of his first niece, Célestine Fevre, as a baby seated in a bathtub, which he inscribed, "Écoutant l'histoire de la bonne Mimi dans son bain / 24 déc. 67,"[4] but he had been presented with the young Fevres gradually. In New Orleans he met six young children at once, all but one for the first time—two by his brother René and their cousin Estelle, three by their cousin Mathilde and her husband, William Bell, and a sixth, Joe Balfour, who was Estelle's child by her first marriage. He described these children to Dihau, "Pierre, René's son, is superb, he is so self-possessed and the mixture of English and French is so quaint![5]—Odile, his little girl, is 12 to 15 months old.[6] Jane [*sic*], the eldest, his wife's daughter, has a real feeling for music; she is beginning to solfa in the Italian solfeggio. There is also little Carrie, daughter of Mathilde, the younger of my cousins.[7] Mathilde also decided to have another boy called Sydney[8] and a little brat of two months called Willy.[9]—

29. Children on a Doorstep (New Orleans)

1872
Oil on canvas
23⅝ × 29½ inches (60 × 75 cm)
Ordrupgaard, Copenhagen (31), Denmark
Lemoisne 309

FIG. 97. Edgar Degas, *Portrait of a Young Girl in a White Bonnet*, ca. 1872–73, oil on canvas, 21⅝ × 15⅜ in. Location unknown. Lemoisne 311.

The whole band is watched over by black women of different shades."[10] Degas's interest in them individually is some indication of his enthusiasm. This could not have been decreased by the birth of his goddaughter Jeanne to René and Estelle on 20 December.[11]

Degas painted a reminder of the New Orleans children and considered it sufficiently important to exhibit in the Second Impressionist Exhibition. (The other New Orleans painting he showed was the now more famous *A Cotton Office in New Orleans* (cat. 31). *Children on a Doorstep (New Orleans)* (cat. 29) shows three of them with a bonneted figure, usually interpreted as a black nanny, seated on a stoop toward the back garden of the Musson house, with a somewhat older girl in a white bonnet leaning against the sill and looking down toward them.

In spite of Degas's description of the six children who had greeted him in New Orleans, it has not been easy to identify them in the painting. It has generally been considered that Joe Balfour at ten would have been too large for the girl standing by the door, and that Carrie, the first surviving child of the Bells, at five and a half would have been too small. [12] In the end, somewhat reinforced by consideration of the independent painting of this standing girl (fig. 97), who wears a bonnet as modest, as concealing, and as restricting as the habit of a nun, it seems possible that she might have been Joe, whom Degas, after all, described to the Danish painter Frölich as "9 years old" when she was ten.[13] It is even more probable that five-year-old Carrie Bell was the girl with her back toward us, with long hair and a ribbon tied around her waist. The very docility of her position as well as the sense of responsibility it suggests toward those who are younger than she, was worked out by Degas first in a small painting (cat. 30). In the large canvas he made her seem more adult by straightening her arm and decorating the sleeves with parallel horizontal bands. Next to her sits a small child with beautiful blond hair looking appealingly toward us. It might be either Odile, the daughter of René and Estelle, age fifteen months, or Sydney, the son of William and Mathilde Bell, age eighteen months.[14] Pierre, the "superb," "self-possessed" boy of two and a half, is generally accepted as the boy in the shadow facing the two seated on the top steps, although he could easily be a black boy who played with the children. Beside them, hardly visible, is the figure dressed in dark grey who must have been some kind of nursemaid.

30. Young Girl in a White Dress
1872
Oil on canvas
$10\frac{1}{2} \times 8\frac{5}{8}$ inches (27.5 × 21 cm)
Private Collection, The Bahamas
Lemoisne 310

Since Degas wrote in his letter to Dihau, "The whole band is watched over by black women of different shades,"[15] we assume she must have been black.

There is still another member of the household on the main axis at the left of the painting—the white mastiff that Degas is credited with naming Vasco de Gama.[16] He helps carry our eyes over the garden wall to a white house across Tonti Street, which looks more like a large suburban "cottage" with sloping roofs than a townhouse in the middle of New Orleans. Even when Degas painted the house, it was recently inhabited by a M. and Mme Olivier and their two children.[17] Mme Olivier taught music, including piano to Joe and the De Gas and Bell children, and was also reputedly hired by René De Gas to read to his blind wife. She and René were to fall in love and to elope in 1878.[18]

In coming to terms with this painting, it is probably important to realize that Degas intended to leave it in what many would consider an unfinished condition. He did sign it,[19] which he did so rarely that it does signify that he believed it was complete. It was rather like his second version of *A Cotton Office,* called *Cotton Merchants in New Orleans* (cat. 32), which he described to Tissot as "less complicated and more spontaneous, better art."[20] And, of course, he exhibited the painting of the children to the public, a rarity in itself for Degas.

The very lack of a sharply focused finish in *Children on a Doorstep (New Orleans)* makes it trance-like, a world in which movements are slow, light is gentle, colors tender. It is not a place for struggle or recriminations. The children gathered around the door are particularly young and vulnerable and yet protected rather than threatened by anything in the foreground. At the same time—almost inevitably—our eyes are led to the body of the dog which carries them back to the dark, closed door in the wall. After its sudden break we find the Oliviers' house. It is as if Degas had anticipated the destructive forces that could be unleashed from that modest dwelling, which would destroy the serenity of those young children in the foreground. We do not know that Degas was as perceptive as René's old friend Harmion Watts[21] or as ready to admit such a perception if he had faced it, but certainly he made these children seem defenseless before that house above.

1. Appendix II, letter to Dihau.

2. Ibid., letter to Rouart.

3. Ibid., letter to Tissot, 19 November 1872.

4. This drawing has no conventional catalogue number, is in a European private collection, and was reproduced in Saint Louis, 1967, no. 52, 89.

5. This letter was written on 11 November 1872, although Degas had arrived in New Orleans a couple of weeks earlier. Pierre (Michel Pierre) had been born on 1 April 1870 and was therefore two and a half. He died in 1881.

6. Odile (Odile De Gas Musson) was born on 27 August 1871 and was therefore fifteen months old. She did not marry and died in 1936. She became a source of information on the New Orleans family for both Lemoisne and Rewald when they (separately) began to investigate Degas's New Orleans connections.

7. Carrie (Mathilde Caroline) was born on 7 February 1867 and was therefore five and a half when Degas arrived. She died in 1937.

8. Sydney (Louis Sidney) was born on 14 April 1871 and was therefore eighteen months. He died in 1941.

9. Willy (William A., "Judge") was born on 25 September 1872. He died in 1896.

10. Appendix II, letter to Dihau.

11. Jeanne De Gas was born on 20 December 1872 and died on 4 October 1878.

12. Odile De Gas Musson, who died in 1936, was consulted by both Lemoisne and Rewald about the identification of the children. It was she who suggested that it was five-year-old Carrie standing and Joe seated, which is clearly an impossibility.

13. Appendix II, letter to Frölich.

14. Odile De Gas Musson identified the seated blond child as herself. On the other hand, it seems more probably a boy and, therefore, Sydney Bell.

15. Appendix II, letter to Dihau.

16. Lemoisne I, 1946–49, 77. The name is that of the Portuguese explorer (1469–1524).

17. Byrnes in New Orleans, 1965, 37–38. They lived at 1221 North Tonti, which is now 2306.

18. By far the fullest and most thoroughly documented account of the elopement of America Durrive Olivier and René De Gas and its aftereffects is to be found in Loyrette, 1991, 324–29.

19. A signature like this by Degas himself needs to be distinguished from the stamps, usually printed in red, which were placed on the works when inventorying his collection after his death.

20. Appendix II, letter to Tissot, 18 February 1873.

21. See Brown, 1991, Box III, folder 13, for the letter Watts wrote Désirée on 25 April 1878 about their love and elopement. See fig. 125.

JOSEPHINE (JOE) BALFOUR
(1863–81)

THE ONLY CHILD FROM NEW ORLEANS Degas knew already when he arrived in October 1872 was Josephine Balfour, the daughter of his cousin Estelle, who had come to France as a baby in the summer of 1863. Afterward, Degas saw her during the two years she spent with her mother, aunt Désireé, and grandmother, whenever he visited them at Bourg-en-Bresse. Désirée wrote how enchanted Degas was with Joe, as she was called, but found her too restless to make a good model.[1] One drawing (cat. 9) may show her as a baby.

Joe was seven when her widowed mother, Estelle Musson Balfour, married for a second time and to their cousin René De Gas. When Joe was little more than two and living in France, she may have anticipated the event by learning to say, "Bonjour, René De Gas."[2] Her mother probably encouraged her to adopt fanciful names since, when she was about a year and a half old, Estelle referred to her in a letter as "Miss Joe,"[3] the "Miss" a reminder that she was not Creole but the daughter of an English-speaking Protestant, Joseph Davis Balfour, who had risen from first lieutenant to major in the Confederate army when he was killed at the battle of Corinth on 4 October 1862. The De Gas–Musson Papers at Tulane University contain many notes by Joe, including one wishing her grandfather Michel Musson happy birthday on 29 September 1869,[4] a little more than two months after the marriage of her mother to René, as she would wish him Happy New Year on 1 January 1871.[5] It is not so much that she was sufficiently loving or well-behaved to have sent those notes—but that she was sufficiently loved that these notes were treasured. René wrote to her on occasion himself as he did on 25 July 1872 saying he expects her to speak French, not English, when he returns to New Orleans. He will leave from Paris where he will buy pretty things for her and pick up Edgar, "who wishes to come with him to hug all of you."[6] She begins to adopt nicknames of her own contriving, as her mother had once called her "Miss" Balfour. She writes on one occasion as Joe "de Burleigh,"[7] and on 19 May 1878 as Joe "de Marie" about a school picnic to her grandfather.[8] There is correspondence with her while she boarded at the Convent of the Visitation in Mobile, Alabama, where she was amused to be called one of the "French girls."[9] The last letter from Joe seemed to be one in which at the age of nineteen she was assuming certain responsibilities in informing her uncle William Bell on 9 April 1881 that his nephew by marriage, Pierre De Gas, age eleven, was ill with scarlet fever.[10] Two days later Pierre died. And a week later Joe followed.

Degas had fortunately seen the restless baby grown—now a charming child of ten when he decided to paint her in New Orleans. Admittedly, his painting of Joe Balfour, which is called *Le Pédicure,* more properly belongs to genre than to portraiture (fig. 98). It shows, however, how loved and cossetted she was in her grandfather's house. A chiropodist has been called in to attend to her feet. Degas may have been amused about how humble his *Le Pédicure* was compared with Rembrandt's great painting of *Bathsheba,* which had just entered the Louvre four years before. Joe, unlike that biblical courtesan, is swaddled in a wonderfully white towel or sheet, only part of her right leg and a little of the bottom of the foot modestly revealed. She is completely relaxed like any child who never has been given any reason to be afraid. The chiropodist is one of Degas's anonymous male figures with a bald pate, this one reflecting a patch of light from the window behind her, which also may have illuminated, if more whitely, her shoulder. Joe is surrounded by a setting that suggests a certain comfort and ease—the delicious calm of the pale, slightly blue-green wall, the dresser with a black jug and a hexagonal ceramic bowl, and a mirror with a narrow gilt frame above. She sits on a comfortable tufted seat of a chintz with a diaper pattern inspired by a trellis of roses. The glimpse of the rug is a deep pink. In the lower right corner there is a round foot bath of the kind that would shortly begin to appear in Degas's prints and pastels of bathers. There are also small paintings hanging on the wall or placed against the wall or mirror. They seem to be landscapes which Degas was certainly not painting in Louisiana, and they seem a little sophisticated to be by Joe herself. But perhaps they are another expression of the indulgence of the world in which she lives. Her face is too shadowed, too trusting to express anything more.

Although Loyrette seems ready to concede that this could have been begun in New Orleans, he is inclined to believe that in spite of its American subject it was painted in France.[11]

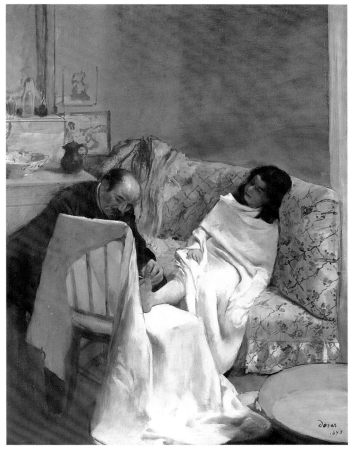

FIG. 98. Edgar Degas, *Le Pédicure,* 1873, essence on paper mounted on canvas, 24 × 18⅛ in. Musée d'Orsay, Paris. Lemoisne 323.

1. Brown, 1991, Box II, folder 16, 5 January 1865.

2. Ibid., folder 9a, letter from Désirée, 31 August 1864.

3. Ibid., folder 11g, 27 October 1864.

4. Ibid., folder 32.

5. Ibid., folder 51.

6. Ibid., folder 46d.

7. Ibid., Box III, folder 7g.

8. Ibid., folder 14.

9. Ibid., folder 11.

10. Ibid., Box IV, folder 11c.

11. Loyrette in Paris, Ottawa, New York, 1988, no. 120, 191–92.

NEW ORLEANS:
THE COTTON OFFICES, 1873

THE WORKS THAT DEGAS PRODUCED in the first part of his stay in New Orleans were given over to the agreeable realm of women and children. It was probably natural, and even more romantic, for Degas to see his mother's birthplace rather idyllically without the intrusion of men. He himself did not always regard these portraits that sentimentally. At one moment when he had diverted his attention to the male world of the cotton offices, he wrote to his friend living in London, the painter James Tissot, about "having wasted time in the family trying to do portraits in the worst conditions of day that I have ever found or imagined."[1] The cotton offices offered an escape.

We do not know whether it was Degas's desire to pursue the male world of business in his paintings or the result of some accident about his passage home to France that kept the artist in New Orleans. It is certain that he had intended to leave in mid-January and hopefully by a French ship to Brest, which might stop in Havana.[2] When this trip was postponed, he was not perfectly clear about the reasons in a letter to Tissot on 18 February, "I should have been in London or Paris about the 15 January . . . But I remained and shall not leave until the first days of March. Yesterday my trunks and Achille were ready but there was a hitch which stopped everything. One misses the train here exactly as at Passy. The Saint-Laurent is leaving without us."[3]

We can speculate about what could have happened. It has been suggested that he stayed to experience New Orleans's famed Mardi Gras. In 1873 the event was devoted to the theme of "The Missing Links to Darwin's Origin of Species," for which René had acted as an advisor in recommending costumes of insects that could be bought in Paris.[4] If Mardi Gras had been the reason, it is odd that Degas would never have mentioned this festival in his letters. Aside from some fortuitous accident, the real reason must have been Degas's desire to pursue a subject in the male world of New Orleans.

From his letters we believe that he stopped in at the offices of his brothers' partnership or his uncle's firm, not too far apart, with regularity, if only to receive mail and sometimes even to send it. As early as 27 November he had written to Frölich about "the lively hum and bustle of the offices."[5] His pride in his brothers showed in the same letter when he wrote, "Achille and René are partners; I am writing to you on their office notepaper. They are making some money and are really in an exceptionally good position for their age. They are much liked and respected here and I am quite proud of them."[6] On 5 December

31. *A Cotton Office in New Orleans*
(Portraits in a Cotton Office)

1873
Oil on canvas
$28\frac{3}{4} \times 36\frac{1}{4}$ inches (73×92 cm)
Musée des Beaux-Arts, Pau (878.1.2)
Lemoisne 320

32. Cotton Merchants in New Orleans
1873
Oil on canvas
$23\frac{5}{8} \times 28\frac{3}{4}$ inches (60 × 73 cm)
Harvard University Art Museums (Fogg Art Museum),
Cambridge, Massachusetts. Gift of Herbert N. Straus
Lemoisne 321

he wrote to his good friend Henri Rouart, "I am in the office of the De Gas Brothers, where it is not too bad for writing. De Gas Brothers are respected here and I am quite tickled to see it. They will make their fortune."[7] There must have been a time that winter when Degas was made aware of exactly how perilous the position of his brothers was and that their uncle Michel was on the brink of bankruptcy. Whether these revelations had something to do with his staying, we shall probably never know.

Once Degas had decided to stay, all his energies were directed toward the two versions of the cotton office paintings. After all, it was only on 18 February when he wrote Tissot, "I have attached myself to a fairly vigorous picture which is destined for Agnew and which he should place in Manchester."[8] And he went on in the present tense, "In it there are about 15 individuals more or less occupied with a table covered with the precious material." In other words the painting was not just a proposal or a dream—but a reality with details such as fifteen men, each different in features, manner and dress, already projected on to the canvas. This makes us realize two things. One is that we really have very little evidence of what Degas did between his writing to Henri Rouart on 5 December and his letter to Tissot of 18 February—over ten weeks. Even Mardi Gras seems to have reached its height with the centerpiece of the Krewe of Comus on 25 February, a week after Degas's letter to Tissot. In the intervening weeks Degas must have been busy peopling his cotton offices with fourteen men—his counting had been wrong—four from his own family, his uncle Michel Musson, his brothers Achille and René, his cousin-in-law William Bell—as well as Michel Musson's partners, James Prestidge and John Livaudais. The other eight are unknown to us but could have been familiar to Degas and even more probably to his family.[9] In arriving at his description of them in the painting, Degas achieved distinguishing features, physiques, postures, gestures, facial expressions, attitudes, and ambitions. Gifted as Degas was, he still must have made preparatory drawings in arriving at the final composition.

One of the wonders of his New Orleans stay is that Degas seems to have managed without the small notebooks (or *carnets*) he customarily used for drawings and other annotations. In spite of the difficulties he had with his eyes in New Orleans's strong sunshine, he could so easily have made fast sketches of the children playing in the garden with Vasco de Gama or of the tropical foliage and the iron balconies that make that city so decorative. But aside from the notebook he carried aboard the *Scotia* (only partially filled) when he traveled from Liverpool to New York (cat. 19), there are very few preparatory drawings and almost no casual sketches known from his voyage to New Orleans.[10] But there simply had to have been preparatory studies for something as complicated as *A Cotton Office in New Orleans*. Their loss seems greater here than the missing links in Darwin's theory.

Although in every case Degas revealed something of the face of each of the fourteen men and never hid one in shadow, very few of the figures are complete—only Achille De Gas at the far left, William Bell, the husband of Mathilde, holding out cotton, and René stretched out reading the newspaper. John Livaudais, the partner in shirtsleeves at the right, is almost full length. Although we see less of Michel Musson seated in the foreground, he gains in proximity even if we do not see his legs. The other partner, James Prestidge, bareheaded, wearing a light fawn coat, which Benfey describes as a duster,[11] is propped on a stool behind René. Although we do catch Prestidge's generous sideburns, we see little of his face. In the other cases the information may be limited, but it is convincing. It is also believable that these men belong to a single tribe with certain demands in dress, which do permit variations, and in behavior, which allows a certain casual informality. The visits to the offices of his brothers and his uncle almost daily since he had arrived in New Orleans have paid off in terms of Degas's understanding of the limitations to their conformity. There are perhaps only two conversations in that room and little noise aside from their voices except from the rustle of the local newspaper that René is reading.[12] It is a quiet, businesslike group of men.

Degas presumably made studies of each figure independently. Very few studies he had made in the past of men in conventional nineteenth-century dress were useful here. He had, of course, made the study *Achille De Gas* (cat. 17), in essence, his brother dashingly dressed in a top hat, leaning on a furled umbrella, the perfect image of the *flâneur* as he had used him for one stage of *At the Races in the Countryside* (cat. 16) before he left for New Orleans. Achille could very easily have been a stock figure. (Degas made another variation of his position with a different model, more heavily bearded, his body more challenging, and his hat a bowler rather than a top, *Standing Man in a Bowler Hat* [fig. 99], but if he had thought of him for one of the outsiders for *A Cotton Office in New Orleans*, he may have found that man too insolent for that company.) The single study (cat. 33) we have for *A Cotton Office* was wrongly and somewhat improbably identified by Lemoisne as René De Gas,[13] whereas it is a study of John Livaudais, Michel Musson's Creole, French-speaking partner,[14] who in the final painting is working on the firm's books at the right.

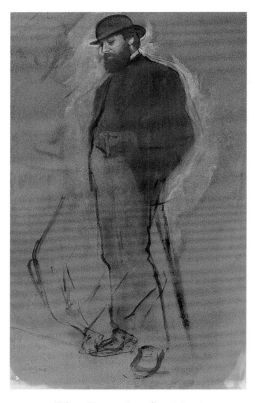

FIG. 99. Edgar Degas, *Standing Man in a Bowler Hat (Achille De Gas)*, essence on paper, (12⅞ × 7⅞ in.). Pierpont Morgan Library, New York. Lemoisne 344.

This drawing on oiled paper of the head and shoulders of Livaudais in profile comes very close to caricature and reminds us that in the final painting, although each man was highly individualized, none is caricatured. In this world that was exclusively male and also exclusively white,[15] Degas had studied the behavior of these (and other) men as they waited, worried, ruminated, pondered, watched, discussed, and even bragged. His next problem was to bring them together.

It is quite clear from his letters to Tissot that Degas was attracted by the narrative illustrations produced by artists of some stature for the English illustrated newspapers and magazines.[16] They were narrative in the sense that they provided the information in a detailed setting and the variety of characters upon which the readers or subscribers could build their own stories. That is essentially what Degas did with *A Cotton Office in New Orleans*. He had provided the characters and would provide the setting upon which we could build a story, an opera, a ballet,[17] or a theory.[18]

Degas naturally thought in terms of the theater when it came to providing a setting for his cast of fourteen. Inevitably it invites comparison with his *Dance Class at the Opéra* (fig. 86), painted the year before in Paris. In both, the architecture provides a box to contain the figures—a box that shows the ceiling, the even more important floor, two principal stretches of walls, one receding diagonally at the left, the other behind, but both providing unexpected vistas by different means. In both there was a certain loyalty to existing architecture, for the dance in the practice rooms in the old Opéra on the rue Pelletier that would burn down after Degas's return to Paris, in the second as Brown in this book has demonstrated[19] in the actual space Michel Musson had occupied with his partners Prestidge and Livaudais on the second floor of their Carondolet Street offices (fig. 41). In addition to her own work reconstructing those spaces, Brown discovered two things with the help of an article in the *Times-Picayune* of 8 June 1975. In the first discovery the photographer, who had attempted to photograph the equivalent space with "an extremely wide-angle lens," found "it was impossible to register a width encompassing the inside shutters and transoms on the left as did Degas."[20] The second discovery was more archaeological. In 1975 the black safe, under the print of the *Alabama and Keersage* on the wall above in the painting, was still there.[21] Although Degas began with those spaces his uncle's offices had occupied, Brown argues that he developed them very freely as he had undoubtedly done the rehearsal rooms in the older Paris Opéra house. As Brown puts it, "Degas's apparently "natural" construction was

33. *Study of John E. Livaudais*

1873
Gouache on paper
$9\frac{3}{4} \times 7\frac{1}{2}$ inches (25 × 19.2 cm)
Pierpont Morgan Library
Lemoisne 322

actually an artificial construction."[22] The spaces for both paintings are nevertheless remarkably self-contained and comprehensive. The room for *A Cotton Office* is more architecturally complex, more measured, and more rapid in its spatial recession, as if Degas were trying in 1873 (as against 1872) to achieve something more tangible and substantial. This goal might be measured by comparing the chairs that are used as a transition in the front of both paintings.

The chair for *The Dance Class* is a conventional wooden chair of the time, its frame and its rush seat light so that it can be moved easily. In short, as it is placed at a slight angle, it seems as delicate and fragile as the young dancers appear to be. The chair beside Michel Musson in the foreground of *A Cotton Office* is a captain's chair and much more substantial. Whereas some dancer has probably casually dropped the red fan and the piece of white fabric on the chair in *The Dance Class,* in *A Cotton Office* the opened package of white cotton was deliberately placed beside Musson, who is examining it. Benfey returns to the matter of this chair twice, once as a symbol of "immortality and the other time of mortality."[23] Degas, who was apparently so little attracted to still life that he only painted one (aside from drawings and paintings of plaster casts),[24] was nevertheless a master at differentiating between glass and plaster or painting paper and ledgers and even a wastepaper basket of discarded envelopes; he could easily have been the "Master of Still Life" for the nineteenth century.

There are moments in which the cast of characters in *A Cotton Office* come very close to still lives themselves. Each is separate, distinct, distinguished by color, form, and texture—and remarkably mute. They are not dramatized with the possible exception of Michel Musson in the foreground—the father-in-law or uncle of the three men placed diagonally behind him—Achille De Gas, a nephew, William Bell, a son-in-law, and René De Gas, nephew, son-in-law, and eventual renegade. But it does seem to be a tour de force of genre painting. Brown, who has undertaken the research that has disclosed the information that can animate the painting, believes herself that it is a commentary on the

FIG. 100. Michel Alexander Agelasto. 1870, Daguerreotype. Collection of Peter Alexander Agelasto III.

nature of a commercial life he found distasteful.[25] The rest of us may feel that it only makes us realize how vulnerable these gentlemen were.

Perhaps most significant, Brown discovered that, even as Degas was painting *A Cotton Office,* it was announced in the 1 February 1873 edition of *The Daily-Picayune* that the firm of Musson, Prestidge, & Co. was now bankrupt and the partnership was being dissolved (fig. 43).[26] That catastrophe probably invited the realization that De Gas Brothers, and in particular René, were heavily in debt to the De Gas bank in Paris and that the French members of the family had been only too ready to follow Michel Musson's advice to acquire Confederate bonds, now worthless paper.[27] The painter, who had been so proud of the business acumen of his young brothers, may have realized how desperate his family's financial position was just as he was about to return to France in January and, consequently, decided to stay and paint a masterpiece that would restore their fortunes. As Brown has shown again, Degas sadly misjudged any potential interest in either America or cotton in the English or French markets.[28] Even when he did sell *A Cotton Office in New Orleans* to the museum in Pau in the south of France through the influence of two of his old friends, Paul Lafond and Alphonse Cherfils, it was for the relatively modest sum of 2,000 francs, which would be a humble contribution to paying off the debt of 40,000 francs to the Bank of Antwerp he and his brother-in-law Henri Fevre had assumed after the death of Auguste De Gas, the painter's father, later in 1873.

On the other hand, this information does illuminate the figures in the painting in other ways. René and Achille are not only outsiders, visitors, but genuinely irresponsible and very ill at ease. John Livaudais, the partner examining the ledgers at the right and placed in front of the safe which Brown points out contains the firm's "secure money,"[29] is diligently trying to assess the damage as he is watched by some hapless clerk. The former partners have literally turned their backs on one another. James Prestidge, perched on a stool, attempts to carry on business by writing something in a notebook for a potential client. Michel Musson sits in unhappy isolation, endlessly feeling the cotton. His son-in-law William Bell, not a partner, seems to believe in the efficacy of action as he holds out cotton to another visitor. We do not know how much Degas actually knew or how much he only sensed, but he makes us suspect their insecurity and even to realize that Michel Musson has removed himself from reality. Like a nineteenth-century Lear, he will mourn over his daughters. But these are just whispers of desperation in what was probably originally intended to be a detached record of ordinary activity in a cotton office in New Orleans, a scene of American business life to appeal to some rich and foreign buyer.

This painting has often been written about, although never with the same understanding of its social and economic significance that it has been given by Marilyn Brown starting with "Degas and 'The Cotton Office in New Orleans,'" in *The Burlington Magazine* in March 1988, further developed in *Degas and the Business of Art* of 1994 and condensed in the essay for this catalogue, "Franco-American Aspects of Degas's *A Cotton Office in New Orleans.*" Degas could have shown the painting at what we now call the First Impressionist Exhibition in 1874, but he decided to wait for what would prove to be the Second in 1876. There this relatively small painting was a sensation, attracting the ire or reluctant admiration or assumed indifference of almost every one of the many critics from newspapers and periodicals throughout France and occasionally from abroad.[30] Its presence was almost always acknowledged, but it was not, as Degas so ardently wished and for reasons Brown has analyzed, sold then or out of other small exhibitions at dealers afterwards. Only when the purchase was encouraged by two of the painter's friends, Paul Lafond and Alphonse Cherfils, was it bought by the provincial museum in Pau in the Pyrenees. When that happened, forty-two-year-old Degas wrote a polite letter of thanks to the curator, Charles LeCoeur,[31] who had been a fashionable architect and belonged to a family that were patrons of Renoir, "I must offer my warmest thanks for the honor you have done me. I must also admit that it is the first time that a museum has so honored me and that this *official* recognition comes as a surprise and is terribly flattering."[32]

Degas did not ignore *A Cotton Office in New Orleans,* once it was sold. He would have seen it when he continued to visit Lafond and Cherfils in Pau, just as they continued to visit him in Paris. Not long after the purchase, he painted a small oil sketch of them as *Les Amateurs* (The Collectors) (fig. 45) examining a painting—perhaps *A Cotton Office*—and inscribed it "Degas à ses chers amis"; it is now in the Cleveland Museum of Art.[33] Cherfils had a son, Christian, who in 1889 dedicated a volume of poems called *Coeurs* to Degas. And very soon after the artist's death, Paul Lafond, who had become curator of the museum in Pau by 1900, wrote a two-volume monograph on the work of the artist who had been his friend.[34]

Occasionally Degas had some differences with Lafond and the museum in Pau. One was over the *Centennale de l'art français,* held in Paris in 1900. In the past Degas seemed to have been very content with large exhibitions, even if he was ready to offer advice to the Salon Jury on its hanging.[35] After all, at the age of nineteen he had persuaded Paul Valpinçon's father to lend his *Valpinçon Bather* by Ingres to the World's Fair of 1855.[36] He had been thoroughly engrossed in the contemporary English painting he found at the World's Fair in Paris of 1867[37]—but toward 1900 we find him writing to Paul Lafond, who had encouraged the first museum to buy his work, "I want to know whether the Pau Museum has been asked to lend its picture of the cotton market to this 'Concentration.' I want to prevent this loan about which I was not consulted."[38]

There are many ways of interpreting this letter. Like many artists further into the twentieth century, Degas may have felt that an artist retained control over the disposition of his work, even after a sale. He might, on the other hand, have had serious objections to the form this centennial exhibition was taking as a grab bag of contemporary work rather than as serious monographic exhibitions of the work of one or two distinguished living artists like those honoring Delacroix and Ingres in 1855. In any case, as with so much connected with *A Cotton Office in New Orleans,* he did not win. The work was exhibited in spite of his objections. He could, after all, have been reluctant to have it sent since it had been painted almost thirty years before and he had done so much that was more modern since. By then the memories of New Orleans must have been dim. Only René, René's stepdaughter by his second wife, Odile Olivier, and the American widow of Achille, who had been born Emma Hermann, were ever in Paris to remind him of his Louisiana connections.[39] All correspondence had long ceased. *A Cotton Office in New Orleans* would have represented painful situations, which by 1900 he might have been permitted to forget—or, if not that, could have been forgiven for not wanting to flaunt at a World's Fair.

Cotton Merchants in New Orleans: Better Art?

Degas has provided at least one level of explanation for the Fogg's *Cotton Merchants,* which is slightly smaller than the *Cotton Office* in Pau. In his letter to Tissot of 18 February 1873 he wrote, after having described Pau's version, "I am preparing another less complicated and more spontaneous, better art, where the people are all in summer dress, white walls, a sea of cotton on the table."[40] There is no question but that the Fogg's painting is less complicated—three figures instead of fourteen, the room reduced to a hint of blue sky through a window in the upper left, a spur wall with a slice of a color print or watercolor of a steamship, matted in white and framed with a strip of gold, the table of cotton that appears to take up a good quarter of the surface of the painting, and the suggestion of the outline of an armchair in the lower right-hand corner. These are Spartan contents for the area of that canvas.

What ingredients there are in the *Cotton Merchants* weigh almost nothing. Instead of the concentrated masses, which are convincingly heavy, of Pau's painting, everything in the Fogg's version, except the cotton covering the table, seems light and almost transparent. Even that table of white frothy stuff—that cotton about which Degas had complained to Tissot in his earlier letter, "Here one speaks of nothing but cotton,"[41] more than in Pau's painting, dominates the composition, although its execution is not quite as lively. It is nevertheless frothy and buoyant, a veritable "sea." The very illusiveness of this material, as Degas painted it here, could be Degas's cynical commentary on it as the basis of Louisiana's economy.

The rest of the painting is even less tangible and enduring than the cotton. The room could easily have been built up by a few fragile Japanese screens. In its very lack of architectural definition like the glass partitions and the shutters in Pau's painting, it defies identification with any place or particular culture. It could be in Borneo as well as New Orleans.

The three men are similarly insubstantial, although they are distinguished one from another. The man in the dark suit, top hat, and black bow tie is undoubtedly Michel Musson, although reduced in girth, density, and, as he leans over tentatively to touch the cotton, we discover that he is very much reduced in importance as well. The most significant figure—although he is also not very tangible—is the man in profile with the red-gold beard, a jacket that might be a duster or summer attire, and a very yellow straw hat with a black ribbon. We might speculate that he looks like an Englishman but also a Frenchman whose chief enjoyment could be boating on a river. And finally the rather meager profile appearing from behind the spur wall, which could have been drawn by a Japanese calligrapher. Degas has sacrificed mass, the clarity of the definition of space, the superiority of individual men to the evocation of his dream of a cotton office that is beautiful but very remote.

Why would Degas have considered this better art? Or perhaps if not exactly as compared with Pau's painting better art but a better direction for art? He has given us two clues. It is "less complicated," which means less information and that his art could concentrate upon what he believed to be essential. He also said it was "more spontaneous" and therefore a more natural and immediate expression of the interests and enthusiasms of the artist. Later in the letter he reminds Tissot to, "remember the art of the Le Nain and all Mediaeval France, Our race will have something simple and bold to offer." And then he refers to the art that had interested him and had inspired Pau's *Cotton Office,* "This English art that appeals so much to us often seems to be exploiting some trick. We can do better than they and be just as strong."[42]

Degas was writing to Tissot what he had discovered in making the two paintings based on cotton offices in New Orleans. His work was at a watershed, and he was ready to return to France and move in the direction of a far simpler, more natural, more spontaneous art. He would probably have arrived at the same place if he had never left Paris, but it was possible in the very exoticism of the surroundings in New Orleans to isolate the issues. He returned to France invigorated, ready to join in the struggle with his colleagues who would work with him on the exhibitions of Independent artists, who would become known in history as the Impressionists. Above all, Degas had learned about the vulnerability of material things in New Orleans.

1. Appendix II, letter to Tissot, 18 February 1873.

2. Ibid., letter to Tissot, 19 November 1872; letter to Frölich; letter to Rouart.

3. Ibid., letter to Tissot, 18 February, 1873.

4. Benfey, 1997, 154, 171–172; Byrnes, in New Orleans, 1965, 76, quoting from a letter of 17 July 1872 from René to Estelle, a section that is not included in Brown, 1991 (Box II, folder 46b) that there is "a coup to be made in buying the costumes in Paris which have been used in this part of the ballet of the Insects, for the Mystik [*sic*] Krewe (of Comus). They are all ravishing, from the ladybug to the roach. They would be very pretty for the procession."

5. Appendix II, letter to Frölich.

6. Ibid.

7. Ibid., letter to Rouart.

8. Ibid., letter to Tissot, 18 February 1873.

9. As the catalogue went to press, we received a letter regarding the possible identification of yet another figure in *A Cotton Office*. George Tucker, a Tidewater Virginia historian had long ago been told by a friend of his, Michael Agelasto, that the latter's father was one of the two men Degas had included in the picture. The man reported to be in the portrait was Michel Alexander Agelasto, 1833–1906. Michel Agelasto, of Greek origin, arrived in New Orleans in the 1850s, and during the 1860s and 1870s was involved in land speculation as well as being a commodity merchant and cotton buyer. His businesses were located during the 1860s and 1870s at various addresses on Carondolet Street and Gravier Street. The Agelasto family lived on Esplanade Avenue. Michel Alexander Agelasto was about thirty-nine years old at the time, and his appearance is recorded in a daguerreotype (fig. 100) taken around 1870. He is said to be the man leaning on the table examining the cotton. Certainly the style of the beards are identical and a resemblance can be seen in the rather shadowed features as well. The identification is surely plausible but it has not been possible to pursue the research necessary to explore it further in time for the catalogue. The information was kindly reported to us by Peter Agelasto III, the great-grandson of Michel Alexander Agelasto. [GF]

10. Reff, Nb. 25, 169, 168, 167, 170, 171, 165, 164, 163, 162, 161.

11. Benfey, 1997, 166, "to protect his clothes from cotton fibers."

12. Brown, 1994, 28, on basis of letter to Lemoisne from Odile Musson, daughter of Estelle and René (Brown, 1991, Box V, folder 3), who wrote of this painting that, "this offers quite a contrast to the hustle and bustle of a modern cotton office."

13. Lemoisne, 1946–49, no. 322.

14. For information about Livaudais, see Brown, 1994, 31, n. 55.

15. Appendix II, letter to Frölich, Degas writes of "the contrast between the lively hum and bustle of the offices with this immense black animal force" (which he does not otherwise define).

16. Paris, 1989, 363, undated letter to Tissot. For evidence and consequences of this, see Ronald Pickvance, "Degas's Dancers," *Burlington Magazine* CV, no. 723 (June 1963): 259–63; Pantazzi in Paris, Ottawa, New York, "The Rehearsal of the Ballet on the Stage," 225–27.

17. Benfey, 1997, discusses the painting in a chapter (nine) called "The Cotton Ballet," 152–70.

18. Brown in this book writes, "the painting's messages about Franco-American relations, interpreted in the context of shifting audiences and patronage, were neither stable nor static, but rather were fluid and sometimes contradictory."

19. See Brown, 1994, 20–27, with photographs, figs. 8 and 9.

20. Brown in this book, 50.

21. Ibid., 53.

22. Ibid., 50.

23. Benfey, 1997, 158, "the empty chair since Roman times a traditional image of immortality" and 166, "the empty chair beside him may suggest, in addition to his own mortality, the recent death of his wife."

24. The only still life (aside from paintings or drawings of plaster casts) attributed to Degas is L 58, *Nature morte au lézard,* owner unknown, recto of L 648, *L'Amateur,* owner unknown.

25. See n. 18.

26. Brown, 1994, 32.

27. Brown in this book, 54.

28. Ibid., 55.

29. Ibid., 50.

30. Berson in Washington, San Francisco, 1986.

31. The curator of the museum at Pau was Charles Clément Le Coeur (1805–97), an architect who was a member of a family of builders and architects who were patrons of Renoir. See Colin B. Bailey, *Renoir's Portraits* (Ottawa, 1997), no. 18, 132, 283.

32. Letter of 31 March 1878, Musée des Beaux-Arts, Pau. Paris, 1989, 428.

33. L 647, Paul Lafond and Alphonse Cherfils examining the painting *Les Amateurs,* 1878–81. Cleveland Museum of Art (see fig. 45).

34. Lafond, 1918–19.

35. Letter addressed to the members of the Salon Jury, 1870, signed "Degas," published in *Paris-Journal,* 12 April 1870.

36. Valéry, as told him by Degas, 22 October 1905, 34–36.

37. Reff, Nb. 21, 30, 31, 31v.

38. Denys Sutton and Jean Adhémar, "Lettres inédites de Edgar Degas à Paul Lafond et autres documents," *Gazette des Beaux-Arts,* 6th series, CLX, no. 1419 (April 1987): 175.

39. Their Franco-American uncles Eugène and Henri Musson were dead, Achille De Gas died in 1893. Even René's second wife, America Durrive Olivier, died. Their mother's quadroon first cousin, Norbert Rillieux, lived in Paris until 1894 and was buried in Père Lachaise.

40. Appendix II, letter to Tissot, 18 February 1873.

41. Ibid., 19 November 1872.

42. Ibid., 18 February 1873.

The Rehearsal of a Song, 1873

34. The Song Rehearsal

1872–73
Oil on canvas
$31\frac{7}{8} \times 25\frac{5}{8}$ inches (81 × 65 cm)
Dumbarton Oaks Research Library and Collection,
Washington, D.C. (H18.2)
Lemoisne 331

ONE OF THE PAINTINGS Degas almost certainly brought from New Orleans unfinished and completed in Paris was *The Song Rehearsal.* From his second surviving letter to Tissot from New Orleans, it is quite clear that Degas was concerned about the transportation and storage of his canvases. He was worried then about the movement of *A Cotton Office in New Orleans,* which on 18 February he expected to finish in two weeks. He wanted to take it to London for Tissot and potential buyers to see but, as he wrote, "it will not be possible for it to leave with me. A canvas scarcely dry, shut up for a long time, away from light and air, you know very well that that would change it to chrome-yellow no. 3."[1] It may have been with the fragility of the paint surface in mind that Degas decided to leave two of his most charming New Orleans paintings, *Le Pédicure* (fig. 98) and *The Song Rehearsal,* to be finished at home.[2]

The exquisite painting *The Song Rehearsal* appears to have taken place in a room in the house that Michel Musson had rented on Esplanade—perhaps even, as Benfey suggests, in the parlour itself.[3] In any case the room has the lofty ceilings, the substantial moldings, the generous doors that we expect of New Orleans mansions. The walls are a beautiful yellow, almost identical to the color of the wall in Washington's portrait of Estelle Musson De Gas (fig. 96); the walls in both are inviting and flattering. The upholstered furniture is covered with the white slipcovers we associate with summer.[4] A casual informality is suggested by the comfortable cushions and the red scarf thrown over the back of a chair in the foreground. The tropical plant in the corner would have been a typical New Orleans decoration. Whether the absence of pictures was characteristic or a matter of discretion on Degas's part, we do not know, but he did complain to Henri Rouart, whose own house was full of works of art, that he would be happier about painting portraits in New Orleans "if the settings were less insipid."[5] Whether pictures were considered desirable or not in New Orleans, a grand piano was de rigueur in such drawing rooms—and René had

35. Young Woman Singing,
Study for The Song Rehearsal
1872–73
Lead point on buff wove paper
19 × 12⅜ inches (48.3 × 31.5 cm)
Cabinet des Dessins, Musée du Louvre (Orsay) (RF 5606)

been looking for a smaller substitute grand piano by Payel for the one made by Chickering on his most recent European trip in 1872.[6]

Degas made drawings for the painting of the two young women singing. It is not impossible that Estelle could have posed for the singer on the right, where she wears a loose jacket that might have been intended to conceal her pregnant condition. Although we have no photographs or drawings of Estelle in profile, this, with the long nose and generous jaw, does not seem impossible. She responds to the singing of the other woman with a certain theatrical éclat. Loyrette writes of both singers, "they affect the exaggerated stereotypical gestures of opera divas."[7]

The other drawing for the woman singing seems to be of someone older, more formally coiffed, whose dress is also more fashionably cut, and is clearly more experienced as a performer. Curiously she has been considered to be the pregnant Estelle.[8] Degas had not as yet achieved the ease with an opened mouth that he would reveal before the 1870s were over.[9] One of the interesting things about these robust preparatory drawings is that the two performers are considerably larger than the same figures in the painting itself.

Degas made certain changes to the two singers when it came to working with paint on canvas. On the whole the positions of the figures were as they had been drawn with very few changes to the figure at the right—but there are some to the singer on the left. Although her right hand holds a small book in both the drawing and the painting, in the drawing she seems to be clutching it to her heart almost melodramatically, whereas in the painting she holds it opened and out from her body. Perhaps more significant, Degas lifted her left hand as if she is beseeching the other singer to pause. In fact there is a more intimate relationship between them dramatically than one would expect from the drawings. But the greatest surprise is that the heads of both singers have changed. They are younger and pretty.

The changes in the ages of the two singers and their physiognomies support the perfectly sensible conclusion that the work was begun in New Orleans and finished in Paris. To make this even more probable, there has been a long tradition that Marguerite De Gas Fevre, the painter's sister, had posed for both figures.[10] And indeed the delicacy, animation, and even prettiness of the features makes this seem possible. Degas was using his sister in a genre composition in which she is playing two roles, rather than painting another portrait

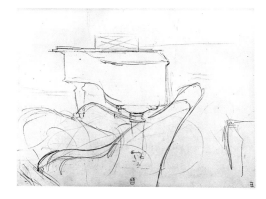

FIG. 101. Edgar Degas, Notebook 22, page 133. Bibliothèque Nationale de France, Paris.

FIG. 102. *20 duos.* Album of sheet music belonging to Estelle Musson. Earl K. Long Library, University of New Orleans.

of her. But she was superimposed over the two women—one a cousin—from New Orleans.

The remaining figure who demands speculation, although he has seldom received it, is the pianist—a shadow with a profile expressing interest and even curiosity. Benfey, in his provocative analysis of the painting, has followed Byrnes's lead in believing him to be René.[11] But he goes even further, believing that *The Song Rehearsal* is "a painting signifying the plight of his brother René, caught between the two women in his life, and cowering behind Mme Olivier and the piano that linked him with her."[12] It is certain that René knew America Durrive Olivier before Degas's arrival in October 1872, and that the house she shared with her husband and family faced the back of the property of the Musson house on Esplanade.[13] There was a friendly rapport between the Olivier and Musson households[14] and evidence that there was a strong attraction between René and America long before they eloped,[15] but it seems out of character for Degas to have produced such a charming painting as an allegory of a relationship that was pulling his New Orleans family apart.

The inclusion of a man in what otherwise is a scene of the enjoyment of leisure by two young women is a departure for one of Degas's paintings of New Orleans, where—possibly following local custom—he kept the sexes separated. It may be significant that the other work that introduces a man into the world of women and children is *Le Pédicure,* which also comes from the end of that American visit and was also presumably taken back to France to be finished there. In both cases also the description of the men verges on caricature. But at least in having brought the two sexes together, while avoiding some of the dangers Degas must have observed in such relationships in his family in New Orleans, he was preparing the way for the license of Paris, which he would observe with pleasure over the next few years while he was tackling some of the most humiliating problems of his life.

36. Young Woman Standing,
Study for The Song Rehearsal

1872–73
Lead point on buff wove paper
$19\frac{1}{2}$ × $12\frac{1}{4}$ inches (49 × 31.2 cm)
Cabinet des Dessins, Musée du Louvre (Orsay) (RF 5607)

1. Appendix II, letter to Tissot, 18 February 1873.

2. Loyrette in Paris, Ottawa, New York, 1988, no. 117, 189, agrees that this was finished in Paris and refers to a preparatory drawing in Reff, Nb. 22, 133 (not reproduced in Reff) (fig. 101).

3. Benfey, 1997, 253.

4. Victoria Cooke investigated and discovered such slipcovers were common in New Orleans, whereas we have been told they were not in France.

5. Appendix II, letter to Rouart. Degas was writing to a friend whose collection provided a handsome setting for his family, as we can see in Degas's painting of the Rouart daughter Hélène in the National Gallery, London (L 869), which includes Egyptian statues, a Chinese wall hanging, a chair made by Mme Rouart's grandfather (a great cabinetmaker), and a drawing by Millet. Although seldom as grand as the Rouart house, Degas's interiors painted in France have, for the most part, a certain elegance and contain other works of art. See, for example, *Interior with Two Figures* (fig. 67) or the pastel of his sister Thérèse in their father's apartment (L 255, private collection), in which a painting by Perronneau can be identified on the back wall. The spareness of the New Orleans interiors is an exception. Either Degas was painting them because he enjoyed the relief of large areas of light colored, uninterrupted walls or because he chose to ignore the works that were hanging on those walls.

There is an oral tradition in the family that Degas had actually brought from France some oil paintings that were copies of Old Masters and that were handed down in the family. Considering Degas's discrimination as a collector, which was demonstrated in the exhibition *The Private Collection of Edgar Degas* at The Metropolitan Museum of Art in 1997–98, and the high quality of the copies he painted as a young man, this tradition is not very convincing. Nevertheless, it has been believed in the family that a painting of the head of Christ

(the artist is unidentified) and one after Raphael were brought by the painter to New Orleans.

After returning to Paris, Degas painted a portrait of his great friend, the collector, amateur painter, engineer, and industrialist Henri Rouart, against a background of his factories (fig. 103). Since by 1869, the Louisiana Ice Works had been built in New Orleans according to Rouart's specifications based on a technology he had invented, it has been proposed by Rebecca R. deMuth ("Edgar Degas, Henri Rouart, Art and Industry," M.A. thesis, University of Pittsburgh, 1982) that Degas painted Rouart against these ice works, which he never actually visited.

6. De Gas–Musson, Box II, folder 45c, letter of 26 June 1872. For the relevant passage see Byrnes in New Orleans, no. 79.

7. Loyrette, 1991, no. 117, 190.

8. Byrnes in New Orleans, 79–80; Benfey, 1997, 256–57.

9. For example, L 380, *The Song of the Dog,* private collection; L 504, *Two Studies of a Music Hall Singer,* private collection; L 478 bis, *Singer with a Glove,* Harvard University Museums.

10. Loyrette in Paris, Ottawa, New York, no. 117, 189, n. 4, indicates that the unpublished memoirs of Louise Halévy, a friend of Marguerite, is one source.

11. Byrnes in New Orleans, 70; Benfey, 1997, 256.

12. For the evidence see Benfey, 1997, 255–56.

13. Byrnes in New Orleans, 38.

14. Benfey, 1997, 255.

15. Brown, 1991, Box III, folder 13f, letter in English to Désirée Musson from Harmion Watts, 25 April 1878 (fig. 125).

After New Orleans, 1873–79

WE DO NOT KNOW EXACTLY how and when Edgar Degas left New Orleans during the spring of 1873, except that it must have been in March and that Achille accompanied him.[1] Nor do we have thank-you letters or an effort by Degas to assess the experience of his five months in America. His uncle Eugène dispensed with the courtesies for him in writing to Michel Musson on 3 April 1873, "Edgar came back enchanted by his voyage, enchanted to have done so many things new to him, but especially enchanted to have made the acquaintances of all his good relatives in America. He is, as you say, an amiable boy who, moreover, will be a very great painter if God preserves his sight and makes him a little less feather-brained."[2]

It is difficult to think of anyone less feather-brained than Edgar Degas, the "boy" approaching forty—unless he possibly cultivated this affectation to protect the time to paint. The five months in New Orleans were remarkably serious. In spite of all the inevitable petty domestic distractions, he managed to paint or draw in pastel at least four portraits, make four sketches of individuals, paint the small but incredibly complex *A Cotton Office in New Orleans* (cat. 31) and the related oil sketch (cat. 32), produce three remarkable genre paintings, *Children on Doorstep (New Orleans)* (cat. 29), *Le Pédicure* (fig. 98), and *The Song Rehearsal* (cat. 34), even if the last two were finished in Paris. Finally it is possible that some of his invalids (cats. 21, 22, 23) were painted in New Orleans. It is difficult under any circumstances to measure the productivity of an artist, but it seems Degas must have produced an exhibitable work at least every ten days after his arrival until February, when he turned his attention to the two versions of the *A Cotton Office* and the initiations of *Le Pédicure* and *The Song Rehearsal*. In spite of the absence of studies for *A Cotton Office,* it is difficult to believe that they did not exist and, on the basis of the one sketch on oiled paper of John Livaudais (cat. 33) and the related sketches of Achille and the gentleman in the bowler hat (fig. 99), that they were not drawings on dark paper with a certain amount of color like the remarkable series Degas had done of jockeys about 1868.[3]

These New Orleans pastels and paintings were serious in mood. The demands (or at least the taste) of the Mussons had been formed on an admiration for the affectations of the double portrait in chalk and wash of the sisters Anne Eugénie Musson de Rochefort and Marie Célestine De Gas by Catherine Longchamps (fig. 5). In addition, there were the expectations on the part of

Degas for a market in England. This meant that the works from New Orleans were decorous; there is rarely anything offensive or even mildly flirtatious. (The one slip was probably the Göteborgs pastel of Mathilde, cat. 26.) Degas, *pace* his uncle Eugène, was not in the least "feather-brained." He was substantial, ready to conform, confronting his New Orleans subjects in the spaces they normally occupied and shared with him as a visitor or a guest and certainly as an equal. He also respected the mores to which they adhered. And he must have come to New Orleans with sober intentions for his life as well as his work. Even his toying with the thoughts of marriage and children as he approached forty was consistent with this attitude to New Orleans and his American family.

New Orleans did not turn Edgar Degas into a landscape painter and, aside from the small sketches stuck against the wall in *Le Pédicure* (fig. 98), there is no evidence of Degas's having painted the small landscapes he sometimes produced on holidays. Perhaps the foliage and the architecture were too large and too bold for that kind of painting. Certainly the sun was, as he complained frequently, too strong. It was not that he did not admire the exotic extravagance of New Orleans; he described it glowingly in his letters. To Tissot he wrote of "villas with columns in different styles, painted white, in gardens of magnolias, orange trees, banana trees, negroes in old clothes . . . rosy white children in black arms, charabancs or omnibuses drawn by mules, the tall funnels of the steamboats towering at the end of the main street."[4] As he advised Henri Rouart, probably quite accurately, "Manet would see lovely things here, even more than I do."[5] Degas, however, was not led astray in Louisiana.

In New Orleans he would paint portraits of the women and children in his family at home and the men at their place of business, the cotton office—the two poles apart except that the industry of the men protected the gentility and the charm of the women and the innocence of the children. To Tissot he justified such family portraits as, "It is the art of giving pleasure and one must look the part."[6] He was not without some doubts about the success of the results, as he wrote Rouart: "A few family portraits will be the sum total of my efforts, I was unable to avoid that and assuredly would not wish to complain if it were less difficult, if the settings were less insipid and the models less restless."[7]

It is curious that Degas apparently did not paint these portraits for his family to be left in New Orleans. There does not even appear to be a sketch Degas made there that has survived in the possession of the descendants of the Degas and Musson families in Louisiana.[8] They may have been largely indifferent to his work, although it is quite clear that René, at least, was sensitive to it. He had written with real feeling about his pleasure, for example, in seeing Degas's portrait of Mme Camus (not a relative but a good friend) the summer he was in Paris before returning with Edgar to New Orleans: "Edgar is doing some charming things. There is a portrait of Mme Camus in profile wearing a dress of garnet velvet, seated in a brown armchair against a rosey background that is, for me, a masterpiece. His drawing is ravishing."[9] Many visitors to the National Gallery of Art in Washington, D.C., where Mme Camus now resides, would agree with his assessment. As Marilyn R. Brown has pointed out in this book, Degas was, however, beginning to think of his work as a commodity.[10] After all, he wrote Tissot: "Here I have acquired the taste for money, and once back I shall know how to earn some, I promise you."[11] Probably considering the financial circumstances of both the Degas and Musson families, what he had acquired was "the need for" rather than "the taste for" money, but he may not have felt himself in a position to give away what he painted in New Orleans.

Some of what he had painted in Louisiana, he intended to have shipped separately as he wrote Tissot about *A Cotton Office*.[12] It is a pleasant conceit to think that, when these works were finally reunited in Paris, Degas might have had an informal *vernissage* in his studio at 77 rue Blanche for his father and friends. The exoticism of New Orleans would only have been inferred from the height of the ceilings in the paintings, their pale walls that seem to reduce the intensity of the light, the pretty muslin dresses, a certain extravagance with flowers, and the openness of Mathilde's balcony. But the women's world and the world of the cotton brokers would balance each other nicely to make Louisiana seem both a charmingly feminine and a virile place. We can wonder whether Degas's imaginary guests would have been slightly amused by the separation of the sexes, the mark of a provincial society. The personalities of the men would probably—at least initially—have seemed stronger, but these visitors would probably have found themselves remembering Mathilde's modest allure or the tension of Estelle's fingers in *The Woman with a Vase of Flowers* or the pathos in *The Invalid* or the domestic protection provided by *The Nurse*. Even the flowers scattered over the table in New Orleans's own large painting could have clung in their memories as a romantic disorder that Estelle is blindly trying to control. They would have noticed how tactfully Degas suggests her blindness and her pregnancy. *A Cotton Office,* on the other hand, would have bowled them over as a tour de force—so convincingly American that, when Degas did exhibit the work in the Second Impressionist Exhibition in 1876, one critic reported that the painter had been born in New Orleans.[13] Although most of the works were conventionally conceived and composed, some undertones of financial and emotional insecurity might have been detected by sensitive spectators before Degas had as yet articulated them for himself.

If there had been any guests at this imaginary vernissage, they probably would have been artists, critics, or collectors, certainly fascinated by the freedom of the painting of the children on the back steps of the Musson house and charmed by the flaxen-haired child who turns toward us. It is even possible that they may have sensed the vulnerability of the children and the menace to them in the house across the way. And having seen a work as free as this, they would have still perhaps been somewhat perplexed by the other version of the cotton offices, his *Cotton Merchants in New Orleans,* which Degas had called "better art."[14] But probably no such vernissage took place because Degas was finding personal and professional matters pressing and may have only shown one or two of these canvases to some of the most intimate of his friends.

In spite of all the documentation we possess, we do not know how much Degas knew of the financial position of his own family in Paris and New Orleans (his brother Achille, as he wrote Tissot, "with one foot over there and the other here").[15] Did he even know that his father had written to Michel Musson in 1864 stating, "I authorize you to sell Edgar's house [in New Orleans] and to convert the proceeds into Confederate bonds?"[16] He may have been an improbable agent, but it is possible that his father, who two years later would be dead, had confessed his financial concerns to the painter, particularly in relation to the business René and Achille shared in New Orleans, and had asked Degas to go there to review their situation. This might explain the artist's "daily" visits to their offices or those of their uncle. It could also explain his obsession with a market for his own works, particularly in England, to compensate for the private income that would be lost. This New Orleans visit could have been troubling for him and somewhat duplicitous. All of this was taking place against a general depression in both Europe and America—the consequences of reparations in France from the Franco-Prussian War and in Louisiana of Reconstruction. In any case, in returning to Paris—whether he knew it or not—Edgar Degas would be facing the consequences.

There were financial and family embarrassments that Degas had to confront before the decade of the 1870s was over. It may have begun with some "loss of face" with the announcement of the dissolution and subsequent liquidation of Musson, Prestidge, & Co. in the New Orleans *Daily Picayune* of 1 February 1873[17] (fig. 13) when Degas was still working on his now famous painting of the interior of their offices (cat. 31). On the other hand, in Paris after the death of the painter's father (in Naples) on 23 February 1874, which left his family and its bank in the same kind of financial disorder,[18] Degas was able to face the liquidation of that small bank and the assumption of a debt to the Bank of Antwerp of 40,000 francs by him and a brother-in-law, Henri Fevre, without any apparent publicity.[19] Nevertheless, unfavorable press coverage did come to the Degas family in Paris through the painter's brother Achille. A friend of Edgar's, the painter Berthe Morisot, reported that her mother-in-law (Manet's mother) "writes us that the gentleman who caused such excitement at the Bourse was Achille Degas; I saw the report of the incident among the sensational news items."[20] Her husband, Eugène Manet, wrote her further about the matter: "I dropped in yesterday at Achille Degas'; he is worried about the outcome of his case. He has been advised to have it tried in the court of assizes. The judges of the Correctionnelle court would find him guilty."[21] In August 1875 Achille had shot (but not seriously wounded) the husband of his former lover, the dancer Thérèse Mallot, in a very public place, the Bourse (the stock exchange in Paris).[22] In the end he was only imprisoned for a month, but the trial was well covered by the sensational press. It was René, however, who provided the next embarrassment (more discretely but also more painfully) by deserting Estelle and their children with their neighbor (over the back fence) America Durrive Olivier, marrying bigamously in Cleveland on 3 May 1878, obtaining a "Utah-type" divorce on 17 June, and marrying legally in New York on 6 February 1879, where a child was born that winter. René returned to France at the end of 1879 but was not forgiven by the painter until 1887.[23] On a more purely professional level Degas was troubled by a contract he had initiated in 1873 with the Opéra baritone and collector Jean-Baptiste Faure, who quite reasonably pressed him to finish the paintings he had promised, which did not happen until he threatened a lawsuit in 1887, the year Degas was reconciled with René.[24] On top of all of this the nagging of the Mussons for the portrait of Mathilde and the care of their uncle Eugène must have seemed insupportable.

Curiously, as an artist Degas overcame these tribulations and embarrassments. Perhaps the return sea journey at the end of, for him, five relatively indolent months in New Orleans gave him the energy (and also the perspective) to deal with them. In returning to Paris, he could shed the need to conform to the customs of his American family. He was on his own again and free to find his own way as an artist and as a man—eccentric and original as it might be. He probably gained strength in returning to his friends—the bassoonist from Lille, Désiré Dihau, and his sister Marie; the expatriate painter in England, James Tissot; the Danish painter, Lorenz Frölich[25]; that gifted engineer, collector, and family man, Henri Rouart (fig. 103), all of whom saved the letters Degas wrote from New Orleans. There were also those others like Berthe Morisot and her husband, Eugène Manet, Manet himself, Dr. and Mme Camus, Ludovic Louis Halévy, and Paul Valpinçon, whose lives enriched his and whose

FIG. 103. Edgar Degas, *Henri Rouart and the Ice Factory*, 1875, oil on canvas, 25⅝ × 19¾ in. Carnegie Museum of Art, Pittsburgh. Lemoisne 373.

children were often also his friends when he was an old man. Perhaps it was because of their support that he became such an aggressive and creative artist, fighting to bring the exhibitions of the work of independent artists to be known as Impressionists into existence. His letters to Tissot, in particular, chronicle his passion for a new "realist movement"—its strength derived from the finest French art of the past. He was sure enough, independent enough, imaginative enough to be one of the most triumphantly creative artists of his time. New Orleans had not broken him. It had even liberated him. In Paris he was once more where he belonged and could forget conformity, good manners, gentility, good taste—and even the need to be gallant.

1. This is implied in a letter that Eugène Musson wrote to Michel Musson on 3 April 1873, Brown, 1991, Box II, folder 52b.

2. Ibid.

3. Lemoisne, 1946–49, nos. 151–62.

4. Appendix II, letter to Tissot, 19 November 1872.

5. Ibid., letter to Rouart.

6. Ibid., letter to Tissot, 19 November 1872.

7. Ibid., letter to Rouart.

8. The children of René did receive some bronzes, which were cast in 1921, the year of René's death. Two tiny drawings of the heads of both M. and Mme Michel Musson are believed to exist—but it is not known whether they were in the possession of the family.

9. Brown, 1991, Box II, folder 45c.

10. Brown in this book, 47–65.

11. Appendix II, letter to Tissot, 19 November 1872.

12. Ibid., 18 February 1873.

13. Charles Bigot, *La Revue Politique et littéraire,* 8 April 1876. See Washington, San Francisco.

14. Appendix II, letter to Tissot, 18 February 1873.

15. Ibid., 19 November 1872.

16. Brown, 1991, Box II, folder 1c.

17. Brown, 1994, 32.

18. Pantazzi in Paris, Ottawa, New York, 1988, 212, under 4 April 1874, reference to a notarized inventory, Private collection, Paris.

19. Rewald, 1946, 122–23.

20. Rouart, 106.

21. Ibid., 110.

22. See McMullen, 1984, 250–51, for the earliest and fullest account based on contemporary newspaper accounts.

23. Most of this information is based on Loyrette, 1991, 324–27 and 735, n. 34.

24. Pantazzi in Paris, Ottawa, New York, "Degas and Faure," 221–23.

25. Lorenz Frölich (1820–1908) is probably best known for his *Study of a Dead Rat* of 1841 in the Ny Carlsberg Glyptotek, Copenhagen, but Degas could have thought of his domestic interiors when he was painting in New Orleans.

EXHIBITING IN PARIS AFTER RETURNING FROM NEW ORLEANS

WHEN DEGAS RETURNED TO PARIS from New Orleans, he may have had to wait for the shipment of canvases he had not finished there, in particular *Le Pédicure* and *The Song Rehearsal.* With *The Song Rehearsal,* he changed the two women he had drawn in New Orleans and replaced them with the single blond young woman believed to have been based upon his sister Marguerite Fevre. This painting does not appear to have left his studio for sale or for an exhibition during his lifetime. On the other hand, although he kept *The Pedicure* for almost twenty years, in 1892 he did sell it to Durand-Ruel, who immediately sold it to a Londoner and bought it back from him six years later, selling it the next month to the great Parisian collector comte Isaac de Camondo, who bequeathed it to the Louvre in 1911.

For Degas his New Orleans works were a private experience, which he was reluctant to share with others. With the exception of *A Cotton Office in New Orleans* an exception for him in many respects, which he would willingly and gratefully sell to the museum in Pau in 1878, and *Woman with a Vase of Flowers,* which, like *The Pedicure,* also made its way into Camondo's collection and became part of Camondo's bequest to the Louvre, Degas kept the portraits he painted in New Orleans. This may not have been just because they were portraits of his American family. In April 1876, in preparing for the Second Impressionist Exhibition, Degas wrote Berthe Morisot, "I want to ask your permission about two things. I expect to show an old sketch of a portrait of your sister, Mme Gobillard, and a portrait of your husband sitting by the side of a road. Of course I shall not do this without your consent."[1] Apparently he considered a portrait to be based on a private relationship between the artist and the sitter, which should be respected. But on another level it may have provided further justification for cutting himself off from New Orleans.

On his return to Paris from America, Degas worked industriously and enthusiastically toward the first exhibition of a group of independent artists who would eventually be known as Impressionists. On some Friday early in 1874 he wrote to his friend James Tissot in London with uncharacteristic fervor,

> Look here, my dear Tissot, no hesitations, no escape. You must exhibit at the Boulevard [des Capucines in a studio once occupied by Nadar]. It will do you good and us too. Manet seems determined to keep

aloof; he may well regret it. Yesterday I saw the arrangement of the premises, the hangings and the effect in daylight. It is as good as anywhere . . . I am getting really worked up and am running the thing with energy and I think a certain success. The realist movement no longer needs to fight with the others. It already *is, it exists,* it must show itself as *something distinct.* There must be a *Salon of realists.* Manet does not understand this. I believe he is more vain than intelligent.[2]

In spite of this letter, Tissot did not join his friend in the exhibition and risked the danger of being considered like Manet "more vain than intelligent." But there were other artists like Cézanne, Monet, Pissarro, and Renoir, who did.

Degas's own contribution to the exhibition was somewhat conservative since, of the ten works he did show, seven had already been purchased from him in the last few years.[3] They would therefore represent those works of his that were most immediately acceptable to the public—a matter of increasing concern to him as his previous financial independence was vanishing. It is not surprising that none of these had been painted in New Orleans. One work in that First Impressionist Exhibition, *At the Races in the Countryside* (cat. 18) was a particular favorite of the critics for its combination of landscape and agreeable color. Jean-Baptiste Faure (1830–1914), the baritone who was a collector with a remarkable eye but so little love for the works that he sold everything he owned by Degas between 1893 and 1898, owned that painting and lent it, as he also did a dance examination at the theater, which has not been identified. Degas's great friend (and one of his New Orleans correspondents), Henri Rouart (1833–1912), lent his *Intérieur de Coulisse,* which Degas later destroyed. Gustave Mühlbacher (1824–1907),[4] a carriage builder whose firm had 250 employees, was a Protestant and a friend of Rouart's but didn't sustain his interest in modern art, lent to this exhibition his almost grisaille oil painting of a *Ballet Rehearsal on the Stage,* which is now in the Musée d'Orsay in Paris. Another lender was a painter, Edouard Brandon (1831–97), whom Rouart claimed as one of his teachers and who specialized in Jewish subject matter. He lent three works, the exquisite tiny *Dance Class,* which is now one of the joys of The Metropolitan Museum of Art, New York, and rather surprisingly, considering the soberly religious character of his own works, two very secular laundresses. These collectors were all approximately contemporaries of the painter—Mühlbacher ten years older— and probably all were impressed by the enthusiasm of Rouart for his friend's work. But the exhibition must have seemed as if Degas had never gone to New Orleans.

PARIS LAUNDRY GIRLS

In one curious way New Orleans was not forgotten. Although Degas must have missed the theater and the dance in Louisiana, the most poignant cry in his letters is for the laundresses of Paris. He had written to Tissot the previous November: "Everything is beautiful in this world of the people. But one Paris laundry girl, with bare arms, is worth it all for such a Parisian as I am."[5] From New Orleans he had even thought of the beauty of their wares and wrote Rouart, "Long live fine laundering in France."[6] (Not even the memory of the boot-blacks he had enjoyed in American pullman trains could distract him from his admiration for his washerwomen who were in fact usually ironing.) He chose for the First Impressionist Exhibition two laundresses, probably painted before he left for New Orleans. (The catalogues for the Impressionist exhibitions have very little information. Sizes are never given and dates very rarely.) One was a pastel (fig. 104) of one of his favorite models, Emma Dobigny,[7] who about 1869 posed for him as she ironed. He also exhibited a painting of a laundress, which has never been identified. It is tempting to think it might be another he painted of Emma Dobigny (fig. 105) but unfortunately this was in his studio when he died whereas the one in the exhibition, like the pastel, had been owned by Édouard Brandon.

The pastel he exhibited in 1874 shows the ironer wearing the scanty, sleeveless blouse (or camisole) we are told the heat of the laundries made essential. She holds out her bare arms with a certain pride so that we can understand Degas nostalgically remembering those "bare arms" when he was in New Orleans. But, although the colors of the pastel are quietly decorative, Degas did not succumb to sentimentality. He tousled Emma Dobigny's normally orderly hair, darkened her eyebrows and rouged her opened lips so that, in that relatively immodest costume, she appears something of a slut. As one of the critics of the exhibition stated, "It is a very robust and very frank pastel representing an ironer."[8] Degas had made it clear that she is in a trade that, like the dancer's, was precipitously close to prostitution.[9]

In the painting (fig. 105), for which Dobigny also posed but which was not in the 1874 exhibition, the ironer is almost defiant as she stands behind her ironing table and in front of laundry hanging from the ceiling. The analysis of this work is somewhat difficult since Degas repainted it—particularly the background and the arms—perhaps as much as twenty years later.[10] Nevertheless, as she looks at us directly, we see the young woman as she was originally conceived. She is independent, perhaps a little sullen and even challenging, but above all she possesses the well-recorded sensual beauty of the model Emma

Dobigny. Degas was neither sentimental nor demeaning. As the poet Stéphane Mallarmé, who would become a good friend of Degas in the nineties, put it much more eloquently in an article he wrote at the time of the Second Impressionist Exhibition, Degas's laundresses have "a strange new beauty." He added, "No voluptuousness there no sentimentality here; the wise and intuitive artist does not care to explore the trite and hackneyed view of this subject."[11] In fact, although artists had painted laundresses before, it was not a common subject, which is why critics commented upon it so often in reviews of the first two Impressionist exhibitions.

Another writer at that time who was captivated by Degas's laundry girls was Edmond de Goncourt, who on 12 February 1874 (before the First Impressionist Exhibition later in the spring), pointed out that "After many attempts, experiments, and thrusts in every direction, he has fallen in love with modern subjects and has set his heart on laundry girls and danseuses . . . Degas showed me his laundry girls while speaking their language and explaining in technical terms the leaning on the iron, the circular ironing etc."[12] Degas's laundresses were a bigger sensation than his New Orleans works would have been.

1. Rouart, 110.

2. Letters 12, 38–38, dated only "Friday, 1974." The original French can be found in Paris, 1989, BN 6 (1), 364–65.

3. These are the Lemoisne numbers and current owners of the works exhibited by Degas as nos. 54–63: no. 54 ?; no. 55, L 297, Metropolitan Museum of Art; no. 56, destroyed; no. 57, L 397, Metropolitan Museum of Art; no. 58 ?; no. 59, L 258 ?, Yale University Art Gallery ?; no. 60, L 340, Musée d'Orsay; no. 61, BR 62, Louvre/Orsay; no. 62 ? ; no. 63, L 281, Museum of Fine Arts, Boston.

4. For the information on Mühlbacher, see Anne Distel, *Impressionism: The First Collectors* (New York, Inc., 1990), 191; his dates are from its index.

5. Appendix II, letter to Tissot, 19 November 1872.

6. Ibid., letter to Rouart.

7. For Emma Dobigny, who would have been eighteen in 1869, see Loyrette in Paris, Ottawa, New York, 1988, no. 86, 148–49.

8. Marius Chaumelin, "Actualités. L'Exposition des intransigeants," *La Gazette des étrangers,* 8 April 1876, 2. See Berson in Washington, San Francisco I, 68.

9. See Lipton, 1986, chap. 3, "Images of Laundresses: Social and Sexual Ambivalence," 116–50.

10. Loyrette in Gary Tinterow and Henri Loyrette, *Origins of Impressionism* (New York, 1994), no. 65, 377, suggests that the repainting was done between 1873 and 1876. Another possibility is that it that it is the painting about which Degas wrote to Durand-Ruel on 28 August 1891, "I should also show you a laundress that I have just finished. You will recognize it." (Paris, 1989, carte-lettre D 24, 448.)

11. Stéphane Mallarmé, "The Impressionists and Édouard Manet," *The Art Monthly Review and Photographic Portfolio* I, no. 9 (30 September 1876): 117–22; reprinted in Washington, San Francisco, 33.

12. McMullen, 1984, 241.

WOMAN IRONING, SILHOUETTE

In the Second Impressionist Exhibition in 1876 in the hospitable galleries of Durand-Ruel, Degas exhibited five canvases of women ironing, all presumably painted since his return from New Orleans. The only one that until recently had been certainly identified is the one he called *Blanchisseuse, Silhouette* (cat. 37), which must have been painted immediately after his return in April 1873 since it was sold to Durand-Ruel in June of that year. In March 1874 this painting was bought back from Durand-Ruel by Jean-Baptise Faure for the artist,[1] who therefore lent it himself to the Second Impressionist Exhibition.

This may have been the work to which Degas referred somewhat obliquely in writing to Durand-Ruel in 1891 about repainting an earlier laundress, which could certainly apply here to the painting of the linen and the laundry hanging in the background (as it could also to Munich's painting of Emma Dobigny as an ironer).[2] The composition was based on a squared charcoal drawing,[3] which makes it clear that from the beginning Degas thought in terms of the silhouette he chose for its title in the exhibition. It is a complete reversal of his painting of the young, confrontational ironer about 1869 after Dobigny (fig. 105). This later ironer is reduced to a shadow and turns away from us so that we do not even see her features. That silhouette, which can remind us of Degas writing to Tissot from New Orleans, "I love silhouettes so much,"[4] nevertheless in its

FIG. 104. Edgar Degas, *The Ironer,* ca. 1869, charcoal, white chalk, and pastel on tan paper, ($28\frac{7}{8} \times 23\frac{3}{4}$ in.), Musée d'Orsay, Paris. Lemoisne supp. 62.

FIG. 105. Edgar Degas, *Ironer,* ca. 1869, oil on canvas, ($35\frac{7}{8} \times 28\frac{7}{8}$ in.). Lemoisne 216.

37. Woman Ironing (Blanchisseuse, Silhouette)

1873
Oil on canvas
$21\frac{3}{8} \times 15\frac{1}{2}$ inches (54.3 × 39.4 cm)
The Metropolitan Museum of Art, New York.
Bequest of Mrs. H. O. Havemeyer, 1929.
H. O. Havemeyer Collection (29.100.46)
Lemoisne 356

harsh outlines emphasizes industry and willpower triumphing over inertia and weariness. We have lost the individuality and daring of the painting based on Emma Dobigny, but we have gained a quiet if more generalized reflection on the fundamental (rather than peripheral) role the ironer plays. That shadowed form against the light of her environment is handled with compassion.

In work on a recent exhibition at the Metropolitan Museum of Art, *Degas Photographer,* its curator, Malcolm Daniel, has identified one of the other paintings of laundresses by Degas in the 1876 exhibition.[5] There should be no doubt about this work since it was described by several critics, including Alex Pothey, as, "two laundresses, one weighing down on the iron in a convincing movement, the other yawning and scratching her arm. It is powerful and true like a Daumier."[6] But there are several paintings of the same subject, clearly painted in the 1880s.[7] However, Daniel uncovered four photographs owned if not taken by Degas of paintings of ironers and one clearly the underpainting of *The Ironers,*[8] which it is believed Degas first exhibited in 1876 and reworked about 1887, when it was bought by Faure, who sold it in 1893. This underpainting satisfies the descriptions of the critics in 1876; it clearly provides an invitation to the visitors to smile at the juxtapositions of the energetic yawn, the bottle of wine, and the witless pressure exerted upon the iron by the second ironer at the right. This was the beginning of Degas's exploration of pairs of ironers, which become more serious and more monumental as he works upon them in the 1880s.

The number of laundresses Degas exhibited in 1874 and 1876, two at the first exhibition and five at the second, suggest that this theme had become almost an obsession. His comment to Tissot about having missed their arms in New Orleans had not been an idle one. Although he never dated the works, there seems to have been an explosion of ironers by Degas in the 1870s in varying sizes and media. They could be petite or heroic, amusing or tragic, isolated or

in a crowded passageway anticipating Zola's *Germinal*.[9] They could be wonderfully good-natured like the actress playing the role of a washerwoman in a play by Ludovic Halévy and Henri Meilhac, which Degas drew in one of the two notebooks he kept at the Halévys and in which he would make drawings when he had dinner with these good friends, whose guests were apt to be some of the wittiest and most gifted men and women in the arts and the theater in Paris.[10]

Laundresses were by no means Degas's only subject at this time. Although he gave up the racetrack temporarily and did not explore any landscapes, Degas did continue seriously and creatively with the dance. But the range in mood of his laundresses and his technical inventiveness was typical of his work in the seventies after he returned from America. In spite of his personal problems, the works he produced between 1873 and 1879 were among the most amusing, surprising, and animated of his career.

1. Pantazzi in Paris, Ottawa, New York, 1988, no. 122. See "Provenance," 224.

2. See n. 10, previous section.

3. Vente III, 269, *Woman Ironing,* charcoal, squared, 42.5 × 30.5 cm, private collection.

4. Appendix II, letter to Tissot, 18 February 1873.

5. Daniel in New York, 1998, 38, figs. 20–23, pp. 38–41.

6. Pothey, 1876; Berson in Washington, San Francisco, 1986, 104.

7. L 687, ca. 1884–85, Norton Simon Museum, Pasadena; L 785, ca. 1884–86, Musée d'Orsay, Paris; L 786, ca. 1891, private collection.

8. L 686, *Les Repasseuses,* underpainting by 1876, repainted by 1887, present owner unknown.

9. See Pantazzi in Paris, Ottawa, New York, no. 122, 223.

10. Reff, Nb. 29, 21, 23, 1879–80, Collection Mr. and Mrs. Eugene V. Thaw, on deposit with the Pierpont Morgan Library, New York.

NEW ORLEANS AT THE SECOND IMPRESSIONIST EXHIBITION

THE TWO NEW ORLEANS WORKS Degas chose to show at the 1876 exhibition of the Impressionists were of two aspects of Louisiana society—one domestic, a group of young children with their nursemaid on the steps of the back walled garden of his uncle's house; the second commercial, men gathered together to buy and sell cotton in the offices of the same uncle. In neither case was anyone identified. The first work on Degas's list was called *Portraits in an Office (New Orleans)* (cat. 31), the second, *Courtyard of a House (New Orleans)* (cat. 29, *Children on a Doorstep*). The critics ignored the second, the children, perhaps because, although Degas did identify it as a sketch on the program, they were disconcerted by the very modernity of the handling. On the other hand, they were startled into emphasizing *A Cotton Office in New Orleans,* which was received with verbal generosity while the other painting was ignored.

A Cotton Office was almost as satisfactory as an ocean voyage in introducing visitors to the exhibition to a commercial world they would otherwise have never experienced. Their reviews were sometimes not too accurate. One wrote, imaginatively: "M. Degas is a surprising artist. He tries to see new things. He was born in New Orleans and has left it to live in Paris. One feels that he sees Parisian life as an observer who has not from his childhood been accustomed to its spectacles."[1] Another critic noted, "M. Degaz [*sic*] gives us an American scene that is in every way remarkable. It is a New York shop where cotton is sold by weight."[2] On the whole it was preferred to his other works. One wrote of his others as "a realism that is the saddest and most regrettable." But he went on typically, "I make an exception, however, for the painting with the least bizarre title, *Portraits in an Office.* The painting thus designated and thus disguised, is nothing but a collection of cotton merchants examining the precious material which is today the source of fortunes in America. It is cold, it is bourgeois, but it has been seen exactly and honestly and rendered correctly."[3] Another more enthusiastic critic wrote, "I do not believe the Salon of 1876 offers us as many interiors as remarkably painted as the painting by Degas with the title, *Portraits in an Office, New Orleans* About the composition there is nothing to say except that the figures are not posed. They are grouped, or rather dispersed, absolutely as if you could see them in a wholesaler on the rue du Sentier." He continues at length and goes on, "This is a subject which is certainly not traditional. Academicians could laugh at it; but it will not displease those who love painting to be exact and frankly modern, who believe that the

conveying of life and delicacy of execution ought to be counted for something
. . . M. Degas seems to have wished to rival the delicacy and cleanliness of
Dutch painters."[4] Zola was surprisingly (and perhaps unjustly critical) in describing the painting as "half-way between a marine and the reproduction in
an illustrated newspaper. His artistic perceptions are excellent, but I fear that
his brushes will never become creative."[5] Another critic found his color in the
painting "dull and not very agreeable."[6] No one was ready to buy it. But the
painting was not ignored. And a little of New Orleans crept into the consciences of the visitors to this exhibition in Paris.

1. Charles Bigot, "Causerie artistique L'Exposition des intransigeants," *La Revue politique et littéraire,* 8 April 1876, 349–52; Berson in Washington, San Francisco, 1986, 60.

2. Pothey, 1876; Berson in Washington, San Francisco, 103.

3. Louis Enault, "Mouvement artistique: L'Exposition des intransigeants dans la galerie de Durand-Ruelle [*sic*]," *Le Constitutionel,* 10 April 1876, 2; Berson, in Washington, San Francisco, 83.

4. Marius de Chaumelin, "Actualités: L'Exposition des intransigeants," *La Gazette des Étrangers,* 8 April 1876, 2; Berson in Washington, San Francisco, 68.

5. Émile Zola, "Deux Expositions d'art au mois de mai," *Le Messager de l'Europe,* June 1876; Berson in Washington, San Francisco, 112–13.

6. Arthur Bagnères, "L'Exposition de peinture par un groupe d:artistes, rue Le Peletier, 11," *L'Echo Universel,* 13 April 1876, 3; Berson in Washington, San Francisco, 54.

THE COTTON OFFICES REMEMBERED:
M. DE CLERMONT

WHEN EDGAR DEGAS WROTE HIS LETTER to thank the director of the museum at Pau, Charles le Coeur,[1] for having bought *A Cotton Office in New Orleans,* he wrote it on the office writing paper of Hermann de Clermont,[2] who was a successful furrier and tanner, the brother of a painter of racetrack scenes, Auguste de Clermont, and the son-in-law of a woman who was very rich in her own right,[3] Mme Dietz-Monin, whose portrait Degas rather famously failed to finish to her satisfaction.[4] It is assumed that Degas knew the tanner through his brother, the painter. It is also assumed that Degas undertook the only commissioned portrait of his career, that of Mme Dietz-Monin, because the Clermonts had given him help when he was so heavily in debt after his father's death. In fact, it is believed that the commission was a tactful effort on the part of that family to reduce his debt.[5] In any case to Degas, Hermann de Clermont represented security and success in the world of business and finance. It may have been to borrow or repay money that Degas was in Hermann de Clermont's office that March day.

At the Second Impressionist Exhibition in 1876, where Degas exhibited *A Cotton Office in New Orleans,* he had already ventured into another area of the business world in showing a pastel he called a "Portrait of M. E. M.," which was of Ernest May with a friend, M. Bolâtre, at the Bourse (or Paris Stock Exchange).[6] It was probably after writing his letter to M. LeCoeur to thank him for the purchase of *A Cotton Office* that he painted another larger version in oil, which he persuaded M. May to lend to the Fourth Impressionist Exhibition in 1879, where he called it, "Portraits à la Bourse,"[7] *A Cotton Office* had obviously led him to the world of commerce—but one cannot claim that it was sustained.

Nevertheless, even thanking M. LeCoeur for having bought *A Cotton Office* for the museum in Pau may have encouraged Degas to make two drawings of de Clermont with one of his pelts in his hands. It is also interesting to discover that in the same Fourth Impressionist Exhibition in which he showed *À la Bourse,* he also exhibited *Portraits de M. et de Mme H. de C. (détrempe à pastel).* The work or works may not have survived. Certainly it is not known. But it is interesting that "détrempe" (probably what today we would call essence) was the medium he used for the unfortunate (but very beautiful) portrait of Mme de Clermont's mother, Mme Dietz-Monin, which was called *Portrait après un bal costumé.* Our only other evidence of Mme de Clermont comes from an inscription on a drawing in one of Degas's notebooks, where she is invisible but

38. *Hermann de Clermont*

ca. 1879
Black chalk with white heightening on blue paper
$18\frac{3}{4} \times 12\frac{1}{8}$ inches (48 × 31.5 cm)
Copenhagen, Statens Museum for Kunst
Department of Prints and Drawings (tu 35.5)

1. Paris, 1989, 428–29. The letter is in the Musée des Beaux-Arts, Pau.

2. Loyrette in Paris, Ottawa, New York, 1988, no. 115, 188, n. 3.

3. Loyrette, 1991, 359. The great fortune was hers, inherited from an uncle.

4. See Brettell in Chicago, 1984, no. 47, 105–9.

5. Brettell uses Dietz-Monnin family papers to explain the circumstances.

6. L 392, no. 38, in the 1874 Impressionist exhibition. Present owner unknown.

7. L 499, Musée d'Orsay. See Brown, 1994, 128–31; and Linda Nochlin, "Degas and the Dreyfus Affair: A Portrait of the Artist as Anti-Semite," in *The Dreyfus Affair* (Berkeley and Los Angeles, 1987).

8. Reff, Nb. 30, 13.

9. There was another drawing framed with this of M. de Clermont in the same position in the Degas sale (Vente III, 168 [1]). Its present owner is unknown.

10. Brown, 1994, 126.

there is the drawing of a physician who is, according to Degas's inscription, "Dr. Lacronique who is prescribing to Mme de Clermont certain remedies with conviction expressed in his right fist and, in particular, the right thumb, but suggesting doubt through the open left hand tapping on the edge of the table."[8] Since Mme de Clermont is invisible on that page, M. de Clermont has to represent the family for us.

The drawing of Hermann de Clermont, which is charcoal, heightened with white, on greyish blue paper, is more impressive in the original than can be suspected from a photograph.[9] It might seem that the strokes are very loose and casual, but they are remarkably effective in suggesting the bulk of Clermont's body and the power of his hands. The head admittedly is flatter, reduced almost to a shadow, but that in itself gives the profile a keener suggestion of intelligence and concentration. The fur in his hand is magnificently rich and soft. The skin cast over the railing is so animate it is disturbing, particularly as an apparent extension of his coat. Although the figure was clearly inspired by the memory of Michel Musson feeling cotton, as Marilyn R. Brown writes there is in the drawing of M. de Clermont "a rather disconcerting quality that seems to arise from the shift from plant fiber to dead animal skins."[10] On the other hand, there is a great deal of relatively empty space in the drawing to absorb the reaction to the animal skins, and there is such assurance in Clermont's gaze and his gestures that we respect his control over his particular enterprise.

The cotton offices of New Orleans may have introduced us to a tannery, but Degas did not go any further in his exploration of the world of commerce. He went on to more purely artistic considerations instead.

A POSTSCRIPT: *The Dance Class*

39. The Dance Class
1881
Oil on canvas
$31\frac{1}{8} \times 30\frac{1}{8}$ inches (81.6 × 76.5 cm)
Philadelphia Museum of Art:
W. P. Wilstach Collection (W´37-2-1)
Lemoisne 479

WHEN MARILYN BROWN WROTE of the drawing of Hermann de Clermont she pointed out that "Degas created a further sense of spatial uncertainty" and that "although the basic lines of composition recall (in reverse) those of the Fogg version of *A Cotton Office* (cat. 32), the effect is more unsettling because the viewer's standpoint is less certainly grounded."[1] In fact, by the end of the seventies, Degas was creating spatial effects that seem irrational and can be disorienting but produce remarkably animated images. This can be seen in a work that has no ostensible connection with New Orleans but does have one echo of a work Degas produced in this city. This is *The Dance Class* (cat. 39), which was bought by the brother of the painter Mary Cassatt, Alexander J. Cassatt, in 1881 and has been in Philadelphia ever since.

No matter how irrational the space appears in *The Dance Class,* it was carefully contrived. Even when Degas, with the dancer at the right with her back to us who is touching her ear, seems to have cut through her body in an arbitrary fashion, he had studied it first in a large drawing of the two dancers on the right.[2] Nothing is actually the result of chance. We do not see much of this rehearsal room, but we do see what seems to be a vast amount of floor between the two groups. That floor rises so high to meet the wall that it appears tilted. The wall is penetrated in the upper left by a view of Paris roofs, which we discover is a quite improbable mirrored reflection of a window behind our backs The three unsteady young dancers—like birds—in the upper left are believably related to each other and the mirror in scale—but in order to give the composition some solidity and weight, Degas has played much more freely with the scale of the two other dancers, the man whose profile appears unexpectedly and the seated woman. In fact, his liberties are such that the dancer with the long hair could seem a giantess when compared with the reading woman. Even the second dancer seems surprisingly smaller than her companion. The head and shoulders of the man are so detached from a body that we do not speculate

too much about his height—but in actuality he is surprisingly short. And the exquisitely painted woman slumping on the chair seems very small indeed. We would appear to be in a fun-fair or a wonderland if Degas's subtle handling of light and atmosphere did not bind the work together and cast a spell on us so that we do not question its eccentricities.

It is the woman, of course, who supplies us with a link with New Orleans. She reads a newspaper with the same indifference to her surroundings that René De Gas revealed in reading *The Daily Picayune* in the middle of all the activity in his uncle's office. Like René she is dressed up—in a blue printed dress with a white collar and a yellow straw hat with a splendid ribbon and bow. Her costume is actually painted with great feeling for the texture of the paint as well as for the fabrics it describes. We see little of her shadowed face, but we can appreciate the delicacy of her wrists as she holds up the newspaper to read. Like René De Gas in *A Cotton Office* she is one fulcrum around which the action takes place. Degas could not have painted her without thinking of his brother in the New Orleans canvas. And since this was not too long after René's elopement—at the very most three years later—Degas may have wickedly enjoyed the transformation of the somewhat disdainful René into this funny (if endearing) little chaperone in Degas's own wonderland. But it is painted with more humor than acrimony.

1. Brown, 1994, 128.
2. L 480, *Two Dancers at Rest,* private collection, Switzerland.

Provenances

Provenances are given as provided by the owners.

1. *Self-Portrait in a Soft Hat*
   Sterling and Francine Clark Art Institute, Williamstown, Massachusetts
   Marcel Guérin, Paris; Daniel Guérin, his son, Paris; bought by Durand-Ruel, New York, 20 April 1948 (stock no. N.Y. 5747), bought the same day by Robert Sterling Clark, New York; his gift to the museum 1955.

2. *Portrait of René De Gas*
   The National Gallery of Art, Washington, D.C.
   René De Gas, Paris; Roland Nepveu-De Gas, Paris, probably by 1931; sale Hôtel Drouot, Paris, 24 November 1964, no. 38, Lemee collection; acquired 1964 by Wildenstein & Co., sold December 1968 to Mr. Paul Mellon; gift to National Gallery of Art, 1995.

3. *René De Gas, The Artist's Brother*
   New Orleans Museum of Art
   René De Gas to his descendants; Tahir Gallery, June 19, 1969, sold to New Orleans Museum of Art.

4. *Marguerite De Gas*
   Museum of Fine Arts, Boston
   Collection D. David-Weill; sold at one of his estate sales at Hôtel Drouot, Paris, 25–26 May 1971, lot 44; bought by C. G. Boener, Düsseldorf; sold to Museum of Fine Arts, Boston, 1973.

5. *Thérèse De Gas*
   Museum of Fine Arts, Boston
   Atelier Degas; René De Gas, the artist's brother, Paris 1918–21 (René De Gas estate sale, Drouot, Paris, 10 November 1927, no. 17, repr.); bought by the museum through Paul Rosenberg, 1931.

6. *Portrait of Mme Edmondo Morbilli, née Thérèse De Gas*
   Collection of Walter Feilchenfeldt, Zürich
   Collection of Henri Fevre, Monte-Carlo; Vente coll. M.X., Hôtel Drouot, 22 June 1925, n. 65; collection of Mrs. Fred W. Davies, New York; coll. Walter Feichenfeldt, Zürich.

7. *Désirée Musson*
   Collection of Mrs. T. Ham, McLean, Virginia
   Atelier Degas; Jean Nepveu Degas, until 1964; acquired by Wildenstein & Co., until 1966, Collection of Mrs. T. Ham.

8. *Mme Michel Musson and Her Daughters Estelle and Désirée*
   The Art Institute of Chicago
   Atelier Degas; Henri Fevre, Nice; Marcel Guérin, Paris; Seligmann and Co., New York; Mary Day Blake, Chicago; acquired by the museum in 1949 as part of the Margaret Day Blake Collection.

9. *Four Studies of a Baby's Head (Joe Balfour?)*
   The Minneapolis Institute of Arts
   Atelier Degas at time of his death; Edmond Sagot, Minneapolis Institute of the Arts, John de Laittre Memorial Collection, Gift of Mrs. Horace Ropes.

10. *Estelle Musson Balfour*
    Walters Art Gallery, Baltimore
    Mary Cassatt, Le Mesnil-Théribus; Henry Walters, Baltimore, 1903; bequeathed to Walters Art Gallery by Henry Walters, 1931.

11. *Young Woman in an Armchair (drawing of Estelle Musson Balfour)*
    Private Collection, The Bahamas
    Atelier Degas; Vente IV, 1919, no. 136b, illus.; sale Galerie Kornfeld, 23 June 1982, no. 149; private collection Sigrid Dassler-Malms, Küsnacht.

12. *Marie Lucie Millaudon*
    Museum Boymans-van Beuningen, Rotterdam
    IIéme Vente 1918, no. 238 (I); Paul Cassirer, Berlin; Franz Koenigs, Haarlem.

13. *Portrait of a Woman (Possibly Mme Ducros)*
    Private collection, on anonymous extended loan to the Portland Art Museum
    Atelier Degas sale, May 6–8, 1918, no. I; Charles Vignier (Sale, May 21, 1931, no. 8 repr.); Bonnemaison; Mrs. R. Thürlimann; Freddy and Regina Homburger, 1957; private collection, on anonymous extended loan to Portland Museum of Art, Maine.

14. *Musicians in the Orchestra, Portrait of Désiré Dihau*
    Fine Arts Museums of San Francisco
    Galerie Georges Petit, Paris, 6–8 May 1918, no. 9; perhaps Ambroise Vollard, Paris by 1933; Galerie Mouradian-Vallotton, Paris, by 1938; Andre Weil Paris, purchased by California Palace of the Legion of Honor in 1952.

15. *Walking Horse*
    New Orleans Museum of Art
    Wax, Atelier of the artist, Degas heirs, 1917; Gaston De Gas Musson and Odile De Gas Musson; gift of the Musson family to the Isaac Delgado Museum (the New Orleans Museum of Art), 1950.

16. *At the Races*
    Collection of Weil Brothers, Montgomery, Alabama
    Degas Vente III, Galerie George Petit, Paris, April 7–9, 1919, lot 36; Vollard, Paris; Sam Salz, New York; Thannhauser Gallery; Ritz, Settignano; Sotheby's, 1 July 1959, lot 76; Arthur Tooth & Sons Ltd., London; Lord Marks; Christie's, New York, 18 October 1977, lot 4 to present owner.

17. *Achille De Gas*
The Minneapolis Institute of Arts
René De Gas, Paris, Vente 1927, no. 81 ill.;
Chester Dale, New York; Parke Bernet
sale, New York, 16 March 1944, no. 38;
Jacques Seligmann Gallery, New York;
Putnam Dana McMillan, Minneapolis,
bequest to Minneapolis Institute of Art.

18. *At the Races in the Countryside*
The Museum of Fine Arts, Boston
Bought from the artist by Durand-Ruel,
Paris, 17 September 1872 (as "La voiture
sortant du champ de courses," stock no.
1910); bought through Charles Deschamps
by Jean-Baptitste Faure, 25 April 1873;
bought by Durand-Ruel, Paris, 2 January
1893 (as "Voiture aux courses" stock no.
2566); deposited with the Durand-Ruel
family, Les Balans, 29 March 1918; bought
by the museum, in New York, 1926.

19. *Notebook 25*
Bibliothèque Nationale de France, Paris
In collection of René De Gas following his
brother's death; given by René De Gas to
Cabinet des Estampes of the Bibliothèque
Nationale in 1920.

20. *Head of a Woman*
Private Collection, on anonymous loan
to Portland Museum of Art, Maine
Sale, Galerie Mott, Geneva (1965), Freddy
and Regina Homburger, 1957; private
collection, on anonymous extended loan
to Portland Museum of Art.

21. *The Invalid (La Malade)*
Collection of John Loeb, New York
Bought from the artist by Durand-Ruel,
Paris (as "La malade" in stock book,
"Convalescente" in journal), 31 January
1887 (stock no. 919); bought by Henry
Lerolle, Paris, 15 February 1888; Mme
Henry Lerolle, Paris; Captain Edward
Molyneaux, Paris; M. Knoedler and Co.,
New York; bought by John Loeb, 2 Janu-
ary 1958; bought by John L. Loeb, Jr. at
Christie's 12 May 1997.

21b.*Young Woman Seated in a Garden*
Private Collection, New York
Atelier Degas (Vente I, 1918, no. 32); Collection Alphonse Kann, Saint-Germain-
en-Laye (confiscated by Nazis in WWII;
recovered at Allies Collection Point in
Munich, 1946; restituted to Kann family
22 October 1948); sold Bernheim-Jeune &
Cie., Paris, 1956; acquired by present
owner July 1956.

22. *The Nurse (La Garde-Malade)*
Private Collection, courtesy of Walter
Feilchenfeldt
Atelier Degas (3e Vente, No. 29, repr.).
Collection Ochsé, Paris. Collection Hector
Brame, Paris; Paul Cassirer, Amsterdam,
1935; Erich Maria Remarque, Porto Ronco,
1935; Collection Feilchenfeldt, Amsterdam
1960; Private Collection, Frankfurt, 1961;
Private Collection (courtesy Walter
Feilchenfeldt).

23. *Woman with Bandage*
The Detroit Institute of Art
Dupuis collection; sale Drouot, Paris, 10
June 1891, no. 16 (as "Chex l'oculiste"),
bought at that sale by Hubert du Puy,
Louviers; Laurent collection, Paris (M.X.
. . . [Laurent] sale, Paris (stock no. 4873);
bought by Raymond Koechlin, Paris,
4 May 1899; Denys Cochin, Paris (sale,
March 1919, no. 9 repr.); Mme Jacques
Cochin, Paris; Robert H. Tannahill, De-
troit, 1949; his bequest to the museum,
1970.

24. *Woman Seated on the Balcony*
Ordrupgaardsmlingen, Copenhagen,
Denmark
Atelier Degas, Collection Wilhelm
Hansen, Copenhagen; bequeathed by
his widow in 1951 to the state toward the
establishment of the Ordrupgaardsam-
lingen, which opened in 1953.

25. *Mathilde Musson Bell*
Collection of Carol Selle, New York
Jeanne Fevre, Nice; Mme Guillaume-
Walter, Paris; John Rewald, New York;
Sotheby's London, 7 July 1960, no. 25,
to Richard and Carol Selle.

26. *Mathilde Musson Bell*
Göteborgs Konstmuseum, Göteborg,
Sweden
Carl Matthiessen, Stockholm; Jean
Jahnssons, Stockholm 1934; Svensk-
Franska Lonstgalleriet, Stockholm;
Göteborgs Konstmuseum, Göteborg,
1940.

27. *Woman with a Vase of Flowers*
Musée d'Orsay, Paris
Michel Manzi, Paris; bought by comte
Isaac de Camondo, 18 June 1894, (as
"La Femme aux fleurs"); his bequest to
the Louvre 1911; exhibited 1914.

28. *Portrait of Mme René De Gas, née
Estelle Musson*
New Orleans Museum of Art
Atelier Degas 1918, Collection Pr. Cremetti,
London; Collection Thannhauser, Zürich;
Collection of Dr. Kurt Oppenheim,
Blonay-Vevey, Switzerland; Peter M.
Samuel, London; E. V. Thaw, & Co., New
York, bought in 1965 by public subscrip-
tion for New Orleans Museum of Art.

29. *Children on a Doorstep (New Orleans)*
Ordrupgaard, Copenhagen, Denmark
Atelier Degas (Vente I, 1918, no. 45 [as
"Enfants assis sur le perron d'une maison
de campagne"]); bought at that sale by
Jos Hessel; Wilhelm Hansen, Copenhagen; bequeathed by his widow in 1951
to the state toward the establishment of
the Ordrupgaardsamlingen, which opened
in 1953.

30. *Young Girl in a White Dress*
Private Collection, The Bahamas
Atelier Edgar Degas, Galerie Georges
Petit, Paris, 1918; Figuet, Paris; Mme
Friedmann, Paris; Ader Picard Tajan sale
9 April 1987; Christie's London, 30 No-
vember 1987, lot 31; private collection,
Küsnacht, Sotheby's 1992, lot 3.

31. *A Cotton Office in New Orleans (Portraits
in a Cotton Office)*
Musée des Beaux-Arts, Pau
Bought from the artist in 1878; on the
occasion of the exhibition organized by
the Société Béarnaise des Amis des Arts at
Pau, by the Musée des Beaux-Arts, Pau,
thanks to Noulibos bequest.

32. *Cotton Merchants in New Orleans*
Harvard University Art Museums (Fogg
Art Museum), Cambridge, Massachusetts
Atelier Degas (Vente I, 1918, no. 3);
bought at that sale by Rosenberg;
Herbert N. Straus, New York; his gift to
the museum.

33. *Study of John E. Livaudais*
Pierpont Morgan Library, New York
Atelier Degas (3e Vente, no. 155, repr.).
Collection Buhler, Paris, Pierpont
Morgan Library.

34. *The Song Rehearsal*
Dumbarton Oaks Research Library and
Collection, Washington, D.C.
Atelier Degas (Vente I, 1918, no. 106 [as
"Deux jeunes femmes en toilette de ville
répétant un duo"]); bought at that sale by
Walter Gay; Mr. and Mrs. Robert Woods
Bliss, Washington, D.C.; their bequest to
the Dumbarton Oaks Research Library,
1940.

35. *Young Woman Singing,* Study for
The Song Rehearsal
Cabinet des Dessins, Musée du Louvre
(Orsay)
Atelier Degas (Vente III, 1919, no. 404.2);
bought at that sale by Marcel Bing with
Woman Singing (cat. 118); his bequest to
the Louvre 1922

36. *Young Woman Standing,* Study for
The Song Rehearsal
Cabinet des Dessins, Musée du Louvre
(Orsay)
Atelier Degas (Vent III, 1919, no. 404.2);
bought at that sale by Marcel Bing with
Woman Singing (cat. 118); his bequest to
the Louvre, 1922.

37. *Woman Ironing (Blanchisseuse, Silhouette)*
The Metropolitan Museum of Art,
New York
Bought from the artist by Durand-Ruel,
Paris, 14 (or 6) June 1873, (stock no. 3132,
stamped on the stretcher); transferred to
Durand-Ruel, London, winter 1873; returned to Durand-Ruel, Paris; bought
back on behalf of the artist by Jean-
Baptiste Faure, Paris, 5 or 6 March 1874;
resold by the artist to Durand-Ruel, Paris,
29 February 1892, (stock no. 2039, inscribed on a label on the back); deposited
with Bernheim-Jeune, Paris, 13 February
1894; sold to Durand-Ruel, New York, 4
October 1894 (stock no. 1204, inscribed
on a label on the back); bought by H. O.
Havemeyer, New York, 18 December 1894;
Mrs. H. O. Havemeyer, New York, 1907–
29; her bequest to the museum, 1929.

38. *Hermann de Clermont*
Copenhagen, Statens Museum for Kunst
Vente III, 1919, no. 162 (2), illus.; Durand-
Ruel, Paris; Ambroise Vollard, Paris;
Feilchenfeldt, Zürich, Copenhagen,
Statens Museum for Kunst.

39. *The Dance Class*
Philadelphia Museum of Art
Painted for Alexander Cassatt; delivered
by the artist to Durand-Ruel, Paris,
18 June 1881, (stock no. 1115, as "Le foyer
de la danse"); delivered by Durand-Ruel
the same day to Mary Cassatt, Paris, for
6,000 francs; Alexander Cassatt, Philadelphia 1881–1906; Lois Cassatt, his widow,
Philadelphia, to 1920; Mrs. W. Plunkett
Stewart, their daughter, to 1931; Mrs.
William Potter Wear, her daughter;
Mrs. Elsie Cassatt Stewart Simmons, her
daughter; bought by the Commissioners
of Fairmont park for the W. P. Wilstach
Collection, 1937.

FIG. 106. Walter Sickert, *Degas at New Orleans,*
ca. 1912–13, pen with black and sepia ink, black
chalk highlighted with white on gray paper,
$15\frac{1}{2} \times 13$ in. Private collection, New Orleans.

Supplemental Objects

S.1. Benjamin Franklin Reinhart, *Portrait of Eugène Henri Musson,* 1850s, oil on canvas, 52 × 40 in., Collection of Ronald Smith, New Orleans. [fig. 8]

> The portrait was executed in the 1850s, some years after the child's death in 1849. The sad course of Eugène Henri's undiagnosed fever is chronicled in detail in an extraordinary sixteen-page letter written by his anguished father, Michel Musson, to his own father, Germain Musson, who was in Mexico (De Gas–Musson, Box I, folder 12). When Eugène Henri died, his parents had a photographer make daguerreotypes so that his image would not be lost to them, and in order to serve as a model for a painted portrait, a common practice at a time when child mortality was so high. Such a daguerreotype may have been used by the Pennsylvania-born Reinhart who visited New Orleans periodically, making portraits of Creole society. His highly finished academic style represents the kind of portraiture to which the Musson family would have been more accustomed, and it provides a sharp contrast to the style of their Parisian cousin.

S.2. Catherine Longchamps, *Portrait of Mme Auguste de Gas, née Musson and her sister comtesse de Rochefort,* 1835, chalk and wash on paper, 9 × 11 in., Historic New Orleans Collection (acc.num.1979.28) [fig. 5]

> This is the surviving portrait of a pair by Longchamps, a Swiss artist who lived in Paris. It represents Marie Célestine Musson shortly after the birth of her son, the painter Edgar Degas; her companion is her sister, Anne Eugénie Musson, the comtesse de Rochefort. Both had married in Europe and this portrait may have been commissioned for their father, Germain Musson, when he returned to New Orleans. The pendant (reportedly destroyed by fire) shows the Musson brothers, Eugène and Henri, who also remained in France (fig. 52). The third brother, Michel, returned to the United States with his father.

S.3. *Portrait of the comtesse de Rochefort and Portrait of Désirée Musson,* 1863, two-sided drawing. Collection of Marie Estelle Moyer. [fig. 107]

> Family tradition attributes the drawing to Edgar Degas while in Italy. The identifications, which are uncertain, are also according to family tradition.

S.4. Adrien Persac, artist and Eugène Surgi, civil engineer, *Plan of a Splendid Property and of two fine lots of ground/ second district,* March 12, 1860, 55 × 30 in., Notarial Archives Plan Book, 5, Folio 18, Courtesy New Orleans Notarial Archives (.18.O.2.317.Sur&Per.60.el). [fig. 2]

> This drawing was made as an auction notice in 1860, when the property was sold by Benjamin Rodriquez to Jean Baptiste Letorey. The drafting was done by Eugène Surgi, who was from Paris and moved to New Orleans in 1845. The painter was Marie Adrien Persac, who was born in Lyon, France, and lived in New Orleans from 1857 to 1872. A celebrated watercolorist, Persac became well known for his work as a painter of plantations. Sally Reeves, archivist of the Notarial Archives of New Orleans, proposes that in this drawing Surgi did the survey work, completed the site plan, the title portion and other lettering, while Persac did the elevation of the house, the sky, and the area confined by the black line in the lower portion of the drawing.

FIG. 107. Attributed by the family to Edgar Degas, *Portrait of the comtesse de Rochefort* and *Portrait of Désirée Musson,* 1863, two-sided drawing. Collection of Marie Estelle Moyer.

FIG. 108. *La Juive,* album of sheet music belonging to Estelle Musson. Earl K. Long Library, University of New Orleans.

S.5. Sheet Music belonging to Estelle Musson. Modern binding, collection ranges in date. Earl K. Long Library, University of New Orleans. Many of the title pages bear the signature "Estelle Musson." The collection was probably bound (original binding lost) before her marriage to Joseph Balfour, rather than after her divorce from René De Gas, as her signature deteriorated with her eyesight over the years.

    a. *La Fille du regiment: Romance.* Lyrics by Saint Georges and Bayard. Music by Gaetano Donizetti.

    b. *Mon Âme à Dieu, mon coeur à toi!: Romance.* Lyrics by F. de Courcy. Music by Louis Clapisson. [fig. 13]

    c. *Le Lac.* Poem of meditation by Alphonse de Lamartine. Music by Louis Niedermeyer.

    d. *L'étoile du nord: prière et barcarolle.* Music and lyrics by Giacomo Meyerbeer.

    e. *Trop tard!* Lyrics by F. Tourte. Music by d'Etienne Arnaud.

    f. *Robert le Diable.* Opera in five acts. Lyrics by MM. E. Scribe et G. Delavigne. Music by Giacomo Meyerbeer.

    g. *La Juive.* Opera in five acts: Bolero. Lyrics by Mr. Eugène Scribe. Music by F. Halévy.

    h. *Robert le Diable.* Opera in five acts. Lyrics by MM. E. Scribe et G. Delavigne. Music by G. Meyerbeer. [fig. 85]

i. *Li marinari; duetto.* Lyrics by C. Pepoli. Music by Gioacchino Rossini.

j. *La Juive.* Opera in five acts. Lyrics by Mr. Eugène Scribe. Music by F. Halévy. [fig. 108]

k. *La Favorite: Duo.* Lyrics by MM. E. Scribe, Alphonse Royer, and Gustave Vaez. Music by Gaetano Donizetti

l. *Soon in the cold neglected tomb.* Words and lyrics by Gaetano Donizetti.

m. *Heard ye that sound.* Music and lyrics by Gaetano Donizetti.

n. *Les amours du diable.* Comic opera in four acts. Music and lyrics by Albert de Grisar.

o. *Le cor des Alpes.* Lyrics by Françaises de Belanger. Music by Heinrich Proch.

p. *La Favorite: Prière.* Lyrics by MM. E. Scribe, Alphonse Royer, and Gustave Vaez. Music by Gaetano Donizetti.

q. *Derniers voeux de Rachel.* Lyrics by d'Edouard Filliol. Music by Giuseppe Concone.

r. *Trois soldats bretons: récit.* Lyrics by d'Émile Barateau. Music by Paul Henrion.

s. *Dernier chant d'une jeune fille: mélodie.* Lyrics by Mr. P. Hédouin. Music by de W. Neuland.

t. *Judith: scène et air.* Lyrics by Mr. Bélanger. Music by Giuseppe Concone.

u. *La calabraise: duo.* Lyrics by Mr. Vimeux. Music by Vincenzo Gabussi. [fig. 102]

v. *La muette de Portici.* Cavatine du sommeil. Lyrics de MM. E. Scribe et Germain Delavigne. Music by D. F. E. Auber.

FIG. 109. *Finger Ring,* gold enamel, diamond and opal, probably French, in the neogothic style, ca. 1870s. Collection of Mrs. Arthur Belge.

S.6. *Finger Ring,* gold enamel, diamond and opal, probably French, in the neogothic style, ca. 1870s. Collection of Mrs. Arthur Belge. [fig. 109]

According to family tradition, the ring was given by René De Gas to his wife, Estelle Musson De Gas, shortly before he eloped with America Durrive Olivier in 1878.

S.7a. *Double Case Hunter Pocket Watch and Key,* 18 karat gold. Lacroix and Falconnet, Geneva, ca. 1855–70. Collection of Hugh Miller. [fig. 54]

The watch belonging to Estelle Musson strikes the hour and quarter hour *(trois heure)* and would have been especially useful to Estelle as her sight was fading to complete blindness.

S.7b. *Gold Watch Chain and Fob-winder,* ca. 1870. Collection of Emma Glenny.

These belonged to Michel Musson and may be the same ones partly visible in his portrait in *A Cotton Office in New Orleans* (cat. 31).

FIG. 110. *Meridienne and Two Side Chairs,* rococo revival, ca. 1845–50. Collection of Mrs. Arthur Belge.

S.8. *Meridienne and Two Side Chairs,* probably French, purchased in New Orleans, rococo revival, ca. 1845–50. Collection of Mrs. Arthur Belge. [fig. 110]

> These pieces are part of what was originally a larger parlor set belonging to the Musson family.

S.9. *Silver Tea Set and Case,* French, ca. 1830–45. Collection of Hugh Miller.

> The tea set belonged to Odile Longer Musson, Edgar Degas's aunt.

S.10. Letters from the De Gas–Musson Papers, Special Collections, Tulane University, ms. 226

> a. Letter to Estelle Musson from René De Gas in New York, Monday, June 3, 1872, on De Gas Brothers Stationery, Box II, folder 45a. [fig. 7]
>
> b. Letter to Estelle Musson from René De Gas in Paris dated July 17, 1872, Box II, folder 46b. [fig. 52]
>
> c. Letter to Michel Musson from Joe Balfour, dated January 1, 1873, wishing her grandfather a happy New Year, Box II, folder 51. [fig. 126]
>
> d. Letter to Désirée Musson from Harmion Watts, dated April 25, 1878, on stationery of Sanders & Blackwood describing the events leading up to René's elopement with America Durrive, Box III, folder 13f. (See Appendix I for partial transcription.) [fig. 125]
>
> e. Letter to Achille De Gas at the New York Hotel, New York, from Désirée Musson dated August 20, 1878, concerning the elopement of René, Box III, folder 16a. [fig. 133]
>
> f. Letter to Désirée Musson, from Achille De Gas in New York, August 24, 1878. Box III, folder 16b. [fig. 134]

g. Telegram to Edgar Degas in Paris sent by Michel Musson on January 25, 1884, returned with response in red ink reporting that Edgar Degas will no longer accept communication from Michel Musson, Box IV, folder 43b. [fig. 56]

S.11. Family photographs, collection of Edmund Martin

a. *Michel Musson,* ca. 1876, cabinet portrait by Washburn, New Orleans, $6\frac{3}{8} \times 8\frac{1}{4}$ in. [fig. 49]

b. *Michel Musson,* ca. 1876, cabinet portrait by Washburn, New Orleans, $4\frac{1}{8} \times 6$ in. [fig. 117]

c. *Odile Musson,* ca. 1864, cabinet portrait by G. Penabert & Cie., Paris, $2\frac{1}{2} \times 3\frac{3}{4}$ in. [fig. 51]

d. *Estelle* (standing) *and Désirée* (sitting) *Musson,* cabinet portrait, by Washburn, New Orleans, $4\frac{1}{4} \times 6\frac{1}{2}$ in. [fig. 55]

e. *Josephine "Joe" Balfour,* ca. 1880, cabinet card, albumen print by Theodore Lilienthal, $4\frac{1}{4} \times 6\frac{1}{2}$ in. [fig. 15]

f. *Pierre De Gas* (son of René and Estelle De Gas), 1870s, cabinet portrait by Washburn, $4\frac{1}{4} \times 6\frac{1}{4}$ in. [fig. 120]

g. *Odile De Gas Musson* (daughter of René and Estelle De Gas), ca. 1880, cabinet portrait by Simon, $4\frac{1}{4} \times 6\frac{1}{4}$ in. [fig. 121]

h. *Odile De Gas Musson* (daughter of René and Estelle De Gas), ca. 1880, cabinet portrait by Simon, $4\frac{1}{4} \times 6\frac{1}{2}$ in. [fig. 111]

i. *Gaston De Gas Musson* (son of René and Estelle De Gas) as an infant, ca. 1876, cabinet portrait by Caranon, 4×6 in. [fig. 47]

j. *Gaston De Gas Musson* (son of René and Estelle De Gas), 1886, cabinet portrait by Simon, $4\frac{1}{4} \times 6\frac{1}{2}$ in. [fig. 122]

k. *William Bell, Jr.* (son of Mathilde and William A. Bell), 1879, cabinet portrait by Theodore Lilienthal, $4\frac{1}{4} \times 6\frac{3}{4}$ in. [fig. 130]

S.12. Family portraits in collection of Adelaide Wisdom Benjamin.

a. *William Bell with his children, Carrie, Sidney and William, Jr.,* 8×10 in. [fig. 132]

b. *Bell children in a rowboat (left to right, Carrie, Sidney and William),* 1879, $7\frac{1}{4} \times 9\frac{3}{4}$ in. [fig. 131]

c. *Mathilde Musson Bell holding Germain Musson Bell,* ca. 1864, 5×7 in. [fig. 128]

d. *Mathilde Musson Bell,* ca. 1864, $3\frac{1}{2} \times 5$ in. [fig. 94]

e. *William A. Bell in Uniform,* $5\frac{1}{8} \times 3\frac{1}{2}$ in. [fig. 129]

f. *William A. Bell,* bust portrait, $5\frac{1}{8} \times 3\frac{1}{2}$ in. [fig. 112]

FIG. 111. Simon, *Odile De Gas Musson,* ca. 1880, cabinet portrait, New Orleans. Collection of Edmund Martin.

FIG. 112. *William A. Bell,* bust portrait, $5\frac{1}{8} \times 3\frac{1}{2}$ in., photograph. Collection of Adelaide Wisdom Benjamin.

FIG. 113. Theodore Lilienthal, *Steamboat Landing, New Orleans 1867: Photographs for Emperor Napoleon III.* Napoleon-Museum Arenenberg.

S.13. *Famille de Gas,* "Patent of Nobility" commissioned by Achille De Gas in 1869 and brought to the United States by René De Gas. $11\frac{1}{2}$ × 18 in. Collection of Edmund Martin. [fig. 4]

S.14. *La Sainte Bible,* 1846, traduite par Lemaistre de Sacy, published in Paris. Musson family Bible with genealogy of the family. Collection of Edmund Martin. [fig. 48]

S.15. Photographs of New Orleans by Theodore Lilienthal, *New Orleans 1867: Photographs for Emperor Napoleon III.* Collection of Napoleon Museum, Arenenberg, Switzerland.

 a. *Lake End Pontchartrain* [fig. 9]

 b. *Steamboat Landing* [fig. 113]

 c. *Steamer Great Republic* [fig. 33]

 d. *Private Residence* [fig. 3]

S.16. *Testimonial Album,* leather cover with engraved silver plate, 1870. "Factor's & Traders Insurance Company to Michel Musson. New Orleans 16 August 1870." Collection of Marie Estelle Moyer.

 Awarded to Michel Musson upon his retirement as president of the Factor's & Traders Insurance Company. The album includes official letters expressing praise and gratitude for Musson's service. One letter advises the family of plans for a surprise party on the occasion of the award, to be held in their residence on Esplanade Avenue.

JAMES B. BYRNES AND
VICTORIA COOKE

APPENDIX I
Degas's Family in New Orleans: A Who's Who

GERMAIN MUSSON AND MARIE CELESTE RILLIEUX: EDGAR DEGAS'S MATERNAL GRANDPARENTS

Born in Port of Prince in the French colony of Saint Domingue, Germain Musson (1787–1853) was the son of Stephan Germain Musson and Anna Madeleine Le Canu (fig. 114). According to family legend, Germain was a French Huguenot. He fled to Louisiana and married a New Orleans Catholic, Marie Celeste Rillieux (1794–1819), a member of a large and influential French-Creole family. Her parents were Vincent Rillieux Sr. (d. 1800) and Marie Tronquet (d. 1824).[1] It is through his maternal grandmother, Marie Celeste Rillieux, that Edgar Degas was related to the black inventor and engineer Norbert Rillieux (1806–94). Marie Celeste's brother Vincent Rillieux Jr. (d. 1833) had a lifelong relationship with Constance Vivant, a free woman of color.[2] Norbert was one of their six children. Edmonde Rillieux (b. 1811), a prosperous businessman and builder was another. Norbert Rillieux (fig. 27), educated in Paris, he became a professor of engineering at the École Centrale at the age of twenty and invented the double evaporation process of sugar refining. We do not know whether Degas knew Norbert, his mother's first cousin, or even knew about his kinship with him.

After the death of his wife, Germain Musson took his children to Europe while continuing to do business in Louisiana. He was in Paris for the birth and baptism of his grandson Edgar Degas in 1834. A few years later, Germain moved to Mexico to look after his investments in silver mines. He lived there until he was killed in 1853, when his coach overturned. In letters his sons expressed concern for him, referring to him often as "solitary, abandoned, far away, without one friend."[3]

FIG. 114. Musson Family Tomb in Saint Louis I Cemetery, New Orleans.

The De Gas–Musson Family Tree

Marie Tronquet
?–1824

Vincent Rilleux, Sr.
?–1800

Marie Eloise Rillieux
1790–?

J. L. M. Reynaud
1785–?

Louise A. Reynaud
1818–?

Vincent Rillieux
?–1833

Alfred Hagen Hopkins

Marie Eugenia Hopkins
1838–?

Constance Vivant
1784–1868

Bartolome Rillieux
1808–?

Maria Reynaud
1814–?

Louis Alfred Hopkins
1841–?

Edmonde Rillieux
1811–?

Marie Celeste Reynaud
1816–?

Micheal Rillieux
1788–?

Norbert Rillieux
1806–1894

Leon Vincent Reynaud

* Marie Celeste Rillieux
1794–1819

Emily Cuckow
1827–1912

Marie Celeste Landry

Melchior Vincent Reynaud
1849–?

Maria Antoinette Rillieux
1784–?

Maria Eugenia Rillieux
1813–1817

Michael Smith

Maria Eloise Rillieux
1816–?

Melchior Rillieux

Louis Eugène Rillieux
1818–

Maria Eugenia Rillieux
?–1808

James Freret
1771–1834

James Freret
1800–?

Mlle D'Aresburg

James Freret
1837–?

Octavia Jeanne Freret
1839–?

William Freret

Maria Eugenia Freret

Juan Antonio Freret

Anne Vienne

Eugenia Freret
1839–?

* For descendants of Degas's grandmother,
Marie Celeste Rillieux, see facing page.

Manette Debuys

Amedee Longer

Odile Longer
1819–1871

Germain Musson
1787–1853

Michel Musson
1812–1885

Michel Eugène Musson
1852–1854

Marie Celeste Rillieux
1794–1819

Eugène Musson

Mathilde Musson
1841–1878

Germain Musson Bell
1863–1865

Henri Musson
?–1883

William A. Bell
1836–1884

Mathilde C. Bell
1867–1937

Anne Musson
1813–1857

Joseph Germain Musson
1855–1859

Louis Sidney Bell
1871–1941

Comte Louis
de Rochefort

Maurice de Rochefort

Germaine Odile Musson
1853–1853

William A. Bell
1872–1942

Marie Désirée Bell
1875–1896

Célestine Musson
1815–1847

Désirée Musson
1838–1902

Jean Marie Bell
1878–1878

René-Hilaire Degas
1770–1858

Auguste Degas
1807–1874

Edgar Degas
1834–1917

Eugène Henri Musson
1840–1849

Aurora Freppa
1783–1841

Achille Degas
1838–1893

Joseph Davis Balfour
1842–1862

Josephine Balfour
1862–1881

Henri Degas
1811–1878

Emma Hermann
1838–?

Estelle Musson
1843–1909

Charles Achille Degas
1812–1875

René Degas
1845–1921

Michel Pierre Degas
1870–1881

Emilie A. Degas
1819–1901

Marguerite Degas
1842–1895

America Durrive
1855–?

Maurice Degas
1879–?

Odile Degas-Musson
1871–1936

Henri Fèvre

Edmond Degas

Jeanne Degas
1872–1878

Jean Edouard Degas
1811–1870

Georges Degas
1835–1837

Lucie Jeanne Arsene
Schumagher

**Edgar Achille Gaston
Degas-Musson**
1875–1953

Candida Carafa
di Cicerale
1833–1869

Marie Thérèse Degas
1840–1912

Odette Degas

M. Estelle Boucher

Rose Adelaide Degas
1805–1878

Rolland Wilhelm
Nepveu

René Henri Degas
1876–1877

Giuseppe de Morbilli

Edmond de Morbilli

Anne Laurette Degas
1814–1887

Gennaro Bellelli
1812–1864

Jeanne Bellelli
1848–?

Julie Bellelli
1851–?

FIG. 115. G. P. A. Healy, *Michel Musson,* ca. 1855–69, $29\frac{1}{2} \times 24\frac{1}{4}$ in. Collection of Emma Glenny.

FIG. 116. G. P. A. Healy, *Odile Musson,* ca. 1855–69, $29\frac{1}{2} \times 24\frac{1}{4}$ in. Collection of Emma Glenny.

FIG. 117. Washburn, *Michel Musson,* ca. 1876, cabinet portrait, New Orleans. Collection of Edmund Martin.

FIG. 118. *Michel Musson as Postmaster,* ca. 1849–53, daguerreotype. From *The Great Mail: A Postal History of New Orleans,* 1949.

MICHEL MUSSON AND ODILE LONGER: THE ARTIST'S UNCLE AND AUNT IN NEW ORLEANS

Michel Musson (1812–85) (figs. 115, 117, 118), Edgar Degas's maternal uncle, was the only child of Germain and Marie Celeste Musson to return to New Orleans. Educated in Europe, he settled in Louisiana and married Odile Longer (1819–71) (fig. 116) from the prominent Longer family. Through Odile, the Musson family was connected to some of the most influential families in the city.[4]

Over the course of his life, Michel Musson pursued several careers. He was the assistant to the postmaster of New Orleans for many years. When asked by the president, his friend Zachary Taylor, to take the position of postmaster general of the United States (fig. 118), he declined and asked to serve in that capacity for the city of New Orleans.[5] While in this position from April 18, 1849, until April 7, 1853, he initiated the use of registered mail and set up a system for mail delivery by paid carriers.[6] He was also an officer of the Citizens Bank, the president of Factors' and Traders Insurance Company, and most significantly, a cotton factor.

Obsessive about recording his correspondence, he kept letterpress copies of letters that he sent to others. Much of the information that we have concerning the relationship between the De Gas family and the Mussons is owed to his habit of saving mail.[7]

Late in life, perhaps as a direct result of several family tragedies and business disasters suffered in a short span of time, Michel Musson became somewhat embittered and apparently emotionally unstable.[8] His obituary described him as having lived his last years as a martyr.[9] He died in debt, owing even his daughter Estelle thousands of dollars.[10]

FIG. 119. Notre Dame de Bon Secours, photograph. Special Collections, Tulane University, New Orleans.

ESTELLE MUSSON AND RENÉ DE GAS: A MARRIAGE BETWEEN EDGAR'S BROTHER AND HIS FIRST COUSIN

In 1868 the close ties between the French and New Orleans families grew stronger when Estelle Musson (1843–1909), the youngest daughter of Michel and Odile Musson, married René De Gas (1845–1921), the youngest son of Auguste (1807–74) and Marie Célestine Musson De Gas (1815–47). If René De Gas's character was impetuous, Estelle Musson was described by her family throughout her life as befitting her first name, "Angelina." This was her second marriage.

On January 20, 1862, an eighteen-year-old Estelle married Joseph Davis Balfour (1842–62), the twenty-year-old nephew of Jefferson Davis, the president of the Confederate States of America. Balfour was a Protestant and the couple was married by a Presbyterian minister in Michel Musson's home. Afterward they made a visiting tour to the family in Mississippi where the Balfours owned property. An officer in the Confederate army, Balfour was killed in the battle of Corinth in October of 1862, just weeks before his only child, Josephine "Joe," was born.

Newly widowed, Estelle met her cousin René in France when she fled Union-occupied New Orleans with her mother and sister during the Civil War. René was determined to escort them on the return trip. He aimed to make his fortune in New Orleans despite his father's objections. René moved in with the Mussons and went to work at his uncle's cotton firm, John Watt & Co. In 1866 his brother Achille De Gas joined him in New Orleans and the two established their own firm De Gas Brothers, an import-export firm, wine being one of their major products.

FIG. 120. Washburn, *Pierre De Gas,* ca. 1870s, cabinet portrait. Collection of Edmund Martin.

FIG. 121. Simon, *Odile De Gas Musson,* ca. 1880, cabinet portrait, New Orleans. Collection of Edmund Martin.

FIG. 122. Simon, *Gaston De Gas Musson,* 1886, cabinet portrait, New Orleans. Collection of Edmund Martin.

In 1869 René married Estelle against the advice of both their fathers and after receiving dispensation from the Catholic Church as they were first cousins.[11] The service was held in Notre Dame de Bon Secours (fig. 119), a church that was favored by the close-knit French-Creole community and where they could be assured the service would be held in French. By all accounts, the couple was initially happy and pleased with their growing family of five children: Pierre, born in 1870 (fig. 120); Odile, in 1871 (fig. 121); Jeanne, born during Edgar Degas's visit in 1872; Gaston, in 1875 (fig. 122); and René Henri, in 1876. Only Odile and Gaston survived the illnesses that ravaged New Orleans in the nineteenth century.

In 1869 the Musson family—which included Michel and Odile, their married daughters with their husbands and children, as well as Désirée (1838–1902)—moved from their Garden District home into the house at 372 Esplanade Avenue (now 2306), which Michel rented for $300 per quarter.[12] At the time, the neighborhood was dominated by French-speaking New Orleanians who preferred a church called St. Rose of Lima, which had a French-Alsatian priest, Father Mittlebronn.[13] Degas attended this church when he stood as godfather to René and Estelle's third child, Jeanne De Gas, baptized on February 5, 1873 (fig. 123).

While living on Esplanade, the Mussons met Leonce and America Durrive Olivier (b. 1845), who lived around the corner. The two families had children who were roughly the same ages and soon became quite close. Musson descendants report that America had been asked to read newspapers, novels, and prayer books to Estelle, whose vision was by this time seriously impaired.[14]

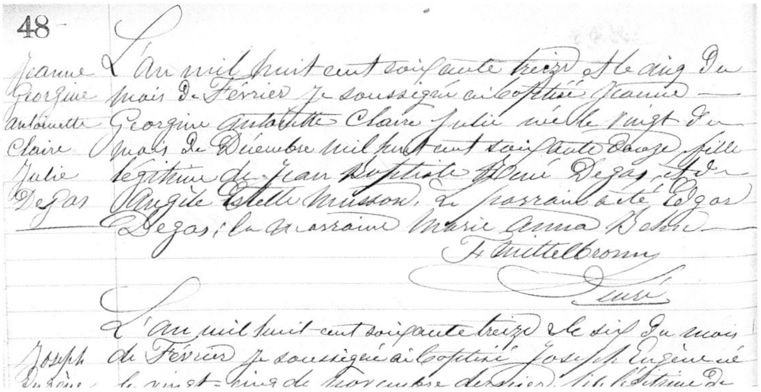

René mentioned Mme Olivier in passing in a letter to Michel Musson in March of 1873 while describing a neighborhood fire.[15] Then in October of 1874, Joe Balfour wrote to her grandfather Michel reporting that they had dined with the Oliviers. In 1875, Leonce Olivier stood as godfather to Marie Désirée Bell, the daughter of Mathilde Musson and William Bell, and America was the godmother to René and Estelle's son Gaston De Gas in 1875 (fig. 124).[16]

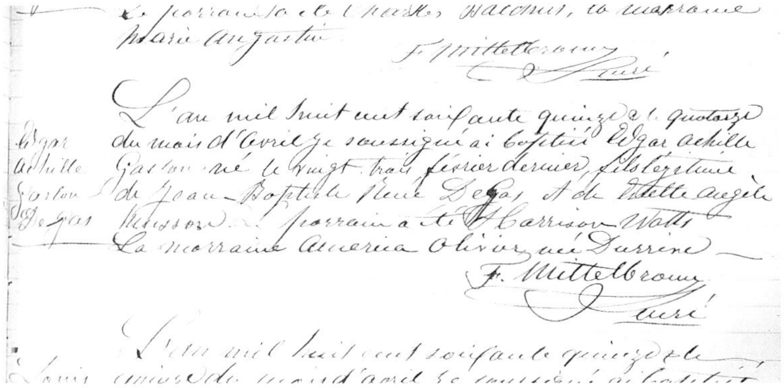

On April 13, 1878, René eloped with America.[17] The couple obtained false divorce papers, called "Utah divorces," in Chicago and married, bigamously, in Cleveland, Ohio.[18] In March of 1879, Estelle was granted a legitimate divorce from René in New Orleans. René then legally married America Olivier in New York. Their first son, Maurice, was born that same year in New York.[19]

Michel and Désirée Musson wrote to Achille and Edgar Degas imploring them to side with the New Orleans family and seeking the address of the errant René. Family friend Harmion Watt wrote to Désirée that he would not reveal the couple's whereabouts: "I ought to keep De Gas address secret, that enough mischief has been done that I ought to prevent further mischief and bloodshed *which would most surely follow*" (fig. 125).[20]

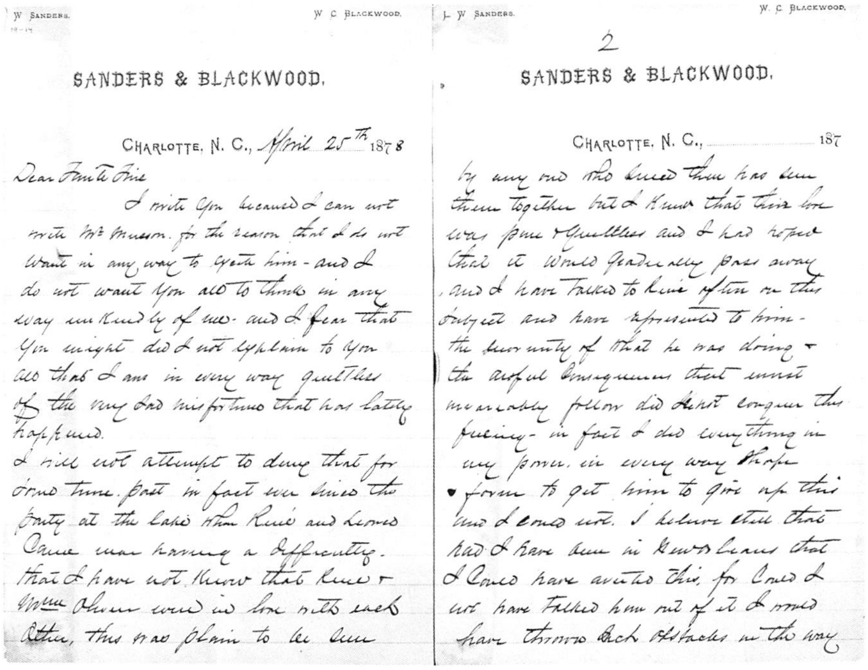

The agreement between René and Estelle's lawyers in September 1878 was for her to receive monthly child support payments for their four surviving children. However, according to Estelle's ledgers (kept by Michel), René sent

FIG. 123. Baptismal record of Jeanne De Gas, 5 February, 1873, *St. Rose of Lima Sacramental Records*. Archives, Archdiocese of New Orleans.

FIG. 124. Baptismal record of Gaston De Gas Musson, 14 April, 1875, *St. Rose of Lima Sacramental Records*. Archives, Archdiocese of New Orleans.

FIG. 125. Letter from Harmion Watts to Désirée Musson, April 25, 1878, De Gas–Musson Papers, ms. 226. Special Collections, Tulane University, New Orleans.

only $2,000 between 1878 and 1883, having missed more payments than he made.[21] René was not allowed to see his American children and apparently made little attempt to do so, although an agent for René did request a visitation, which was summarily denied.[22] Meanwhile, Michel Musson filed suit to adopt his grandchildren in May of 1883. He then changed their last name to Musson while retaining the name De Gas as their middle names.[23] The children, according to family legend, were instructed never to speak of their father again.

The code of silence persisted in the De Gas family as well concerning the New Orleans relatives. René and America's three children were unaware of their surviving half-brother Gaston (1875–1953) and half-sister Odile (1871–1936) until these New Orleans children contacted the French court after René's death to contest his will.[24]

After the *année terrible* of 1878, which was further darkened by several deaths, including that of Edgar Degas's godchild Jeanne of yellow fever, the Musson family moved. Mathilde and William Bell settled into their own house on Canal Street between Hagan Avenue and Telemachus. Michel, Désirée and Estelle, as well as the surviving children, moved temporarily to North Rampart Street in the Old Quarter, while her cousin, architect James Freret, built a house for Estelle at 125 Esplanade Avenue (now 1019-17), where they lived from 1881 until Désirée's death in 1902.[25]

In 1933 while compiling the *catalogue raisonné* for Degas, Paul Lemoisne wrote to Estelle and René's daughter Odile in the hope that she could identify subjects and locales in Degas's New Orleans pictures. She described her mother in the kindest and most poignant terms: "[She was] of a gay nature—despite all that she had suffered she liked to laugh. She died the 18th of October 1909, as she had lived, full of courage and pardoning all."[26]

In 1879, René De Gas returned to France and lived out the remainder of his life in Paris with his second wife and their new family. America had brought her two children from her first marriage, Odile (1870–1957) and Frédéric (1873–94), with her when she eloped with René, and they were to find their new life a bit difficult.[27] René and America afterward had three children, Maurice, Edmond, and Odette. René may never have achieved success in business, but eventually he did reconcile with Edgar. The artist visited René and his family weekly. When Edgar died, René inherited half of his estate. René oversaw the sale of works in his brother's studio after the painter's death.

Josephine Balfour: Edgar Degas's Niece

The only child of Estelle Musson and Joseph Davis Balfour, Josephine (Joe) Balfour (1862–81) (fig. 15) had her own distinct identity within the family. She was born within weeks of her father's death and spent her first years in France, where she learned to say "Bonjour, René De Gas."[28] Although René became her stepfather while she was still quite young, he did not adopt her and her name remained Balfour. There are several letters from her in the De Gas–Musson Papers, mainly good wishes and holiday greetings on monogrammed stationery from Joe to her grandfather Michel Musson as well as to her mother (fig. 126).

Although her father was Protestant, Joe was raised Catholic and attended the Convent of the Visitation in Mobile, Alabama. Many New Orleanians sent their children to boarding school, but Joe apparently found herself one of the few Creoles and told her grandfather that she was called one of the "French girls."[29] When her stepfather left her mother, the fifteen-year-old Joe Balfour was probably away at school. Almost three years to the day later, Joe Balfour died of scarlet fever at the age of eighteen.

Désirée Musson: Edgar Degas's Cousin

Désirée Musson (1838–1902) was the eldest child of Michel and Odile Musson (fig. 127). Her role in the family seems to have been as surrogate mother and insightful confidant. Throughout the family's various troubles, it was Désirée who emerged as a savvy and tactful diplomat, particularly when she intervened during her father's rages later in life. She was the only Musson sister to remain unmarried.

Désirée also may have possessed a certain insight into the characters of those around her. When the Musson women fled to France during the Civil War and René became a permanent fixture in their French household, Désirée called him *l'enfant terrible*.[30]

William and Mathilde Musson Bell: Edgar Degas's Cousin and Her Husband

The middle daughter of Odile and Michel Musson was Mathilde (1841–78), who married William A. Bell (1836–84) on February 26, 1862.[31] Mathilde sat for Degas while he was in New Orleans, but he complained that she was often distracted by the needs of her three youngsters (cats. 24, 25, 26). William, pictured leaning across the table of cotton in *A Cotton Office in New Orleans* (cat. 31), was not a member

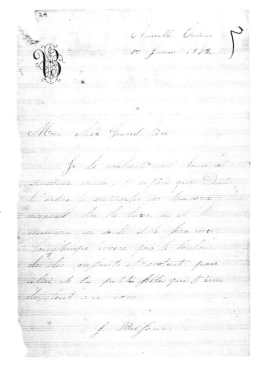

FIG. 126. Letter from Joe Balfour to Michel Musson, January 1, 1873, De Gas–Musson Papers, ms. 226. Special Collections, Tulane University, New Orleans.

FIG. 127. *Désirée Musson*, ca. 1855, photograph.

FIG. 128. *Mathilde Musson Bell holding Germain Musson Bell*, ca. 1864, photograph. Collection of Adelaide Wisdom Benjamin.

FIG. 129. *William Bell in Uniform*, 19th century, photograph. Collection of Adelaide Wisdom Benjamin.

FIG. 130. Theodore Lilienthal, *William Bell, Jr.*, 1879, cabinet portrait. Collection of Edmund Martin.

of the firm, but rather a partner in his own business that manufactured and sold bagging and ties (fig. 129).[32]

The Bells had six children, only three of whom survived to adulthood (fig. 131). The first, Germain Musson Bell, whose birth in 1863 prevented Mathilde from accompanying her sisters and mother to France, is shown in one of the few photographs of her that survived (fig. 128). Germain died at the age of two. Carrie Bell (1867–1937) is one of the children thought to be depicted in *Children on a Doorstep* (cat. 29) as is her brother, Louis Sidney Bell (1871–1941) (figs. 131, 132). Another child, William A. Bell (1872–1942) (figs. 130, 132), was born shortly before Edgar Degas came to New Orleans. Two other children were born after Degas's visit, Marie Désirée (1875–96) and Jean Marie Bell, who died shortly after her birth in 1878, followed by her mother.

ACHILLE DE GAS

Achille De Gas (1838–93) was the middle son of Auguste and Marie Célestine, four years younger than Edgar and four years older than René. He was no less a character than his brothers. Like René, he moved to New Orleans

FIG. 131. *Bell children in Row Boat (left to right, Carrie, Sidney and William)*, 1879, photograph. Collection of Adelaide Wisdom Benjamin.

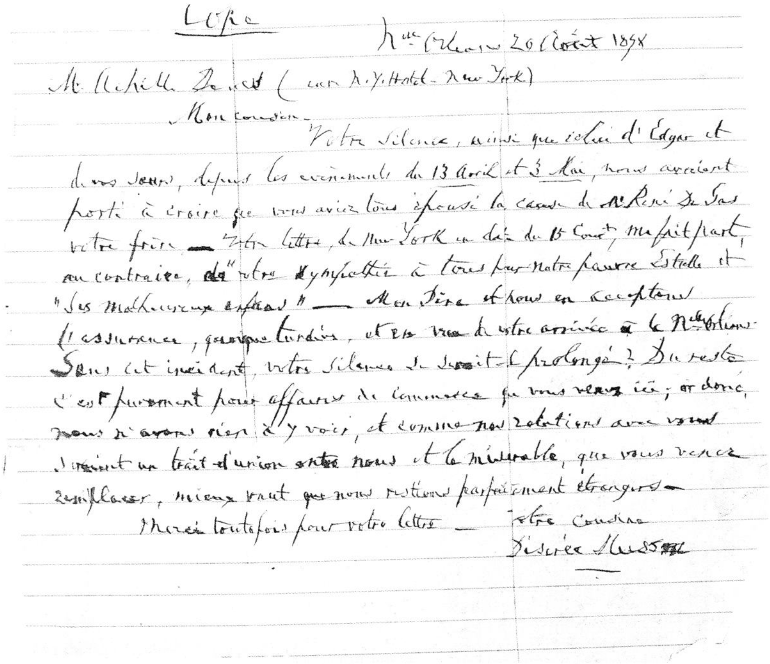

to make his fortune and, like René, he had his share of romantic scandals. In Paris in 1876, Achille was assaulted by the husband of his ex-lover (a dancer named Thérèse Mallot). Achille wounded him with his revolver and got off with a light sentence.[33]

Achille's business took him back and forth between New Orleans and Paris, and occasionally to New York as well.[34] In the mid-1870s, Achille had moved back to Europe. However, in 1878, after René's elopement, Achille returned from Paris to America in an atttempt to straighten out René's affairs. He stopped in New York and wrote to his cousin Désirée hoping to prepare the way to reconciliation. Unfortunately, the correspondance makes clear that his unwillingness to divulge René's address and sever his relationship with his wayward brother marked him a traitor in the view of the Mussons (figs. 133, 134).

It was at this time, in New York, that a romance developed between Achille De Gas and Emma Hermann (b. 1838). Emma was Odile Musson's niece, and Achille met her in New York in the late 1860s, where she had moved with her first husband, Edward Heilbuth. There she entertained members of her New Orleans family and their French relatives.[35] It was Emma who prevented a complete break between the New Orleans and the Parisian families after the fateful events of 1878.

FIG. 132. *William Bell with his children, Carrie, Sidney and William, Jr.*, 19th century, photograph. Collection of Adelaide Wisdom Benjamin.

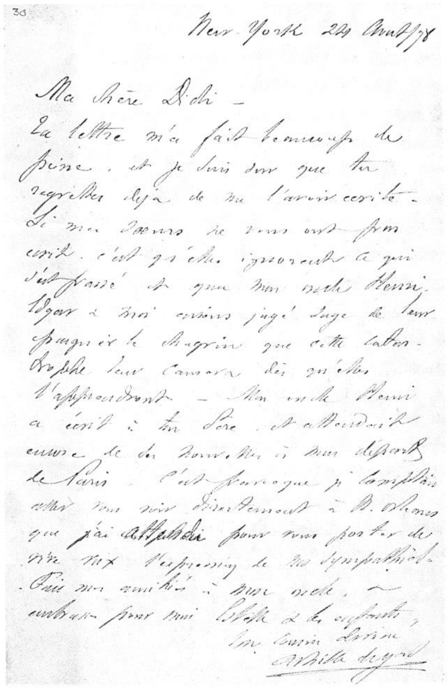

FIG. 133. Letter to Achille De Gas from Désirée Musson, August 20, 1878, De Gas–Musson Papers, ms. 226. Special Collections, Tulane University, New Orleans.

FIG. 134. Letter to Désirée Musson from Achille De Gas, August 24, 1878, De Gas–Musson Papers, ms. 226. Special Collections, Tulane University, New Orleans.

Achille De Gas and Emma Hermann married in New York on October 22, 1881.[36] Emma's continuing relationship with her Musson cousins gave Achille reason to hope that she could reconcile him to the Mussons. Emma found herself in the rather awkward position of remaining on close terms with the Mussons while dealing with René and his new Parisian family. Emma was the granddaughter of a Jewish immigrant to the United States and may have been present in Paris during Edgar's rather vehement anti-Semitic response during the Dreyfus affair, which would have been awkward as well. [37]

Achille and Emma then moved to Switzerland in 1882. In 1889 he suffered a mild stroke, followed by another in 1891, which left him paralyzed. He died in 1893.[38] Emma, joined by her brother Emile Hermann and her sister Georgine Luling, lived out the remainder of her life in Paris, close to her late husband's family.

1. Vincent Rillieux Sr. was successful as a real estate developer and was responsible for several commercial buildings, including two banks. One was built in 1795 at what is now 417 Royal Street. In 1805 it became the Banque de la Louisiana and is presently the location of Brennan's Restaurant. Vincent Sr. died in 1800. The family had been living at the corner of Bourbon and Toulouse Streets in the Vieux Carré; however, the widow Rillieux, Marie Tronquet, bought a house from Joseph Reynes on Bayou St. John. The Rillieux family remained in this house five years, whereupon she sold it with other lands to James Pitot, the first mayor of New Orleans. It is now known as the Pitot House and open to visitors.

2. This relationship does not seem to have been one of the famous *plaçage* arrangements, often associated with the quadroon balls. Constance Vivant belonged to a prominent black family and rather than being a mistress "kept" in a house or apartment separate from Vincent Jr.'s home, the couple lived together throughout their lives and Vincent acknowledged their children. He also saw to their education, ensuring that they would have their own successes in life. For further information on these children, particularly the engineer Norbert Rillieux, see Benfey, 1997, and Ed Koppeschaar, *Norbert Rillieux: commémoration du Centenaire de la mise en marche de la pre-*

mière installation d'évaporation dans le vide à triple effet à la Louisiane en 1834.

As is evident from the Sacramental Records of the Archdiocese of New Orleans, Vincent's sister Marie Eloise Rillieux was godmother to at least two of Vincent's children with Constance, while her husband, J. L. M. Reynaud, was godfather to at least one. Another sister, Maria Eugenia Rillieux, who married James Freret, asked her brother Vincent Jr. to be godfather to at least one of her sons.

3. Letter from Michel Musson to Germain Musson dated 8/9 September 1849, De Gas–Musson, Box I, folder 12.

4. King, 1921, 388–89. Odile was one of eight sisters. "It is of tradition that every eligible man in the city offered himself to one or the other of them. Their choice was decided by the mother's sagacity. All were married well to men of standing in the community, and all were happy in their marriages and blessed by children worthy of them. Not to know the names of the married Longer ladies is regarded in the Creole city as proof of unpardonable social ignorance. Eulalie became Mrs. Samuel Bell; Adele married Florian Hermann; Odile, Michel Musson; Armide married Amedée de Saulles; Amelie, James Behn; Angèle, Evan Jones McCall; Heda, Charles Kock; Helena, Charles Luling."

The Mussons' connections, both through family and business, are far reaching. One such connection yet to be explained is that of John Bell Hood, the retired Confederate general and sometimes cotton factor who moved to New Orleans following the Civil War. In 1876, he named a daughter Odile Musson Hood. It is possible that he is related to either William A. Bell or to Samuel Chambers Bell and thus a cousin of the Mussons. *Hood Relief Committee Appeal for Donations* (Historic New Orleans Collection) published a list of the children of the deceased general and his wife in hopes of finding an adoptive home for them in 1879.

5. Leonard Huber, *The Great Mail: A Postal History of New Orleans* (State College, Pa., 1949), 105–7.

6. This occupation earned him a place in the *Ripley's Believe It or Not!* published on July 22, 1964, which expressed amazement that Musson "spurned the job of Postmaster General in 1849, preferring to serve as Postmaster of New Orleans, LA."

7. According to family tradition, much of what René De Gas left behind when he deserted his wife and children was burned, including much correspondence. However, many of his letters to Estelle survive in the De Gas–Musson Papers.

8. See, for example, correspondence in 1879, following the death of Mathilde Musson Bell, between her father, Michel, and her husband, William Bell. The letters from this time indicate that Michel, under the weight of a lifetime of disappointments, was showing signs of mental distress. After a misunderstanding between Musson and his son-in-law William Bell concerning a visit by the Bell children, Musson launched a written attack on the family of his late daughter's husband. Bell, alarmed, asked Désirée to intervene. This was not apparently the first time such an imagined slight had enraged Michel Musson. Bell wrote to Désirée: "It again becomes my unpleasant duty to inform you that I cannot find words to express my astonishment and indignation at the perusal of the documents penned by your father during my short absence. . . . Mr. Musson's reply after a week's reflection, and in which he seems to have concentrated

all the hatred and bitterness of his nature, and resorted even to threats, only makes the breach all the wider and more difficult to heal." Bell also complained that Michel Musson had accused him of undermining his reputation with the insurance company where Musson served as president by falsely accusing him of mismanagement.

9. Published in *L'Abeille de la Nouvelle-Orléans*, a French newspaper on 5 May, 1885. "Ses dernières années ont été véritablement celles d'un martyr . . . "

10. One interesting item in the De Gas–Musson Papers is the list of Michel's pall bearers scribbled in pencil on a piece of paper. Copied on the back is a French poem by Octave Feuillet declaring suicide to be an act of cowardice. A coincidence perhaps, but given Michel's state of mind at the end of his life, it raises the question.

11. The Musson and De Gas families had a habit of marrying inside their close circles. Thérèse married an Italian cousin and Achille would eventually marry a cousin-in-law. René and Estelle's marriage certificate was witnessed by members of every branch of the family: Manette Longer (Odile's mother), J. L. M. and Célestine Reynaud (relatives through the Rillieux family), Adèle and Emile Hermann (Odile's sister and brother-in-law), as well as business associates Harmion Watts and John Livaudais, who appears in *A Cotton Office in New Orleans*.

12. The street numbers have since changed and the house has been altered considerably. However, one can still see the house at 2306 Esplanade Avenue; it has recently been restored as "The Degas House" bed-and-breakfast. Information concerning the house, including the rent, is in the Notarial Archives of New Orleans. Achille De Gas moved to Royal Street in the French Quarter.

13. Roger Baudier, *St. Rose of Lima Parish: A Parish History* (New Orleans, 1957).

14. Dora Miller, the great-granddaughter of Gaston De Gas Musson.

15. De Gas–Musson, Box II, folder 52a.

16. Parish records of St. Rose of Lima.

17. While the news of this event shocked the family, it seems that there had been some prior intimations of an attraction. Harmion Watts, a close family friend and Gaston De Gas's godfather, described the events that led up to this sudden disappearance: "I will not attempt to deny that for some time past in fact ever since the party at the lake. . . . that René and Mme Olivier were in love with each other. This was plain to be seen to any one who knew them or has seen them together but I knew that their love was pure and guiltless and I had hoped that it would gradually pass away." De Gas–Musson, Box III, folder 13f.

18. Jean Boggs recently obtained a copy of the fraudulent marriage record of René and America, which was found by Harvey Buchanan. In the certificate each of them was required to swear that they had no living spouses.

19. Loyrette, 1991, 326.

20. De Gas–Musson, Box III, folder 13f.

21. To prepare for his suit to adopt his grandchildren, Michel Musson kept a ledger account of the payments along with other household expenses. This ledger includes an inserted note adding up the payments René had sent. De Gas–Musson, Box VI.

22. Brown, 1991, Box III, folder 25. "Letter to Michel Musson from Henri Musson in Paris, November 9, 1878 . . . responds to a request from René that the children be taken North or West by asking 'with whom?'"

23. In the court case, he outlines the events leading up to the divorce and repeatedly referred to Madame Olivier as René's "concubine." All legal records concerning this case can be found in the Civil Court case records in the New Orleans Public Library. There are perhaps several reasons for Michel Musson's decision to adopt his grandchildren. His own male children had died at early ages and the Musson name continued only as a result of this adoption. He may have feared for the future of his daughter, who may have been particularly vulnerable in a custody battle because of her blindness. In letters concerning René's desertion of her, she is often referred to as "poor blind Estelle," a phrase that seems to refer both

to her physical condition and her blindness to her husband's true nature.

24. They were the only survivors of the De Gas–Musson children. Their sister and Edgar Degas's godchild Jeanne died of yellow fever in 1878. In 1881 the family lost both Joe Balfour and Pierre De Gas.

25. The street numbers have changed over the years: 125 Esplanade Avenue is now 1015 and 1017 Esplanade. 291 North Rampart is now 1225, between Barracks and Governor Nichols.

26. De Gas–Musson, Box V, folder 3a; translation courtesy of James B. Byrnes. While Lemoisne had asked Odile for information, in a postscript, she, in turn, made a poignant request of him: "Would you do something for me. For a long time I have been wanting to know my second cousins in France but I always hesitated to make the first move not knowing their attitude toward us. Should you write to Miss Fèvre, tell her what I told you, and that I would be so happy if her heart desires to correspond with me. I thank you very much." Unfortunately, this never came to pass.

27. Loyrette, 324–29.

28. De Gas–Musson, Box II, folder 9.

29. Ibid., Box III, folder 11.

30. Ibid., Box I, folder 70b.

31. Bell was a Protestant and, while he did not convert, he did agree to raise his children in the Catholic faith of his wife. Therefore, he and Mathilde were married by the Catholic Archbishop, but in the Musson's home rather than in the church. The Mussons were insistent that the children be raised Catholic, even after Mathilde's untimely death in 1878.

32. Bell was also an officer at the Jockey Club and later the treasurer of the White League. For more information on Bell's various activities in the community, see Benfey, 1997, 85–86.

33. These events are detailed in Loyrette, 320–23. It seems that Achille had fathered a child by the dancer and had paid some support for the infant, who later died.

34. Achille appears in the city directories intermittently between 1869 and 1882. After the dissolution of De Gas Brothers, he worked for John Leisy & Company which seems to have had business dealings in New York.

35. New York was a major thoroughfare for ships traveling to America from Europe. René and Achille De Gas had several business acquaintances there. René writes of visiting with Emma in New York in 1872 on his way to France.

36. At this time it is unclear if Emma was divorced or widowed.

37. The Hermanns were prominent businessmen in New Orleans although their fortunes took a bad turn in the 1830s with the cotton market crash in London. Samuel Hermann, Sr. was a German-Jewish immigrant who moved to Louisiana's German coast in 1804. He married Emeranthe Becnel and appears to have converted to Catholicism as the couple married in the Church and raised their children as Catholics. At the same time, Hermann remained active in the Jewish community in New Orleans, and he donated money to his family's synagogue in Germany. In Bertram Wallace Korn, *Early Jews in New Orleans* (Waltham, Mass., 1969), the author explains that the Jewish community in New Orleans often practiced Catholicism but identified with their heritage.

In addition to Loyrette, there is a study of Degas's attitudes during this political controversy by Linda Nochlin, "Degas and the Dreyfus Affair: A Portrait of the Artist as Anti-Semite," in *The Politics of Vision*.

38. The details of his illness and death are recounted in an unpublished letter from Edgar Degas to an unnamed woman (probably Mme Camus), Archives of the History of Art, The Getty Center for the History of Art and Humanities, Los Angeles, no. 860070, partly translated in Paris, Ottawa, New York, 488.

Degas's Letters from New Orleans

To Désiré Dihau

De Gas Brothers, New Orleans
11 Nov. 1872

My Dear Dihau,

Thank you for your good letter. It is the first. Already they are forgetting me over here. Please forgive me; I should have guessed your promptness in writing to me and have at least written to you from New York. All the same I am expecting a second edition from you before you receive this.

We had an excellent journey. Ten days at sea is a long time; particularly on an English boat where there is so much reserve. If we could have taken the French boat of the 10 October we should have found some traveling company in which the women at least would have helped us to kill time. No more seasickness for the one than for the other and for my part an appetite such as I had never known and which had every appearance of permanency; it is falling off here; I eat next to nothing. 30 hours wait at New York. Left Thursday at 6 o'clock, we were due at New Orleans at 11 o'clock on Monday with several hours wait at Louisville, as fresh and fatter than when we left. You must have heard of the Wagon Lits; but you have never seen one, you have never traveled in one and so you cannot imagine what this marvelous invention is like: You lie down at night in a proper bed. The carriage which is as long as at least 2 carriages in France is transformed into a dormitory. You even put your shoes at the foot of your bed and a kind negro polishes them whilst you sleep.—What luxuriousness you will say. No, it is simple necessity. Otherwise it would be impossible to undertake such journeys at a stretch. And then the ability to walk all round your own coach and the whole train, to stand on platforms is immensely restful and diverting. Everything is practical and very simply done here, so simply that the trains leave almost without warning.—Well I was with René[1] who is from these parts and I did not miss anything.

Lord how we laughed at your story of the innovations and of the manager of the crémerie.[2]

You gave us a real treat, and being so far from Paris makes it all the more precious.—What part did my dear little Maury play among the cooks? that of Mathilde by any chance? If it really is that, she deserved what you said of her.—The rascal, not one word from her yet.

So the good Simon has not yet had my letter written at sea and posted at the tip of Ireland where we caught mail for Europe. This letter posted there on the 13th should have reached her on the 15th or 16th. Mlle Malot[3] has just replied to a letter from René posted in the same way. I thanked her warmly for all her goodness to me. Why does she wish me more calmness in my ideas? Am I then an unusually excitable person?

I shall beg forgiveness from my Lille friends when I am back. There is a touch of malice in their reply and that does not do any harm. If you have not already been to Lille by January I shall go with you and assume an attitude of courteous submission.

You will certainly have seen my cruel friend again[4] and I am sure that a letter from you is already on the way. Every morning at my brother's office I await the arrival of the mail with more impatience than is altogether fitting.[5]

Ah! my dear friend, what a good thing a family is; we were met at the station. My uncle looked at me over his spectacles; my cousins, their six children were there. The surprise that René had planned for them by not saying that I was with him failed; as there had been some talk of yellow fever still persisting at New Orleans he had telegraphed to Achille asking if that meant there would be any danger for a stranger and the cat was out of the bag. All day long I am among these dear folk, painting and drawing, making portraits of the family. My poor Estelle, René's wife, is blind as you know.[6] She bears it in an incomparable

manner; she needs scarcely any help about the house. She remembers the rooms and the position of the furniture and hardly ever bumps into anything. And there is no hope!—Pierre, René's son, is superb; he is so self-possessed and the mixture of English and French is so quaint!—Odil, his little girl is 12 to 15 months old. Jane, the eldest, his wife's daughter, has a real feeling for music; she is beginning to solfa in the Italian solfeggio. There is also a little Carrie, daughter of Mathilde, the youngest of my cousins. Mathilde also decided to have another young boy called Sydney and a little brat of 2 months called Willy.—This whole band is watched over by negresses of different shades.[7] We are awaiting the arrival, today or tomorrow, by the ship Le Strassbourg, of a French nurse whom René engaged in Paris.

Mlle Sangalli[8] will doubtless remain all the winter. I shall thus be able to enjoy her on my return. What you tell me about Vittoq (?) delights me.

Give my regards to our friends of the orchestra. If you see Gard[9] put in a word for me with this tyrant.

Greetings to Piot,[10] Demarquette, Ziegler etc. and to the distinguished patroness.—What you tell me about Madier gives me great pleasure. Here in the French company we have a Mlle Winke (?) who was a dancer at the Français and whom Madier wanted me to meet in Paris because of my dance picture and of the roguish air of the lady. I regret very much not being quite introduced.

Goodbye, believe in my friendship.—If you see Clotilde ask her to write and tell me what is happening at home.

Degas

To Tissot

De Gas Brothers, New Orleans
19 Nov. 1872

My dear Tissot, what do you say to the heading? It is the paper of the firm. Here one speaks of nothing but cotton and exchange. Why do you not speak to me of other things? You do not write to me. What impression did my dance picture make on you, on you and on the others?—Were you able to help in selling it? And the one of the family at the races, what is happening to that? Oh how far from so many things one is here.

Excellent journey. New York has some charming spots. We spent scarcely two days there. Monet and Pissarro would make mis talk [*sic*] there. What a degree of civilization! Steamers coming from Europe arrive like omnibuses at the station. We pass carriages, even trains on the water. It's England in her best mood.

After four days in the train we arrived at New Orleans. You cannot imaging a wagon-lit sliping car [*sic*]. A real dormitory. Behind curtains one can undress down to one's chemise if one wants to, and then climb into a real apple-pie bed. Everything is done simply except for some points of taste, one says to oneself: it's true, it's just what I needed. The practical Englishman seems to be bristling with mania and prejudices. One feels at once that there is rivalry with the mother country.—Mother country? But Germans are arriving in their thousands, half the shops in Broadway have names like Eimer and Wolf, Schumaker and Vogel, etc. Texas is full of Germans. The other day a French maid whom René had engaged before leaving arrived on a small German boat. In the hold, like [negroes] in Biard's pictures, were 651 German emigrants fleeing the Vaterland, misery and a new war with Russia or fair France. Fair France still has a quarter of a foot in Louisiana. The Creole cannot measure strength with the Yankee.

Villas with columns in different styles, painted white, in gardens of magnolias, orange trees, banana trees, negroes in old clothes like the junk from *La Belle Jardinière* or from Marseilles, rosy white children in black arms, charabancs or omnibuses drawn by mules, the tall funnels of the steamboats towering at the end of the main street, that is a bit of local colour if you want some, with a brilliant light at which my eyes complain.

Everything is beautiful in this world of people. But one Paris laundry girl, with bare arms, is worth it all for such a pronounced Parisian as I am. The right way is to collect oneself, and one can only collect oneself by seeing little. I am doing some family portraits; but the main thing will be after my return.

René has superb children, an excellent wife who scarcely seems blind, although she is, almost without hope, and a good position in business. He is happy, it is his country perhaps even more than France.

Achille has one foot over there and the other here. I still do not know and he does not know himself if he will come with me in January.

And you, what news is there since the 700 pounds? You with your terrible activity would be capable of drawing money out of this crowd of cotton brokers and cotton dealers, etc. I shall not attempt to earn anything here.

May this letter of mine cross something from you. Did you get my photographs? Here I have acquired the taste for money, and once back I shall know how to earn some I promise you.

If you see Millais, tell him I am very sorry not to have been able to see him and tell him of my appreciation for him. Remember me to young Deschamps, to Legros, to Whistler who has really found a personal note in that well-balanced expression, mysterious mingling of land and water.

I have not yet written to Manet and naturally he has not sent me a line. The arrival of the mail in the morning really excites me. Nothing is as difficult as doing family portraits. To make a cousin sit for you who is feeding an imp of two months is quite hard work. To get young children to pose on the steps is another job of work which doubles the fatigues of the first. It is the art of giving pleasure and one must look the part.

A good family: it is a really good thing to be married, to have good children, to be free of the need of being gallant. Ye gods, it is really time one thought about it.

Goodbye. See you soon. Write to me. I shall not leave the country before the middle of January.

Your friend,
Degas

To Frölich[11]

De Gas Brothers, New Orleans
27 Nov. 1872

It is only today, November 2nd, that I receive your affectionate letter, my dear Frölich. These most accurate Americans had read Norwick Connecticut where in your handwriting New Orleans was written quite clearly. And so through their fault this paper has traveled around a fortnight too long.

The ocean! how vast it is and how far I am from you. The *Scotia* in which I traveled is an English boat swift and sure. It brought us (I was with my brother René) in 10 days. The *Empire City* even takes 12 from Liverpool to New York. What a sad crossing. I did not know any English, I hardly know any more, and on English territory, even at sea, there is a coldness and a conventional distrust which you have perhaps already felt.

New York, great town and great port. The townsfolk know the great water. They even say that going to Europe is going to the other side of the water. New people. In America there is far more disregard of the English race than I had supposed.

Four days by train brought us here at last.—Borrow an atlas from your dear little daughter and take a look at the distance. Well (I have certainly not the strength of Thor), I was fatter than on my departure. Air—There is nothing but air.—How many new places I have seen, what plans that put into my head, my dear Frölich! Already I am giving them up, I want nothing but my own little corner where I shall dig assiduously. Art does not expand, it repeats itself. And, if you want comparisons at all costs, I may tell you that in order to produce good fruit one must line up on an espalier. One remains thus all one's life, arms extended, mouth open, so as to assimilate what is happening, what is around one and alive.

Have you read the *Confessions* by J. Jacques Rousseau? I am sure you have. Then do you recall his manner of describing, his wealth of humour, after he has retired to the île du Lac de St. Pierre in Switzerland (it is toward the end) and that he is telling how he used to go out at daybreak, that whichever way he went, without noticing it, he examined everything, that he started on work that would take 10 years to finish and left it without regret at the end of 10 minutes? Well that is my case, exactly. Everything attracts me here. I look at everything, I shall even describe everything to you accurately when I get back. I like nothing better than the negresses of all shades, holding in their arms little white babies, so white, against white houses with columns of fluted wood and in gardens of orange trees and the ladies in muslin against the fronts of their little houses and the steamboats with two chimneys as tall as factory chimneys and the fruit vendors with their shops full to bursting, and the contrast between the lively hum and bustle of the offices with this immense black animal force, etc. etc. And the pretty women of pure blood and the pretty 25 year olds and the well set up negresses!

In this way I am accumulating plans which would take ten lifetimes to carry out. In six weeks time I shall drop them without regret in order to regain and never more to leave *my home.*

My dear friend, thank you a hundred times for your letters and for your friendship. That gives such pleasure when one is so far away.

My eyes are much better. I work little, to be sure, but at difficult things. The family portraits, they have to be done more or less to suit the family taste, by impossible lighting, very much disturbed, with models of full affection but a little *sans-gêne* and taking you far less seriously because you are their nephew or their cousin. I have just messed up a large pastel and am somewhat mortified.—If I have time I intend to bring back some crude little thing of my own but for myself, for my room. It is not good to do Parisian art and Louisiana art indiscriminately, it is liable to turn into the *Monde Illustré.*—And then nothing but a really long stay can reveal the customs of a people, that is to say their charm.—Instantaneousness is photography, nothing more.

Have you seen Mr. Schumaker whom you sent to me? He thought I should have been able to help him more easily. He wanted to be rubbed down by a French hand, like at the Turkish baths, immediately, after having sweated a little. I told him that it took time to sweat out our vices (well done?).

I shall probably be back in January. I shall travel via Havanna. But you, you will soon be leaving us you say?—I do hope it is for your old mother's sake, in which case it is a duty.—However we shall see a lot of

each other until the spring. Your little daughter will play for me—I need music so much.—There is no opera here this winter. Yesterday evening I went to a rather monotonous concert, the first of the year. A Madame Urto played the violin with some talent but rather monotonously accompanied and there is not the same intimacy at a concert, here especially where the applause is even more stupid than elsewhere.

Clotilde must have been delighted to spin you a yarn about the master's journey. I am sure she did not hide her satisfaction. She is a real servant out of a play, but she has her points. I threatened not to take her back on my return and I am afraid to do so. She is too young for a bachelor and her self-assurance is really too strong a quality. You must still have your Swedish woman, she seems to be so devoted to you that you will not be able to part with her.

You only knew Achille, I believe, and only met him for a moment. My other brother, René, the last of the three boys, was my traveling companion, even my master. I knew neither English nor the art of traveling in America; therefore I obeyed him blindly. What stupidities I should have committed without him! He is married and his wife, our cousin, is blind, poor thing, almost without hope. She has borne him two children, she is going to give him a third whose Godfather I shall be, and as the widow of a young American killed in the war of Secession she already had a little girl of her own who is 9 years old. Achille and René are partners; I am writing to you on their office notepaper. They are earning very nicely and are really in an exceptionally good position for their age. They are much liked and respected here and I am quite proud of them.

Politics! I am trying to follow my native France in the Louisianian papers. They talk of little but the supertax on houses, and they give Mr. Thiers experts' advice on republicanism.

Goodbye, your proverbs are nearly as abundant as those of Sancho; given his gaiety you would increase them threefold. How healthy a thing is laughter, I laughed at them a lot.

It is true, my dear friend Frölich, one feels young in spirit. That is what David said in Brussels on the eve of his death. But enthusiasm, good humour and vision, one is bound to lose a little of these. You are in a better way than I am.

You can write me when you get this; your answer will still find me at Louisiana.—A kiss for your little one. I clasp your hand and thank you for your friendship.

Degas

My regards to Manet and his family.
I have reread my letter. It is very cold compared to yours. Do not be angry with me.

To Henri Rouart

Nlle Orléans, 5 Dec. 1872

You will receive this, my dear Rouart, on New Years Day. You will then wish Mme Rouart a happy New Year and embrace your children for me, including the new born.[12] Out of this you will also take a bit for yourself.

I shall certainly be back in January. To vary my journey I intend going back via Havanna, the French transatlantic lines dock there. I am eager to see you again at my house, to work in contact with you. One does nothing here, it lies in the climate, nothing but cotton, one lives for cotton and from cotton. The light is so strong that I have not yet been able to do anything on the river. My eyes are so greatly in need of care that I scarcely take any risk with them at all. A few family portraits will be the sum total of my efforts, I was unable to avoid that and assuredly would not wish to complain if it were less difficult, if the settings were less insipid and the models less restless. Oh well, it will be a journey I have done and very little else. Manet would see lovely things here, even more than I do. He would not make any more of them. One loves and gives art only to which one is accustomed. New things capture your fancy and bore you by turns. The beautiful, refined Indian women behind their half opened green shutters, and the old women with their big bandanna kerchiefs going to the market can be seen in a different light to Biard.[13] But then what? The orange gardens and the painted houses attract too and the children all dressed in white and all white against black arms, they too attract. But wait! Do you remember in the Confessions, toward the end, Rousseau on the île de St. Pierre on the Lac de Brienne, at last free to dream in peace, observing impartially, beginning work that would take 10 years to finish and abandoning it after 10 minutes without regret? That is exactly how I feel. I see many things here, I admire them. I make a mental note of their appropriation and expression and I shall leave it all without regret. Life is too short and the strength one has only just suffices.—Well then, Long live fine laundering in France.

I have had a slight attack of dysentery for the last two days, and that tires me no end. Nitrate of bismuth will get rid of that. Also, devil take it, we are having temperatures in December which we would be pleased to have in June, 24 or 25 degrees at least, not to mention a sirocco that kills you. Climate that must be unbearable in the summer and is somehow deadening during the other seasons. One has to be of the country or in the everlasting cotton, otherwise beware.

A fortnight ago Mr. Bujac dined at our house. Naturally we talked of you and all that was good that was said surprised nobody. He looks very sad and worried, poor man! And he has good cause.—One day I shall go to the [ice] factory with him.

So you are scarcely more of a writer than I am. Why did you not write a few words yourself? In the morning when the post comes there is very rarely a letter for me and I cannot get used to that.

You see, my dear friend, I dash home and I commence an ordered life, more so than anyone excepting Bouguereau, whose energy and makeup I do not hope to equal.[14] I am thirsting for order.—I do not even regard a good woman as the enemy of this new method of existence.—A few children for me of my own, is that excessive too? No. I am dreaming of something well done, a whole, well organised (style Poussin) and Corot's old age. It is the right moment, just right. If not, the same order of living, but less cheerful, less respectable and filled with regrets.

René is here with his family, he is only slightly homesick. His wife is blind, but she has mastered her misfortune. The third child is on the way. I shall be its godfather, but it will not have my obsession. But this is a secret even though the date is the 15th, do not mention it to anyone; we do not speak about it to anyone. I am not even writing about it to my sister. This is an order. Papa wishes the world to end just as if we were not there to make order in it.

The lack of an opera is a real privation. Poor Estelle who is a musician was counting on it. We should have hired a box for her and she would never have missed going except during the actual confinement. Instead we have a company for comedy, drama, vaudevilles, etc. where there are some quite good people and a great deal of Montmartre talent.

The women here are almost all pretty and many have even amidst their charms that touch of ugliness without which, no salvation. But I feel that their heads are as weak as mine, which *à deux* would prove

a strange guarantee for a new home. Alas, I have just let out something which is nothing and yet could earn me an atrocious reputation. Beware Rouart, on your honour never repeat in such a manner that it might be reported to people from here or to people who know people from here that I told you that women of New Orleans were weak minded. This is serious. There is no joking here. My death would not wipe out such an insult and Louisiana must be respected by all her children and I am almost one of them. If in addition I were to tell you that they must also be good, the insult would be complete and by repeating that as well you would have delivered me up once and for all to my executioners. I am exaggerating a little, the Creole women really have something attractive; just now I spoke of Rousseau, I am reading him in the evenings and I like quoting him.

Julie d'Etange was beloved because she showed herself ready to be loved (reread a letter from Claire to her friend): there is the tenderness of the 18th century in their manner. Of the families here several came over in knee breeches[15] and that flavour has not yet disappeared.

Goodbye, I wanted to fill four pages, be grateful for that, I wished to please you; if I have not succeeded punish me in the same way. And then I am in the office of the De Gas Brothers where it is not too bad for writing. De Gas Brothers are respected here and I am quite tickled to see it. They will make their fortune.

In conclusion I repeat my wishes for a happy New Year to Mme Rouart, I embrace your children once again and clasp your hand.

Your devoted
Degas

Greetings to Levert,[16] to your friends, to Martin, to Pissarro with whom I shall have some long talks about here . . . I was forgetting your brother and Mignon.

There is a person here called Lamm who has invented an instrument said to be rather ingenious, which sets buses in motion at the top of the town by means of steam with which it supplies itself. There was a lot of talk about tramways in Paris, I shall bring you a description of this contraption.

To Tissot

De Gas Brothers, New Orleans
18 Feb. 1873

Tissot, my dear friend, I intended, I was going to reply to your good letter in person. I should have been in London or Paris about the 15 January (such a distance has become immaterial to me, no space must be regarded as great except the ocean). But I remained and shall not leave until the first days of March. Yesterday my trunks and Achilles were ready but there was a hitch which stopped everything. One misses the train here exactly as at Passy. The Saint-Laurent is leaving without us.

After having wasted time in the family trying to do portraits in the worst conditions of day that I have ever found or imagined, I have attached myself to a fairly vigorous picture which is destined for Agnew and which he should place in Manchester: For if a spinner ever wished to find his painter, he really ought to hit on me. *Intérieur d'un bureau d'acheteurs de coton à la Nouvelle Orléans, Cotton buyers office.*

In it there are about 15 individuals more or less occupied with a table covered with the precious material and two men, one half leaning and the other half sitting on it, the buyer and the broker, are discussing a pattern. A raw picture if there ever was one, and I

think from a better hand than many another. (Canvas about 40 it seems to me). I am preparing another less complicated and more spontaneous, better art, where the people are all in summer dress, white walls, a sea of cotton on the tables. If Agnew takes both from me all the better. I do not, however, wish to give up the Paris plan. (This is my present style). In the fortnight that I intend spending here I shall finish the said picture. But it will not be possible for it to leave with me. A canvas scarcely dry, shut up for a long time, away from light and air, you know very well that that would change it to chrome-yellow no. 3. So I shall not be able to bring it to London myself or to have it sent there before about April. Retain the good will of these gentlemen for me until then. In Manchester there is a wealthy spinner, de Cotterel, who has a famous picture gallery. A fellow like that would suit me and would suit Agnew even better. But let's be cautious how we talk about it and not count our chickens too soon.

You are getting on like a house on fire! 900 pounds, but that's a fortune? Ah! if ever! But why not? What a lot of good this absence from Paris has done me in any case, my dear friend. I made the most of it. I have made certain good resolutions which (you will laugh) I honestly feel capable of carrying out. The exhibition at the Academy will have to do without me and I shall mind more than it will. Millais does not understand my little Anglo-American excursion. Anyhow we shall get along all right in spite of that. How much shall I have to tell you about art. If I could have another 20 years time to work I should do things that would endure. Am I to finish like that after having come close to so many methods of seeing and acting well? No. Remember the art of Le Nain and all Mediaeval France. Our race will have something simple and bold to offer. The naturalist movement will draw in a manner worthy of the great schools and then its strength will be recognized. This English art that appeals so much to us often seems to be exploiting some trick. We can do better than they and be just as strong.

I really have a lot of stuff in my head; if only there were insurance companies for that as there are for so many things here, there's a bale I should insure at once. This youthful? headpiece of mine is really my greatest asset.

I am very much afraid that Deschamps did not succeed in selling any of my pictures. For the sake of my relationship with Durand-Ruel it is high time that something positive appeared on the debit side of the free-realist stock. From Hirsch I heard that Fantin's picture the *Parnassiens* was sold in London. All the better, he has skill and talent, has Fantin, but too little taste, too little variety, too few ideas. You keep on insisting that over there the place is prepared for a certain number of us. I do believe you, but in my opinion one should go over there oneself to sweep the said place a little and clean it by hand.

What lovely things I could have done, and done rapidly if the bright daylight were less unbearable for me. To go to Louisiana to open ones eyes, I cannot do that. And yet I kept them sufficiently half open to see my fill. The women are pretty and unusually graceful. The black world, I have not the time to explore it; there are some real treasures as regards to drawing and colour in these forests of ebony. I shall be very surprised to live among white people only in Paris. And then I love silhouettes so much and these silhouettes walk.

Goodbye, see you soon. The moment I get to Paris I shall write you. I intend to take a French boat which docks at Brest. If I take an English one I disembark at Liverpool, in which case I shall see you in London.

That fellow Whistler really has something in the sea and water pieces he showed me. But, bless me, there are quite different things to be done!

I feel that I am collecting myself and I am glad of it. It took a long time, and if I could have Corot's grand old age. But my vanity is positively American! Good health to you and some 900 pounds more. My brothers are well, their business too. The family has increased by a daughter whose godfather I was. This daughter is, of course, René's.

I advise you to paint motifs of a varied nature and intensity.

I think we are too fond of the *demi-plein mince*.[17]

I often lecture myself about this and am passing it on to you.

Ever your,

Degas

Regards to Millais whom I do not know. Love to Legros, Whistler and to Deschamps if you see him.

Ah! but I nearly forgot something. Go at once to Deschamps. If he still has the *Danseuses* and if Durand-Ruel gives his permission and if there is still time to get him to send them to the Paris exhibition, before the 20 March. It is the only picture I could exhibit.

All letters reprinted from Guerin, 1947, 13–32.

1. René De Gas (1845–1920), the artist's youngest brother.

2. A small restaurant.

3. Mlle Malot [Mallot], dancer at the opera. Degas did two portraits of her which are among his best: Coll. J. E. Blanche (pastel) and II. Vente Degas, no. 48.

4. This probably refers to Mlle Marie Dihau, sister of Désiré Dihau.

5. This is the office represented by Degas in his famous picture in the Museé de Pau.

6. See fig. 96 and cats. 27 and 28.

7. The picture no. 25 of the first Vente Degas, representing children on the steps of a country house, was certainly painted in New Orleans (see cat. 29).

8. Rita Sangalli, famous opera dancer who created the role of Sylvia in Léo Delibes's ballet, *Sylvie ou la Nymphe de Diane.*

9. Gard, producer of dance at the Paris Ópera; he figures in the picture *l'Orchestre* (Louvre).

10. Piot-Normand, artist and friend of Degas. He figures in the same picture.

11. Lorenz Frölich, Danish painter and designer, who lived in Paris from 1851 to 1872 when he returned to Denmark.

12. Louis Rouart.

13. The French painter, François Auguste Biard (1799–1882). He made numerous journeys in the Mediterranean, to Spitznbergen and Brasil.

14. Is this a sincere or an ironic tribute? In any case Degas and his friends used to say of an excessively finished and over 'slick' picture that it was 'Bouguereauté'.

15. The costume of the French Noblemen in the eighteenth century.

16. Landscape painter who exhibited at the third and fifth exhibitions of the Impressionists. Degas did a portrait of him.

17. This is an expression coined by Degas and presumably refers to technique. Unlike most of the Impressionists Degas laid his color on very thinly and gave full plastic form to his figures.

Selected Bibliography

D'ALMBERT 1856
Alfred d'Almbert. *Flânerie parisienne aux Etats-Unis.* Paris, 1856.

ARMSTRONG 1991
Carol Armstrong. *Odd Man Out: Readings in the Work and Reputation of Edgar Degas.* Chicago, 1991.

BENFEY 1996
Christopher Benfey. "Degas and the 'Black World': Art and Miscegenation in New Orleans." *The New Republic* (21 October 1996): 25–30.

BENFEY 1997
Christopher Benfey. *Degas in New Orleans: Encounters in the Creole World of Kate Chopin and George Washington Cable.* New York, 1997.

BERKELEY 1962
Jean Sutherland Boggs. *Portraits by Degas.* Berkeley and Los Angeles, 1962.

BOGGS 1956
Jean Sutherland Boggs. "'Mme. Musson and Her Two Daughters' by Edgar Degas." *The Art Quarterly* XIX (spring 1956): 60–64.

BOGGS 1963
Jean Sutherland Boggs. "Edgar Degas and Naples." *Burlington Magazine* CV, no. 723 (June 1963): 273–76.

BOGGS 1965
Jean Sutherland Boggs. "Degas: The Painter in New Orleans." In New Orleans 1965.

BOGGS AND MAHEUX 1992
Jean Sutherland Boggs and Anne Maheux. *Degas Pastels.* New York, 1992.

BOSTON, PHILADELPHIA 1984
Sue Walsh Reed and Barbara Stern Shapiro. *Edgar Degas: The Painter as Printmaker.* Exh. cat., Boston, Museum of Fine Arts; Philadelphia, Philadelphia Museum of Art; Arts Council of Great Britain, Hayward Gallery. Boston, 1984.

BRAME AND REFF 1984
Philippe Brame and Theodore Reff, with the assistance of Arlene Reff. *Degas et Son Oeuvre: A Supplement.* New York, 1984.

BROWN 1988
Marilyn R. Brown. "Degas and *A Cotton Office in New Orleans.*" *Burlington Magazine* CXXX (March 1988): 216–21.

BROWN 1990
Marilyn R. Brown. "The De Gas Musson Papers at Tulane University." *The Art Bulletin* LXXII (March 1990): 118–30.

BROWN 1991
Marilyn R. Brown. *The De Gas–Musson Family Papers: An Annotated Inventory.* New Orleans, 1991.

BROWN 1994
Marilyn R. Brown. *Degas and the Business of Art: A Cotton Office in New Orleans.* University Park, Pa., 1994.

BRUNS 1975
Mrs. Thomas Nelson Carter Bruns. *Louisiana Portraits.* New Orleans, 1975.

BYRNES 1965
James B. Byrnes. "Degas: His Paintings of New Orleanians Here and Abroad." In New Orleans 1965.

CHICAGO 1984
Richard Brettel et al. *Degas in the Art Institute of Chicago.* Exh. cat., Chicago, 1984.

DE GAS–MUSSON PAPERS
De Gas–Musson Papers. Ms. 226. Special Collections, Howard–Tilton Memorial Library, Tulane University, New Orleans, Louisiana.

DENIS 1901
Samuel Denis, editor. *Paris de 1800–1900.* In t.iii, *Histoire Contemporaine.* Paris, 1901, unpaginated.

FEVRE 1949
Jeanne Fevre. *Mon Oncle Degas.* Geneva, 1949.

GUERIN 1947
Marcel Guerin, editor. *Degas Letters.* Translation by Marguerite Kay. Oxford, 1947.

HALÉVY 1964
Daniel Halévy. *My Friend Degas.* Middletown, Conn., 1964.

KING 1921
Grace King. *Creole Families of New Orleans.* New York, 1921.

LAFOND 1918–19
Paul Lafond. *Degas,* 2 volumes. Paris, 1918–19.

LEMOISNE 1921
Paul-André Lesmoisne. "Les carnets de Degas au Cabinet des Estampes." *Gazette des Beaux-Arts* LXIII (April 1921): 219–31.

LEMOISNE 1946–49
Paul-André Lesmoisne. *Degas et son oeuvre,* 4 volumes. Paris, 1946–49.

LIPTON 1986
Eunice Lipton. *Looking into Degas: Uneasy Images of Women and Modern Life.* Berkeley, 1986.

LOYRETTE 1991
Henri Loyrette. *Degas.* Paris, 1991.

MCMULLEN 1984
Roy McMullen. *Degas: His Life, Times, and Work.* Boston, 1984; London, 1985.

MOREAU-NÉLATON 1926
Ètienne Moreau-Nélaton. *Manet raconté par lui-même.* Paris, 1926.

NEW ORLEANS 1965
James Byrnes et al. *Edgar Degas: His Family and Friends in New Orleans.* Exh. cat., New Orleans, Isaac Delgado Museum of Art. New Orleans, 1965.

NEW YORK 1997
Ann Dumas et al. *The Private Collection of Edgar Degas,* 2 volumes. Exh. cat., Metropolitan Museum of Art. New York, 1997.

NEW YORK 1998
Malcolm Daniel et al. *Edgar Degas, Photographer.* Exh. cat. New York, 1998.

PANTAZZI 1988
Michael Pantazzi. "Lettres de Degas à Thérèse Morbilli conservées au Musée des Beaux-Arts du Canada." *Racar* XV, no. 2 (1988): 128.

PARIS 1989
Musée d'Orsay. *Degas inédit: Actes du colloque Degas.* Paris, 1989.

PARIS, OTTAWA, NEW YORK 1988
Jean Sutherland Boggs et al. *Degas.* Exh. cat., Paris, Galeries Nationales du Grand Palais; Ottawa, National Gallery of Canada; New York, Metropolitan Museum of Art. New York and Ottawa, 1988.

PINGEOT 1991
Anne Pingeot. *Degas Sculptures.* Paris, 1991.

POTHEY 1876
Alex Pothey. "Chronique." *La Presse* (31 March 1876): 3.

RAIMONDI 1958
Riccardo Raimondi. *Degas e la sua famiglia in Napoli: 1793–1917.* Naples, 1958.

REFF 1976
Theodore Reff. *The Notebooks of Edgar Degas: A Catalogue Raisonné of the Thirty-Eight Notebooks in the Bibliothèque Nationale and Other Collections.* Oxford, 1976.

REWALD 1946
John Rewald. "Degas and His Family in New Orleans." *Gazette des Beaux-Arts* XXX (August 1946): 105–26. Reprinted in New Orleans 1965.

REWALD 1985
John Rewald. *Studies in Impressionism.* London and New York, 1985.

ROME 1984
Henri Loyrette et al. *Degas e l'Italia.* Exh. cat., Rome, Villa Medici. Rome, 1984.

ROUART 1986
Denis Rouart, editor. *The Correspondence of Berthe Morisot.* Translation by Betty W. Hubbard. London, 1986.

SICKERT 1917
Walter Sickert. "Degas." *Burlington Magazine* XXXI (November 1917): 182–91.

SIGWALT 1988
Edouard Goulon Sigwalt. "Les ancêtres paternels d'Edgar Degas." *Cahiers du centre de généalogie protestante* 22 (2nd trimester, 1988): 1188–91.

ST. LOUIS 1967
Jean Sutherland Boggs. *Drawings by Degas.* Exh. cat., City Art Museum of St. Louis. St. Louis, 1967.

TOLEDANO 1995
Roulhac Toledano. "Double Mysteries, Double Cultures: Family History Collides with Art History." Unpublished manuscript, 1995.

VALÉRY 1960
Paul Valéry. *Degas Manet Morisot.* Translation by David Paul. New York, 1960.

VARNEDOE 1980a
Kirk Varnedoe. "The Artifice of Candor: Impressionism and Photography Reconsidered." *Art in America* (January 1980): 66–78.

VARNEDOE 1980b
Kirk Varnedoe. "The Ideology of Time: Degas and Photography." *Art in America* (summer 1980): 96–110.

VOLLARD 1924
Ambroise Vollard. *Degas.* Paris, 1924.

VOLLARD 1986
Ambroise Vollard. *Degas: An Intimate Portrait.* Translation by Randolph T. Weaver. New York, 1986.

WASHINGTON 1998
Jean Sutherland Boggs et al. *Degas at the Races.* Exh. cat., Washington, D.C., National Gallery of Art. Washington, D.C., 1998.

WASHINGTON, SAN FRANCISCO 1986
Charles S. Moffett et al. *The New Painting: Impressionism 1874–1886.* Exh. cat., Washington, D.C., National Gallery of Art; San Francisco, M. H. de Young Memorial Museum. San Francisco, 1986.

ZÜRICH 1994–95
Felix Baumann and Marianne Karabelnik, editors. *Degas Portraits.* Exh. cat., Zürich, Kunsthaus; Tübingen, Kunsthalle. London, 1994

PHOTOGRAPH CREDITS

Every effort has been made to contact the copyright holders for the photographs in this book. Any omissions will be corrected in subsequent editions.

Except when noted, photographs have been supplied by the owners or custodians of the works reproduced; the courtesy of all is gratefully acknowledged. Additional photography credits follow:

Frankfurt, Germany, Ursula Edelmann, cat. 22.

Washington, D.C. Lee Stallsworth, cat. 7.

James B. Byrnes, figs. 11, 38, 70, 74, 114, 115, 116, 127.

Peissenberg, Germany, Jürgen Hinrichs, fig. 83.

Napoleon-Museum Arenenberg, courtesy of South-eastern Architectural Archives, figs. 9, 18, 31, 33.

National Gallery of Art, Washington, D.C., figs. 68, 69, 76, 77, 79, 89, 90, 91, 101.

Provided by the authors, figs. 40, 41, 44, 45, 46, 81, 103, 104.

Other photography by Judy Cooper, New Orleans Museum of Art